Frederick Douglass in Britain and Ireland, 1845–1895

Edited by Hannah-Rose Murray and
John R. McKivigan

EDINBURGH
University Press

Edinburgh University Press is one of the leading university presses in the UK. We publish academic books and journals in our selected subject areas across the humanities and social sciences, combining cutting-edge scholarship with high editorial and production values to produce academic works of lasting importance. For more information visit our website: edinburghuniversitypress.com

Edinburgh University Press Ltd
The Tun – Holyrood Road, 12(2f) Jackson's Entry, Edinburgh EH8 8PJ

First published in hardback by Edinburgh University Press 2021

Typeset in 10.5/13 Goudy Oldstyle Std by
IDSUK (DataConnection) Ltd, and
printed and bound by CPI Group (UK) Ltd
Croydon, CR0 4YY

A CIP record for this book is available from the British Library

ISBN 978 1 4744 6041 5 (hardback)
ISBN 978 1 3995 1110 0 (paperback)
ISBN 978 1 4744 6042 2 (webready PDF)
ISBN 978 1 4744 6043 9 (epub)

Contents

Part I: "To Tell His Own Story": Frederick Douglass and the British Isles

Part II: "Men Naturally Love Liberty"

Part III: "A Sunbeam into the Darknesses of the Hour":
The Responses to Great Britain

List of Illustrations

Note on the Text

All of the documents here have been transcribed verbatim from the original text. The letters, poems, and songs were reprinted in antislavery newspapers and the Victorian press but some of the speeches and first-hand accounts are from Douglass's own hand. The majority of speeches published in this volume, however, do come from British and Irish newspaper accounts. In these cases, we have to be aware of how Douglass's testimony was viewed, edited and shaped through a white correspondent's pen. Several note that it was difficult to transcribe his speech while others mention a lack of column space. It is thus inevitable that correspondents failed to capture every word, theme or sentiment that Douglass expressed as notes were hastily written down and then written up for publication. Performances were also ephemeral, often impossible to describe and capture, which is particularly prescient when we consider the implications of a white correspondent reporting on a speech from a Black activist. It is very likely correspondents misheard, misunderstood or misread Douglass's performative techniques and failed to capture them effectively. Therefore, the documents here should be treated with some caution.

The English spelling used in British newspaper reports is retained, but American spelling is used for the Introduction and Douglass's own writings. For the benefit of the reader, annotations have been kept to a minimum.

Content Warning

Much of the material presented here discusses or references racism, physical and sexual violence, rape, lynching, torture and trauma. This will be potentially emotionally challenging to deal with, and may be triggering to some.

Acknowledgments

Hannah-Rose Murray: I have incurred many debts over the course of this ten-year project. Thanks to Zoe Trodd and Matthew Pethers for looking over the proposal when several publications rejected it; Alan Rice for pointing me towards this subject all those years ago, and Mike Gardner for designing my website. Thanks also go to Celeste-Marie Bernier, Richard Blackett, David Blight, Leigh Fought, John Stauffer, Manisha Sinha, Lisa Merrill, Fionnghuala Sweeney, Sarah Meer, Martha J. Cutter, John Oldfield, Robert Levine, David Silkenat, Susanna Ashton, Maurice Williams, Bridget Bennett, Kelvin Wilson, Jeff Green, Alasdair Pettinger, Ann Coughlan, Caroline Schroeter, Kristin Leary, Adrian Mulligan, Aaron Barnhart, Leslie Park, Amy Cools, Janet Black, Laura Tomlinson, Jak Beula, Liz Davies, Hannah Jeffery, Minh Dang, Emily Pharez, Adam Smith, Nick Batho, and Kenneth B. Morris, Jr.

We both appreciate the support from archives and institutions including the University of Nottingham, University of Edinburgh, University of Manchester, University of Southampton, the British Library, the National Library of Scotland, St. Ives Museum, Cumbria Archive, Whitehaven Archives, Bristol Archives, Dorset History Centre, Essex Record Office, Indiana University, Library of Congress, Boston Public Library, the Beinecke Library at Yale, New York Public Library, New York Historical Society, Widener Library, and Archive.org.

Thank you to Michelle Houston and Edinburgh University Press for your patience and kindness when we extended our deadline, and during the COVID-19 pandemic.

Thank you to Dakota Burks, Jacob Fulgham, Patrick Hanlon, and Hannah Yi, who helped check my transcriptions of Douglass's speeches, and to John for your unfailing support with this book and the Frederick Douglass Papers!

As always, thank you to my wonderful Mum and Dad, Jen and Mick, and Alexandra for being the best partner in life.

Last but not least, I dedicate this book to Celeste-Marie Bernier. Your inspiring intellectual vision and insight into Douglass (and his family) are a constant source of admiration to me. I have learned so much from you and your research as a PhD student, a postdoctoral fellow, and as a friend. I count myself blessed to have your unfailing support, kindness, and endless encouragement, and I am honoured to work alongside you in Edinburgh and hopefully beyond.

John R. McKivigan: Significant labor in transcribing and proofreading the documents reproduced below is owed to a dedicated team of student researchers at Indiana University-Perdue University Indianapolis: Dakota Burks, Jacob Fulgham, Patrick Hanlon, and Hannah Yi. Various resources at our university and at its Institute of American Thought speeded their work considerably. Members of the Frederick Douglass Papers staff, particularly Jeffery Duvall and Brandon Spaulding, generously lent us their expertise in handling these documents. They all have earned our gratitude.

The collection of many of the documents employed in Part 3 was begun by my predecessor as editor of the Frederick Douglass Papers, John W. Blassingame, who was my mentor in documentary editing. Our project is especially dedicated to the National Historical and Records Commission for nearly five decades of unflagging support to the collecting, editing, and publishing of Douglass works. Hannah has been an absolute delight to work with as we discovered our mutual passion to learn more about this iconic figure.

Finally, I am grateful to Heather L. Kaufman, my wife and frequent scholarly collaborator, for encouraging me to pursue this project, and to my children, Charlie and Aurora, for tolerating the many hours that I spent on my computer while "supervising" their play. I am immensely pleased that they know that this was definitely one Black Life That Mattered.

Timeline of Frederick Douglass's Life

1818

February — Frederick Augustus Washington Bailey was born sometime in February at Holme Hill Farm plantation at Tuckahoe, near the town of Easton, Talbot County, on the eastern shore of Maryland. He was rumored to be the son of Captain Aaron Anthony, who enslaved his mother, Harriet Bailey.

1824

August — Sent to live in the home of his enslaver Aaron Anthony, overseer of the Wye Plantation of the powerful Lloyd family.

1826

March — Sent to the Fells Point district of Baltimore to work for Hugh Auld, a ship carpenter and the brother-in-law of Aaron Anthony's daughter, Lucretia Auld.

1827

November — Became the "property" of Thomas Auld, son-in-law of Aaron Anthony, after Anthony's death. Remained in the household of Hugh and Sophia Auld, where he was taught rudimentary reading skills by Sophia, who ceased the lessons at her husband's insistence.

1831

Bought a used copy of Caleb Bingham's compilation of speeches, *The Columbian Orator*, which he memorized to hone his reading and speaking skills.

1833

6 December	William Lloyd Garrison founded the American Anti-Slavery Society in Philadelphia.

1834

January	Began year as a rented field hand on a farm under the watch of Edward Covey, known as the "slave-breaker."
August	Repelled a physical attack by Covey and was never whipped or beaten again.

1836

2 April	Led a failed escape plan from the farm of William Freeland.

1837

Joined the "East Baltimore Mental Improvement Society," a free black debating club, and there met Anna Murray, who encouraged him to save money and plan an escape.

1838

3–4 September	Escaped from Maryland by borrowing papers from a free black sailor to take a train from Baltimore to New York City.
15 September	Married Anna Murray in New York City.
18 September	Moved to New Bedford, MA, where he changed his name to Douglass.

1839

Subscribed to the *Liberator*, an abolitionist weekly edited by William Lloyd Garrison.

Obtained a license to preach from the African Methodist Episcopal Zion Church.

1841

10–12 August	Spoke on his experience as an enslaved individual at a Massachusetts Anti-Slavery Society convention in Nantucket, MA, after which he was invited to become a paid itinerant lecturer.

1843

15–19 August	Successfully opposed a resolution by Henry Highland Garnet at the National Convention of Colored Citizens in Buffalo, NY, urging the enslaved population to rebel.
16 September	Beaten by a mob during an outdoor antislavery meeting in Pendleton, IN.

1844

May	Joined the majority at the annual meeting of the American Anti-Slavery Society in endorsing Garrison's condemnation of the Constitution as pro-slavery.
Winter	Began work on his autobiography.

1845

28 May	Published his first autobiography, *Narrative of the Life of Frederick Douglass, an American Slave, Written by Himself*, which sold 4,500 copies by September.
16 August	Sailed from Boston to avoid recapture, leaving his family behind, and began a twenty-one-month tour of Great Britain and Ireland.
28 August	Arrived in Liverpool, England, and traveled from there to Ireland.
31 August	Began a three-month lecture tour of Dublin, Cork, Limerick, and Belfast.
September	Lectured in Dublin on behalf of the Hibernian Anti-Slavery Society.
29 September	Attended meeting of the Loyal Repeal Association in Dublin's Conciliation Hall and met Daniel O'Connell.
Late September	Richard D. Webb published the first Dublin edition of the *Narrative*. Rapid sales helped finance Douglass's British travels.
October	Lectured several times in Cork.
20 October	Delivered a speech in support of the temperance movement at Cork Temperance Institute, founded and directed by Father Theobald Mathew.
25 October	"Sold" by Thomas Auld to his brother Hugh for $100.
December	Delivered abolitionist addresses in Belfast, assailing the Free Church of Scotland for accepting contributions from the American South.

1846

January–early May	Toured Scotland as part of the "Send Back the Money" campaign against the Free Church of Scotland.
February	Richard D. Webb published second Dublin edition of the *Narrative* with a letter by Douglass rebutting white Marylander A. C. C. Thompson's attacks on its veracity.
18 May	Addressed the annual meeting of the British and Foreign Anti-Slavery Society in London.
Late May–early August	Lectured in Scotland, Northern Ireland, and the Midlands.
7 August	Created controversy at World's Temperance Society convention in London by exposing discrimination faced by free Black temperance groups in the US.
10 August	Joined by William Lloyd Garrison in London, where they helped organize the Anti-Slavery League, a British abolitionist society.
Late August–mid-October	Toured England, Scotland, Wales, and Ireland with Garrison.
November	Pressured by Garrisonians to extend his antislavery tour in the UK. Responded in press to attacks by the Reverend Samuel H. Cox regarding his criticism in the UK of American churches' tolerance of slavery.
12 December	British abolitionist admirers, notably Anna and Ellen Richardson of Newcastle, negotiated the legal purchase and manumission of Douglass from Hugh Auld for the sum of just over $700.
25 December	Visited Newcastle-upon-Tyne with Anna and Ellen Richardson, who introduced him to Julia Griffiths, a British woman active in the antislavery cause.

1847

January	Criticized by Henry Clarke Wright and other Garrisonians for permitting his manumission.
February–March	Conducted a final tour of southern England in anticipation of his departure.
30 March	Guest of honor at a farewell soirée in his honor in London.
4 April	Left Liverpool to return to the United States.

Late September	Used just over $2,000 raised by British and Irish friends to purchase a printing press.
November	Arrived in Rochester, NY, with the intent of establishing a newspaper.
3 December	Published the first issue of his weekly newspaper, the *North Star*, in partnership with Martin R. Delany.

1848

| 19–20 July | Attended the Seneca Falls Women's Rights Convention, where he signed the Declaration of Sentiments. |
| 29 August | Attended convention in Buffalo, NY, which resulted in the formation of the Free Soil Party. |

1849

| May | British reformer Julia Griffiths joined the staff of Douglass's newspaper as its unofficial business manager. |

1850

| May | Douglass assaulted in a New York City park while accompanying Julia and Eliza Griffiths. |

1851

April	Agreed to merge the *North Star* with wealthy New York abolitionist Gerrit Smith's struggling *Liberty Party Paper*, accepting Smith's financial support and his antislavery interpretation of the Constitution.
9 May	Broke with Garrison openly over the issue of political action to end slavery, which Garrison opposed.
26 June	Converted the *North Star* into *Frederick Douglass' Paper*, a pro-Liberty Party newspaper, with the motto "All Rights for All!"

1852

| 5 July | Delivered "What to the Slave Is the Fourth of July?" at a meeting of the Rochester Ladies' Anti-Slavery Society. |
| 14 October | Addressed the Free Democratic Party convention, the successor to the Free Soil party, in Pittsburgh and endorsed John P. Hale, its presidential nominee, in *Frederick Douglass' Paper*. |

1853

January
Published his novella, "The Heroic Slave," in the gift book *Autographs for Freedom*, a collection of antislavery writings edited by Julia Griffiths and sold to raise funds for *Frederick Douglass' Paper*.

March
Visited Harriet Beecher Stowe's home in Andover, MA, and requested that she fundraise for an industrial school for African Americans while touring Great Britain.

6–8 July
Organized and hosted the Colored National Convention in Rochester, NY, where he was criticized by several Black leaders for his industrial school proposal on the grounds that it would promote segregation.

Winter
Garrison's *Liberator* alluded to Julia Griffiths having caused "much unhappiness" in the Douglass household; Douglass responded heatedly.

1855

Mid-June
Julia Griffiths departed Rochester to return to Great Britain.

August
Second autobiography, *My Bondage and My Freedom*, published with chapter recalling his first tour of Britain and Ireland.

1856

15 August
Endorsed the Republican party's presidential ticket as the most electable antislavery ticket, in an editorial in *Frederick Douglass' Paper*.

1857

3 August
Delivered his most widely disseminated West Indian Emancipation Day Celebration orations in Canandaigua, NY.

1858

Late January–early February
John Brown resided at Douglass's Rochester home for three weeks, planning his raid on Harpers Ferry.

June
Launched new periodical, *Douglass' Monthly*, aimed largely at British readers.

1859

19–21 August
Met with John Brown at Chambersburg, PA, but chose not to join the plot to attack the Harpers Ferry Arsenal because he believed the plan would ultimately fail.

16–18 October	John Brown attempted to start an armed slave revolt by seizing the US arsenal at Harpers Ferry, VA.
19–21 October	Warned that he might be placed under arrest following the failure of the Harpers Ferry Raid, Douglass fled from Philadelphia to Rochester, and finally to Canada.
12 November	Sailed from Quebec and then on to Great Britain, for greater safety, because of his prior close connections with John Brown.
24 November– c. 15 January 1860	Used the homes of Julia Griffiths Crofts and other friends as bases for an extensive lecturing campaign across central and northern England.
22 December	Addressed meeting of the Leeds Anti-Slavery Society and defended actions of John Brown.

1860

28 February	In a Glasgow address, George Thompson criticized Douglass's change of position on the relation of the US Constitution to slavery.
13 March	Douglass's youngest daughter, Annie, died at the age of ten years, eleven months, and twenty-one days.
26 March	Douglass traveled to Glasgow to answer Thompson's attacks.
Late March	Douglass finally learns of Annie's death but continues to speak publicly.
Mid-April	Returned to the United States, arriving in Portland, ME.
August	Due to financial difficulties, Douglass was forced to cease publication of his weekly, *Frederick Douglass' Paper*.

1861

April	Denounced secession but called on Lincoln administration to make the goal of war emancipation as well as reunion. Contemplated visiting Haiti to investigate conditions for prospective African American emigrants.
12–14 April	The Civil War officially began with the attack on Fort Sumter in the harbor of Charleston, SC, by Confederate forces.

1862

Summer	US Ambassador Charles Francis Adams warned Washington, DC that the British government was seriously considering formally recognizing the Confederate States of America.

November	"Slave's Appeal to Great Britain" was published in the *New York Independent* and then reproduced and circulated widely by his British admirers.
31 December	Attended celebration of the issuance of the Emancipation Proclamation in Boston.

1863

February–July	Traveled extensively in the North to recruit Black soldiers for Union army regiments being raised by Massachusetts.
1 August	Resigned as army recruiter after protesting the lack of equal pay and promotion opportunities given Black Union soldiers.
Mid-August	Returned to Rochester and issued the valedictory issue of *Douglass' Monthly* in anticipation of receiving a military commission that never arrived.

1864

19 August	Met with President Lincoln in the Executive Mansion (White House), Washington, DC, to discuss means to recruit enslaved people and fugitives to the Union army.
4–6 October	Presided over the National Convention of Colored Men at Syracuse, NY, and gave a lukewarm endorsement to Lincoln's re-election.

1865

4 March	Attended Lincoln's second inauguration in Washington, DC.
9 April	General Robert E. Lee surrendered the Confederate Army of Northern Virginia, effectively ending the American Civil War.
14 April	President Lincoln shot by John Wilkes Booth.
6 December	Thirteenth Amendment ratified.
29 December	William Lloyd Garrison published the final issue of the *Liberator*.

1866

7 February	Part of a Black delegation that had a contentious interview with President Andrew Johnson at the Executive Mansion, Washington, DC.

1868

9 July	Fourteenth Amendment ratified.

27 August	Publicly endorsed the Republican ticket of Ulysses S. Grant and Schuyler Colfax.

1870

3 February	Fifteenth Amendment ratified.
1 July	Moved to the District of Columbia and began editing the *New National Era* to advance Black civil rights as well as other reforms.

1872

13 April	Endorsed Grant's re-election in the *New National Era*.
6 June	Douglass was nominated by Victoria Woodhull, the first woman to run for president, to run as vice president on the Equal Rights Party presidential ticket. Douglass neither acknowledged nor accepted the nomination.
28 November	Turned over editorship of the *New National Era* to his sons.

1874

Late March	Appointed president of the Freedman's Savings Bank and campaigned to keep public trust in the institution.
29 June	Voted along with the bank's board of trustees to close the Freedman's Savings Bank, which they believed was no longer solvent.

1877

Spring	Appointed United States Marshal of the District of Columbia by President Rutherford B. Hayes. Douglass was the first African American to receive a federal appointment requiring Senate approval.
17 June	Visited former enslaver, Thomas Auld, on his deathbed in St. Michaels, MD.

1878

Purchased a fifteen-acre estate that he and Anna named Cedar Hill in the Anacostia neighborhood of the District of Columbia.

1879

Douglass's criticism of the "Exoduster" movement of thousands of African Americans from the former Confederate states into Kansas and other Midwestern states generated international controversy.

1881

May 1881 — Appointed recorder of deeds for the District of Columbia by President James A. Garfield.
Published his third autobiography, *The Life and Times of Frederick Douglass*, with the Park Publishing Company of Hartford, CT.

1882

February — John Lobb published a British edition of *Life and Times* with a preface by John Bright.

4 August — Anna Murray Douglass died.

1884

24 January — Married Helen M. Pitts, a younger white woman. Their interracial relationship provoked public controversy as well as disapproval from members of both families.

1886

14 September — Sailed from New York City with Helen Pitts Douglass aboard the *City of Rome*, arriving in Liverpool on 24 September.

October — Gave addresses in St. Neots and Bridport, England, and a lengthy interview to the *London Daily News*.

November–
February 1887 — The Douglasses toured major cities in France and Italy.

1887

February–
March — Continued tour by visiting Egypt and Greece.

April–August — Helen Pitts Douglass returned to US to tend ill mother; Douglass remained in the UK and Ireland to visit with old abolitionist friends.

11 August — Returned to the United States.

1889

July — Accepted President Benjamin Harrison's appointment as United States minister resident and consul general to Haiti.

1891

3 July — Returned to the United States, by way of New York City, on leave from Haitian post. Resigned in August.

1892

October — Accepted appointment from the government of Haiti to serve as commissioner of the Haitian pavilion at the World's Columbian Exposition.
Published an expanded version of *Life and Times*.

1893

29 April — Joined Ida B. Wells and other activists in protesting the lack of African American representation at the World's Columbian Exposition.

1894

9 January — Delivered oration on "Lessons of the Hour" in Washington, DC, condemning lynching; British friends praised and circulated this.

Summer — Sent British friends an endorsement of Ida B. Wells's speaking tour of the UK.

1895

20 February — Died at his Cedar Hill home in Washington, DC, after attending a women's rights convention.

Map of Frederick Douglass's Speaking Locations

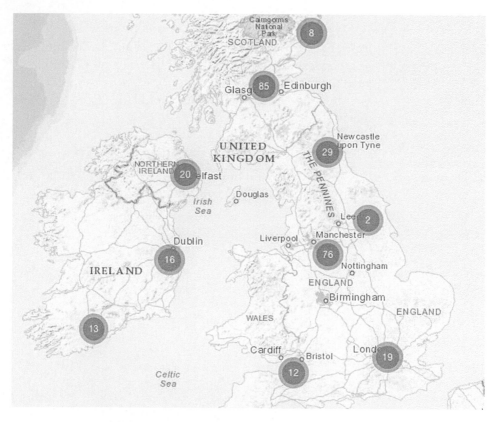

Map of Frederick Douglass's speaking locations (Hannah-Rose Murray, www.frederickdouglassinbritain.com).

List of Frederick Douglass's Speaking Locations

In compiling this timeline we have built and expanded upon the work of numerous scholars: the brilliant team behind the Frederick Douglass Papers (including John W. Blassingame); Celeste-Marie Bernier; Alasdair Pettinger; Christine Kinealy; Gerald Fulkerson; and Hannah-Rose Murray. We have also consulted Frederick Douglass's writings, the letters of George Thompson and William Lloyd Garrison (to name but two), and newspapers both digitized and on microfilm at the British Library.

August 1845	*Cambria* steamship	Atlantic Crossing
31 August 1845		Celbridge
3 September 1845	Royal Exchange	Dublin
9 September 1845	Friends' Meeting House, Eustace Street	Dublin
10 September 1845	Royal Exchange	Dublin
12 September 1845	Friends' Meeting House, Eustace Street	Dublin
16 September 1845	Richmond Gaol	Dublin
17 September 1845	Music Hall, Abbey Street	Dublin
21 September 1845	Royal Canal Harbour	Dublin
23 September 1845	Music Hall, Abbey Street	Dublin
29 September 1845	Conciliation Hall	Dublin
1 October 1845	Music Hall, Abbey Street	Dublin
3 October 1845	Music Hall, Abbey Street	Dublin
7 October 1845		Wexford
8 October 1845		Wexford
9 October 1845		Waterford
13 October 1845	Temperance Hall, Global Lane	Cork
14 October 1845	Lloyd's Hotel, *morning*	Cork
14 October 1845	City Court House, 2 p.m.	Cork

17 October 1845	Wesleyan Chapel, Patrick Street, *afternoon*	Cork
17 October 1845	Independent Chapel, *evening*	Cork
20 October 1845	Temperance Institute	Cork
21 October 1845		Cork
23 October 1845	Imperial Hotel, *afternoon*	Cork
27 October 1845	Independent Chapel	Cork
8 October 1845	St. Patrick's Temperance Hall	Cork
3 November 1845	Independent Chapel, George's Street	Cork
10 November 1845	Independent Chapel, Belford Row	Cork
21 November 1845	Philosophical Rooms, Glentworth Street	Limerick
5 December 1845	Independent Church, Donegall Street	Belfast
9 December 1845	Wesleyan Methodist Church	Belfast
11 December 1845	Presbyterian Meeting House, Donegall Street	Belfast
12 December 1845	Presbyterian Church, Rosemary Street	Belfast
16 December 1845	Town Hall	Birmingham
23 December 1845	Independent Meeting House, Donegall Street	Belfast
26 December 1845	Presbyterian Meetinghouse, Donegall Street	Belfast
29 December 1845	Presbyterian Church	Lisburn
31 December 1845		Holywood
1 January 1846	Wesleyan Meeting House, Donegall Street	Belfast
2 January 1846	Methodist Meeting House, Donegall Street	Belfast
6 January 1846	Commercial Rooms, *morning*	Belfast
6 January 1846	Lancesterian School Rooms, *evening*	Belfast
15 January 1846	City Hall	Glasgow
22 January 1846	City Hall	Glasgow
23 January 1846	City Hall	Perth
24 January 1846		Perth
25 January 1846		Perth
26 January 1846	City Hall	Perth
27 January 1846	School Wynd Chapel	Dundee
28 January 1846	School Wynd Chapel	Dundee
29 January 1846	School Wynd Chapel	Dundee
30 January 1846	Bell Street Chapel	Dundee
9 February 1846	Tay Square Chapel	Dundee
10 February 1846	Trades' Hall	Arbroath
11 February 1846	Abbey Church	Arbroath
12 February 1846	Abbey Church	Arbroath

18 February 1846	City Hall, *afternoon*	Glasgow
18 February 1846	City Hall	Glasgow
26 February 1846		Montrose
27 February 1846		Montrose
28 February 1846		Montrose
March 1846		Dundee
March 1846		Dundee
Early March 1846	Music Hall, George Street	Aberdeen
Early March 1846	Assembly Rooms, Union Street	Aberdeen
1 March 1846	Assembly, *afternoon*	Glasgow
9 March 1846	Rev. H. Hyslop's Chapel	Montrose
10 March 1846	School Wynd Chapel	Dundee
12 March 1846	City Hall, *afternoon*	Perth
12 March 1846	City Hall	Perth
17 March 1846	Rev. William Nisbet's Church, Abbey Close	Paisley
19 March 1846	Rev. William Nisbet's Church, Abbey Close	Paisley
20 March 1846	Rev. William Nisbet's Church, Abbey Close	Paisley
23 March 1846	Relief Church	Ayr
24 March 1846	Relief Church	Ayr
30 March 1846	Secession Church, Abbey Close	Paisley
31 March 1846	Secession Church, Abbey Close	Bonhill
5 April 1846	Secession Meeting House	Fenwick
6 April 1846	Secession Church, Abbey Close	Paisley
10 April 1846	West Blackhall Street Chapel	Greenock
17 April 1846	Exchange Rooms	Paisley
21 April 1846	City Hall	Glasgow
23 April 1846	Assembly Rooms, *afternoon*	Glasgow
23 April 1846	Assembly Rooms, *evening*	Glasgow
28 April 1846	Rev. Mr. Gilchrist's Church, Rose Street	Edinburgh
29 April 1846	Rev. Mr. Gilchrist's Church, Rose Street, *afternoon*	Edinburgh
1 May 1846	Waterloo Rooms, *afternoon*	Edinburgh
7 May 1846	Rev. Mr. Gilchrist's Church, Rose Street	Edinburgh
8 May 1846	Music Hall	Edinburgh
18 May 1846	Freemason's Hall	London
19 May 1846	Finsbury Chapel	London
20 May 1846	Crown and Anchor Tavern	London

21 May 1846	Exeter Hall	London
22 May 1846	Finsbury Chapel	London
25 May 1846	Music Hall	Edinburgh
26 May 1846	Music Hall	Edinburgh
27 May 1846	Music Hall	Edinburgh
28 May 1846		Leith
1 June 1846	Bethelfields Chapel	Kirkcaldy
2 June 1846	Music Hall	Edinburgh
3 June 1846	Music Hall	Edinburgh
4 June 1846	Music Hall	Edinburgh
16 June 1846	Rev. Nelson's Church, Donegall Street	Belfast
29 June 1846	Ebenezer Chapel	Birmingham
30 June 1846	Lecture Room, Natural History Society	Worcester
2 July 1846	Town Hall, *morning*	Manchester
3 July 1846		Manchester
5 July 1846		Belfast
8 July 1846	Primitive Wesleyan Chapel	Belfast
10 July 1846	Methodist Chapel, Donegall Place	Belfast
13 July 1846	First Presbyterian Church	Bangor
22 July 1846	Independent Church, Donegall Street	Belfast
31 July 1846	Brighton Street Church	Edinburgh
August 1846?		Cullercoats
August 1846?		Stockwell
2 August 1846		Newcastle
3 August 1846	Salem Methodist Church, Hood Street	Newcastle
4 August 1846	Baptist Chapel, Howard Street	North Shields
6 August 1846	Literary Institution, Aldersgate Street	London
7 August 1846	Covent Garden Theatre	London
10 August 1846	Crown and Anchor Tavern	London
13 August 1846	Salem Methodist Church, Hood Street	Newcastle
14 August 1846	Athenaeum, Lowther Street	Carlisle
17 August 1846	Crown and Anchor Tavern	London
19 August 1846	Meeting of the London Flogging Abolition Society	London
21 August 1846	Athenaeum, Lowther Street	Carlisle
24 August 1846		Bristol
25 August 1846	Blind Asylum	Bristol

25 August 1846	Victoria Rooms, *evening*	Bristol
26 August 1846	Victoria Rooms	Bristol
27 August 1846	Victoria Rooms	Bristol
28 August 1846	Subscription Rooms	Exeter
29 August 1846	Subscription Rooms	Exeter
30 August 1846	Public Hall	Taunton
31 August 1846	Public Rooms	Bridgwater
2 September 1846	Public Rooms, Broadmead	Bristol
3 September 1846	Lecture Room, Natural History Society	Worcester
4 September 1846	Livery Street Chapel	Birmingham
5 September 1846		Birmingham
6 September 1846		Birmingham
7 September 1846	Athenaeum, Lowther Street	Carlisle
8 September 1846	Baptist Chapel	North Shields
10 September 1846		Sheffield
11 September 1846	Friends' Meeting House	Sheffield
14 September 1846	Exeter Hall	London
18 September 1846	Athenaeum Hall	Sunderland
22 September 1846		Greenock
23 September 1846	Secession Church, George Street	Paisley
24 September 1846	Brighton Street Church	Edinburgh
25 September 1846	*Evening*	Edinburgh
28 September 1846	Bell Street Chapel	Dundee
29 September 1846		Edinburgh
30 September 1846	City Hall	Glasgow
October 1846		Southport
1 October 1846	*Afternoon*	Glasgow
1 October 1846	*Evening*	Glasgow
2 October 1846	Eagle Temperance Hall, *morning*	Glasgow
2 October 1846	*Afternoon*	Kilmarnock
3 October 1846	Music Hall	Belfast
6 October 1846	Independent Church, Donegall Street	Belfast
7 October 1846	Music Hall	Dublin
9 October 1846	Town Hall	Wrexham
12 October 1846	Free Trade Hall, Peter Street	Manchester
14 October 1846	Public Hall	Rochdale

15 October 1846	Public Hall	Rochdale
16 October 1846		Newcastle
19 October 1846	Concert Hall	Liverpool
21 October 1846	Brighton Street Church	Edinburgh
22 October 1846		Kirkcaldy
23 October 1846	James's Chapel, Bell Street	Dundee
24 October 1846	*Morning/afternoon*	Perth
26 October 1846	Concert Hall	Perth
28 October 1846	City Hall	Glasgow
29 October 1846		Edinburgh
10 November 1846	Public Hall	Rochdale
11 November 1846	Public Hall, *morning*	Rochdale
11 November 1846	Public Hall, *evening*	Rochdale
13 November 1846		Stockport
17 November 1846		Warrington
23 November 1846		Bacup
25 November 1846		Oldham
1 December 1846	Corn Exchange, Hanging Ditch	Manchester
4 December 1846	Corn Exchange, Hanging Ditch	Manchester
10 December 1846		Ashton-Under-Lyne
11 December 1846		Ashton-Under-Lyne
Mid December 1846		Birmingham
22 December 1846		Manchester
23 December 1846		Leeds
28 December 1846	Music Hall, Albion Street	Newcastle
29 December 1846	Music Hall, Albion Street	Newcastle
30 December 1846	Music Hall	Sunderland
31 December 1846		Hexham
December 1846 or January 1847		Gateshead
1 January 1847		Hexham
2 January 1847		Carlisle
4 January 1847		South Shields
11 January 1847	Assembly Rooms	Darlington
13 January 1847		Kirkstall
14 January 1847	Music Hall, Albion Street	Leeds
18 January 1847	Corn Exchange	Manchester

19 January 1847	Baptist Chapel, Grosvenor Street	Manchester
21 January 1847		Coventry
24 January 1847	Vicar Lane Chapel	Coventry
2 February 1847	St. Mary's Hall Chapel	Coventry
10 February 1847	Hall of Commerce	London
12 February 1847	British School Room	Pentonville
13 February 1847		Leamington
23 February 1847		Leamington
25 February 1847	Independent Chapel	Winchester
26 February 1847	Mansion House Chapel	Camberwell
Early March 1847		Wakefield
9 March 1847	Mechanics' Lecture Hall	Warrington
2 March 1847	New Hall	Leicester
4 March 1847	Friends' Meeting House	Colchester
5 March 1847	Mansion House	Camberwell
8? March 1847	Exchange Rooms	Nottingham
16 March 1847	Court House	Cockermouth
25 March 1847	Theatre	Sheffield
29 March 1847	New Hall	Northampton
30 March 1847	London Tavern	London
31 March 1847	Philosophical Hall	Huddersfield
January–March 1847?		Bradford
January–March 1847?		Halifax
January–March 1847?		Doncaster
January–March 1847?		Mansfield
January–March 1847?		Derby
January–March 1847?		Rugby
1 April 1847	Broadmead Rooms	Bristol
29 November 1859	Mechanics' Hall	Halifax
30 November 1859	Mechanics' Hall	Halifax
7 December 1859	Mechanics' Hall	Halifax
13 December 1859	Mechanics' Hall	Halifax
19 December 1859	Temperance Hall, Townhead Street	Sheffield
22 December 1859	Music Hall	Leeds
28 December 1859	Mechanics' Hall	Halifax
December 1859 or January 1860		Manchester

December 1859 or January 1860		Stockport
December 1859 or January 1860		Oldham
December 1859 or January 1860		Huddersfield
December 1859 or January 1860		Hull
December 1859 or January 1860		York
4 January 1860	Mechanics' Hall	Halifax
6 January 1860	Mechanics' Institute	Bradford
12 January 1860	Corn Exchange Buildings	Wakefield
16 January 1860	Temperance Hall, Townhead Street	Sheffield
19 January 1860	Hope Hall, Hope Street	Liverpool
Late January 1860		Perth
Late January 1860		Arbroath
Late January 1860		Kilmarnock
26 January 1860	Abbey Close	Paisley
30 January 1860	Queen Street Hall	Edinburgh
31 January 1860		Glasgow
February 1860		Gateshead
February 1860		Aberdeen
February 1860		Greenock
3 February 1860		Paisley
6 February 1860		Paisley
7 February 1860	Free Church	Falkirk
9 February 1860	Free Church	Dalkeith
10 February 1860		Montrose
13 February 1860	Corn Exchange Hall	Dundee
14 February 1860	John Street United Presbyterian Church	Glasgow
15? February 1860	High Meeting House	Berwick
19 February 1860	Lecture Room, Nelson Street, *afternoon*	Newcastle
21 February 1860	Albion Assembly Rooms, Norfolk Street	North Shields
22 February 1860	Scotch Church	Hexham
23 February 1860	Lecture Room, Nelson Street	Newcastle
24 February 1860	Independent Chapel	Morpeth
25 February 1860	Infant School	Cullercoats

28 February 1860	New Church, Square Road	Halifax
9 March 1860	Wesleyan Free Church, Greenside	Wortley
12 March 1860		Leeds
13 March 1860	Mechanics' Institute	Bradford
16 March 1860	Stock Exchange Hall	Leeds
26 March 1860	Queen's Rooms	Glasgow
28 March 1860	East Campbell Street Church	Glasgow
29 March 1860		Glasgow
Late March 1860	UP Church, Cathcart Street	Ayr
5 October 1886	Julia Griffiths Crofts' School for Girls	St. Neots
12 October 1886	Corn Exchange	St. Neots
15 October 1886	Town Hall	Bridport
July 1887	Helen Bright Clark's House	Street

Part I

"To Tell His Own Story": Frederick Douglass and the British Isles

During a speech in Newcastle in 1846, Frederick Douglass—formerly enslaved African American and radical advocate of social justice—attacked the institution of slavery in a two-hour speech. Using his own position as a fugitive to share his testimony of America's greatest sin, he held the audience spellbound by his rhetoric:

> I wish the slave owners to know that one of their slaves has broken loose from his chains and is going over the length and breadth of England, spreading before the people the damning deeds, that are perpetrated under the veil of slavery. I want them to know that one who has broken through the dark incrustation of slavery, is lifting the veil by which the abominations of the slave system in the United States has been so long hidden . . . I have known something of slavery from my own experience; I have known what it was to feel the biting lash, I have known what it was to feel the longings after freedom to which the slaves are constantly subject . . . I know what it is to feel the lash all marked with blood; to look back over those of my brethren who have preceded me, and to see them generation after generation going down to slavery; all hopes of emancipation shut out, all aspirations crushed, all hope annihilated.[1]

Douglass relayed in blistering language that only one who had experienced the brutal lash could describe its evils. He had escaped and drew back the "veil" protecting enslavers and their deeds to expose them to the light of truth. Douglass, as the fugitive carrying such a burden, enlisted the help of his audience to hold back the veil with him to understand what slavery was. Employing moral suasion, he wanted his audience to raise their voices with him and shame enslavers, with Douglass personally highlighting his own heroism in performing such a task. Targeting racists, pro-slavery defenders and those in the British Isles who claimed slavery existed there, he completely overturned their arguments, citing that the real satanic nature of US slavery was a complete ownership over not just the body, but the mind, soul and heart. Using repetitive phrases such as "I have known," he reinforced that only a fugitive from slavery could understand its harsh realities; oblivious to the freedom and citizenship they took for granted, his audience could never understand the meaning of liberty *because* it had never been brutally removed from them. For Douglass, freedom had always been tantalizingly out of

---

1 *Newcastle Guardian*, 8 August 1846, p. 2.

reach, and thus he could never forget those who had died or were currently living a life with "all hope annihilated."

After the publication of his celebrated *Narrative of the Life of Frederick Douglass, an American Slave* in 1845, written in part to answer charges that he had never been enslaved, Massachusetts abolitionists quickly arranged for Douglass to travel to the British Isles, both for his own protection and to proselytize for the antislavery cause. Since he had divulged his true identity, friends warned him that he was not safe from a rendition effort by his former enslaver. Arriving in England in the summer of 1845, Douglass began an extensive and exhausting lecture tour during which his own eyewitness accounts served as the basis for his speeches and his fame: formerly enslaved individuals had lectured across the British Isles before, but none so effectively or persuasively. He used his radical language against slavery, enslavers, and in particular Southern religion, to paint the region as un-Christian and demonic: those who denied liberty to millions, those who tortured and raped women, those who sold mothers away from their children were inescapably and unequivocally corrupted by the sinful nature of slavery. In making such a case, Douglass left no room for argument. As a fugitive who had witnessed such cruelty, who had seen and felt first-hand the torture he described, he alone could rally his transatlantic brethren to join him in the suppression of an institution that had woven itself, tentacle-like, into American soil.

Between 1845 and 1847 Douglass became the leader of the transatlantic antislavery movement, and his impact on the British Isles was incalculably significant. British abolitionists sang his praises and correspondents wrote feverishly about his speeches and, inevitably, his appearance. Since the 1980s, historians such as Richard Blackett, Celeste-Marie Bernier, Alan Rice, Martin Crawford, Fionnghuala Sweeney, Alasdair Pettinger, David Blight, Leigh Fought, Laurence Fenton, and Christine Kinealy – to name but a few – have written on Douglass's literary and oratorical success in the British Isles. Such expert interest has led to numerous academic discoveries surrounding Douglass's networks and hosts, his relationship with abolitionists, the development of his oratory, his *Narrative*, his relationship with family thousands of miles away, and, notably, the activists he inspired on British soil. Douglass nurtured British and Irish connections for the rest of his life, and they often sustained him and his activism in hours of dire need. Douglass found a second home in Britain, a place that represented a spiritual and often physical freedom he had never experienced before. He chose to flee to Britain after the Insurrection at Harpers Ferry, and made the nation his start and endpoint for his honeymoon with second wife Helen Pitts in 1886–7. Throughout his illustrious activist career, British and Irish newspapers constantly printed his speeches, opinions about the United States, and letters to friends. As the foremost and most famous African American of the nineteenth century, his oratorical, literary, and visual genius endlessly fascinated newspaper correspondents and their readers, who were gripped by the details of his heroism and unceasing fight to champion racial equality.

Frederick Augustus Washington Bailey was born in Talbot County, Maryland, in 1818. Like most of the enslaved population, and as part of the dehumanizing brutality of slavery, he never knew his date of birth. His first enslaver, Aaron Anthony, an overseer for the wealthy Lloyd family on Maryland's Eastern Shore, assigned Douglass to be a companion to a scion of his employer. Later, he was sent to live in Baltimore with the family of Hugh Auld, a brother of Anthony's son-in-law, Thomas Auld. In Baltimore, Douglass associated with the city's free Black population and began to teach himself to read. These youthful experiences made him resistant to the discipline of rural slavery when, on Anthony's death, he was inherited by Thomas Auld. During one transformative moment in his life, Douglass was sent by Auld to work for Edward Covey, a notorious "slave-breaker," who severely beat the sixteen-year-old until he fought back. Frederick Bailey attempted to escape slavery twice before he was eventually successful in 1838 with the instrumental help of his future wife, Anna Murray. Inspired by a character from Walter Scott, Bailey changed his name to Frederick Douglass, inserting an extra "s" for differentiation. He soon attracted the attention of abolitionist William Lloyd Garrison, the leader of the American Anti-Slavery Society, who invited him to speak at a meeting in 1841. Douglass became a paid agent of the Society and lectured across the eastern United States to thousands of people. He escaped mobs and would-be lynchers, and converted numerous people to the cause of abolition with his inspiring oratory.[2]

He relied on traditional forms of storytelling from his African heritage, honed through years of teaching, speaking, and preaching sermons that gave him the tools in which to construct visuals of oppression and stir the hearts and minds of his audiences. For example, he used techniques such as call and response to invite audience participation.[3] Learning from such influences, Douglass changed the pitch of his voice and relied on impassioned rhetoric and gestures to illustrate his lectures. He began his early speeches slowly, with limited hand gestures and a quieter tone in

---

2 For biographies of Douglass and his works, see, for example, Andrews, *Frederick Douglass: The Oxford Reader*; Barnes, *Frederick Douglass: A Life in Documents*; Bernier and Lawson, *Pictures and Power*; Douglass (ed. Bernier), *Narrative* and *My Bondage and My Freedom*; Blight, *Frederick Douglass: Prophet of Freedom*; Buccola, *The Political Thought of Frederick Douglass*; Burke, *Frederick Douglass: Crusading Orator*; Chesebrough, *Frederick Douglass: Oratory from Slavery*; Dilbeck, *Frederick Douglass: America's Prophet*; Foner, *Frederick Douglass*; Fought, *Women in the World of Frederick Douglass*; Kinealy, *Frederick Douglass and Ireland*; Lampe, *Frederick Douglass: Freedom's Voice*; Lawson and Kirkland, *Frederick Douglass: A Critical Reader*; Lee, *The Cambridge Companion to Frederick Douglass*; Levine, *The Lives of Frederick Douglass*; McFeely, *Frederick Douglass*; Martin, *The Mind of Frederick Douglass*; Quarles, *Frederick Douglass*.
3 Lampe, *Frederick Douglass: Freedom's Voice*, pp. viii–ix; 1–15.

his voice. He would then speak more loudly, accompanying the change in amplification with more hand gestures and bold language.[4] His attention to detail in his rhetoric filtered down to his facial expressions and clothing, and he orchestrated entire performances that included turning up the lights so audiences could fully see him and amplifying his voice to reach the back of the lecture hall.[5] Throughout his life, Douglass revered the power of oratory; he declared: "Speech! Speech! The live, calm, grave, clear, pointed, warm, sweet, melodious, and powerful human voice is [the] chosen instrumentality." While pro-slavery defenders could use print culture to circulate their foul ideology – "ink and paper have no shame" – they were well aware that "slavery is a poor orator when confronted by an abolitionist and they wisely kept silent."[6]

After spending nearly two years in the British Isles, Douglass returned to the United States to lecture and edit a newspaper, *The North Star*, which caused considerable tension with his Garrisonian friends. In 1851, he officially broke with Garrison over his embrace of political activism and decision to regard the Constitution as an antislavery document. In part to escape the shackles of a white racist schema both within and outside the movement, Douglass was a prolific writer: his first autobiography, *Narrative of the Life of Frederick Douglass*, published in 1845, remains one of the most successful slave narratives. In the first four months after its publication, 4,500 copies were sold, and 20,000 copies were sold from 1845 to the early 1850s. A second autobiography, *My Bondage and My Freedom*, followed in 1855; then a third, *Life and Times*, in 1881, with a revised edition in 1892. As well as his literary masterpieces, Douglass wrote countless pamphlets, hundreds of editorials, thousands of letters, and poetry – and he penned a work of fiction, *The Heroic Slave*, in 1853.[7]

During the American Civil War, Douglass was a prominent figure in the fight for African Americans to join the Union Army, urging his two sons to enlist in the now famous 54th Massachusetts Regiment. While the end of the war may have brought legal emancipation, the legacies of slavery still remained; Douglass continued his fight to advocate for justice and spoke publicly on his abhorrence at the rising racial violence across America. As the most famous and recognized African American in the US and beyond, he held several political appointments until the end of his life: he was a member of a US commission to the Dominican Republic; Recorder of Deeds for the District of Columbia; a US Marshal; and US Minister to Haiti. In the private sector after the war, Douglass served as president of the Freedman's Savings Bank, a private institution designed to help African Americans who had been freed

---

4 Blassingame, *Douglass Papers—Series One: Vol. 1*, pp. xxiv–xxxi.
5 Stauffer, "Douglass's Self-Making and the Culture of Abolitionism," p. 17.
6 Blassingame, *Douglass Papers—Series One: Vol. 1*, p. xxv.
7 Levine, *The Lives of Frederick Douglass*, pp. 14–15; 72–75. See Douglass's multiple writings, and the collected *Frederick Douglass Papers* (ed. Blassingame and McKivigan).

after the Civil War; he also became an editor of a weekly newspaper in the nation's capital of Washington; and, as a trustee of Howard University, he played a part in providing quality higher education to African American students.[8]

Douglass could not have led such a successful life of activism without the support of his family. While providing obvious emotional and moral support, Anna Murray Douglass and their children, Rosetta, Lewis Henry, Frederick Jr., Charles Remond, and Annie (who tragically died in 1860) were all activists in their own right, and had a significant impact on the antislavery and civil rights movements. Anna Murray Douglass was the chief conductor on the Underground Railroad, managed the family finances, and established familial and kinship networks within the local community. The four eldest children were all employed in proof-reading, typesetting, printing, and even distributing Douglass's paper, which would later shape their own activist careers. Behind his very public and celebrated public persona were six family members who toiled relentlessly to aid and allow him to pursue speaking engagements and political appointments, and to travel abroad. After Anna Murray Douglass's death in 1882, he married Helen Pitts, a white woman, which invited tensions within his family and insidious racism from national newspapers.[9]

*

In the last forty years, there has been a significant growth in scholarship focusing on Douglass's experiences abroad. Benjamin Quarles, Phillip Foner, George Shepperson and John Blassingame were among the first to analyze his British sojourns, and devoted chapters or articles to key moments such as the riot on the *Cambria*, the Evangelical Alliance, the World's Temperance Convention, and the Free Church of Scotland. Richard Blackett's *Building an Antislavery Wall* (1983) was groundbreaking in its focus on Black transatlantic abolitionism, including a detailed chapter on Douglass's first tour to the British Isles.[10] In terms of scope, however, Alan Rice and Martin Crawford's *Liberating Sojourn: Frederick Douglass and Transatlantic*

---

8   See Douglass, *Life and Times*; Blight, *Frederick Douglass: Prophet of Freedom*; Douglass (ed. Bernier), *Narrative of the Life of Frederick Douglass*.

9   Bernier and Taylor, *If I Survive*, pp. lxvi–lxix. See the forthcoming volumes by Bernier: *The Anna Murray and Frederick Douglass Family Papers, Volume 1: A Family Biography*; *The Anna Murray and Frederick Douglass Family Papers, Volume 2: Unpublished Papers*; and *The Anna Murray and Frederick Douglass Family Papers, Volume 3: Published Papers* (2021). See also Fought, *Women in the World of Frederick Douglass*; Blight, *Frederick Douglass: Prophet of Freedom*.

10 Blassingame, *Douglass Papers—Series One: Vol. 1*; Quarles, *Frederick Douglass*; Foner, *Life and Writings of Frederick Douglass, Vol. 1*, Ripley, *The Black Abolitionist Papers*; Blackett, *Building an Antislavery Wall*, Fulkerson, "Frederick Douglass and the Anti-Slavery Crusade" and "Exile as Emergence"; McFeely, *Frederick Douglass*; Sinha, *The Slave's Cause: A History of Abolition*; Fisch, *American Slaves in Victorian England*; Taylor, *British and American Abolitionists*.

Reform (1999) was the first comprehensive work on Douglass's experience in the British Isles as a whole. Based on an international conference, the co-edited volume explored Douglass's Scottish and Irish campaigns, his association with the Chartist movement, his connections to British Unitarians, and his 1859 visit, which acted as a catalyst for scholars to begin fully examining Douglass's relationship with the Atlantic.[11] However, since its publication, only Laurence Fenton's brilliant work *I was Transformed: Frederick Douglass – An American Slave in Victorian Britain* (2018) studies Douglass's Atlantic experience in its entirety.

Most scholarship focuses on specific events or regions of his journey, particularly his relationship with Ireland. There are many reasons for this, but primarily, Douglass's Irish visit was the first part of his 1845 tour and so was the starting point for dramatic changes in his self-fashioning. For the first time in his life he experienced an alternate form of citizenship and freedom, and his often relentless schedule proved representative of his later travels; he cultivated abolitionist networks and important dignitaries in order to lecture on slavery whenever possible. Douglass's new *Narrative* edition was also printed in Dublin, which represented his growing independence from the Garrisonian movement. In *Frederick Douglass and the Atlantic World* (2007), Fionnghuala Sweeney brilliantly analyzes Douglass's relationship with Ireland, examining his performative engagement with his audiences and the crucial networks he helped to forge. Tom Chaffin and Laurence Fenton have written detailed narratives of Douglass's time in Ireland, and Christine Kinealy has published two in-depth anthologies of his speeches, letters, and editorials that pertain to his relationship with the Emerald Isle.[12]

Douglass's notorious campaign against the Free Church of Scotland has also received seminal analysis and commentary. Alasdair Pettinger's *Frederick Douglass in Scotland* (2018) marked years of extensive and meticulous research into the Scottish archives to fully comprehend Douglass's tour, and radically updates Douglass's speaking itinerary. His digital humanities project also contains an examination of his trip, interaction with other abolitionists, and spotlights key cities Douglass visited. Iain Whyte (2012) provides extensive detail on the American abolitionist

---

11 Rice and Crawford, *Liberating Sojourn*; Rice, "Transatlantic Portrayals"; Fenton, "*I was Transformed*"; Murray, *Advocates of Freedom*. See also Amy Cools' excellent website, *Ordinary Philosophy*: <https://ordinaryphilosophy.com/2018/09/06/following-frederick-douglass-in-the-british-isles/> (last accessed 11 October 2020).

12 Sweeney, *Frederick Douglass and the Atlantic World*; Kinealy, *Frederick Douglass in Ireland*; Fenton, *Frederick Douglass in Ireland*; Chaffin, *Giant's Causeway*; Quinn, "'Safe in Old Ireland'"; Kerr-Ritchie, "Black Abolitionists, Irish Supporters, and the Brotherhood of Man"; Ferreira, "Frederick Douglass and the 1846 Dublin Edition of His Narrative"; Ritchie, "'The Stone in the Sling'"; Mulligan, "As a Lever Gains Power." Robert Levine dedicates an entire chapter to the Dublin edition in *The Lives of Frederick Douglass*. See also the brilliant PhD thesis by Ann Coughlan, "Frederick Douglass and Ireland, 1845: The 'Vertiginous Twist[s]' of an Irish Encounter."

campaign against the Free Church, building on and revising George Shepperson's groundbreaking research from the 1950s.[13]

Celeste-Marie Bernier has published numerous articles and books on Frederick Douglass over the last two decades, and in recent seminal works such as *Pictures and Power: Imaging and Imagining Frederick Douglass 1818–2018* (2017); *Narrative of the Life of Frederick Douglass, An American Slave: A 2018 Bicentenary Edition* (2018); and *If I Survive: Frederick Douglass and Family in the Walter O. Evans Collection* (2018), she analyzes the Irish publication of his *Narrative*, his relationship with international abolitionists, and the impact of his transatlantic travels. In Edinburgh, Bernier has organized numerous community events to permanently memorialize Douglass's legacy in Scotland, including the erection of a heritage plaque, an exhibition, digital maps, and walking tours.[14]

International biographies have also contained essential writings about Douglass's visits abroad. In his 2018 prizewinning book *Prophet of Freedom*, David Blight devotes two chapters to Douglass's first visit to the British Isles, and Leigh Fought examines his integral networks with British and Irish women in *Women in the World of Frederick Douglass* (2017). In particular, she includes new material on Julia Griffiths Crofts, the Jennings sisters, and the Richardson family, many of whom became lifelong supporters of Douglass and were crucial to his activism in the United States.[15]

In conjunction with these works, our volume focuses on the rediscovery and amplification of Douglass's testimony in Britain and Ireland: we publish several speeches, writings and poetry that have never been published before. Our book does not explore every connection he made nor every speech, but is structured to provide close readings of the themes he espoused across the Atlantic, particularly in these rediscovered sources. Between 1845 and 1847 he spoke to numerous audiences across class, racial, religious, and gender lines in crowded churches, town halls, and schoolrooms, which launched his international career. His electrifying oratory and performative engagement with his audiences set the stage for his future successes, and many of his speeches rival the thematic content of addresses like "What to the Slave is the 4th of July?" (delivered in 1852). His lectures were live performances, site-specific interactions between speaker and audience, which changed nightly depending on the composition of the audience, their reaction, and whether any interruptions took place. His speeches were deliberate and often rehearsed but any disruptions allow us to

---

13 Whyte, *Send Back the Money!*; Pettinger, *Frederick Douglass and Scotland*; and Pettinger's digital humanities project, "Douglass in Scotland," at <https://www.bulldozia.com/douglass-in-scotland/> (last accessed 11 October 2020). See also Shepperson, "The Free Church and American Slavery," and Shepperson, "Thomas Chalmers, The Free Church of Scotland and the South."

14 Bernier and Lawson, *Pictures and Power*; Bernier (ed.), *Narrative of the Life of Frederick Douglass*; and Bernier and Taylor, *If I Survive*. See also Bernier's website focusing on her project, "Our Bondage and Our Freedom," <https://ourbondageourfreedom.llc.ed.ac.uk> (last accessed 11 October 2020).

15 Blight, *Frederick Douglass: Prophet of Freedom*, and Fought, *Women in the World of Frederick Douglass*.

comprehend his on-the-spot reactions and his blistering rhetoric, blinding sarcasm, wit, and even anger. By examining this performative engagement and his literary and oratorical testimony, we can analyze the themes he focused on during his three visits. These included, but were not limited to: the brutality of slavery; the auction block; slaveholding religion; US imperialism through the annexation of Texas; the American jeremiad; religious assemblies, such as the Evangelical Alliance and the Free Church; the suffrage movement; temperance; Black masculinity and heroism; social inequality; women's rights; John Brown; and racism and segregation. The nature and range of such speeches delivered on British or Irish soil should delineate new readings on themes that Douglass carried with him for the rest of his life.[16]

Often during his speeches, for example, he personified slavery as a large monster which would soon awaken to destroy the United States. The entire nation, then, was corrupted and polluted by its influence. Implicit in this ideology was Douglass laying down the metaphorical gauntlet for his British and Irish audiences to wield against their American brethren: their ancestors had perpetuated slavery and their white privilege simultaneously protected them from and reinforced the system, which meant that – enlightened with Douglass's testimony – their ignorance or silence was now impossible. They should renounce fellowship with enslavers and churches that supported slavery, champion true Christianity, educate others, and perform their duty, for all of their hands were soaked with the blood of his enslaved brethren. In the US, Douglass's narrative was symbolic of the Black American jeremiad, which proscribed America's destiny toward disaster if the racial scars on the landscape continued to be reopened. If this racial injustice was cured, the nation could fulfil its divine invocation and begin to heal. In his writings and speeches, Douglass employed the jeremiad trope to convince his audiences that he was making a divine intervention to warn the people that the nation was polluted under the weight of slavery and for the nation's survival, slavery must be destroyed.[17] In Britain, Douglass extended this metaphor to implicate his transatlantic audiences not only with the sin of slavery, but also the future destiny of the United States.

Unsurprisingly, most scholarship tends to concentrate on his new-found freedom and independence in the British Isles, particularly in Ireland.[18] As Rice and Crawford note, Douglass's journey led to a "refiguring of the Atlantic crossing from a historically enslaving experience into a literally liberating one." He came to Britain

---

16 See Murray, *Advocates of Freedom*, and numerous transcriptions of Douglass's speeches in Blassingame, *Douglass Papers—Series One: Vol. 1*.

17 Andrews, *To Tell a Free Story*, pp. 123–28. See also Blight, *Frederick Douglass: Prophet of Freedom*; Howard-Pitney, *The African American Jeremiad*; and Harrell Jr., *Origins of the African American Jeremiad*.

18 For example, see Quarles, *Frederick Douglass*; Foner, *Frederick Douglass*; Fulkerson, "Exile as Emergence"; Rice and Crawford, *Liberating Sojourn*; Chesebrough, *Frederick Douglass: Oratory from Slavery*; Sweeney, *Frederick Douglass and the Atlantic World*; Blight, *Frederick Douglass: Prophet of Freedom*; and Kinealy, *Frederick Douglass in Ireland*.

a "raw material" and would return to America as "the finished independent man cut from a whole cloth and able to make his own decisions about the strategies and ideologies of the abolitionist movement."[19] There is no doubt Douglass left the British Isles a changed man: he experienced a completely different form of citizenship and liberty in Britain and Ireland. His level of mobility, for one, was extremely different to what it had been in the US, and he was not mobbed, beaten, or threatened with torture, kidnap, or assassination on the platform. Few individuals could resist being changed after a nearly two-year trip abroad, and this experience had a deep impact on Douglass's identity and his concept of nationhood. As he repeatedly stated, to enjoy true freedom he had to travel thousands of miles away and celebrate it under the flag of monarchy rather than republicanism.

Instead of focusing solely on Ireland as one of the central points in his dramatic self-fashioning, however, we enlarge the scope to view his sojourn in its entirety and complicate his declarations of freedom. We do not deny the liberty he felt in Britain compared to the US, but we also place great focus on the racialized rhetoric he experienced in the British Isles surrounding Blackness, race, and minstrelsy, together with the racism directed toward him from the press, critics, religious ministers, and his own abolitionist friends. The trip abroad did lead to an eventual split with the Garrisonians, but only because of the build-up of numerous microaggressions that had taken place before 1845, together with those that were compounded thousands of miles away from home and within a short and concentrated period of time. The desire to control his own lecturing schedule, his *Narrative*, the purchase of his legal freedom, and the lack of respect from certain abolitionists infuriated him. Thus, the British Isles gave him the space, the opportunity, and the time away from the epicentre of Garrisonian abolitionism in New England to develop and nurture a radical antislavery philosophy, shaped by his experiences abroad but not forged there entirely. By reshaping his own ideology through a transatlantic lens, he completely rejected the white constraints of his Garrisonian peers, who wanted him to merely state the facts of his life; by combining his testimony as a fugitive with a visual philosophy of antislavery, he convinced thousands of people on both sides of the Atlantic about slavery's realities. His first trip provided the first falling domino in an often tumultuous position within the antislavery movement, one that would be further strained in the 1850s and beyond.

It is important to note, then, that Douglass was already his own man *before* he crossed the Atlantic, his radical *Narrative* being an example of a literary tour de force that rejected white enslaver ideology and by extension the white racial schema.[20] He was no carbon copy of Garrison and had always differed from him on subjects

---

19 Rice and Crawford, "Triumphant Exile," p. 3.
20 In her thesis, Ann Coughlan challenges the "raw material" analogy: see Coughlan, "Frederick Douglass and Ireland, 1845." See also McDaniel, *The Problem of Democracy in the Age of Slavery*, and Bernier (ed.) for an extensive discussion on the *Narrative* (2018).

such as non-violence; while he was against murder and war, there were "circumstances when it would not only be right – but our bounden duty to use Physical force to restrain persons bent upon the commission of crime."[21] As a critical and radical philosopher his independence manifested itself before his journey to Britain, as he later expressed his displeasure at echoing "the same old story month after month, and to keep up my interest in it." On the Garrisonian platform, he rejected the passive label of a "chattel" and carved a space for himself within a movement that often restricted the voices of Black lecturers.[22]

What his Atlantic visits gave him instead was the opportunity to assert his authorial and oratorical independence more fully and reject abolitionist tropes with which he had never been fully comfortable. Abroad, he had the space to creatively practice and hone his performative engagement with his audiences and to continue creating his antislavery philosophy away from his Garrisonian mentors. For example, James Buffum, a traveling companion sent along by the Boston abolitionists to keep an eye on Douglass, soon abandoned his mission and returned home. And by mid-1846, any previous reliance on or instruction by Garrisonian abolitionists to exhibit whips and chains, sing antislavery songs, or even use minstrelesque language ceased to be part of his repertoire. In many of his English speeches from October 1846 to April 1847, he refused to employ such tactics and instead relied purely on his voice. Instead of focusing solely on his Irish trip, as other studies have done, we shift our focus to his English lectures and study his two-year sojourn as a whole to fully comprehend these changes and his experiences abroad.

The difficulties of navigating such tensions revealed itself in later trips, too, and the speeches and analysis presented here offer an opportunity to revise the monolithic image of Douglass as a celebrity and see a crack in his lionized facade. Suffering severely from depression, miles away from his family, performing for hours on end – sometimes nightly – meant his tour almost broke him. Such immense abolitionist activism revealed an inherent cost in pursuing such a hectic schedule, a battle between the public and private spheres which he struggled with for the rest of his life. Nowhere is this more apparent than in 1860, when Douglass attempted to deliver public speeches after being given the heartbreaking news of his youngest daughter's death. The echo of such tragedies, together with his traumatic past, constantly plagued him throughout his life, and forces us to recognize Douglass the *human* activist instead of the celebrated image.

Together with new sources and other famous documents, we hope that this book provides a comprehensive resource on his relationship with the British Isles,

---

21 Frederick Douglass to Elizabeth Pease, 6 July 1846, in McKivigan, *Douglass Papers—Series Three: Vol. 1*, pp. 141–43.

22 Selby, "The Limits of Accommodation"; Douglass (ed. Bernier), *My Bondage and My Freedom*, p. xxiii.

offering scholars, students and activists the chance to conduct their own close readings of Douglass's speeches and to view his sojourn in entirely new ways. We also want to redress the balance of previous scholarly focus: while his first visit will be covered in detail, his second and third sojourns will also receive an unprecedented in-depth analysis. British press coverage during his three visits shows how Douglass employed various mediums – letters, speeches, interviews, and his autobiographies – to convince the transatlantic public not only that his works were worth reading and his voice worth hearing, but also that the fight against racism would continue after his death.

In 1847, Douglass declared that the slaveholder could no longer hide what slavery truly was, for "the slave now broke loose from his chains and went forth to tell his own story, and to make known the wrongs of his brethren."[23] There was no alternative career for him: after a brief contemplation of a life in England, there was no serious move to bring his family across the Atlantic. While his fellow brethren toiled in enslavement or in the bitter unfreedom of emancipation, he refused to give up the dedication to liberty that was ingrained into his mind, body, and soul, and devoted every waking hour to the abolition of slavery and racial injustice. To British audiences, he epitomized a radical heroism where he refused to be silenced by racists or pro-slavery defenders, placing his literary, visual, and oratorical testimony at the forefront of the antislavery movement and social justice struggles throughout the nineteenth century.

The structure of this book reflects Douglass's extensive transatlantic relationships from his trip in 1845 to his death. The first section is a detailed overview of Douglass's visits to Britain and Ireland. The second publishes eighteen of Douglass's speeches in the British Isles between 1845 and 1886, which point to controversies revolving around the Free Church of Scotland, the Evangelical Alliance, and the World's Temperance Convention. They highlight how he began to reach out beyond the narrow base of British supporters of William Lloyd Garrison's perfectionist brand of abolitionism to reach a broader audience, more sympathetic to religious and political antislavery tactics anathema to the Garrisonians. Covering Ireland, Scotland, and England, these speeches testify to Douglass's gruelling lecturing schedule as he sought to capitalize on the popularity of abolition and his oratorical brilliance. As alluded to above, this section will redirect focus toward his activism in England, which has received comparably less attention than his Irish and Scottish tours. We should note here that Douglass did give one speech in Wrexham, Wales, which is not covered in this volume; instead, we point readers to Daniel Williams's *Black Skin, Blue Books: African Americans and Wales 1845–1945* (2012), which offers extensive analysis on this successful lecture.

---

23 Blassingame, *Douglass Papers—Series One: Vol. 2*, pp. 8–19.

Several of Douglass's speeches from 1847 are published here for the first time and contain clues as to *why* Douglass was so successful, and the ways in which he crafted his celebrity to remain famous even after his departure. By contrast, Douglass's brief return in 1859–60, to escape arrest in the wake of John Brown's raid, was not as successful as his previous visit. While he had long contemplated a visit to the British Isles, Brown's rebellion forced Douglass's hand, and he arrived in England in November 1859. However, his close association with Brown's violent assault frightened away Quakers and other potential antislavery listeners with pacifist inclinations. Estranged from the Garrisonians since the early 1850s because of his endorsement of political abolitionist tactics, Douglass did not have an established hosting network to arrange his speaking engagements, save Julia Griffiths Crofts, who had laid extensive groundwork for his planned visit. Finally, one speech is included from 1886, before Douglass and his second wife, Helen Pitts, traveled to France on their honeymoon.

The third section focuses on Douglass's observations about Britain and Ireland from his speeches in the US, journalism, letters, and autobiographies, which provide an additional layer of context to understand the speeches. They include his thoughts regarding British contributions to various reform causes, class and race relations in the British Isles, the British–Irish conflict, and his hope for cordial interactions between the US and UK based on shared values. These selections also document the evolution of Douglass's thinking on such issues, from his abolitionist advocacy following his 1840s visit to his reminiscences almost a half-century later.

The last section includes a selection of nineteenth-century songs, poetry, images, newspaper articles, and obituaries. We publish eighteen poems, many for the first time since their nineteenth-century appearance in the local press, including works inspired by his antislavery campaign and his *Narrative*. Adding significantly to scholarship focusing on Douglass's 1880s travels, we publish an extensive interview Douglass gave in *The London Daily News*, which provides an in-depth glimpse into Douglass's melancholy that the promise of Emancipation remained unfulfilled. Finally, we include an obituary once again published by *The London Daily News* that not only illustrates the important and proliferating print culture surrounding Douglass, but also his impact on British society as a whole.

In a letter reprinted in this volume for the first time since 1865, Douglass wrote that "the thought of some day visiting England again flits across my mind like a sunbeam into the darkness of the hour, but I dare not allow it a long stay . . . England has entered deeply into my life ever since, and happily so. My friends there have been more thoughtful for me, in my works than anywhere else."[24] Throughout his long

---

24   *Manchester Times*, 20 May 1865, p. 5.

life, Douglass traveled thousands of miles across the British Isles, and his personal and political life would have been very different without the support of his British and Irish friends. His oratorical brilliance performed across four countries reflected not only his urgent desire to bring freedom to millions of his enslaved brethren, but also his radical belief in equality and social justice. As proved by numerous African American activists during the course of the nineteenth century, the very act of traversing the Atlantic was a radical move in itself, as they – Douglass included – defied their former enslavers and enlightened the transatlantic public as to the true nature of slavery. While Douglass was perhaps the most successful of them all, he never forgot how his British and Irish experience shaped his future career – nor how the bond shared with transatlantic friends, and with the nation as a whole, became a part of his identity until the day he died.

Chapter 1

"To Remove the Mask from Her Face": 1845–1847

During the mid-nineteenth century, there was a steady stream of American abolitionists who visited the British Isles and used the transatlantic crossing to make a statement about American slavery. Since advances in transportation shortened the journey to a mere couple of weeks, the bonds between abolitionists grew stronger: how could American slavery exist, argued abolitionists, when Britain – a nation which had fought hard to remove slavery – was only a short voyage away? The journey encouraged correspondence with letters, pamphlets and newspapers sent to and fro in an unprecedented capacity. Douglass and other Black abolitionists couched the voyage in terms of a passage from American racism to British freedom: if African Americans experienced racial discrimination or injustice on board a steamship, the unusual ideological space between two countries (one with slavery and one without) could often make confrontations tense. Never one to miss an opportunity, Douglass used this experience as a political lens through which to examine the differences between the freedoms he experienced on British shores and the racism he endured in the United States.[1]

The rise of William Lloyd Garrison's radical abolitionism and his supporters in Britain ensured a growing network of like-minded individuals who were prepared to offer help, support and their homes to Black activists. Garrison's party, the American Anti-Slavery Society, was created in 1833, with its unofficial newspaper, *The Liberator*, founded two years previously; Garrison constantly networked, shared information and exchanged antislavery pamphlets, and such transatlantic correspondence formed an integral part of the newspaper's coverage.[2] These

---

1 McDaniel, "Saltwater Anti-Slavery," pp. 142–46.
2 Ripley, *The Black Abolitionist Papers*, pp. 6–10; *Freeman's Journal and Daily Commercial Advertiser*, 27 June 1840, pp. 2–4. See also Blackett, *Building an Antislavery Wall*, and Taylor, *British and American Abolitionists*.

networks were formed and nurtured at events such as the World's Anti-Slavery Convention in 1840, organized by the British and Foreign Anti-Slavery Society (BFASS). That event was attended by more than five hundred people from around the globe, with an additional 5,000 who visited or listened to the debates; men and women such as Daniel O'Connell, Joseph Sturge, William Lloyd Garrison, George Thompson, Henry Stanton, Elizabeth Cady Stanton, and Lucretia Mott were present, and the latter three individuals were famous for their protest against the BFASS's refusal to allow women to take part as delegates.[3] Formed in 1839, the BFASS was based at 27 New Broad Street, London, where the secretary (John Scoble up until the mid-1850s) worked on correspondence, compiled reports, and edited their newspaper, *The Anti-Slavery Reporter*.[4] The BFASS's membership drew heavily from Quakers and other nonconformists, but the group was troubled by the bitter criticism many Garrisonians launched against religious institutions for condoning slavery. In particular, Scoble's combative nature thwarted productive alliances with Garrisonian groups across the country. In 1840, Scoble even went so far as to distribute inflammatory material about Garrison's character and targeted his unwillingness to compromise, particularly when it came to concepts such as perfectionism.[5]

Members of the Garrisonian network, meanwhile, were loyal and committed to the cause. Douglass would soon work with Richard D. Webb in Dublin; Ralph Varian and the Jennings family in Cork; John Murray, Andrew Paton, and William Smeal in Glasgow; the Estlin family in Bristol; Elizabeth Pease in Darlington; Mary Brady in Sheffield; the Hilditch sisters, Sarah and Blanche, in Wrexham; and Eliza Wigham in Edinburgh.[6] When Douglass met Ellen Richardson in August 1846, she introduced him to her cousins Eliza Nicholson and Jane Carr, and Anna, her sister-in-law; as kinfolk and as Quakers, the Richardsons had extensive relations across the country.[7] Garrison exploited transatlantic connections with abolitionists, newspaper editors, journalists, writers, poets, and anyone of influence that could lend support to the antislavery cause. He maintained such working relationships and friendships with numerous people across the Atlantic, and each time he visited Britain, he cultivated connections to friends in high places to raise awareness of American slavery and maximize readership for *The Liberator*.[8]

---

3   Bric, "Debating Slavery and Empire," pp. 61–63. See also McDaniel, *The Problem of Democracy in the Age of Slavery*.

4   Temperley, *British Antislavery 1833–1870*, pp. 34–40.

5   Heartfield, *The British and Foreign Anti-Slavery Society*, pp. 32–39; 55.

6   Blassingame, *Douglass Papers—Series One: Vol. 1*, p. liv; Ripley, *The Black Abolitionist Papers*, pp. 6–18.

7   Fought, *Women in the World of Frederick Douglass*, pp. 84–90.

8   Morgan, "The Political as Personal"; Blackett, "'And There Shall Be No More Sea,'" pp. 15–17; 22–23.

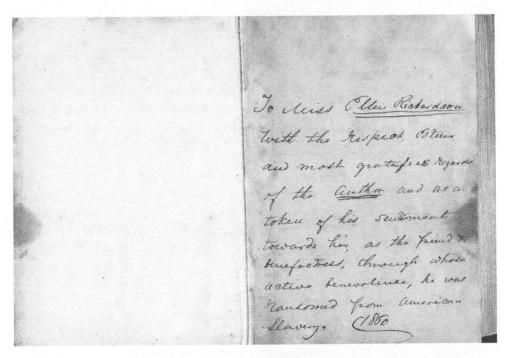

Figure 1.1 Inscription to Ellen Richardson from Frederick Douglass, *My Bondage and My Freedom* (Stanford University).

These networks gave Douglass the opportunity to speak in numerous locations, from large industrial towns to small fishing villages on the coast. He wrote on his return to America that he had "made use of all the various means of conveyance, by land and sea, from town to town, and city to city" and traveled the length and breadth of the country.[9] He had "journeyed upon highways, byways, railways, and steamboats" and stated, "I have myself gone, I might say, with almost electric speed."[10] The rapidity of the railway boom, along with other methods of technology, communication, and transport, was unprecedented and transformed British society: journeys were faster, time was standardized, ship-building increased, trade was made easier and quicker between towns and the countryside. In recognition of this, Douglass argued in Leeds in 1846 that "what is uttered this day in the Music Hall of Leeds, will, within fourteen days resound in Massachusetts."[11]

---

9 Frederick Douglass to William Lloyd Garrison, 21 April 1847, in McKivigan, *Douglass Papers— Series Three, Vol. 1*, pp. 202–03.

10 Frederick Douglass, 30 March 1847, in Blassingame, *Douglass Papers—Series One: Vol. 2*, p. 49.

11 Frederick Douglass, 23 December 1846, in Blassingame, *Douglass Papers—Series One: Vol. 1*, p. 174.

Douglass recognized the importance of the railway and took full advantage of the developing network across the country. He may have been one of the first passengers on certain lines: on 18 March 1847, he wrote to John Gibson – postmaster of Whitehaven – that he was visiting the town "on the day of opening the Rail Road from Whitehaven to Carlisle."[12] A few months earlier, in Newcastle, anticipation for Douglass's lecture was so high that a special train was scheduled to leave at quarter past ten to allow people from Sunderland and Shields to attend and then return home.[13] His connections to the stalwart abolitionist Richardson family in Newcastle indicate why he spoke there several times and perhaps explain this railway connection, as it is very likely they had some influence in arranging the extra train. Regardless, the concept of traveling to a meeting outside an immediate location was novel. It highlighted the growing importance of the railway to local towns and how it allowed for greater communication and a chance for people to physically travel to see a famous figure.

Thus, the organization of a lecture tour was an impressive enterprise that had to be carefully planned. Abolitionists would arrange to meet Douglass at a train station or hotel, and he was introduced to local activists or friends of the movement. They would orientate him around a city and sometimes lead or chair antislavery meetings.[14] The Belfast Anti-Slavery Society paid for Douglass's room at the Victoria Hotel for several weeks, and as per the arrangement, Douglass lectured at least six times on their behalf. In Wexford, Webb organized for Douglass to stay with his cousin's family and coordinated two lectures in early October. Webb then arranged for him to stay with the Jennings family in Cork, who advertised Douglass's lectures and invited influential people to attend.[15] When Douglass spoke to 6,000 people at Exeter Hall in London on 14 September, abolitionists helped pay nearly $250 for the building's rental, advertisements, and placards, providing Douglass with opportunities that were closed to some Black abolitionists like Moses Roper, who was traveling around Britain at the same time without such networks of kinship.[16]

*

---

12 Frederick Douglass to John Gibson, 18 March 1847, in John Gibson, "Autograph album, Vol. 1: 1747–1880s," Daniel Hay Collection, c. 17th–c. 20th, Cumbria Archive.

13 *Newcastle Guardian*, 12 December 1846, p. 4.

14 *The Freeman's Journal*, 13 September 1845, p. 4. When Douglass visited Bristol, John B. Estlin met him at the train station and brought him back to his house for dinner with abolitionist friends. See Estlin to Samuel May, 1 September 1846, in the Boston Public Library Anti-slavery Collection (available via <www.archive.org>; hereafter BPLAC), identifier: lettertomydearsiooestl_1.

15 Chaffin, *Giant's Causeway*, pp. 71–72; 98.

16 Frederick Douglass, Speech on 14 September 1846, in Blassingame, *Douglass Papers—Series One: Vol. 1*, pp. 407–16; William Lloyd Garrison to Helen Garrison, 17 September 1846, BPLAC, identifier: lettertomydearwioogarr21. For Roper's antislavery networks, see Murray, *Advocates of Freedom*.

Before embarking on his journey to the British Isles in the summer of 1845, Douglass had but three days to pack after a long tour speaking nightly to audiences across New York.[17] Exhausted and with little idea that he would be leaving his family for nearly two years, he boarded the steamship *Cambria* on the 16th of August in company with James Buffum and the Hutchinson Family, an abolitionist singing troupe. Unable to purchase a first-class cabin and confined to steerage, Douglass and Buffum – who had joined him in solidarity – passed the voyage together. The day before arriving in Liverpool, Douglass was permitted to speak by Captain Charles Judkins on the deck of the ship, where most of the passengers had gathered to listen. As he began to read the slave laws of the Southern states pro-slavery Americans "actually got up a mob – a real, American, republican, democratic, Christian mob and that too, on the deck of a British steamer." One enslaver "shook his fist in my face, and said 'O, I wish I had you in Cuba!'" and threatened to throw him overboard, but an Irishman intervened to defend him, while the "clamor went on, waxing hotter and hotter, till it was quite impossible for me to proceed."[18]

Writing in *The Boston Times*, an American passenger charged Douglass with ruining the peace and was disgusted at his "outrageous abuse" against his native land. Placing the blame firmly on Douglass's shoulders, he denounced him as an agitator who had been "permitted to vomit his foul stuff" upon deck.[19] According to another eyewitness, Douglass's lecture forced the passengers "into a dozen stormy groups . . . with their fists almost in each other's faces; while threats and curses were poured forth in all directions." Douglass, the "demon of discord," swiftly left the deck and returned to his cabin, leaving a "dire tumult" in his wake.[20] Reflecting on the incident in *My Bondage and My Freedom*, Douglass wrote that men "do not take bowie-knives to kill mosquitoes, nor pistols to shoot flies; and the American passengers who thought proper to get up a mob to silence me, on board the *Cambria*, took the most effective method of telling the British public that I had something to say."[21]

When he reached Ireland, Douglass took great delight in recounting this story and tailored his performances to different cities. He declared in Belfast that the English captain had protected and allowed him to speak, and his story caused "con-

17 Frederick Douglass to Wendell Phillips, 13 August 1845, in McKivigan, *Douglass Papers—Series Three*, Vol. I, p. 560. See also editions of *The Liberator*, 27 June 1845 and 18 July 1845.

18 For coverage of the *Cambria*, see Douglass to Garrison, 1 September 1845; *The Liberator*, 26 September 1845. See also McDaniel, "Saltwater Anti-Slavery"; Chaffin, *Giant's Causeway*; Pryor, *Colored Travelers*; Blight, *Frederick Douglass: Prophet of Freedom*; Fenton, "I was Transformed"; and Pettinger, *Frederick Douglass and Scotland*.

19 *The Liberator*, 3 October 1845, p. 2.

20 Warburton, *Hochelega*, pp. 358–61. Thanks to Alasdair Pettinger for bringing this to my attention.

21 Douglass, *My Bondage and My Freedom* (1855), p. 381.

siderable merriment" from the audience.[22] In Dublin, he embellished the story and emphasized how it was the "noble-hearted Irishman" who had saved him from the pro-slavery mob, and greatly pleased the audience when he told how the captain had threatened to put the men in irons.[23] In a deliberate performative decision that smacked of anglophilia, Douglass did not allude to the captain's previous history as an enslaver, as this would have jarred with the contrast he tried to create between a free, monarchical Britain and hypocritical republican America.[24] Furthermore, the captain had ousted a Black passenger from one of his ships a year previously to this incident; but if the abolitionists knew about this, they wisely kept silent lest it destroy their rhetorical arguments.[25]

Ireland

In early September 1845, Douglass arrived in Dublin and stayed with militant Garrisonian abolitionist Richard D. Webb. Within a matter of days, he had spoken in the prison where Daniel O'Connell had been confined, given a temperance address, and was introduced to O'Connell himself. Over the course of his journey, he recounted the brutalities of slavery, read extracts from Southern newspapers and slave laws, rejected Black inferiority and racism in both the US and Irish press, addressed temperance meetings, celebrated the heroism of Black men such as Madison Washington, began his campaign against the Free Church of Scotland, and even discussed the Texas annexation, which was "a conspiracy from beginning to end . . . for the purpose of upholding and sustaining one of the darkest and foulest crimes ever committed by man."[26] In a transatlantic exchange of print culture between Douglass and Irish and American abolitionists, his speeches, letters and travels were frequently published in *The Liberator*.[27]

---

22 *The Belfast Newsletter*, 9 December 1845, p. 1.
23 *The Freeman's Journal*, 13 September 1845, p. 4; Frederick Douglass to William Lloyd Garrison, 1 September 1845, Frederick Douglass Papers (FDP), Digital Collection, Library of Congress.
24 *Spectator*, 4 October 1845, p. 1.
25 Pettinger, "Send Back the Money," p. 47.
26 Frederick Douglass, Speech on 2 January 1846, in Blassingame, *Douglass Papers—Series One: Vol. 1*, pp. 118–25. For more of Douglass's travel in Ireland, see Riach "Daniel O'Connell and American Anti-Slavery"; Fenton, *Frederick Douglass In Ireland*; Sweeney, *Frederick Douglass and the Atlantic World*; Chaffin, *Giant's Causeway*; Coughlan, "Frederick Douglass and Ireland"; Kerr-Ritchie, "Black Abolitionists, Irish Supporters"; and Kinealy, *Frederick Douglass and Ireland*.
27 See for example, numerous editions of *The Liberator* between September 1845 and July 1847, including 26 September 1845, p. 3; 17 October 1845, p. 24; 7 November 1845, pp. 1–3; 1 January 1846, p. 2; 14 May 1847, p. 1.

In one of his first meetings in the Music Hall in Dublin, Douglass was joined by the Lord Mayor (who acted as chairman), James Haughton from the Hibernian Anti-Slavery Society, and the Hutchinson Family. In his speech, which is reprinted in this volume, Douglass "shewed the fallacy of the argument so frequently resorted to by slave-holders, that the negro race were unfit for freedom, owing to their mental inferiority to the European nation." He blisteringly attacked all religious groups, including Quakers, who "conspired to keep [the enslaved] in degrading subjection, and had refused to admit them on equal terms into the house of that God." In a distinct performative tactic and to "tremendous cheering," he then alluded to Catholics, who "never denied to them the privileges of the Christian faith, and the offices of brotherly love, but had opened to them their churches without any distinction."[28] From the beginning, Douglass's lectures attracted numerous audiences on all sides of class, religious, and regional lines; as Adrian N. Mulligan summarizes, Douglass was an "astute reader of his specific environs" and "tailored his speeches accordingly" to working-class Catholic audiences in Dublin who supported Daniel O'Connell and Irish Repeal, many of whom helped to set up Douglass's meetings.[29] In Belfast, he distanced himself from O'Connell and downplayed his support for Repeal, sensitive to the large number of Protestants in his audience, although this did not stop him from exposing the Presbyterian links to the Free Church.[30]

In his subsequent speeches in Dublin, Douglass waxed lyrical about his meeting with O'Connell on 29 September at Conciliation Hall. O'Connell had invited Douglass up to the platform to give a short speech, referring to him as the Black O'Connell. Douglass was deeply impressed with O'Connell's lecture, which Garrison later used to encourage Irish Americans to sympathize with the enslaved, as they were part of a global system of oppression since their fellow Irish brethren suffered under a colonial empire.[31] Douglass was also impressed by another Irish luminary in Cork, Father Theobald Mathew, who was a strong advocate of teetotalism and had administered his temperance pledge to over half of Ireland's population. Douglass spoke alongside him, had breakfast in his home, and took the pledge.[32]

---

28   *The Freeman's Journal*, 24 September 1845, p. 4.
29   Mulligan, "'As a Lever Gains Power,'" p. 406. Kerr-Ritchie, "Black Abolitionists, Irish Supporters," pp. 603–04; Fenton, *"I was Transformed,"* p. 56.
30   Quinn, "'Safe in Old Ireland,'" pp. 548–49. See also Jenkins, "Beyond the Pale."
31   Chaffin, *Giant's Causeway*, pp. 117–19; Kinealy, *Daniel O'Connell*, pp. 134–36; Quinn, "'Safe in Old Ireland,'" pp. 540–43; Kerr-Ritchie, "Black Abolitionists, Irish Supporters," p. 607.
32   Fenton, *Frederick Douglass In Ireland*, pp. 107–08.

While in Dublin, Douglass also exposed the evils of a Southern Christianity polluted by slavery. He declared in one speech:

> I love the religion of Jesus which is pure and peaceable, and easy to be entreated. I ask you all to love this religion, but I hate a religion which, in the name of the Saviour, and which prostitutes his blessed precepts to the vile purposes of slavery, ruthlessly sunder all the ties of nature; which tears the wife from the husband – which separates the child from the parent – which covers the backs of men and women with bloody scars – which promotes all manner of licentiousness.[33]

Douglass was careful to dwell on the distinct differences between the form of Christianity he (and the audience) subscribed to and that of Southern enslavers. Connecting violence, rape, and plunder with so-called Christian enslavers, he painted this religion as dark, evil, and sinful. He described true Christianity as the light and ultimately, the form of truth and moral righteousness which would destroy slavery. The twisted form of Christianity in the South ignored religious teachings and represented brutality in all its forms. Slavery was the Devil's work and it poisoned religion; he therefore implored his audience to urgently do something about slavery and demanded they support the true principles of Christ, regardless of what sect they belonged to. If such unity of religious support could be gathered, abolition was inevitable.

After meetings in the Royal Exchange and Friends' Meeting House, Douglass wrote privately that his "success here is even greater than I had anticipated." His subsequent lecture at the Music Hall was kindly donated to him for free, saving Douglass and the organizers roughly $50. He was also surprised at the "total absence of all manifestations of prejudice against me" and noted that the "change of circumstances is particularly striking."[34]

However, when Douglass attacked the Methodist Church for their lack of criticism against American brethren, fellow Methodists in Dublin took offense and refused Douglass entry into their meeting houses. He mocked their actions in a speech shortly afterwards and declared "he would not sacrifice his friends now in chains, and perhaps writhing under the lash while he spoke, to any fear of personal inconvenience." In a formidable performative technique, he used his opponent's words against them, molding them to suit his own ends. The Methodists had closed their doors and it merely proved the truth of his attacks against American Methodists.[35] Although abolitionist

---

33 *The Freeman's Journal*, 4 October 1845, p. 4.
34 Douglass to William Lloyd Garrison, *The Liberator*, 10 October 1845, p. 3.
35 *The Freeman's Journal*, 18 September 1845, p. 4; Quinn, "'Safe in Old Ireland,'" pp. 538–40; Sweeney, *Frederick Douglass and the Atlantic World*, p. 31.

John B. Estlin remarked in a letter that "friends in Dublin had been scandalized by the violent denunciations uttered" by Douglass, he refused to compromise.[36]

From Dublin, Douglass travelled to Wexford, where he stayed with Joseph Poole, Webb's cousin, who like his relative knew how to maximize the antislavery cause through every medium possible. After his meeting, Poole described Douglass's lecture in the local newspaper and asked them to print a series of resolutions passed against slavery.[37] Poole also introduced Douglass to a family member in Waterford, who helped organize another meeting that did not receive as much support as they hoped. The lack of interest inspired a sonnet in the local press (reprinted in this volume) chastising the town for its apathy.[38]

In Cork, Douglass stayed with the Jennings family, who were "brimming over with good nature, courtesy, hospitality and philanthropy." He worked closely with Isabel, the secretary of the Cork Ladies' Anti-Slavery Society, and her sisters Mary and Jane.[39] Douglass paid tribute to Charles Lenox Remond, who had visited Cork a few years beforehand, as his "labors here were abundant, and very effective." During one meeting in the city, Douglass capitalized on this sentiment and gave an address at the St. Patrick's Temperance Hall. He compared the path of the abolitionists to religious odysseys, describing how during the early 1830s they "literally passed through a sea of blood; their houses were burned, their property confiscated, and in some instances even their lives were sacrificed." Contrasting the stark difference between violence enacted against American abolitionists with his reception in Ireland, he "continued to enforce upon the meeting the necessity of renewed efforts in the cause of abolition" and sang a song, "to the infinite amusement of the company."[40]

On 14 October, Douglass spoke at the City Courthouse with the Mayor as chairman. Employing the metaphor of a shining light to expose the horrors of slavery, he argued that the infernal system "feeds and lives in darkness, and like a tree with its roots turned to the sun, it perishes when exposed to the light." If enough light – supported by Irish and British public opinion – was concentrated on the Southern region, slavery would implode as if hit by "a thunderbolt." Douglass emphasized the brutality of slavery by reading extracts from the Black Codes of slave states ("for visiting a plantation without a written pass – *ten lashes*") and recounted the

---

36   John Estlin to Richard D. Webb (?), 5 November 1845, in Taylor, *British and American Abolitionists*, pp. 240–41.

37   Fenton, *Frederick Douglass In Ireland*, pp. 118; 124–27.

38   Fenton, *"I was Transformed,"* p. 57.

39   Fought, *Women in the World of Frederick Douglass*, pp. 84–90.

40   Frederick Douglass to William Lloyd Garrison, 28 October 1845, in McKivigan, *Douglass Papers—Series Three, Vol. 1*, pp. 59–63; *The Southern Reporter*, 30 October 1845, p. 4.

torture of a woman whose ear had been nailed to a post and then ripped off. He then "assumed the attitude and drawling manner so characteristic of the American preachers" and caused shouts of laughter with a "slaveholder's sermon."[41] First used in the US, his parodic rendition in the British Isles was very successful – no doubt owing in part to Douglass's incredible oratorical ability, but also because audiences took great delight in shaming Americans for their hypocrisy. Using the religious reading "servants, be obedient to your masters" as his text, he mimicked Southern enslavers who used the Bible to justify their brutality. In doing so, he highlighted the sheer impossibility that any religious teaching could be used to perpetuate slavery.[42]

Douglass barely contained his frustration at criticisms regarding descriptions of religious enslavers. In response to Methodists in Cork who were also angered by Douglass's remarks, he believed that "there was an over-sensitiveness on the part of some persons" who dismissed his testimony as fraudulent and false. He defended his position, but cautioned his audience that they should investigate the links of their brethren in the US, for it was likely they were defending callous enslavers who beat Douglass's cousin "until she was crimsoned with her own blood from her head to the floor." His decision to employ such sectarian and sometimes regional arguments often inflamed his hearers and he "pushed the boundaries of where he could safely use particular language." However, Douglass connected his audience to the torturous brutalities of slavery; he demanded they open their eyes and ears to the sounds of whips, chains and blood on the floor. His audience were not just implicated in the system of slavery, but practiced a form of heresy if they refused to acknowledge their privileged position or Douglass's words.[43] Despite the criticism, Isabel Jennings believed "there never was a person who made a greater sensation in Cork amongst all religious bodies."[44]

From Cork, Douglass travelled to Limerick, where he extolled the transformative journey across the Atlantic and described his experience of a new form of freedom and citizenship. In a speech reprinted in this volume, he pointed out that a mere seven years earlier he had been "an object of merchandise – dragged and ranked with beasts to be sold in the market or auction mart . . . oh, what a transition it was to be changed from the state of a slave to that of a freeman!" Directly appealing to his audience for their moral countenance and protection, he stated that if he returned to the

---

41   Frederick Douglass, Speech on 14 October 1845, in Blassingame, *Douglass Papers—Series One: Vol. 1*, pp. 39–45.

42   Selby, "Mocking the Sacred," pp. 329–33.

43   Frederick Douglass, Speech on 17 October 1845, in Blassingame, *Douglass Papers—Series One: Vol. 1*, pp. 45–54; Grace, "Infidel America," p. 741.

44   Isabel Jennings to Maria Weston Chapman, 1845, BPLAC, identifier: lettertodearmrscoojenn5.

US he "would be taken and bound in slave chains. He must plant himself, therefore, under the protection of the Irish and British people." Celebrating his own politicized and radical journey across the Atlantic, he also described "the various battles won for America by negro blood, and depicted in glowing colours the base ingratitude with which they were rewarded." Commemorating the bravery and masculinity of other Black heroes, Douglass challenged conceptions of Black inferiority and exposed the white supremacist ideology to which his audiences subscribed.[45]

Unfortunately, Douglass's speeches in Belfast were also marred by criticism. Upon his arrival, he was greeted at the train station by Francis Calder and was taken to the Victoria Hotel ready for his first meeting in the city on 5 December.[46] He wrote that ministers from Cork and Dublin "have written here against me," causing him "no bed of roses" for the campaign. By slandering his character, the ministers aligned themselves with enslavers in the US, but they would face and "take the consequences" of such an unholy alliance, since Douglass's testimony would expose them to international audiences.[47] Writing in early December, Douglass was determined to stay longer in Belfast; for, as he put it, the "field is ripe for the harvest" and a "blow can be struck here" more effectively than anywhere else in Ireland, particularly against the Free Church.[48]

In a speech on 23 December, Douglass denied rumours that he was an imposter and criticized those who slandered his character. He urged his audience to have "no union with the slave-holder," for there could "be no union between light and darkness." An enslaver was no "common criminal" and was indeed far worse because he was a "murderer of the body . . . [and] a murderer of the soul."[49] Douglass elaborated on the "painful" duty he performed when exposing the connections between slavery and religion:

> The only way of purifying our church from the deep damnation into which she was plunging was to expose her deeds to the light. But in exposing those deeds, I do not wish to place myself in the position of an enemy. Let no man rank me among the enemies of the church, or of religion because I dare to remove the mask from her face and give nations of the earth a peep at her enormities. It is for her salvation and purification I do it and for the redemption and disenthralment of my race.[50]

---

45 *The Limerick Reporter*, 25 November 1845, p. 2.

46 See Ritchie, "'The Stone in the Sling.'"

47 Frederick Douglass to Richard D. Webb, 5 December 1845, BPLAC, identifier: lettertofearfri-oodoug_1.

48 Frederick Douglass to Richard D. Webb, 6 December 1845, BPLAC, identifier: lettertomydearfr-oodoug_1.

49 Frederick Douglass, Speech on 23 December 1845 in Blassingame, *Douglass Papers—Series One: Vol. 1*, pp. 103–18.

50 *Belfast Newsletter*, 26 December 1845, p. 1.

Douglass risked the charges of heresy because he dared to expose the true evils of slavery. The churches were possessed by the devil of slavery, and enlisting the support of his audience abroad was the only way to exorcise its satanic influences and save her from eternal pollution. Casting himself as the saviour and using language almost akin to that of a divine prophet, Douglass was the warrior bold enough to save the church, his race, and the US nation as a whole. His language shocked audiences and he reassured them he was not one of "the enemies of the church or of religion," but simply chose to "remove the mask from her face."[51] The exposition of this relationship was complex and he admitted it was "one of the most painful duties he had been called on to perform"; it was necessary, however, to ensure "the light of truth be permitted to shine into [the church's] dark recesses."[52]

As numerous scholars have noted, Douglass was among many Black abolitionists who reframed their concepts of freedom and equality abroad since their ability to travel, to speak, to eat, and to stay was not restricted or segregated in the British Isles.[53] Such a transformation inevitably occurred in Ireland, the first region where Douglass stayed for a considerable amount of time. In a letter to Garrison, Douglass wrote, "as to a nation, I belong to none. I have no protection at home, or resting-place abroad." The US cast his identity solely as a fugitive and despite "her bright blue sky – her grand old woods – her fertile fields," his "rapture was soon checked, my joy is soon turned to mourning." The American nation was forever altered by the stain of slavery and how the blood, sweat, and tears of his enslaved brethren fertilized the landscape. In contrast, he had "spent some of the happiest moments of my life" in Ireland and marvelled at the stark contrast: "I seem to have undergone a transformation. I live a new life."[54] When travelling abroad, Douglass shifted his identity to that of an exile who could not return to America in safety because of the imminent threat of danger or kidnap into slavery. He criticized Americans for their inability to comprehend his own fugitive identity, and in doing so, represented the voices of millions of his enslaved brethren who could not challenge Americans themselves.[55]

Douglass tried to encapsulate this transformation within his Irish speeches. When enslaved, he recounted the numerous erosions of liberty and declared that if he ever tried to reach for that freedom, as was his birthright, "he would be taken up and hung upon the first lamp-post." Ever the versatile and virtuoso performer,

---

51   *The Belfast Newsletter*, 26 December 1845, p. 1; Burke, *Frederick Douglass: Crusading Orator*, pp. 32–33.
52   *The Northern Whig*, 25 December 1845, p. 1.
53   Pryor, *Colored Travelers*, pp. 150–51.
54   Frederick Douglass to William Lloyd Garrison, 1 January 1846, in McKivigan, *Douglass Papers— Series Three, Vol. 1*, pp. 72–79.
55   Eckel, "'A Type of his Countrymen,'" pp. 1–6; 12.

he then "erected himself to his full height, and in a tone of commanding eloquence exclaimed . . . O! I thank God that I stand upon British soil." Careful to appeal to "British" sentiment in this particular location – Belfast – the contrast between the tortuous system of slavery and where Douglass now stood as a freeman on the platform, instead of limp in a hangman's noose, was as stark as the difference between light and dark itself. His audience could never understand the "happiness I now feel," for "you must have been freed from the brutality of a tyrant master, and all the bloody paraphernalia of slavery, before you can judge of my feelings aright."[56] Douglass marvelled at the comparative lack of discrimination he then felt, but used the opportunity to point to their white privilege: despite problems of poverty and oppression, slavery did not exist on Irish or British soil and they could never appreciate the value of their freedom – or the position Douglass spoke from – unless they were Black and had been enslaved.

Save from two letters to Garrison, Douglass did not discuss the poverty in Ireland or the beginnings of the Great Hunger, in part as a performative strategy to avoid unnecessary conflict or anger some of his middle- to upper-class Irish friends. As numerous scholars like Sweeney and Jenkins have pointed out, his relationship with Ireland and its people was incredibly complex, and he chose not to specifically engage with the effects of the Great Famine, which had already wreaked havoc across the landscape.[57] Writing from Montrose, Douglass admitted to Garrison that he "dreaded to go out of the house" and witness how "the streets were almost literally alive with beggars, displaying the greatest wretchedness." He was distressed at the abject poverty, particularly among children, which in some ways caused him to compare it to "the same degradation as the American slaves."[58] As he would make clear in most of his British and Irish speeches, though, slavery did not exist on this side of the Atlantic, and even the poorest Irishman or woman could count themselves free from tyrannical enslavers. Throughout his trip, Douglass publicly minimized the sufferings of the Irish poor and continued to do so throughout his later autobiographies.[59]

The most symbolic change in Douglass's self-fashioning, however, occurred with the publication of his *Narrative*. His sojourn to the British Isles was in part a result

---

56 *Belfast Newsletter*, 9 December 1845, p. 1.

57 Sweeney, *Frederick Douglass and the Atlantic World*, pp. 72–74; Jenkins, "Beyond the Pale," pp. 69–83; Kinealy, *Frederick Douglass and Ireland*, pp. 49–55; McKivigan, *Douglass Papers—Series Three, Vol. 1*, pp. 93–98; Coughlan, "Frederick Douglass and Ireland," pp. 115–18.

58 Frederick Douglass to William Lloyd Garrison, 26 February 1846, in McKivigan, *Douglass Papers—Series Three, Vol. 1*, pp. 93–98.

59 Ibid. See Quinn, "'Safe in Old Ireland,'" pp. 535–50; Buccola, *The Political Thought of Frederick Douglass*, pp. 18–19. See also Sweeney, "Common Ground"; Coughlan, "Frederick Douglass and Ireland," p. 117.

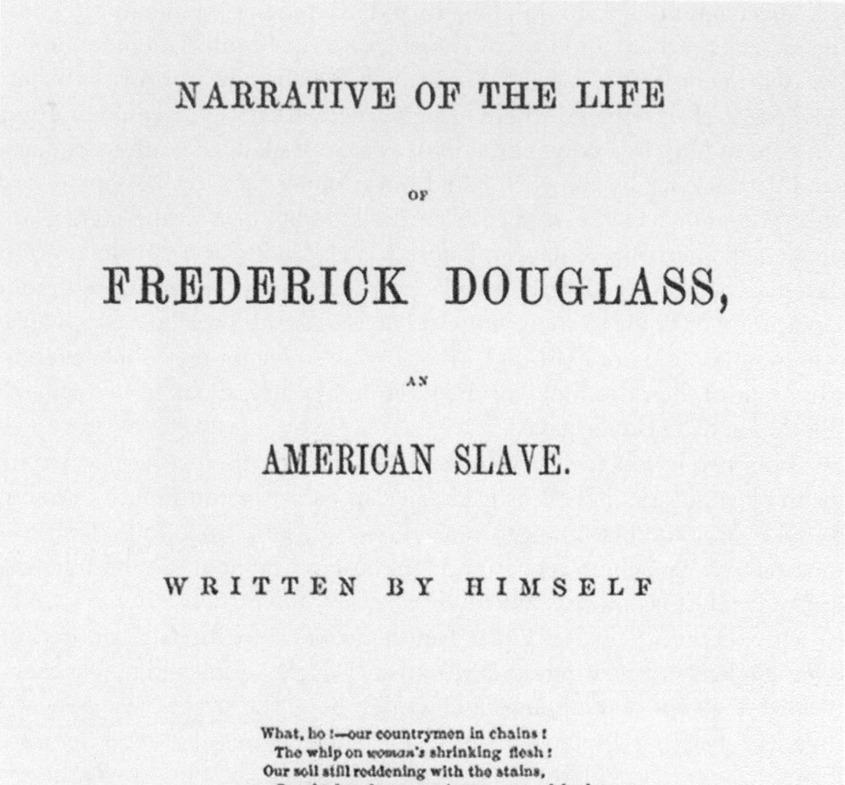

NARRATIVE OF THE LIFE

OF

FREDERICK DOUGLASS,

AN

AMERICAN SLAVE.

WRITTEN BY HIMSELF

What, ho!—our countrymen in chains!
The whip on woman's shrinking flesh!
Our soil still reddening with the stains,
Caught from her scourging, warm and fresh!
What! mothers from their children riven!
What! God's own image bought and sold!
Americans to market driven,
And barter'd, as the brute, for gold:—Whittier

DUBLIN:
WEBB AND CHAPMAN, GT. BRUNSWICK-STREET.
1845.

Figure 1.2 Frederick Douglass, *Narrative of the Life of Frederick Douglass* (Dublin, 1845). British Library, as digitized by Google.

of the furore surrounding its US publication; the book sold well in New England and by the end of 1847, the *Narrative* had reached its ninth edition and sold over eleven thousand copies. On the eve of the Civil War, it had sold at least thirty thousand.[60] The book enjoyed comparable success in Britain and Ireland, too: one critic wrote that "every Englishman should read" the "wonderfully written" narrative, while another extolled the "very remarkable little volume . . . remarkable as being the production of a slave, and one of that people whom it has always been the cue of slaveholders to represent as incapable of intellectual vigour and ability" and called it "one of the most thrilling and absorbing imaginable."[61]

When Douglass arrived in Ireland, he entered into an agreement with Richard D. Webb to publish an Irish edition, and in September two thousand copies were distributed across the Garrisonian network. The Hilditch sisters in Wrexham were "fired to tenfold zeal" by Douglass's book, and immediately sent donations to the cause as a result.[62] This formed the basis of a very successful meeting there a few months later, which was "universally acknowledged the <u>best</u> meeting in our town on any occasion and until nearly midnight the speakers were listened to with rapt attention."[63] In Rochdale, William Logan implored Douglass and Garrison to hold a meeting in his town, as he had organized several gatherings "on the subject of 'American manstealing' . . . [as] the subject is almost new to the people." Before Douglass's arrival, he read extracts from the *Narrative* to antislavery meetings which "produced a powerful impression on the audience."[64] Before Douglass's first meeting in Bristol, the Estlin family sold over one hundred and fifty copies of his *Narrative* to "ensure him a welcome and a numerous audience."[65] The circulation of print culture had a formidable impact, as Douglass himself acknowledged in a speech in Cork: a local minister read his work, and had then subsequently preached an antislavery sermon.[66]

Noting that six hundred copies of the *Narrative* had been sold in two months, Webb was impressed, considering the "whole of this sale has been private, and with hardly any assistance from the booksellers."[67] Douglass sold numerous copies at the

---

60 Blight, *Frederick Douglass: Prophet of Freedom*, p. 139.

61 *Woolmer's Exeter and Plymouth Gazette*, 13 March 1847, p. 4.

62 Richard D. Webb to Maria Weston Chapman, 26 February 1846. BPLASC, identifier: lettertomydearfroowebb28.

63 Sarah Hilditch to Maria Weston Chapman, 31 October 1846. BPLASC, identifier: lettertomydearmroohild; Williams, *Black Skin, Blue Books*, pp. 29–33; 40–44.

64 William Logan to William Lloyd Garrison, 28 September 1846, BPLAC, identifier: lettertodearfrieoologa_0.

65 Mary Anne Estlin to Maria Weston Chapman, 1 March 1846, BPLAC, identifier: lettertomydearmrooestl4.

66 *Supplement to the Cork Examiner*, 7 November 1845, p. 1.

67 *The Liberator*, 26 December 1845, p. 3.

end of his meetings; emboldened by his recent success in Belfast, he remarked to Webb: "my Books went last night at one blow. I want more I want more, I have every thing to hope and nothing to fear."[68]

The encouraging sale of the *Narrative* did not please everyone, and John Estlin of Bristol objected to certain sections of the narrative. In a shocking display of white editorial paternalism, he edited and even cut paragraphs that referenced slave breeding. He refused to allow the women in his household to read the book without tampering with the pages first and was fearful that it would shock respectable classes or harm the sale amongst women. Webb defended the passages and refused to edit it, leaving Estlin to presumably disfigure his own copies before reluctantly selling others to his friends and associates. Whether Douglass was aware of this remains to be seen, but Estlin's controlling actions were a microcosm of future problems concerning white abolitionist editorship and charges of violent discourse or inauthenticity.[69]

Despite Webb's defence of the *Narrative*, his relationship with Douglass became increasingly tense over the first printing of the Dublin edition. Without Douglass's permission, Webb used an engraving by Henry Adlard based on a drawing of Douglass by James Haughton's relative Bessie Bell. Adlard created a steel plate of the image, which was then sent back to Webb. After seeing the image, Douglass wrote a letter to Webb "full of abuse of the portrait to which he applied every epithet of deprecation he could think of." Confused, Webb assured Douglass that his abolitionist friends in Dublin were happy with the portrait and it was not worth creating divisions between them, but Douglass replied that if their friendship "consisted in endeavouring to force a thing on him he did not like [then] it was of too pictorial a nature to be worth much." Webb was stung, but Douglass merely stated: "I am cirtain the engraving is not as good, as the original portrait. I dont like it, and I have said so without heat or thunder."[70] In a move demonstrating Douglass's independence and literary control over his *Narrative*, in the second Irish and the third London edition the publishers reverted to the frontispiece used in the Boston version.[71]

Using a multitude of literary strategies, Douglass used his revised *Narrative* to challenge the white supremacist thought that underpinned the system of slavery as

---

68   Frederick Douglass to Richard D. Webb, 6 December 1845, BPLAC, identifier: lettertomydearfr-oodoug_1. See also McKivigan, *Douglass Papers—Series Three, Vol. 1*, pp. 69–71.

69   John B. Estlin to Samuel May, 10 November 1845, BPLAC, identifier: lettertomydearmooestl1; Fisch, *American Slaves in Victorian England*, pp. 1–8.

70   Pettinger, *Frederick Douglass and Scotland*, pp. 224–28; McKivigan, *Douglass Papers—Series Three, Vol. 1*, pp. 79–80.

71   Douglass (ed. Bernier), *Narrative of the Life of Frederick Douglass*, pp. 174–75; Levine, *The Lives of Frederick Douglass*, pp. 86–88. See also Bernier, *Characters of Blood*; Bernier and Lawson, *Pictures and Power.*

well as the abolitionist movement. He wanted full editorial control over his own written and visual testimony, and placed his own frontispiece at the beginning to challenge racialized images of Black bodies.[72] As Robert S. Levine notes, Douglass's reliance on print pathways through his autobiographical writings in particular "suggests he was well aware that the voice carries only so far and certainly does not survive the speaking body." Thus, Douglass reframed and personalized his subsequent *Narrative* editions to celebrate his editorship and control over his own literary work. In doing so, Douglass showed that Garrison, Webb, or other white transatlantic abolitionists did not need to endorse his narrative, or by extension, his oratorical voice on the lecturing stage.[73]

Within the revised edition, Douglass added a new preface that highlighted the main reasons for his presence in the British Isles; composed and published in Ireland, it therefore added a new dimension to his identity as a fugitive and as an American.[74] The edition also included testimonials from Irish ministers including Reverend Isaac Nelson (to answer the charge of Douglass's religious infidelity on account of his attacks against Southern religion), a notice for the American Anti-Slavery Society's annual antislavery bazaar, and reviews from both the American and British press.[75]

In the preface, Douglass reiterated his position on religion after numerous charges of heresy were directed against him. Some of these attacks had occurred in Dublin, and in a savvy site-specific refutation of these attacks, he clearly and boldly stated he was no "opponent of all religion." While the arguments in his speeches could be taken out of context, edited, misreported, or misunderstood, he wanted to use his own literary masterpiece to ensure the people of Dublin – and those of the British Isles and beyond – knew that he was a deeply religious man and spoke only of the *"slaveholding religion."* If one believed in the "pure, peaceable and impartial Christianity of Christ" then they should morally "hate the corrupt, slave-holding, women-whipping, cradle-plundering, partial, and hypocritical Christianity of this land." In graphic language, Douglass denounced the hypocrisy of so-called religious enslavers who sold men to buy Bibles, separated children from mothers, whipped the defenceless, and practiced sexual violence against women, as they stood "forth as the pious advocate of purity." He employed graphic imagery and even sound – "the slave auctioneer's bell and the church-going bell chime in with each other" – to implore his audience to note the irreconcilable contrasts between religions. In the

---

72   Douglass (ed. Bernier), *Narrative of the Life of Frederick Douglass*, pp. 22–23.
73   Levine, *The Lives of Frederick Douglass*, pp. 10; 77–89.
74   Sweeney, *Frederick Douglass and the Atlantic World*, pp. 15–17.
75   Ritchie, "'The Stone in the Sling'"; Douglass (ed. Bernier), *Narrative of the Life of Frederick Douglass*, p. 43; Levine, *The Lives of Frederick Douglass*, pp. 86–88.

churches of the South, one could hear the "clanking of fetters" alongside the sound of hymns; "religion and robbery" were interwoven together in a covenant of hell.[76]

Such an emphasis on the religious hypocrisy of enslavers foreshadowed the second significant editorial piece in the Dublin edition, Douglass's refutation of A. C. C. Thompson's diatribe against the authenticity of the *Narrative*. Thompson, a Maryland farmer acquainted with both Douglass and his enslaver Thomas Auld, had slandered Douglass's testimony in an open letter to the press and was outraged at the "glaring falsehoods" contained within it. According to Thompson, as an African American and so-called fugitive Douglass was mentally incapable of writing such a work; and he dismissed eyewitness accounts of brutality, for there were "no such barbarities committed on their plantations." Furthermore, Covey – instead of the murderous slave-breaker described in the *Narrative* – was a "plain,

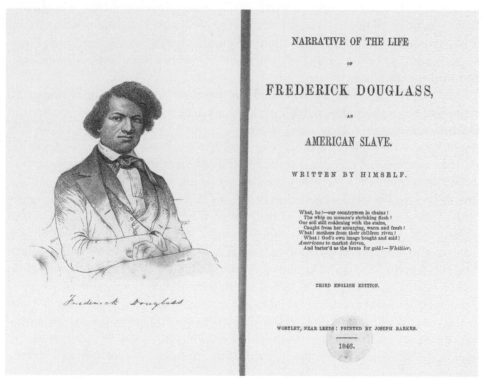

Figure 1.3 Frederick Douglass, *Narrative of the Life of Frederick Douglass* (Wortley, 1846). University of Southampton.

---

76 Douglass, *Narrative* (1846), pp. 118–22. See also Ferreira, "Frederick Douglass and the 1846 Dublin Edition," pp. 59–62; Douglass (ed. Bernier), *Narrative of the Life of Frederick Douglass*, p. 28; Kinealy, *Frederick Douglass and Ireland*.

honest farmer" and at heart a religious man. In reply, Douglass used Thompson's letter as a piece of propaganda for the antislavery cause, a shining indictment of the system of slavery. He thanked Thompson for confirming some of the details in his *Narrative*, for few in the US or in the British Isles could now doubt his identity or his facts. In exposing such truths, he had acted in Douglass's favor for "silencing these truly prejudicial rumours and hurtful slanders."[77] Emblematic of the famous exchange between enslaver and enslaved in *The Columbian Orator*, a popular primer Douglass had obtained as a child, he inserted the correspondence between himself and Thompson, removing it from a transatlantic newspaper context to give his *Narrative* a new meaning, in part because he had full control over his own response.[78]

Tensions and disagreements with Webb led Douglass to enter into a contract with a publisher for an English edition. In late September 1846, Douglass informed Joseph Barker, a printer in Leeds, that he had "just entered into an agreement with Mr. Swan Engraver to print 5,000 portraits for the forthcoming Edition of my Narrative – two thousand copies of which be Sent you in the Course of a fortnight."[79] A London edition was printed too; Garrison's preface was removed and the *Narrative* printed virtually by itself, together with Douglass's Finsbury Chapel speech delivered in May 1846.[80] Here, Douglass had exercised his authorial voice over the publication of his own testimony, which no doubt was a factor in making an editing career more attractive: with his own newspaper, for example, he could frame and edit his testimony as he saw fit.

The Free Church of Scotland

After a successful tour in Ireland, Douglass arrived in Glasgow in mid-January 1846. Douglass stayed with William Smeal and worked under the auspices of the Glasgow Emancipation Society, led by Smeal and John Murray. While American Garrisonian Henry Clarke Wright had made some headway with the campaign against the Free Church, his radicalism had alienated most audiences.[81] Over the course of several months, Douglass lectured on the American press (one paper had called him a "glib-tongued scoundrel"), the plight of Jonathan Walker, the history of the abolitionist

---

77 Douglass, *Narrative* (1846), pp. cxxiv–cxxviii; Frederick Douglass to William Lloyd Garrison, 27 January 1846, in McKivigan, *Douglass Papers—Series Three, Vol. 1*, pp. 81–85.

78 Levine, *The Lives of Frederick Douglass*, p. 100.

79 Frederick Douglass to Joseph Barker, 22 September 1846, in McKivigan, *Douglass Papers—Series Three: Vol. 1*, p. 562.

80 Levine, *The Lives of Frederick Douglass*, p. 113.

81 Fulkerson, "Frederick Douglass and the Anti-Slavery Crusade," p. 95; Pettinger, *Frederick Douglass and Scotland*, p. 37.

movement, the Texas Annexation, the life of Madison Washington, and the temperance movement.[82] He traveled to numerous places in Scotland including Aberdeen, Ayr, Glasgow, Greenock, Kilmarnock, Dundee, the Vale of Leven, and Edinburgh. In Ayr he visited Robert Burns's birthplace, met his sister, and in a distinct performative strategy quoted his poetry in numerous Scottish meetings, dropping it from his repertoire when he went south of the border.[83]

Most of his speeches, however, concerned the exposure of slavery and its links with the Free Church. The issue of non-fellowship with proslavery or slaveholding churches in the US had been debated in Britain since the 1830s, but Douglass added a new dimension to this when he framed his philosophy on behalf of his enslaved brethren, "those who cannot speak for themselves."[84] He had begun his campaign in Belfast – a deliberate strategy, as the city represented a stronghold of Presbyterianism and had strong connections to Scottish churches, including the Free Church.[85] Douglass's initial efforts in Scotland, however, were exhausting. He sometimes "found the people for the most part cold and indifferent" and in Glasgow he was advised "not to agitate the question there, and for a time, I confess my hands hung down – I felt almost incapable of prosecuting my work." His relationship with the Garrisonians, particularly Henry Clarke Wright, could have been the cause for this, as when Douglass first arrived he had expected Wright's extensive campaign against the Church to have roused considerable support. He was disappointed, however; Wright's radicalism and uncompromising tone seemed to have alienated rather than united the Glaswegian population. To avoid Wright's rhetorical strategies and to engage the people, he philosophized that in their acceptance of the money, the Free Church had acted as a bulwark for American slavery; and he used his own fugitivity to dramatize the impact on his enslaved brethren like no other abolitionist could.[86]

In 1843, Thomas Chalmers and his supporters separated from the established Church of Scotland to form the Free Church. To raise money for their new organization, Chalmers sent a small deputation of missionaries to America, some of whom, including the Reverend George Lewis, were sent south. The mission raised

---

82 Frederick Douglass, Speech on 17 April 1846, in Blassingame, *Douglass Papers—Series One: Vol. 1*, pp. 215–31. Once again, *The Liberator* reprinted numerous newspaper articles, reports of speeches, and letters from transatlantic abolitionists. Douglass was convinced that the furore surrounding the Free Church would cause proslavery defenders—especially the church—"to be filled with shame and confusion of face," and would "give another staggering blow to the monster of Slavery." (*The Liberator*, 29 May 1846; 12 June 1846; 19 June 1846).

83 Pettinger, *Frederick Douglass and Scotland*, pp. 135–38. See also Sood, *Robert Burns and the United States of America* and Sood, "The Burnsian Palimpsest," pp. 55–57.

84 Frederick Douglass, Speech on 12 February 1846, in Blassingame, *Douglass Papers—Series One: Vol. 1*, pp. 156–64; Blackett, *Building an Antislavery Wall*, pp. 82–83.

85 Ritchie, "'The Stone in the Sling,'" pp. 245–48.

86 Pettinger, *Frederick Douglass and Scotland*, pp. 52–54.

ten thousand pounds, a third of which came from Southern enslavers, which deeply offended abolitionists on both sides of the Atlantic; Wright and the Glasgow Emancipation Society urged the Church to renounce their fellowship with enslavers.[87] In the United States, both Garrisonians and their abolitionist rivals demanded that religious denominations expel all enslavers from their communion tables as sinners and refuse to accept any financial contributions from them. This brought the militant abolitionists into conflict with many Northern antislavery "moderates" who believed the churches could convert enslavers to emancipation by appealing to their consciences.[88] During this commotion, Thomas Chalmers wrote privately that although slavery was a great evil, he renounced the notion of non-fellowship with enslavers and would not sympathize with those who "would unchristianize that whole region."[89] These words would soon haunt him, magnified by Douglass's presence in Scotland itself and the "Send Back the Money" campaign.

Within two weeks of giving his first lecture in Glasgow, Douglass spoke in Dundee at the City Hall on 30 January. Anticipation was so high that tickets had to be issued. Once on the platform, Douglass began his speech by reading from the book of Isaiah: "And when ye spread forth your hands, I will hide mine eyes from you: yea, when ye make many prayers, I will not hear: your hands are full of blood." In doing so, he pointed to the blood-stained hands of US enslavers and, by extension, the Free Church who had accepted their money. He predicted that divine punishment would follow their actions, considering this "state of pollution" fuelled the "gross and dark infidelity" of so-called religious enslavers. Their religion was an "Atheism . . . of lawless murder and plunder." Once again employing rhetorical questions to his audience, Douglass thundered, "Does the Free Church represent your views on the question of slavery?" to loud shouts of "No!" Throughout this speech, Douglass used the quotation from Isaiah to frame his argument and constantly referred to the blood-stained gold, how the Free Church ministers were blood-soaked and all that they possessed was "the result of the unpaid toil of the poor fettered, stricken and branded slave." Upon hearing dissent and hissing in the audience, he used such disapprobation against them and merely said that "when the cool voice of truth falls into the burning vortex of falsehood there would always be hissing."[90]

---

87 Whyte, *Send Back the Money!*, pp. 9–18; 33–45; Pettinger, "Send Back the Money," pp. 31–56; Pettinger, *Frederick Douglass and Scotland*, pp. 46–48. For more on the Free Church, see Shepperson, "The Free Church and American Slavery," and Fenton, *"I was Transformed."*

88 McKivigan, *The War Against Proslavery Religion*, pp. 18–35.

89 Thomas Chalmers to Thomas Smyth, November 1844, "Correspondence of Lewis Tappan," *Journal of Negro History*, 12:2 (1927), pp. 305–29.

90 Frederick Douglass, Speech on 30 January 1846, in Blassingame, *Douglass Papers—Series One: Vol. 1*, pp. 144–56. Douglass also read from Isaiah in Arbroath: see Blassingame, *Douglass Papers—Series One: Vol. 1*, 12 February 1846, pp. 156–64. Dilbeck, *Frederick Douglass: America's Prophet*, and Pettinger, *Frederick Douglass and Scotland*, also discuss this rhetoric.

Douglass connected these brutalities to the Free Church and used his position as a fugitive in a deeply personal narrative that no white abolitionist could describe. As one correspondent phrased it, "the novelty of a slave addressing a Scottish audience, altogether apart from the interest felt in the subject, could not fail to draw together a numerous assembly" as he opened up the secrets of the "dark prison house of slavery as it exists in the southern states of the union."[91] After reading numerous advertisements from Southern newspapers detailing runaway slave notices and the barbarity of slavery, he noted a eulogy of Chalmers in a Southern newspaper criticizing the abolitionists. Brandishing the paper in his hand, he asked his audience rhetorically, "did they think Dr. Chalmers would ever have said this, if, like him, he had had four sisters and one brother in bondage?" Chalmers's white privilege – and, by extension, that of the audience before him – made Douglass the only one to understand slavery's horrors and how he could ill afford to cease his duty in exposing it. By connecting the deeds of the Free Church with enslavers, he successfully showed to a captivated audience that Scottish support for slavery would have severe consequences for his enslaved brethren. Ultimately, he accused Chalmers of being in league with those at the slave auction, the slave-breakers, the slave-catchers, and enslavers as a whole.[92]

Douglass held several crowded meetings in Dundee and recounted slavery's brutalities, read slave laws, and as in Ireland, graphically described how one woman had attempted to escape but was "dragged back again, when her ear was nailed by her master against a post." In one speech republished in this volume, he continued:

> The practice of branding slaves in America was as common as the custom of marking sheep was in this country. The slave was taken out for the purpose, the furnace was heated, the branding-iron placed in the midst of the fire, and, when heated, taken sparking from it, and applied to the ear. His cheek was scorched all over . . . He had known a girl about seventeen years of age, who was held in slavery; her keepers came to her prison to feed her, along with other slaves; they let bread fall to her; she picked it up while they passed on to other slaves. The gate of the prison had been left open; she dropped the bread, and, before they were aware, she had cleared the gate; pursuit was made after her by the keeper; she gained a bridge; two Virginian slave-holders were coming up; meeting her, the poor girl stood; she saw slavery before her and worse than death behind; she clasped her hands, as if beseeching mercy, and then sprung over the parapet into the water, – at once preferring to appear before God, in all her sins, rather than

---

91 *Dundee Courier*, 3 February 1846, p. 2.
92 Frederick Douglass, Speech on 30 January 1846, in Blassingame, *Douglass Papers—Series One: Vol. 1*, pp. 144–56.

again endure slavery. He was forbidden by the presence of the audience before him to tell all the secrets of his prison house; they could not endure to hear him, because these secrets were so horrible.[93]

Douglass related atrocity after atrocity in short, sharp sentences, leaving his audience with no breathing room. Enslavers tortured women, men, and children relentlessly and were sanctioned by the government, and his visually illustrative language conjured images of the sparks from the flames and the sound of the whip. In pointing to the young woman's flight, he reiterated the argument that there could only be death or liberty, and celebrated her bravery when she realized that only in death would she be granted true freedom. Regardless of his efforts, however, he could never tell his audience all the "secrets" of the prison house of bondage, for their liberty was safe on British soil and protected by their white privilege. Douglass used the word "forbidden" as a performative tactic – the gathering was too *respectable* to hear or comprehend such horrors – but it also signified his trauma and the inability of language to describe the horrors he had witnessed.

In another example of this, Douglass created an imagined scene where he was enslaved in Maryland and Reverend George Lewis, who had traveled to the South to raise money for the Free Church, called on Thomas Auld. Much to the audience's enthusiasm, he recounted the "speech" by Lewis, who implored Auld to give money to "religious freedom in Scotland." Douglass's ear was pressed to the door and could hear Auld agree to give the minister money through the sale of an enslaved person. To much applause, Douglass imagined that Lewis accepted the "bounties produced by the blood of the slave watered by the sweat and enriched by the blood of the half-famished negro." When the minister was ready to leave, Douglass imagined himself as the enslaved individual "tied behind the carriage" who was taken away to be sold on the auction block. Five hundred dollars was bid, and Douglass lambasted Lewis's greed to much laughter from his audience. The ministers then built churches in Scotland with this money, and Douglass argued how "brother Lewis daringly stands up here in Scotland and makes light of it."[94] Using mimicry as a performative strategy, Douglass mocked the Free Church in a way that no white abolitionist could: Lewis and other Free Church representatives had arrogantly and hubristically accepted blood-stained donations from enslavers, who then had the audacity to defend their conduct to the Scottish people, and more importantly, to a formerly enslaved person whose brethren were at that very moment fighting for

---

93 *Dundee, Perth and Cupar Advertiser*, 30 January 1846, p. 3.

94 *Dundee Courier*, 17 March 1846, p. 2. Pettinger refers to this performance as a "monopolylogue, a form of entertainment . . . in which a solo performer takes the part of several characters." Pettinger, *Frederick Douglass and Scotland*, p. 21.

survival. They had disgraced the name of a *Free* church and in a series of accusations, Douglass charged the institution with accepting money from "well-known thieves" who had "taken the counsel and followed the bidding of slaveholders and their guilty abettors, whilst they turned a deaf ear to the bleeding and whispered slave."[95] By accepting the money, the ministers signed a contract written in blood and sold their souls to the devil: Douglass specifically referenced the instruments of torture – which he had experienced himself – to highlight that their unholy alliance was one of violence and brutality. By accepting the money, the Church defended and even sustained the infernal system of slavery.[96]

The response to the campaign was unprecedented. Thousands crammed into town hall and church venues, the newspapers clamored to write descriptions of Douglass's speeches, and numerous poems and songs were composed (some of which are published in this volume). In a letter to Francis Jackson, Douglass wrote that the meetings had "been of the most soul changing character" and "Scotland boils like a pot" under the heat of their campaign.[97] Mary Welsh, a fellow Garrisonian abolitionist in Edinburgh, wrote that his tactics appeared to be working as he and his supporters had "done wonders in opening the eyes of the public" to slavery.[98] A Free Church Anti-Slavery Society was formed, and news of the controversy spread, with the *London Daily News* reporting that Scotland was "the scene of a movement provocative alike of mirthful and dolorous emotions" and Douglass's mantra of "Send Back the Money!" had created a "perfect hurricane of indignation."[99]

Despite the success, Douglass thought the controversy was "rather unfavourable to the sale of my book" but still vowed to continue "with unabated zeal to sound the alarm" amongst the Scottish people.[100] Henry Clarke Wright noted that in Arbroath, the words "'THE SLAVE'S BLOOD' were painted in black on Free Church buildings . . . They could not wash, nor scrape off the bloody spots, nor the black letters. It seemed like the blood of the murdered victim, that could not be washed out." They were taken like tourists to see the graffiti, which had become a monument to their activism on a walking tour of the town. In Edinburgh, Douglass

---

95   *Dundee Courier*, 17 March 1846, p. 2.

96   Frederick Douglass, Speech on 19 March 1846, in Blassingame, *Douglass Papers—Series One: Vol. 1*, pp. 186–90.

97   Frederick Douglass to Francis Jackson, 29 January 1846, BPLAC, MS.A.1.2V.16, p. 13; McKivigan, *Douglass Papers—Series Three, Vol. 1*, pp. 89–92.

98   Mary Welsh to Maria Weston Chapman, 17 May 1846, BPLAC, identifier: lettertomydearmroowels5.

99   Frederick Douglass to William Lloyd Garrison, 2 January 1847, in McKivigan, *Douglass Papers—Series Three, Vol. 1*, pp. 190–95; *London Daily News*, 29 June 1846, p. 1; Whyte, *Send Back the Money!*, p. 129.

100 Frederick Douglass to Richard D. Webb, 10 February 1846, BPLAC, MS.A.1.2V.16P. 16; McKivigan, *Douglass Papers—Series Three, Vol. 1*, pp. 92–93.

walked the streets to find "Send Back the Money" placards spread throughout the city, and along with Eliza and Jane Wigham, carved the slogan into Arthur's Seat in protest.[101] Douglass later recalled that "'SEND BACK THE MONEY!' stared at us from every street corner; 'SEND BACK THE MONEY!' in large capitals, adorned the broad flags of the pavement; 'SEND BACK THE MONEY!' was the chorus of the popular street songs; 'SEND BACK THE MONEY!' was the heading of leading editorials in the daily newspapers."[102]

The campaign affected the daily lives of Scottish people in various ways: in Leith, a sign to advertise lodgings added a postscript "none need apply who is a member of a church which encourages slavery."[103] Furthermore, at a monument dedication to John Knox in May 1846, great crowds of people began to chant "Send back the money" and the police attempted to keep the streets clear, particularly in light of a rumor that people were planning to interrupt the procession.[104]

In response to the campaign, members of the Free Church tried to defend their position. John MacNaughtan dismissed the abolitionist agitation and argued that the Church had made its position against slavery clear. Furthermore, the small amount donated by enslavers was inconsequential, and if the abolitionist logic was to be extended, then "we must go a great deal farther with them than sending back the money . . . we must not buy their cotton, nor wear it; we must not use their rice, nor purchase their tobacco, – the stamp of slavery is on them all."[105] In a similar vein, one correspondent for the *Fife Herald* wrote that "Mr Frederick should be detained a few years longer in bonds" and pointed out that many churches in Scotland were "partially erected by West India planters . . . it would have been very silly to have declined those degrees and dollars."[106] Even Garrison noted the criticism, writing in one letter that Douglass's speech in Greenock "caused some hissing among the snakes" who supported the Free Church, "but this was trifling, in comparison with the amount of applause bestowed."[107]

In response, Douglass linked his own personal history with the Free Church which had made itself complicit with slavery, and declared that "the man whose

101 Fulkerson, "Frederick Douglass and the Anti-Slavery Crusade," pp. 99–107; *The Liberator*, 3 April 1846, p. 1.

102 Douglass, *My Bondage and My Freedom* (1855), pp. 383–86.

103 *Caledonian Mercury*, 15 June 1846, p. 3.

104 *Fife Herald and Kinross, Strathearn and Clackmanan Advertiser*, 21 May 1846, p. 4; Shepperson, "The Free Church and American Slavery," p. 129.

105 MacNaughtan, *The Free Church and American Slavery*, pp. 2–5.

106 *Fife Herald*, 14 May 1846, p. 3.

107 William Lloyd Garrison to Henry Clarke Wright, 23 September 1846, BPLAC, identifier: lettertodearhenroogarr12.

pockets are lined with the gold with which I ought to have been educated, stands up charging me with ignorance and poverty." The Free Church practiced heresy, and no true Christian would sanction the acceptance of money stained with the blood of the enslaved.[108] Back in March, Douglass had also defended himself against attacks from *The Northern Warder*, a Free Church-supporting newspaper, and quoted Robert Burns ("the De'il has business on his hands") to loud cheers from his audience. Once again, he cast those who stood against the abolitionists as aiders and abettors of enslavers and argued that the *Warder* "would deliberately stand by and see your wife taken from your bosom and sold on the auction block, and would strike hands with the robber after he did it." The printer's ink was stained with blood, much like the treasury of the Free Church.[109]

In the midst of such agitation, the Free Church held its annual assembly in May 1846 and George Thompson, James Buffum, and Douglass took their seats in the audience. The chairman stated that remonstrances had been sent from the Glasgow Emancipation Society, the British and Foreign Anti-Slavery Society, and the Ladies' Anti-Slavery Society in Edinburgh against the Church's conduct in relation to slavery. Drs. Thomas Chalmers, William Cunningham, and Robert Candlish reiterated their defence of the Church in that, while slavery was a sin, it was possible that "a man might sometimes be a slaveholder in circumstances in which he could not possibly help it." Unfortunately, their arguments regarding a distinction between "slaveholding" and "slave-having" were easily derided by the abolitionists. Incensed, Douglass easily exposed its illogical argument, causing hearty laughter amongst his audiences when he suggested that society should spare the murderer or the gambler, but denounce the crime.[110]

In Edinburgh shortly afterwards, a meeting was held by Douglass, Buffum, Thompson, and Wright to "review" the assembly; Douglass rose and declared that "he had never heard, even in the United States, more open and palpable defences of slave-holding . . . [and] anything more calculated to steel the consciences of slave-holders than the remarks then made."[111] Condemning Free Church ministers who had accused the abolitionists of disturbing the peace, he turned the argument around to state that the disturbance was necessary because "they allied themselves

108   Frederick Douglass, Speech on 25 April 1846, in Blassingame, *Douglass Papers—Series One: Vol. 1*, pp. 240–43. See also Douglass's criticism of MacNaughtan in a speech on 1 May 1846 in Blassingame, *Douglass Papers—Series One: Vol. 1*, pp. 243–49.

109   Frederick Douglass, Speech on 10 March 1846, in Blassingame, *Douglass Papers—Series One: Vol. 1*, pp. 171–82.

110   Blackett, *Building An Antislavery Wall*, pp. 88–89; *Caledonian Mercury*, 1 June 1846, pp. 2–3. See also *Free Church Alliance with Manstealers*, pp. 21–23. Other pamphlets published include *The Free Church of Scotland and American Slavery: Substance of Speeches Delivered in the Music Hall* (Edinburgh: Published for the Scottish Anti-Slavery Society).

111   *Dundee, Perth and Cupar Advertiser*, 5 June 1846, p. 1.

to manstealers." In blistering language, Douglass denounced the Free Church minister who "had no sympathy with the man who was burning in the fire; but they were well able to sympathize with the man who was making up the fire around him." In doing so, he rendered the ministers complicit in the lynching of his enslaved brethren. Instead, they had more sympathy for the souls of the murderers who took pleasure in wrenching the life from the writhing victims, or "the monster who was applying the lash to his back." Douglass framed his argument that the ministers were, in their silence, quite literally encouraging such demonic activity, as if they held the whips themselves.[112]

Reminiscing on this campaign in his second autobiography, *My Bondage and My Freedom*, in 1855, Douglass mournfully reported that the Free Church "held on to the blood-stained money" and "lost a glorious opportunity for giving her voice, her vote, and her example to the cause of humanity; and to-day she is staggering under the curse of the enslaved, whose blood is in her skirts." Despite this, however, the campaign was a success in that it provided an opportunity for making the Scottish people aware of the nature of slavery.[113]

Alliances, Leagues and Conventions

Riding on a wave of popularity from his campaign against the Free Church, Douglass arrived in London in mid-May 1846. Over the next six months, he travelled hundreds of miles on trains, omnibuses, and stagecoaches, returning to Scotland and Ireland for short stretches before remaining exclusively in England between November and 1 April 1847.[114]

Over the course of his lectures, Douglass spoke on a variety of subjects including the Free Church, the Evangelical Alliance, and the World's Temperance Convention (discussed below), as well as larger topics such as war, colonialism, temperance, suffrage, worker's rights, and Black heroism. Within a week of his arrival in London, he spoke at a meeting of the London Peace Society, the Metropolitan Complete Suffrage Association, and the annual meeting of the National Temperance Society in Exeter Hall.[115] He went to Cremorne Pleasure Garden with his London host,

---

112   Frederick Douglass, Speech on 4 June 1846, in Blassingame, *Douglass Papers—Series One: Vol. 1*, pp. 300–06. Douglass had elaborated on lynching in a lecture here: *Caledonian Mercury*, 11 May 1846, p. 3.

113   Douglass, *My Bondage and My Freedom* (1855), pp. 383–86; Pettinger, *Frederick Douglass and Scotland*, pp. 87–88.

114   Blight, *Frederick Douglass: Prophet of Freedom*, pp. 168–89; Murray, *Advocates of Freedom*, pp. 166–67; 201–02.

115   Murray, *Advocates of Freedom*, pp. 159–60. See also Frederick Douglass's speeches in Blassingame, *Douglass Papers—Series One: Vol. 1*.

George Thompson; became a member of the exclusive Free Trade Club; visited museums and galleries with "no distinction on account of color"; and attended Parliament to hear the speeches of John Bright, Robert Peel, Lord Henry Brougham, and Lord John Russell.[116] While numerous historians have pointed to Douglass's respect for O'Connell, few have highlighted his admiration for Brougham. Douglass declared that he was "the most wonderful speaker of them all." Once again demonstrating his savviness with print and aural pathways, he wondered how newspaper correspondents could record Brougham's speeches, for "listening to him was like standing near the track of a railway train, drawn by a locomotive at the rate of forty miles an hour. You are riveted to the spot, charmed with the sublime spectacle of speed and power, but can give no description of the carriages, or of the passengers at the windows." When Brougham resumed his seat, "you felt like one who had hastily passed through the bewildering wonders of a world's exhibition."[117]

While he extolled white men like Brougham and O'Connell, he demonstrated his commitment to Black solidarity and radicalism by speaking alongside other Black men in England. In Newcastle, John Joseph briefly addressed the meeting alongside Douglass and shared his experience of slavery.[118] In Manchester in October 1846, Thomas Wilson spoke on the platform and brandished a whip, simultaneously demonstrating his politicized desire to share his own experience and authenticate Douglass's words too.[119] In Liverpool, J. R. Bailey briefly confirmed Douglass's statements and declared he only exposed "one millionth part of the truth."[120] In the same city, Douglass by chance met another survivor of slavery, Harry, whom he had known in Maryland. While he framed Harry's story to celebrate the freedoms they both enjoyed under a British flag, Douglass related how even on English soil the US crew of the ship Harry had sailed upon tried to drag him back to America. Thus, his transatlantic audiences should be vigilant in protecting survivors of slavery, and their own soil as well, from the corrupting influence of enslavers.[121] While such shared platforms were a rare occurrence, the testimony of two fugitives on the platform enabled each to authenticate the other's testimony instead of relying on white abolitionist networks.

By the end of May, Douglass had spoken at two meetings supported by the British and Foreign Anti-Slavery Society, the second and most successful at Finsbury Chapel.

---

116 Frederick Douglass to William Lloyd Garrison, 23 May 1846, in McKivigan, *Douglass Papers—Series Three, Vol. 1*, pp. 127–40.

117 Douglass, *Life and Times* (1892), p. 297; Fenton, *"I was Transformed,"* p. 102.

118 *The Liberator*, 5 February 1847.

119 *Manchester Times*, 16 October 1846, pp. 4–6.

120 Frederick Douglass, Speech on 19 October 1846, in Blassingame, *Douglass Papers—Series One: Vol. 1*, pp. 466–74.

121 *The Liberator*, 25 December 1846, p. 1.

Douglass would later include this speech in his second autobiography as an example of his oratory in the British Isles, which was published as a pamphlet to reinforce its success yet further. Wielding Theodore Weld's antislavery work *Testimony of a Thousand Witnesses*, adverts from Southern newspapers, and Charles Dickens's *American Notes* to substantiate his words, Douglass urged his audience to make enslavers aware that "the curtain which conceals their crimes is being lifted abroad." He described how slavery was "a system of wrong, so blinding to all around, so hardening to the heart, so corrupting to the morals, so deleterious to religion, so sapping to all the principles of justice in its immediate vicinity, that the community surrounding it lack the moral stamina necessary to its removal." Thus, he stood before a British audience to demand their help in advocating for its demise. He would not compromise or be silent, for he was "bound by the prayers and tears and entreaties of three millions of kneeling bondsmen." He exposed slavery in Britain and Ireland "because to expose it is to kill it. Slavery is one of those monsters of darkness to whom the light of truth is death." By ripping the mask from its face it would be exposed to the sun, and with a "wall of anti-slavery fire" it would melt away from the land.[122]

The speech contained numerous themes that Douglass would expand upon throughout his English tour. As described above, he personified slavery as a monster that cast a corrupting shadow over the enslaved *and* enslavers as it spread across the South, and even to the British Isles. As a deft rhetorical ploy, he then demanded the help of his audience to immediately stop it before they were infected too.[123] While Douglass exposed the hypocrisy of Southern Christianity in Finsbury Chapel and elsewhere, he urged his audiences to reject the teachings of false prophets – particularly those who travelled to the British Isles under the guise of this false religion – and encouraged them to follow the true teachings of Christ instead. In order to do so, he had to withstand charges of heresy as he ripped off the mask to reveal the evils underneath.[124]

Throughout his sojourn, exposing the relationship between slavery and American churches was a core theme of Douglass's speeches, and he perfected the art of attacking Southern churches as part of his performative strategy. In England, ministers at the World's Anti-Slavery Convention of 1840 had tried to uphold that slavery was a sin and any religious man or institution who supported such a practice should be excommunicated, but several American delegates were deeply offended, feeling that British ministers had no right to interfere with American affairs and knew little of the intricacies surrounding slavery in the United States.[125] Concerned

---

122   *American Slavery: Report of a Public Meeting Held at Finsbury Chapel*, p. 21. Blackett, in *Building an Antislavery Wall*, uses this theme to describe Douglass's "moral cordon" around the British Isles.

123   Chesebrough, *Frederick Douglass: Oratory From Slavery*, pp. 90–96.

124   Dilbeck, *Frederick Douglass: America's Prophet*, pp. 63–75.

125   Bric, "Debating Slavery and Empire," pp. 64–66.

by American apathy, many British ministers were swayed by Douglass's rhetoric to challenge American churches.[126] He exploited this and in almost every speech (especially in England) he pointed to the church as a foundation stone of slavery and cruelty in the South. In one speech in Liverpool, he declared:

> [Slaveholders] had men sold to build churches, women sold to support missionaries, babes sold to buy bibles to send to the heathen. The slaves' prison and the church stand in the same street – the gates of heaven and the gates of hell being in the same avenue. The pulpit and the auctioneer's block are in the same neighborhood, and the blood-stained gold, received from the sale of human flesh on the auction block, goes to support the pulpit, while the pulpit, in return, governs the infernal business with the garb of Christianity. Under the drippings of the American sanctuary slavery has its existence. Whips, chains, gags, blood-hounds, thumb-screws, and all the bloody paraphernalia of slavery lie right under the drippings of the sanctuary, and instead of being corroded and rusted by its influence, they are kept in a state of preservation. Ministers of religion defend slavery from the Bible – ministers of religion own any number of slaves – bishops trade in human flesh – churches may be said to be literally built up in human skulls, and their very walls cemented with human blood – women are sold at the public block to support a minister, to support a church – human beings sold to buy sacramental services, and all, of course, with the sanction of the religion of the land.[127]

In graphic, radical, and electrifying language, Douglass painted the American slaveholding church not as a safe haven but as an accomplice and enemy of true Christianity. Churches and plantations existed in the same location, and the church – instead of being a light in the darkness – was part of the evil system of slavery. Douglass mocked the fact that the church and auction block existed in the same street, and invited his audience to agree with him on this judgment without actually asking them: this relationship was obviously morally wrong and incomprehensible. He went further and described how both coexisted in the same community and profited from each other. When an enslaved individual was sold, the profit went directly to the church, which pretended to respect and honor the Savior when in reality it made a mockery of it. The violence of slavery and the instruments of torture, such as whips and chains, were protected instead of shunned by the church, and the term "dripping" conjured images of bleeding wounds. The structures of the South – physically, morally, and mentally – were saturated in blood, right to its foundation's heart. Churches were built by this

---

126   Harwood, "British Evangelical Abolitionism and American Churches," pp. 288; 295.
127   *The Liverpool Mercury Supplement*, 23 October 1846, p. 4.

blood and were sites of death, violence, and rape. A minister could not truly be a Christian if he preached to a congregation on Sunday in a blood-stained institution, only to return to his enslaved population afterwards. In another meeting, Douglass once again espoused the same themes and argued that slaveholders were "devils dressed in angels' robes."[128] In the employment of such language, Douglass heightened tensions surrounding American national identity. As an American on British soil, he ridiculed American boasts of freedom and presented his own version of American history and identity, one that severely lacked in civil rights for Black people. Douglass exploited any opportunity to ridicule American slavery and the nation's hypocrisy, despite facing criticism for this on both sides of the Atlantic.[129]

Douglass used oratorical techniques such as pathos and antithesis to cast light on the injustice of slavery and the hypocrisy of the US nation. Antithesis in particular was a staple of Douglass's oratory in Britain and Ireland, for it allowed him to educate ignorant audiences on the stark contrast between Americans' professions of freedom and the soul-destroying realities of slavery.[130] He painted America as an imperialist power that brutally oppressed his enslaved brethren, criticized American nationalism at its core, and argued that the nation could not progress morally or intellectually as long as slavery still existed. He went further and stated that if a formerly enslaved individual escaped slavery, he or she was hunted and likely to be killed by that very nation. He targeted not only the American ideological foundations of freedom but also the cultural myth that it was the freest nation under heaven.[131]

In a forecast of his 1852 "What to the Slave is the 4th of July?" speech, Douglass attacked the hypocrisy surrounding Independence Day. He lambasted the anniversary for "under the eave-droppings of their chapels, were heard the clank of the fetters and the rattling of the chains which bound their miserable slaves together." He recounted hypocrisy after hypocrisy, one violent act after another, and in repetitive statements sarcastically claimed the US was a "land of civil and religious liberty!"[132] Similarly, in Liverpool he exposed such truths to an international audience because Americans would "see the cancer that was eating into

---

128   *The Newcastle Guardian*, 8 August 1846, pp. 2–3.

129   Eckel, "'A Type of his Countrymen,'" pp. 3–6; 12; Chesebrough, *Frederick Douglass: Oratory From Slavery*, pp. 83–96.

130   Leeman, "Frederick Douglass and the Eloquence of Double-Consciousness"; McDaniel, *The Problem of Democracy in the Age of Slavery*, pp. 81–82. See also Taylor, *British and American Abolitionists*; Blackett, *Beating Against the Barriers*.

131   Eckel, "'A Type of his Countrymen,'" pp. 12–16.

132   Frederick Douglass, Speech on 25 August 1846, in Blassingame, *Douglass Papers—Series One: Vol. 1*, pp. 341–52.

their vitals, and that all their vaunted independence was a lie." The celebration of Independence Day "was regarded as an absolute profanity . . . [and] utter blasphemy." If the true character of slavery was to be known, British Christians would instead choose to link "themselves to a pirate ship" rather than an American church.[133] With his radical rhetoric, he lambasted the symbols of American freedom, "for where was there a nation on the earth that made such a boast of liberty as she? On every coin, from the cent to the dollar, was stamped 'Liberty'; on every star-spangled banner was the liberty-cap; and on the return of each anniversary of her independence, the roar of every cannon, and the sound of every 'church-going bell' greeted a nation proud of its freedom."[134]

Earlier in the year, Douglass had also lambasted *physical* monuments of freedom which he could not claim as his own. When he looked upon the American Revolution site, he could be dragged back to the jaws of slavery from that very spot. In no corner of America was Douglass safe, in complete contrast to the platform where he then stood. By placing the gauntlet of responsibility at their feet, he charged his audience with an abolitionist mission and asked rhetorically, "who would hold fellowship with the man-stealing, cradle-robbing, woman-beating American slaveholder?" Now enlightened to the realities of slavery, his audience could no longer plead obliviousness to the frightening visuals Douglass had painted, nor the sounds of the "clanking" of fetters; he had released them from a prison of ignorance and it was their duty to rise up together and help abolish slavery. In making such a stark comparison, Douglass repeatedly denied that slavery existed in the British Isles; while poverty and exploitation did exist on this side of the Atlantic, he used his testimony as a fugitive to educate his audience and based his description on the complete oppression of mind, body and soul.[135]

To further cement the notion that slavery did not exist in the British Isles, he argued in Newcastle that its very foundation rested on the investment of "property in the body and soul of another man:"

This is slavery – having a mind, he may not cultivate and improve it; having a soul, he may not call it his own; having moral appreciations, he may not be guided by them; having a conscience, he may not walk by its admonitions; having an immortal spirit and a soul to aspire, he may not aspire, humbly as his

---

133   Frederick Douglass, Speech on 19 October 1846, in Blassingame, *Douglass Papers—Series One: Vol. 1*, pp. 466–74.

134   Frederick Douglass, Speech on 25 March 1847, in Blassingame, *Douglass Papers—Series One: Vol. 1*, pp. 8–19.

135   Frederick Douglass, Speech on 15 January 1846, in Blassingame, *Douglass Papers—Series One: Vol. 1*, pp. 131–44.

Master did . . . The whip must be there – the chain must be there – the gag must be there – the thumb screw must be there – the fear of death must be there, in order to induce the slave to go to the field and labour for another man without wages. Men do not suffer themselves to be robbed, their wives torn from their bosoms, sold at a returnless distance from them; men do not allow their children to be sold on the auction-block, whipped in their presence, driven away, with the fear of death hanging over them in the event of resistance . . .[136]

Violence was one of the central pillars of slavery, and Douglass targeted advocates of racial inferiority who implied African Americans were enslaved because it proved a "better" condition. The very nature of slavery involved the oppression of the mind, body and soul and dehumanized a person into a beast. Unlike his present audience, he could not make his own decisions, work for and keep a wage, marry whomever he chose, or even be guided by moral and Christian virtues. The enslaver removed these decisions from him.

In similar fashion, he was also forced to enlighten new audiences on the brutality of slavery. In another speech from Newcastle reprinted in this volume, Douglass dwelled upon one of his most painful memories, the whipping of his Aunt Hester, and recounted how "he was awakened by the sound of the whip, and dreadful shrieks." Hearing her screams and watching the blood drip at her feet "made an impression upon [my] mind that could never be erased."[137] The decision to focus on the female corporeal would have struck a chord with a Victorian audience: a woman's role was in the private sphere, and these stories disrupted social norms and were a horrifying affront to femininity and Victorian gentility. Exploiting the strain of sentimentalism in transatlantic culture, Douglass argued that in relation to these stories about women, Britons would be filled with such horror that they would be motivated to act. Douglass and other Black men tried to avoid descriptions of passive, enslaved men, as this threatened their masculinity, but in refocusing their attention on women they played into gender stereotypes and used accounts of white men violating Black women to stir sympathy from their audiences.[138]

Having been scarred for life upon witnessing such a horrific scene, Douglass used sound and visual allegories to describe his experience. He reimagined for his audience the screams of his aunt together with the brutal sounds of the whip, and performed a similar tale of horrific violence when he described how he had seen women "with their frantic children surrounding them, tied to a post, and lashed by an overseer until their blood covered their garments. The children were screaming

---

136   *Newcastle Guardian*, 8 August 1846, p. 2.
137   *Newcastle Guardian*, 15 August 1846, p. 5.
138   Hamilton, "Frederick Douglass and the Gender Politics of Reform," pp. 77–84.

for the release of their mother," while the whip was then applied to their father. One could hear the screams of the children, see the splatter of blood on bodies, clothes and even the children themselves as their loved ones were brutally tortured in front of them.[139] As Tom F. Wright argues, Douglass was "principally drawn to images of voice" that highlighted his "increasingly sophisticated awareness of reprint pathways." Well aware of his relationship with print culture, he "projected a vision of public opinion formed most powerfully through the combined sway of oratorical charisma, through the contagion of peer response, and crucially, through the symbolic depictions of such acts of collective listening in print."[140]

In speech after speech, Douglass reiterated that his white audience could never understand the horrors of slavery, and shortly afterwards, in Leeds, he urged them to "bring it before your mind." A naked woman, man or child was "tied hand and foot to a stake, and a strong man standing behind with a heavy whip, knotted at the end, each blow cutting into the flesh, and leaving the warm blood dripping to the feet (sensation)." To reinforce such a graphic image, Douglass read one after the other from a list of punishments "for being found in another person's negro-quarters, forty lashes . . ."[141] In Sheffield, when describing another scene, Douglass focused on a lynching where the murderers slowly drew out the man's death "while the blood was boiling in his mouth, and his lips were burning to a cinder." He described in excruciating detail how after an enslaved person was whipped, their backs were rubbed with brine and then tied up to a post; "the driver is made to take a live cat, and drag its claws over the closing wounds, and tear them open again." He discussed such barbarities because he wanted enslavers to know that their conduct was being exposed to *true* Christians in the British Isles.[142]

In another performative tactic, Douglass relied on moral suasion to chastise the English for their abandonment of antislavery principles. He urged the people to take action against the bloody institution of American slavery and asked rhetorically how British audiences could "remain silent" when his enslaved brethren were "within fourteen days' sail of them, shut up in prison for no crime" and "having tongues and not allowed to speak." If anyone doubted whether Englishmen should interfere, they should remind themselves of this fact and "remember that the slave was a man, and had rights."[143] Citing the immense improvements in technology and

---

139 Frederick Douglass, Speech in Sheffield on 11 September 1846, in Blassingame, *Douglass Papers—Series One: Vol. 1*, pp. 398–407.

140 Wright, *Lecturing the Atlantic*, pp. 58–68.

141 Frederick Douglass, Speech on 23 December 1846, in Blassingame, *Douglass Papers—Series One: Vol. 1*, pp. 474–85.

142 Frederick Douglass, Speech on 25 March 1847, in Blassingame, *Douglass Papers—Series One: Vol. 1*, pp. 8–19.

143 *Leicester Mercury*, 13 March 1847, p. 1.

communication during the 1840s, he pointed to the short geographical distance that existed between America and Britain to highlight the urgency of his mission: millions of women, men and children were enslaved and tortured only a few weeks' sail away. Douglass also blamed Britons for their part in the slave trade, which dealt "in the thews and sinews of their fellow-men" and it was their duty "to effect that foul blot . . . [and] redeem the errors of your race."[144] Hence, British people were in a unique position where they could use moral suasion to convince Americans of their crime. Carefully phrased so as not to provoke hostility from listeners, his words cajoled British audiences into the acceptance of their moral and physical responsibility to do something about American slavery. While the government may have ended slavery in the Empire, it seemed to care little about the consequences of the slave trade in America. The "foul blot of American slavery calls upon you, cries aloud to you, demands of you" to "enter your assistance and co-operation in bringing about . . . abolition."[145] Douglass empowered his audience to be activists even in small ways, as he knew how much hope it would give to his enslaved brethren. No white abolitionist could say this with the same conviction; it was his unique experience as a formerly enslaved individual that allowed him to make this claim.

To represent Britain as a land of freedom in direct contrast to America's self-professed declarations, Douglass employed anglophilia as an assimilationist tactic. He played to Britain's moral superiority and jingoistic pride when he stated that Britain had a unique and powerful influence on America, and argued that the state of freedom was synonymous with the nation.[146] His invocation of British liberty was a common performative strategy both for himself and numerous other African Americans on the Victorian stage.[147] When he first arrived in 1845, he had been shocked at the differences compared to the United States: "I am seated beside white people – I reach the hotel – I enter the same door – I am shown into the same parlor – I dine at the same table – and no one is offended."[148] In numerous meetings, he highlighted this distinct contrast, and sang the praises of Britain's antislavery history, citing famous abolitionists such as Thomas Clarkson, William Wilberforce, and Lord Henry Brougham to stir his English audiences.[149]

---

144 *The Vindicator*, 10 December 1845, p. 1. See also Bennett, "Frederick Douglass and Transatlantic Echoes," pp. 106–10.

145 *The Leeds Times*, 26 December 1846, p. 7.

146 Huzzey, *Freedom Burning*, pp. 37–39; 80–82.

147 When he returned to the US, Douglass employed a similar rhetorical strategy in numerous annual "West Indies Emancipation Day" celebrations. See McKivigan and Silverman, "Monarchical Liberty and Republican Slavery," pp. 7–19.

148 Frederick Douglass to William L. Garrison, 1 January 1846, in Foner, *Life and Writings of Frederick Douglass*, Vol. 1, p. 125. See also McKivigan, *Douglass Papers—Series Three, Vol. 1*, pp. 72–79.

149 *The Newcastle Guardian*, 2 January 1847, p. 6.

Although Douglass did experience racism on British soil, he exposed the hypocrisy of a nation that fought for freedom in the American Revolution but consistently denied freedom to thousands of African Americans. His speeches, which contained comparisons between republican America and monarchical Britain, implied that Britain was a racial paradise for Black people. He conveniently ignored the success of Blackface minstrel shows and, more importantly, the racism that was directed towards him. This "strategic anglophilia" (a term used by Audrey Fisch and Alan Rice) allowed Douglass and other African Americans to systematically discredit American white mainstream society while at the same time garnering support via their appeals to British patriotism.[150] Britain was inevitably an important place in the Black transatlantic abolitionist mind: it had destroyed slavery in the Empire and had taken active steps towards the end of slavery in the rest of the world. Thus, Douglass argued that slavery and racism were counter to the British ideal of civilized respectability.[151]

Douglass's anglophilia and attempts to praise British freedom were ironic given how the nation sought to colonize and Christianize Black people across the world. Britain's antislavery past and its apparent tolerance of Black people was mirrored by a nation that espoused imperialism, prejudice, and racism.[152] He also ignored Britain's fascination with colonized peoples, and the commodification of non-white individuals that was commonplace on the British national stage. In May 1847 (a month after Douglass had returned to America), Robert Knox exhibited several Africans on stage at Exeter Hall. Known amongst reformers as a symbol of abolitionist activity – and an institution at which Douglass himself had spoken – the Hall oversaw the exhibitionism of Black bodies.[153]

In his English speeches, Douglass also spoke on equality, feminism, his support for Home Rule, and British political affairs. In a public letter written to William Lloyd Garrison, he was convinced that "the next great reform will be that of complete suffrage" in England, and celebrated the success of the Anti-Corn Law League.[154] Douglass befriended activists such as Richard Cobden and John Bright, and attended meetings with Chartists Henry Vincent and William Lovett. While Chartism as a movement largely began in 1837, between 1845 and 1846 most Chartist groups underwent a significant period of restructuring, and Lovett and Vincent were key

---

150   Frederick Douglass, Speech on 12 February 1846, in Blassingame, *Douglass Papers—Series One: Vol. 1*, p. 159. For discussions on anglophilia, see Rice, *Radical Narratives of the Black Atlantic*, and Tamarkin, *Anglophilia*.
151   Tamarkin, *Anglophilia*, pp. xxii–xxx; 180–82; 203–04.
152   Dickerson, *Dark Victorians*, pp. 2–20; 40–50.
153   Qureshi, *Peoples on Parade*, pp. 1–4.
154   Frederick Douglass to William Lloyd Garrison, 23 May 1846, in Foner, *Life and Writings of Frederick Douglass, Vol. 1*, p. 165. See also McKivigan, *Douglass Papers—Series Three, Vol. 1*, p. 129.

players alongside other activists such as the Black British reformer William Cuffay. While there is no hard evidence that Cuffay and Douglass actually met (possibly because the former supported political violence), both Lovett and Vincent were present at the foundation of the Anti-Slavery League, and Douglass attended a meeting of the London Flogging Abolition Society in August 1846 where Vincent spoke. Douglass, William Lloyd Garrison, and Henry Clarke Wright spent at least one evening at the home of Lovett, accompanied by Vincent, and while all five men placed great value on political, moral, and social education, they would have inevitably clashed over Lovett's hesitation to support universal suffrage and Vincent's strong belief that wage slavery equated to American slavery.[155]

Douglass's position as a fugitive and his persuasive oratorical techniques led to the creation of a new antislavery society on 10 August, 1846, at the Crown and Anchor Tavern: the aforementioned Anti-Slavery League (ASL). Supported by William Lloyd Garrison (who had traveled to Britain in the wake of Douglass's success) and his international networks, the organization was designed to rival the British and Foreign Anti-Slavery Society led by John Scoble. Scoble and Garrison had been at war with each other since the 1840 World's Anti-Slavery Convention, and Garrison's supporters saw the ASL as a chance to usurp the power of the BFASS in London.[156] The League endorsed the Garrisonians' perfectionist antislavery tactics in both the political and religious spheres. In particular, it loudly demanded the Free Church of Scotland send back donations from Southern enslavers. Throughout the rest of 1846 and early 1847, Douglass traveled around the country with Robert Smith – the ASL's secretary – to raise support; but his refusal to engage in petty squabbles and his desire to work with abolitionists, Garrisonian or otherwise, meant that audiences followed his platform rather than any factional divides.[157] Nevertheless, Garrison organized meetings with influential individuals to support the League and his own American society, particularly those involved with some form of print culture like editors, journalists and printers who could have a significant impact on public opinion. As he stated in a letter to Edmund Quincy, it was his mission "as far as practicable, to become personally acquainted with those who have the control of the press in this country, or who, by their literary efforts, are molding the public sentiment, in order to secure their co-operation with us."[158] Garrison befriended the editor of the London *Daily News*

---

155   Bradbury, "Frederick Douglass and the Chartists," pp. 170–84. Frederick Douglass, "Chartists," *North Star*, 5 May 1848, p. 2; Benjamin Fagan, "The North Star and the Atlantic 1848," *African American Review*, 47:1 (Spring 2014), p. 61.

156   *Dundee, Perth and Cupar Advertiser*, 21 August 1846, p. 1; *London Daily News*, 19 August 1846, p. 4.

157   Blackett, "'And There Shall Be No More Sea,'" pp. 28–30.

158   William Lloyd Garrison to Edmund Quincy, 14 August 1846, in Merrill, *The Letters of William Lloyd Garrison*, Vol. 3, pp. 369–73.

and the editor of *Punch* magazine, Douglas Jerrold, who reprinted articles from *The Liberator*.[159] The editor of the *Daily News* in particular was a useful ally who would "inform the public mind, from time to time, through his columns, of the workings of slavery in America." Garrison tasked Richard D. Webb with cutting articles from *The Liberator* to send to the newspaper, "as far as the editor may find room and inclination for their insertion."[160]

As a result, the League initially met with great success; small branches were established in at least forty towns, including Rochdale, Manchester, Liverpool, Oldham, Stockport, Southport, Newcastle, Gateshead, Sunderland, Hexham, Carlisle, and South Shields.[161] Unitarian reformers welcomed Douglass to Exeter, Bridgewater, Taunton, and Leeds, often organizing auxiliary societies in support.[162] Unfortunately, when Douglass (as the main leader) returned to the United States, the League faded into obscurity after its first annual meeting in 1847.[163]

Douglass's speeches in England were often focused around two international events that took place in August, the same month the League was founded. The first was the World's Temperance Convention, held in Covent Garden from 4–8 August, 1846. Eight hundred delegates from Britain and fifty from all over the globe discussed the major successes and barriers to temperance in front of a 7,000-strong audience. In his opening address, the chairman – Samuel Bowly of Gloucester – welcomed the delegates, but also issued a warning that they should "preserve as much unanimity as possible" in the forthcoming proceedings. Sensitive to Douglass's antislavery campaign and the furore he had caused over the Free Church of Scotland, Bowly was desirous of keeping the peace, particularly in the presence of his American guests. On several occasions, he averted discussion on slavery.[164]

Ann Coughlan reveals the complexity behind Douglass's temperance campaign, noting that he used his status as a delegate from Newcastle to point to the exclusion of Black temperance advocates from white societies, and how his position would thus be null and void in the United States.[165] By refusing to acknowledge from the outset the racial disparities between white and Black temperance societies, the

---

159   Ibid. pp. 326–28.

160   William Lloyd Garrison to Edmund Quincy, 14 August 1846, in Merrill, *The Letters of William Lloyd Garrison*, Vol. 3, pp. 369–73.

161   Fulkerson, "Frederick Douglass and the Anti-Slavery Crusade," pp. 129–34.

162   Turley, "British Unitarian Abolitionists, Frederick Douglass, and Racial Equality," p. 58.

163   Frederick Douglass to William Lloyd Garrison, 2 January 1847 in McKivigan, *Douglass Papers—Series Three, Vol. 1*, p. 193.

164   *The Proceedings of the World's Temperance Convention* (London: Charles Gilpin, 1846), pp. 4–8; 20–21. Blassingame, *Douglass Papers—Series One: Vol. 2*, p. 57; Coughlan, "Frederick Douglass and Ireland," pp. 125–35.

165   Coughlan, "Frederick Douglass and Ireland," pp. 132–33.

Convention was not only doomed to failure but also highlighted the strength of racism within temperance, abolitionist, and other reformist movements. Douglass's speech threatened the survival of the Convention yet exposed the hollowness of its commitment to freedom and democratic expression of thought, reflecting the transatlantic conflict over slavery.[166]

During one evening discussion, Douglass was invited to the platform to speak. In his allotted fifteen minutes, he lectured on the present condition of temperance societies in America, highlighted the racial segregation between groups, and pointedly addressed the American delegates about their white privilege and lack of commitment to African Americans.[167] In particular, Douglass referred to an incident in Philadelphia in 1842, when Black temperance advocates in the Moyamensing Temperance Society had been mobbed while peacefully parading. The insidious racism of the white community had destroyed a peaceful reformist display, and such a response illustrated beyond doubt how slavery and racism were intertwined together.[168] His testimony caused some commotion on the platform, but when the chairman whispered in Douglass's ear (merely to inform him the apportioned time had passed), he had evidently won over the crowd, for the "vast audience simultaneously shouted – 'Don't interrupt! Don't dictate! Go on! Go on! Douglass! Douglass!'" The confusion continued for several minutes, until he very briefly proceeded and thanked the assembly for the opportunity to speak.[169]

Dr. Samuel Hanson Cox, an American Presbyterian minister and apostate abolitionist who had crossed the Atlantic to attend the Convention, was outraged at Douglass's speech. In an attempt to publicly shame him, Cox angrily wrote a public letter and charged that the "moral scene was superb and glorious" until Douglass came onto the platform. He had been paid by the abolitionists to disrupt the meeting and had spoken against temperance societies in "abominable" terms. With a supercilious strain of racial paternalism, he objected to the "revengeful missiles" Douglass had launched at America and was incensed at being talked down to "as if he had been our schoolmaster." Instead of helping the true cause of abolition, Douglass, together with his Garrisonian friends, all but hindered it.[170]

As Douglass later said, "I did not allow the letter of Dr. Cox to go unanswered through the American journals, but promptly exposed its unfairness."[171] Disgusted

---

166   Ibid. pp. 127–29.
167   *Correspondence Between The Rev. Samuel H. Cox and Frederick Douglass*, pp. 7–17.
168   Yacovone, "The Transformation of the Black Temperance Movement."
169   *Correspondence Between The Rev. Samuel H. Cox and Frederick Douglass*, pp. 7–17.
170   Ibid. pp. 5–7. See also Blackett, *Building an Antislavery Wall*, pp. 104–06, and Fulkerson, "Exile as Emergence," pp. 120–23.
171   Douglass, *Life and Times* (1892), p. 309.

at Cox's self-professed notions of abolitionism, Douglass wrote in reply that he was the representative of his enslaved brethren and as a result had a right to speak on their behalf. He was only able to do so on British soil thousands of miles away from the "foul clutch" of enslavers, and he slowly and deliberately dissected every charge Cox made, with particular focus on his credentials of antislavery and philanthropy. If Cox were a true abolitionist, he "would have been delighted at seeing one of Africa's despised children cordially received." He objected to the charges of payment but turned Cox's words against him, as a failure to speak on behalf of his enslaved brethren would be "selling my birthright for a mess of pottage." Casting his antislavery mission as one of lightness against the inherent evil and darkness of slavery, he argued that his testimony was an opportunity to smite the "demon" of slavery and "rebuke this evil spirit, where my words would be borne to the shores of America." Ultimately, Cox's vicious malignity "tells the whole story of your abolitionism, and stamps your pretensions to abolition as brazen hypocrisy or self-deception." To amplify Douglass's message and maximize support for the antislavery campaign, Douglass and the Garrisonians decided to publish the exchange as a separate pamphlet; they wanted to expose Cox's hypocrisy and use this as an example of Northern religious ministers who aided and abetted enslavers, and perpetuated racism itself.[172]

A few weeks later, a second international event provided another opportunity to intensify Douglass's philosophy of non-fellowship. More than eight hundred religious ministers gathered from around the world in an attempt to form a global Evangelical Alliance. This event took place in London between 19 August and 2 September and among its attendees were several of the individuals, including Drs. Cunningham, Candlish, and Cox, whom Douglass had recently and so publicly challenged. At a preliminary meeting months before, the furore over the Free Church had led to discussions of membership, and it was decided in a rather lacklustre fashion that American enslavers should not be invited despite the fact that most of the invitations had already been sent out.[173] In the first few days, slavery was barely mentioned, but on the ninth day, British and Foreign Anti-Slavery Society representative Reverend J. H. Hinton objected to silencing the convention on slavery and questioned the organizing committee, who had professed antislavery principles and banned enslavers from membership, only to later accept them to the meeting. Enslavers were menstealers and should not be recognized as Christians, but Hinton was clear to differentiate himself from Garrison (whom he named directly)

---

172   *Correspondence Between The Rev. Samuel H. Cox and Frederick Douglass*, p. 17. This correspondence was printed in *The Liberator*, 1 January 1847 and 29 January 1847.

173   *Report on the Proceedings of the Evangelical Alliance*, pp. 11–19. See also Blackett, *Building an Antislavery Wall*, pp. 88–89, and Dilbeck, *Frederick Douglass: America's Prophet*, pp. 63–75.

and his radical views.[174] Several Americans objected to Hinton's position and to Douglass's and Garrison's activism in the British Isles, "which utterly misrepresented the great mass of the Christian community." Another American concurred and reminded his British brethren that "the price of a slave in Louisiana is always regulated by the price of a pound of cotton at Liverpool."[175] Several Americans refused to attend the following morning in protest; eventually the committee decided that each international branch should declare for themselves whether American enslavers could be members. While the original idea of a united international organization had failed, the abolitionists succeeded in pressurizing the British section to practice non-fellowship with enslavers.[176]

In response to the meeting, Douglass believed that the Alliance ministers were "misled and cajoled" as "they had it in their power to have given slavery a blow which would have sent it reeling to its grave."[177] Building on his testimony against the Free Church, Douglass charged the Alliance with "infidelity" and accused them of endorsing slavery by their silence. Douglass stated: "I stand here as the representative of three millions of human beings in slavery. I was not in the Alliance; but the money, the blood-stained dollars, were in their pockets."[178] He criticized the meeting for "its unprincipled shrinking from all denunciation of the crime of slavery" and unsparingly castigated the ministers as "Man-eaters."[179] Although support for Douglass was not unanimous, the controversy over the Evangelical Alliance demonstrated the power of his antislavery campaign: he had directly affected two organizations, and one dissolved because of his pressure against it.[180]

British and Irish newspapers were divided in their reportage of both controversies. *The Patriot* wrote that "American slavery has proved to be the 'great difficulty' of the Evangelical Alliance" and "on this rock, it has well nigh split, and may yet be wrecked."[181] One anonymous correspondent to *The Western Times* thanked Douglass and Garrison for bringing the public's attention to the true horrors of slavery, but regretted the "very painful position in which the dissenters of England (especially the Wesleyans) were placed by the uncourteous, unqualified expressions, made use of by *Frederick Douglas* the fugitive slave of America." He had given the impression

---

174   *Report on the Proceedings of the Evangelical Alliance*, pp. 290–97.
175   Ibid. pp. 300–17.
176   Ibid. pp. 289–317; 338–85; Ripley, *The Black Abolitionist Papers*, pp. 160–75. See also McKivigan, *The War against Proslavery Religion*, pp. 125–26.
177   *Farewell Speech of Mr. Frederick Douglass*, p. 12.
178   Frederick Douglass, Speech on 24 September 1846, in Blassingame, *Douglass Papers—Series One: Vol. 1*, pp. 434–70.
179   *Northampton Mercury*, 3 April 1847, p. 3.
180   Blackett, *Building an Antislavery Wall*, pp. 88–110.
181   *Bradford Observer*, 3 September 1846, p. 7. Originally from *The Patriot*.

that Wesleyan churches supported slavery, despite the fact that it was declared a universal sin at a recent conference of Wesleyan Methodist Ministers in Bristol.[182] A week later, another anonymous correspondent lambasted "the incompetent judgment of these itinerant adventurers," who delivered biting "anathemas and entreaties to excommunicate the American churches, because, forsooth, they contain a few unhappy apologists for slavery." Douglass was deliberately targeted for vilifying the Free Church in particular and had chosen to ignore the nation's abolitionist history.[183] In a dark and menacing twist, pro-slavery defenders in Sheffield were reported to have carved "Death to Abolitionists" on bowie knives as a stark warning to Douglass and his activist friends.[184]

When Douglass returned to Belfast with William Lloyd Garrison in early October 1846, *The Belfast Newsletter* was similarly unimpressed with their rhetoric against both religious organizations: one article described them as "American Antislavery Agitators" and another recorded how one meeting resulted in such "disapprobation . . . that, as the only means to put a stop to the confusion, thanks were voted to the chairman, and the meeting broke up." In one newspaper article reprinted in this volume, although most of the criticism was saved for Garrison, Douglass was described in racialized terms as the "'curled darling' of the ladies" who in another meeting led to such "a mournful exhibition of bad taste and worse feeling" that the correspondent refused to write what Douglass had said.[185]

As a result, several meetings in England became rowdy and turbulent. In Manchester, Douglass spoke alongside Garrison, George Thompson, and Henry Clarke Wright, but the local correspondent was disgusted at their attempts to "put the Evangelical Alliance on its trial and to ask for a verdict of 'guilty' against it." While some members of the audience tried to interrupt Thompson and Garrison, most of the crowd became frustrated and immediately left.[186] Speaking by himself in Sunderland, Douglass was constantly interrupted by ministers who supported the Alliance. When he declared the organization had missed opportunities to denounce slavery as a crime, one minister shouted "They did so" to loud cries of "Order." Douglass refused to acquiesce and referred to the Free Church of Scotland to support his religious arguments against the Alliance.[187] Comparable disapprobation happened in Darlington, and he later wrote he was "somewhat dissatisfied" with his speech but was pleased to know from Elizabeth Pease that "the cause has suffered no real injury

---

182   *The Western Times*, 5 September 1846, p. 7.

183   *The Western Times*, 12 September 1846, p. 8.

184   Fenton, *"I was Transformed,"* pp. 157–58.

185   *Newcastle Guardian*, 16 January 1847, p. 5. See also the *Belfast Newsletter* on the following dates: 2 October 1846, p. 2; 6 October 1846, pp. 1–2; 9 October 1846, pp. 1–2.

186   *Manchester Times*, 16 October 1846, pp. 4–6.

187   Frederick Douglass, in Blassingame, *Douglass Papers—Series One: Vol. 1*, pp. 417–25.

by my visit." Cautious of the impact of damaging newspaper reports, he wanted to reschedule another meeting to give himself "a fair opportunity for making the people . . . somewhat better acquainted with the merits of our great enterprise."[188] Demonstrating his awareness of print pathways and how his speeches were reported, Douglass refused to let white reporters or correspondents corrupt and malign his testimony, and often incorporated their attacks into his speeches. Subverting the words of one correspondent in Carlisle named only as "A.B." (who had accused him of libeling the Free Church), he waved the *Carlisle Journal* in his hand, "dissected A.B's defence and held up his apology to ridicule."[189]

Such rebukes were not always possible when he faced pressure from his hosts to curtail his opinions. During a series of lectures in Bristol, he was not above issuing clarifications to previous speeches, particularly if his position "did not seem to be clearly understood," but was forced to issue an apology to Reverend George Armstrong, who demanded a retraction of Douglass's statements against the Unitarian church.[190] The commotion upset local abolitionists, and Garrison wrote to their host John Estlin that "Frederick was unguarded in one of his expressions, in regard to the Unitarian communion table, I am certain it was far from his intention to make an invidious fling."[191] Mary Carpenter, too, wrote of her disappointment with Douglass's speech and his "sarcastic and unnecessarily offensive manner" but expressed her satisfaction with his written apology.[192] Reflecting back on his experience, Douglass later wrote: "My speeches in Great Britain were wholly extemporaneous, and I may not always have been so guarded in my expressions, as I otherwise should have been," which may indicate his regret at certain remarks he had made in cities like Bristol.[193]

Anti-Racist Interventions

The intense notoriety surrounding Douglass attracted charges of inauthenticity and falsehood. When he returned to Belfast in June 1846, he was surprised to find rumors circulating that he was an imposter. To certify his authenticity, he waved a paper

---

188 Frederick Douglass to Elizabeth Pease, 3 and 11 March 1847, BPLAC, MS.A.1.2V.17, p. 19 and p. 21. For coverage of the meeting itself, see *Newcastle Guardian*, 16 January 1847, p. 5.

189 *Carlisle Journal*, 12 September 1846, p. 4. For the letter in question, see *Carlisle Journal*, 29 August 1846, p. 4.

190 Frederick Douglass, Speech on 29 August 1846, in McKivigan, *Douglass Papers—Series Three*, Vol. 1, pp. 161–65.

191 William Lloyd Garrison to John B. Estlin, 8 September 1846, BPLAC, identifier: lettertomyesteemoogar.

192 Mary Carpenter to William Lloyd Garrison, 3 September 1846, BPLAC, Ms A.1.2 V.16, p. 83.

193 Douglass, *My Bondage and My Freedom* (1855), pp. 377–80.

"containing a threat, by my former master, that so sure as Frederick Douglass set his foot on American soil, he shall be taken back to slavery." Since he had proved his identity as a formerly enslaved individual, Douglass then demanded "the right to speak in reference to whatever sustains or upholds American slavery."[194]

These charges became far more sinister when they were connected with stereotypes of the sexually aggressive Black male. Reverend Thomas Smyth, an Irishman working as a minister for the Second Presbyterian Church in Charleston, South Carolina, spread a rumor that Douglass had emerged from a brothel in Manchester. Smyth had supported Thomas Chalmers and the Free Church since 1843 and had traveled to the British Isles in 1846. When he visited Belfast, he was incensed to find the city was "in a hub-bub about this said Douglass" and that he had been personally mentioned in one of his speeches. In the first few days of July, Smyth responded by slandering Douglass's character and branded him an infidel. Reverend Isaac Nelson and several members of the Belfast Anti-Slavery Society met with Smyth personally to force him to retract the slander, but when he refused, entered into negotiations with a solicitor. Smyth eventually issued an apology, which was reprinted in the British and the American press via *The Liberator*.[195] Smyth could have solely charged Douglass with fraud, but by focusing the rumor on a brothel, he played on racialized stereotypes and class prejudices. Considering the countless white women Douglass corresponded with, spoke to, or stayed with, Smyth's rumour was potentially damaging enough to derail his visit, and it was likely his presence had led to placards reading "Send back the nigger" across Dublin and Belfast.[196] All criticisms towards Douglass were grounded in a white racist schema and invoked stereotypes of supposed African barbarity, or the fact that Black people "belonged" in slavery.

In an attempt to control the fallout from Smyth's slander and his subsequent apology, Douglass said to his solicitors and friends in Belfast that "the retraction should first appear there" (the site of the libel itself).[197] The episode had done its damage, however: Douglass admitted that his stay in Belfast was "marred by the malignant slanders of Dr. Smyth. I ought not to have permitted this to have disturbed me, but one cannot always command their feelings." Concerned that Smyth

---

194   *The Belfast Newsletter*, 19 June 1846, p. 1.

195   Blackett, *Building an Antislavery Wall*, pp. 85–86; J. F. Maclear, "Thomas Smyth, Frederick Douglass, and the Belfast Antislavery Campaign," p. 286.

196   Fought, *Women in the World of Frederick Douglass*, pp. 85–86; Richard D. Webb to Maria Weston Chapman, 16 July 1846, BPLAC, identifier: lettertomydearfroowebb30.

197   Frederick Douglass to William Smeal, 1 August 1846, in McKivigan, *Douglass Papers—Series Three: Vol. 1*, p. 562; Frederick Douglass to James Standfield, 2 August 1846, in McKivigan, *Douglass Papers—Series Three: Vol. 1*, p. 155.

would jeopardize his mission, Douglass was also weary of the constant charges of fraud and racist insult.[198]

From the beginning of his tour, Douglass objected to the racism he experienced on an almost daily basis. As we noted above, Douglass did experience greater freedoms in the British Isles than ever before, but was forced to endure a myriad of instances of white paternalism from his fellow abolitionists, racist descriptions of him in the press, and offensive accusations of racial inferiority. He would later write in *Life and Times*: "I have often been bluntly and sometimes very rudely asked, of what color my mother was, and of what color was my father? In what proportion does the blood of the various races mingle in my veins, especially how much white blood and how much black blood entered into my composition?"[199] Douglass was asked endlessly about his racial heritage, and nowhere was this more apparent than in newspaper descriptions of him. The racialized climate of Victorian society meant that press descriptions focused on Douglass's intelligence, eloquence, and the corporeal self. Several newspaper descriptions emphasized Douglass's body, his physique, face, hair, skin, and even the aura that surrounded him – occasionally at the expense of reporting what he actually said. Audiences relied on their white privilege to train their spectatorial gaze on his body, but Douglass refused to be viewed and treated like an enslaved figure on the abolitionist block. Instead, he used the opportunity to refer to Madison Washington, a man whom he fervently admired as a leading example of Black heroism and manhood.[200]

British newspapers offered extensive commentary on the lectures of African Americans and in many cases reflected the prevalent racial stereotypes as espoused by racial thinkers such as Thomas Carlyle.[201] For example, one correspondent for *The Leeds Times* employed racial stereotypes to describe Douglass's "woolly head, his prominent thick lips, and high cheek bones," but *despite* these characteristics felt he represented the height of nobility. Raising Douglass so high on a racialized pedestal confined his fellow African Americans to a life of inferiority, as it was apparently rare that someone of mixed heritage could attain such intelligence and skill.[202] In a similar fashion, *The Manchester Examiner* referred to his "great muscular strength" and labelled him a "Negro Hercules"; with a deliberate reference

---

198   Frederick Douglass to [Mary Carpenter?], 30 July 1846, in McKivigan, *Douglass Papers—Series Three: Vol. 1*, pp. 561–62.

199   Douglass, *Life and Times* (1892), p. 621.

200   Fanuzzi, "The Trouble with Douglass's Body," pp. 27–30; DeLombard, "'Eye-witness to the Cruelty,'" pp. 270–71; Blassingame, *Douglass Papers—Series One: Vol. 1*, pp. xxviii–xxx; Celeste-Marie Bernier, "From Fugitive Slave to Fugitive Abolitionist."

201   See Carlyle, "Occasional Discourse on the Negro Question."

202   *Leeds Times*, 26 December 1846, p. 7.

to his racial heritage, the correspondent clearly believed he was "not of the pure Negro race. In his veins evidently flows the blood of the white man, co-mingled with that of the African" and it was this "mixing" that explained Douglass's oratorical gifts.[203] In a speech reprinted in this volume, a correspondent in Carlisle captured the astonishment of the audience, too, when "he gave unmistakeable signs of extraordinary talent, his impassioned eloquence taking the majority of his hearers, to whom he was a stranger, by surprise."[204] In his private diary, Joseph Adair noted that the "Audience were extremely pleased" with Douglass's lecture in Cockermouth: "the lecture was far beyond what was expected from a negro, all seemed to concur with the opinion that it would have done credit to any [learned] englishman [sic]." In a letter to fellow abolitionist Francis Jackson, Douglass touched on this and wrote: "I am hardly black enough for British taste, but by keeping my hair as woolly as possible I make out to pass for at least half a Negro at any rate."[205] Despite Douglass's self-proclaimed fair treatment, he still had to combat British racism when audiences did not believe him to possess "African blood," and he sarcastically referred to his hair as this seemed to give his true heritage away. Beneath the joke, however, lay Douglass's frustration with people expecting him to appear as a caricature, rather than himself.

Incensed at such descriptions, Douglass challenged and exposed this racism whenever he could. In Limerick, he objected to a local actor impersonating Jim Crow and "was sorry to find that one of these apes of the negro" had been welcomed to the city.[206] More specifically, in October 1845, the *Cork Examiner* stated: "the hue of his face and hands is rather a yellow brown or bronze, while there is little, if anything, in his features of that peculiar prominence of lower face, thickness of lips, and flatness of nose, which peculiarly characterize the true Negro type."[207] Douglass despised this stereotype, a false impression against which he fought on a daily basis. In response to a similar charge from the Irish newspaper *Constitution*, he objected to the description because it was "the mode of advertising in [America] a slave for sale."[208] By publicly highlighting the incident, he refused to tolerate such casual but unconscionable discrimination and also made a stand against other reporters who

---

203 *The Manchester Examiner*, 11 July 1846, p. 5.

204 *Carlisle Journal*, 22 August 1846, p. 4.

205 Frederick Douglass to Francis Jackson, 29 January 1846, in Foner, *Life and Writings of Frederick Douglass, Vol. 1*, p. 25. See also McKivigan, *Douglass Papers—Series Three, Vol. 1*, pp. 89–82.

206 Frederick Douglass, Speech on 10 November 1845, in Blassingame, *Douglass Papers—Series One: Vol. 1*, pp. 76–86; Sweeney, "Mask in Motion," p. 34.

207 Frederick Douglass, Speech on 15 October 1845, in Blassingame, *Douglass Papers—Series One: Vol. 1*, p. 36.

208 Frederick Douglass, Speech on 27 October 1845, in Blassingame, *Douglass Papers—Series One: Vol. 1*, p. 59.

had used similar language to describe him.[209] However, in a patronizing tone that demonstrated the racism among white abolitionists, Garrison addressed Douglass's reaction to this in the pages of *The Liberator*. If Douglass had only "understood the world-wide difference . . . in meaning and spirit, in the use of the term 'negro' on that and on this side of the Atlantic," he would not have betrayed "so much sensitiveness." According to Garrison, the term in the US was "generally used in a contemptuous and vile manner" but in Britain, it was "used with all possible respect."[210] Douglass does not offer a rejoinder to this, but such dismissiveness to his experience of racism would only provide more fuel to the growing gap between himself and the Garrisonians, who had no idea of the exhausting realities he was facing – or, if they did, often belittled it.

Restricted by his public performances and his reliance on the Garrisonian network, Douglass could do little to expose the numerous counts of racism he experienced from his friends during his British and Irish tour. He continued to defend Garrison, the movement, and his friends, in part to prevent further divisions.[211] However, as Alan Rice notes, "Douglass was not prepared to act as second fiddle in an ensemble orchestrated by others."[212] For example, his experience at a Birmingham temperance meeting highlighted the white authenticity politics of the movement. After grudgingly deciding to go to the meeting midway through his first tour of Belfast in 1845, he was displeased with the effort: a meeting with renowned minister Reverend John Angel James provoked ill-feeling, as he demanded to see Douglass's testimonials and was not only "cold toward me but absolutely suspicious of me." Joseph Sturge, too, was also very cautious, and when Douglass finally met the meeting's organizer – John Cadbury – he discovered his name had been left off the placards advertising the meeting, for Cadbury feared he would not turn up. Their initial meeting together left Douglass with the distinct impression that he would fail "to interest the audience," and that evening he remained on the platform for three hours until he was asked to second a resolution.[213] The supercilious strain of white antislavery politics decreed that Black lecturers were forced to carry testimonials to their character: white abolitionists were wary of charges of inauthenticity, and rigorously checked the facts of each lecturer they hired to certify the truth of their testimony. White lecturers, of course, suffered no such treatment.

---

209   Frederick Douglass, Speech on 17 October 1845, in Blassingame, *Douglass Papers—Series One: Vol. 1*, pp. 45–54, and Cork, 23 October 1845, pp. 59–70.

210   *The Liberator*, 28 November 1845.

211   Blackett, *Building an Antislavery Wall*, pp. 107–08.

212   Rice, *Radical Narratives of the Black Atlantic*, pp. 174–75; Levine, *The Lives of Frederick Douglass*, pp. 108–09; Fulkerson, "Exile as Emergence," p. 80.

213   Frederick Douglass to Richard D. Webb, 20 December 1845, BPLAC, identifier: lettertomydearfroodoug_2.

The frustrations Douglass had experienced while editing the Dublin edition of his *Narrative* in particular were magnified tenfold over the next few months of his trip. Garrisonians sought to control his speaking engagements, how long he should stay in Britain, and his financial rewards, with a complete disregard for his personal or family needs. As Celeste-Marie Bernier summarizes, he "realized only too well that he was being bought and sold in abolitionist campaigns that traded in shamelessly sensationalist, dehumanizing and derogatory language when it came to Black women and men."[214] Even before he had left the US, Boston-based abolitionist Maria Weston Chapman believed he should be warned away from doing "anything for himself in the preservation of philanthropic enterprise" and was skeptical of the management of his own fame. Chapman saw Douglass as an untrustworthy child who might wreak havoc or be led astray from the Boston Society's influence. So far, he had taken the right course, but he should follow in the footsteps of Garrison and Wendell Phillips, who spurned fame or notoriety in favour of the antislavery cause. He should not "yield to temptation" and sacrifice the cause of abolition – a patronizing comment that implied a formerly enslaved Black man would forget about slavery more quickly than a white abolitionist.[215] British abolitionists were not above stirring such fears, as John B. Estlin noted even after Douglass returned home that several friends were "anxious to detach him" from the Garrisonian movement.[216] Even Isabel Jennings recognized this control, and remarked, "some <u>dictated</u> to him" too much.[217]

In 1846, Chapman again expressed her fears and declared Douglass should not become "drunk with vanity": if he used common sense and steered on the right course (i.e., what the Garrisonian abolitionists wanted), then "all will be well."[218] The bitterness between Douglass, Chapman, and Webb existed for months, and Douglass had to repeatedly reassure them that he remained an "old organized Garrisonian abolitionist," sometimes to his own detriment.[219] According to Webb, Douglass was "the least loveable and the least easy of all the abolitionists" and treated members of his family "in such a contemptuous, uncourteous manner." He was a "child – a savage" and "a wild animal."[220]

---

214   Douglass (ed. Bernier), *Narrative of the Life of Frederick Douglass*, pp. 21; 50–51.

215   Maria Weston Chapman to Richard D. Webb, 29 June 1845, BPLAC, identifier: extractsofthree-loochap. Fought, *Women in the World of Frederick Douglass*, pp. 79–81.

216   John B. Estlin to Samuel May, 17 October 1847, BPLAC, identifier:lettertomydearmrooestl_27.

217   Isabel Jennings to Maria Weston Chapman, 2 August 1847, BPLAC, identifier: lettertomydearm-roojenn8.

218   Maria Weston Chapman to Richard D. Webb, 23 January 1846, BPLAC, identifier: extractsoft-hreeloochap.

219   Frederick Douglass to Richard D. Webb, 29 March 1846, BPLAC, identifier: lettertomydearfr-oodoug_7.

220   Richard D. Webb to Maria Weston Chapman, 16 May 1846, BPLAC, identifier: lettertomydear-froowebb29; McKivigan, *Douglass Papers—Series Three, Vol. 1*, pp. 98–102.

White abolitionists constantly referred to Douglass in racialized language. Webb sneered at the "petting he gets from beautiful, elegant and accomplished women."[221] John B. Estlin observed this too and wrote: "You can hardly imagine how he is noticed, – *petted* I may say by *ladies*. Some of them really exceed a little the bounds of propriety." Douglass would "face a craving void" when he returned home to his wife, whom both Webb and Estlin believed was uneducated and inferior compared to the middle- or upper-class white English women who swarmed around Douglass. Estlin was also skeptical about Douglass's work ethic, and was convinced he would shy away from working too hard since he had become used to "sailing on [the] tide of popularity."[222] Estlin's disgust at interracial relationships, together with his belief that African Americans sorely needed the interference or patronization of white men and women, revealed that white abolitionists were not free from investing in narratives of white supremacist thought.[223] Infuriated by these accusations, which were shared with him at some point, Douglass objected to the notion that he was "spoiled" by all the attention and soon enough he would be home to "encounter again the kicks and cuffs of proslavery." Fully aware of the paternalistic attitudes of white abolitionists and their concerns that he would no longer be fit for the role in which they proscribed him, he reminded his friends and benefactors of the constant racism to which he was subjected, and dismissed patronizing claims that he would soon forget his past as an enslaved individual amidst all the attention.[224]

Smaller but no less grating microaggressions compounded these growing tensions. During one speech in Paisley in 1846, Garrison interrupted the flow of Douglass's lecture to read a short speech of one of the Free Church ministers; with forced politeness, Douglass resumed and reminded the audience of what he was going to say.[225] In August, Douglass was "weighed down, oppressed, and almost overcome by constant effort – by engagements, public and private, growing out of immediate contact with deeply interested friends here." He compared the white privilege of other abolitionists to his position as a fugitive, which "subjects me to many calls and questions from which other lecturers would be comparatively free." It was near impossible to rest from his speaking engagements and the constant activity, together with the endless paternalism he suffered from friends and strangers simultaneously

---

221 Richard D. Webb to Maria Weston Chapman, 31 October 1846, BPLAC, identifier: lettertomydearfroowebb31.

222 John Estlin to Samuel May, 12 January 1847, BPLAC, identifier: lettertomydearmrooestl_21.

223 Rice and Crawford, "Triumphant Exile," pp. 7–8; Rice, *Radical Narratives of the Black Atlantic*, pp. 174–87.

224 Frederick Douglass to Francis Jackson, 29 January 1846, in Foner, *Life and Writings of Frederick Douglass*, Vol. 1, p. 25; McKivigan, *Douglass Papers—Series Three*, Vol. 1, pp. 89–92.

225 Frederick Douglass, Speech on 23 September 1846, in Blassingame, *Douglass Papers—Series One: Vol. 1*, pp. 426–33.

suspicious of and fascinated by his position.[226] To illustrate this further, at an anti-slavery meeting in London Douglass was surprised when George Thompson mentioned a subscription to bring Douglass's family over to Britain. The "result was entirely unexpected to me. I had not even mentioned my desire for any such thing to the meeting." The confusion may have arisen from Douglass mentioning that he could not be absent from his family for longer than a year, but it also demonstrated that Thompson and other abolitionists had made up their minds about extending his lecturing tour before consulting him – that the movement could ill afford to spare him, so the only option was to bring his family over, instead of Douglass returning to the United States. His surprise – and presumably the pressure to maintain his composure at a public meeting – possibly hid a deeper resentment towards his colleagues for making life-changing and alarming statements without proper consultation or action.[227] Besides, Douglass never seriously entertained the thought of remaining in Britain. In July 1846, he wrote that "no inducement could be offered strong enough to make me quit my hold upon America as my home."[228] Garrison did force Douglass to extend his trip, however: Anna Murray Douglass had reportedly asked him to "come home," and he had planned to sail back to America on 4 November. Under pressure from his Garrisonian friends, he relented, knowing the decision would "cost her some pain." Not only did he extend his tour by five months, the constant lecturing schedule only increased and caused him to be ill in December that year.[229]

Such tensions were exacerbated when Douglass – in an attempt to control his own lecturing schedule – spoke at two meetings under the BFASS umbrella in May 1846. Before this, he had avoided igniting sectional strife between rival abolitionist groups, and constantly assured his American colleagues that he "acted in every way independent of [the London Committee]" despite the fact it jeopardized his potential success.[230] When Douglass first received the invitation he sent his apologies, aware that his Garrisonian supporters – particularly those who were currently providing homes and networks for him – would be displeased. However, it was George Thompson who suggested he accept and was thus unprepared for the storm of criticism he received from several of the US-based Garrisonians, including, of

---

226 Frederick Douglass, Speech on 18 August 1846, in McKivigan, *Douglass Papers—Series Three*, Vol. *1*, pp. 158–60.

227 Frederick Douglass to William Lloyd Garrison, 23 May 1846, in McKivigan, *Douglass Papers—Series Three*, Vol. *1*, pp. 127–40.

228 Frederick Douglass to James Wilson, 23 July 1846 in McKivigan, *Douglass Papers—Series Three*, Vol. *1*, pp. 145–46.

229 Douglass (ed. Bernier), *Narrative of the Life of Frederick Douglass*, pp. 50–51.

230 Frederick Douglass to Wendell Phillips, 28 April 1846, in McKivigan, *Douglass Papers—Series Three*, Vol. *1*, pp. 117–19. See also Pettinger, *Frederick Douglass and Scotland*, p. 241.

course, Garrison himself.[231] The displeasure seemed misplaced, considering that at several of his speeches – including the one to the BFASS itself – he proclaimed his loyalty to the Garrisonian wing of the movement.[232]

After the meeting, however, Webb read Douglass a private letter from Maria Weston Chapman accusing him of speaking there for money. Douglass refused to apologize for this, stating that he lectured there because "good friends" advised him to do so, and implied Chapman did not have his best interests at heart. He was deeply offended by the accusation of "money temptations," declared he would "speak in any meeting where freedom of speech is allowed," and promised to do "anything to expose the bloody system of slavery."[233] He was also displeased with abolitionist divisions. After discussions with Sturge, he scolded Garrison when he discovered the latter did not send a copy of his paper to the BFASS. Knowing full well that the societies were sworn enemies, Douglass politely told the BFASS that he believed the reports "had been miscarried, or that some accident had befallen them" as he rhetorically stated to Garrison that he could think of "no reason for withholding them."[234] Douglass was impatient with any form of rivalry that threatened the success of the antislavery cause, and highlighted the hypocrisy of a society that refused to share information with other groups. While petty white abolitionists squabbled, formerly enslaved women, men, and children were, at that very moment, being brutalized, raped, tortured, and killed amidst the hell of slavery.

The purchase of Douglass's freedom also spoke to this complicated relationship with white abolitionist networks. Ellen and Anna Richardson, based in Newcastle, wrote to Hugh Auld via a lawyer in New York and organized a bill of sale for £150 or $750 for Douglass's legal freedom. Eventually, on 12 December 1846, Douglass's free papers were signed.[235] This decision ruffled Garrisonian abolitionist feathers on both sides of the Atlantic, as it was a "compromising of principle" and appeared to give sanction to the idea that human beings were property. Douglass could not operate by sheer belief alone, and this incident not only highlighted the large gulf between white and Black abolitionists, but also how the Garrisonians could not control Douglass in the way they wanted.[236]

---

231   Fulkerson, "Frederick Douglass and the Anti-Slavery Crusade," p. 108.

232   Blackett, "'And There Shall Be No More Sea,'" pp. 31–32.

233   Frederick Douglass to Maria Weston Chapman, 18 August 1846, BPLAC, identifier: lettertomydearmroodoug.

234   Frederick Douglass to William Lloyd Garrison, 23 May 1846, in McKivigan, *Douglass Papers—Series Three, Vol. 1*, pp. 127–35. See also *The Liberator*, 26 June 1846, p. 2.

235   Douglass (ed. Bernier), *Narrative of the Life of Frederick Douglass*, pp. 48–49.

236   Catherine Paton to Maria Weston Chapman, 17 November 1846, BPLAC, identifier: lettertodearmuchoopato2.

In a letter to Elizabeth Pease Nichol, Garrison himself wrote that several Americans were "loudly protesting against his ransom by the English friends, as though it were a violation of principle." He was surprised that so many had objected to it, for although he disagreed with the notion of compensation, he had never believed it was "wrong to ransom one held in cruel captivity."[237] He noted such criticism in editions of *The Liberator*: the Philadelphia Female Anti-Slavery Society decried the purchase, recommending the money be sent towards "Ireland's starving millions" instead, for it now removed "one of the strongest claims to the sympathy of the community." Such arguments confirmed Douglass's position in the antislavery movement: a man whose power came from his fugitivity only, where he was expected to grace the platform with facts and use his position to advocate change. Once that "status" was altered, he was of little use and was thus ironically regarded as a free man, not a chattel, with less value to the cause.[238] Militant Garrisonian Henry Clarke Wright went so far as to write a public letter to Douglass and denounce the proceedings. While Douglass was always free, the confirmation of legal freedom meant he would be less effective to the antislavery cause and he was "shorn of your strength" when advocating for the freedom of others. Wright believed that Douglass had already "escaped the grasp of the Pirate Auld," who thus held "no power" over him; it was therefore pointless to "ask the sacrilegious villain to set a price" upon him.[239]

Setting aside Wright's ignorance of the trauma Douglass experienced during slavery, Wright was infuriated that the ransom did not comply with his theoretical views concerning disunionism and freedom in general. Douglass, however, could not afford to operate within such principles. In reply, he argued that without the ransom, Auld, *aided by the American Government*, can seize, bind and fetter, and drag me from my family, feed his cruel revenge upon me, and doom me to unending slavery." His English friends worked to establish as much safety as possible and to free him "from a liability full of horrible forbodings to myself and family." The £150 was paid not to confirm legitimacy upon a "remorseless plunderer" but "to release me from his power, not to establish my *natural right* to freedom, but to release me from all legal liabilities to slavery." He bristled at Wright's racial paternalism, in particular the same language Maria Weston Chapman had used a few months earlier, suggesting that he would somehow become a different person and desert the antislavery cause. Douglass assured him he would "be Frederick Douglass still"; no ransom could ever make him "forget nor cease to feel the wrongs of my enslaved fellow-country-men."

---

237   William Lloyd Garrison to Elizabeth Pease Nichol, 1 April 1847, BPLAC, identifier: lettertobe-lovedfoogarr9.

238   *The Liberator*, 19 March 1847, pp. 2–3.

239   Wright and Douglass, *Letter to Frederick Douglass*, pp. 1–3.

His knowledge of slavery and his experience of trauma would remain the same and he pointedly clarified to Wright that he had never made his "suffering the theme of public discourse"; he had framed his lectures around the inherent evil of slavery and his appeals on behalf of those currently enslaved. The money was simply proof of his legal freedom and that his friends had been "legally robbed" in order to secure his liberty. The bill of sale was representative of the "plundering character of the American government" and was a "brand of infamy, stamping the nation in whose name the deed was done, as a great aggregation of hypocrites, thieves and liars." After a year of rising tension, disagreements over money and infighting largely caused by inherent racism from certain Garrisonians, Douglass took a public stand against Wright and by extension all those who disagreed with a decision that affected him alone. It was another nail in the coffin for Douglass's relationship with the Society; and such a public renunciation of Garrisonian principles at this early stage of his career could only happen so fiercely on *British* soil, far from the hotbed of Garrisonianism.[240]

Reacting against the abolitionist desire to control him through a white paternalist ethos, Douglass fiercely denied his experience would change, as he could not so easily forget the trauma of enslavement and it was an insult to suggest that he would renounce the abolitionist cause.[241] It demonstrated Douglass's sense of self-mastery in a private context and his deliberate dissent against both enslavers and white networks. Douglass sanctioned the purchase of his freedom because it legally protected him and his family, but the controversy served as yet another reminder to white abolitionists that they could not control him. As he summarized in *My Bondage and My Freedom*, while his "uncompromising friends" failed to see the wisdom in such a ransom, he was fully aware that it was necessary for his return home. He could have remained in the British Isles, but he had "a duty to perform – and that was, to labor and suffer with the oppressed in my native land." He could not afford to be a "private person" with a life in England, and although his growing celebrity invited more danger to himself and his family, he had no choice but to share his testimony and expose the evil of slavery.[242] Such language revealed on a colossal scale the tensions between Douglass and white abolitionists, the racism of those who felt Douglass would "lose" the power of his oratory or position within the antislavery movement, and the miscomprehension by white people on both sides of the Atlantic who had no idea of the lived realities of racism and white supremacy.

In his speeches and writings, Douglass always framed the purchase as an act stemming solely from the Richardsons' generosity, and did not mention his part within it. In August 1846 he had written to Anna Richardson from London, and

---

240   Ibid. pp. 1–2. Douglass also published a letter in the press: *Durham Chronicle*, 22 January 1847.
241   Douglass (ed. Bernier), *Narrative of the Life of Frederick Douglass*, pp. 20–21.
242   Douglass, *My Bondage and My Freedom* (1855), pp. 375–76.

was clearly aware of her attempts to secure his legal freedom. He longed to see his family and hoped to return to the US that autumn, but wanted to ensure his travel did not "interfere in any way with your correspondence with my owner – as whether you succeed or fail good may come of the effort."[243] Decades later, the letters of Ellen Richardson reveal a different side to this incident.

Writing to Helen Pitts Douglass in 1894, Ellen Richardson's visit to Whitley-by-the-Sea just outside of Newcastle prompted memories of Douglass's ransom: "At a short distance from here I see the spot when the thought first [came to] me that <u>Frederick must be free!!</u>" She was often reminded of the events when "Frederick my sister and myself sat opposite Cullercoat sands with the sea rolling on the beach . . . that was one of the best days works I ever did when I look at the result of Frederick's freedom."[244] Reminiscing in her later years, she wrote to Douglass that she could not "<u>recollect</u> that I <u>ever</u> wrote to you on the subject which seems a little remarkable but as you say I wished to spare your feelings on what I deemed was to you an <u>unwelcome</u> subject and that the responsibility <u>should not rest on you.</u>"[245] She expanded on this and even regretted that Douglass

> never knew your friends who subscribed to the Ransom . . . it was all done so <u>quietly without your sanction</u> that <u>you did not know</u> who effected it for <u>years afterwards.</u> My reason for this was that I was <u>afraid you would not allow yourself</u> to be purchased and I was <u>determined you should.</u> I did not dare to tell my sister Anna for some time for I believed <u>she</u> sympathised in this feeling and I was afraid she might question it . . . Then I came to a <u>stand still</u> what was to be done? I knew not how to deal with that Thos Auld or in what way to get a <u>legal purchase</u> effected. Here it was my <u>sister</u> came to help us through . . . [Anna Richardson] <u>knew</u> a Gentleman she thought would make the attempt . . . I do not like to allude to all this now But it is to explain to you and if need be to <u>apologise to my friends</u> for letting you remain in ignorance of your <u>benefactors</u> . . . I knew the Garrison Party opposed it in principle and in as much as you were so identified with them I was afraid they would <u>influence</u> you against it. Now I think you will understand the case <u>as it was.</u>[246]

Richardson "felt some compunction" that she had not asked Douglass's permission, and wished to partially make amends for her conduct. Her fear of the Garrisonian

243   Douglass (ed. Bernier), *Narrative of the Life of Frederick Douglass*, pp. 50–51.

244   Ellen Richardson to Helen Pitts Douglass, 28 September 1894, FDP Digital Collection, Library of Congress.

245   Ellen Richardson to Frederick Douglass, undated [possibly 1886/87], FDP Digital Collection, Library of Congress. Pettinger, *Frederick Douglass and Scotland* mentions that Richardson did not speak to Douglass first, pp. 78–83.

246   Ellen Richardson to Frederick Douglass, May? 1892, FDP Digital Collection, Library of Congress.

party the Auld family, and her doubt over Douglass's views on the subject, forced her hand. Richardson remarked that she "well remember[ed] how <u>astonished</u> you were in my drawing room when I told you how the ransom had been effected you leaned back in the arm chair and exclaimed 'well I <u>never knew this!!</u> I never knew this before'!!"[247]

As we have seen from Douglass's own hand, Ellen is perhaps misremembering the particulars. This does not take away from her memories, or the fact that Douglass may not have known all the details surrounding the ransom and those involved within it. Perhaps Ellen does not remember informing him because Anna did so instead; she mentions her sister-in-law's key role, and Anna may have felt uneasy at trying to arrange this without Douglass's permission, advice, or acknowledgment. The passage of time and some guilt had weighed on Ellen's shoulders, despite the fact that Anna had taken matters into her own hands and had clearly discussed it with him. Privately, Douglass urged the Richardson family on with their mission for all of the reasons outlined above, but publicly he always pointed to the Newcastle sect for their integral role to highlight British philanthropy as a performative and rhetorical tactic against "republican" slavery, and perhaps to allay tensions with the Garrisonian movement, who may have given Douglass more grief for proposing it in the first place. Douglass gave them his blessing for all the reasons outlined above, and he never forgot his Newcastle benefactors, who had given him the ability to return home safely to his family.[248]

Douglass correctly anticipated that part of the frustration over the loss of his "slave" status meant that white abolitionists could no longer introduce him to a meeting as such. In *My Bondage and My Freedom*, he wrote that on the antislavery platform: "I was generally introduced as a '*chattel*' – a '*thing*' – a piece of southern '*property*' – the chairman assuring the audience *it* could speak."[249] In a discernible attempt to exercise his oratorical muscles away from the constricting Garrisonian platform, Douglass changed his repertoire in the last six months of his trip, particularly when he spoke alone. While many scholars have focused on the dramatic moments of self-fashioning in his Irish trip, few have pointed to his extended time in England – and thus time away from Garrisonian thought in Boston – and the influence such experiences had on his tour. While in Ireland, James Buffum or Richard D. Webb accompanied Douglass many times on the antislavery platform and either encouraged him, exhibited alongside him weapons of torture, or sang antislavery songs. A year later, Douglass dismissed both from his performances, together with a removal of anything resembling minstrelesque

---

247   Ibid.
248   Murray, "'The Birth Place of <u>Your</u> Liberty.'"
249   Douglass (ed. Bernier), *My Bondage and My Freedom*, p. 247.

language, which troubles previous analyses that focus entirely on Ireland as the site of the most change in his identity or performance.

Since the eighteenth century, Black and white abolitionists had displayed whips, manacles, and chains as a way of teaching audiences about slavery and encouraging their support for the abolitionist movement. Formerly enslaved individuals challenged the white paternalist ethos of Josiah Wedgwood's "Am I Not A Man And A Brother?" and used their oratory or literary talents to tell their experiences through their own lens. Black activists relied on their voices to highlight their independence from a white paternalist ethos, and men such as David Walker, Robert Wedderburn, and Jupiter Hammon used their rhetoric to challenge antislavery or proslavery imagery that cast Black people as physically and mentally inferior. Several abolitionists exhibited whips and chains together with the use of fiery rhetoric to illustrate the brutality of slavery; in Britain, the reliance on such instruments of torture or visual culture surrounding slave ships was more pronounced than in America.[250]

In his third autobiography, *Life and Times* (first published in 1881), Douglass admitted to a lack of control on the abolitionist circuit and stated that he was "called upon to expose even my stripes, and with many misgivings obeyed the summons and tried thus to do my whole duty."[251] There is little evidence to suggest he did this in Britain, and Douglass deliberately rejected literary and visual abolitionist discourse that depicted the suffering Black body as much as possible. At a meeting in May 1846, for example (in remarks reprinted in this volume), Douglass deliberately refused to "show them the stripes on his back" and instead chose to read Southern newspaper advertisements depicting the cruelties.[252]

When Douglass first arrived in Ireland, he often lectured with James Buffum and at least twice in the first couple of months both men "exhibited, amid great sensation, several instruments of torture in common use in the slave states."[253] In Limerick, Douglass exhibited other weapons of torture including an iron collar, hand-cuffs, and chains, and he did the same for the first few months of his Scottish tour in 1846.[254] Similarly, in Cork Douglass was recorded as singing "a beautiful sentimental air." Alasdair Pettinger can find no evidence of singing in his Scottish meetings, and speculates the descriptions from Irish newspaper correspondents of

---

250 Bernier, "'Iron Arguments.'" For discussions on whipping, scars, and exhibition of torture see Putzi, "'The Skin of an American Slave,'" pp. 184–87; Mailloux, "Re-Marking Slave Bodies," pp. 102–03; Wood, *Slavery, Empathy, and Pornography*, pp. 21; 409–27.

251 Bernier, "'His Complete History,'" p. 595.

252 *Caledonian Mercury*, 11 May 1846, p. 3.

253 *The Freeman's Journal*, 18 September 1845, p. 4. Douglass also exhibited instruments of torture in Dublin (*The Freeman's Journal*, 4 October 1845, p. 4).

254 Frederick Douglass, Speech on 10 November 1845, in Blassingame, *Douglass Papers—Series One: Vol. 1*, pp. 76–86; Pettinger, *Frederick Douglass and Scotland*, p. 106.

him singing "a nigger song" may account for this.[255] It does not appear that Douglass performed any music in his English meetings, although according to William Lovett he "sang a number of negro melodies" at a private gathering alongside Lovett, Henry Vincent, Wright, and Garrison. Whether he felt obliged to or could not refuse is unknown, but the significant lack of music in his later public meetings would suggest a discomfort with using it as a performative strategy.[256] Besides, on many occasions Douglass counter-argued the notion that songs and music performed by the enslaved were a sign of happiness. On the contrary, these sorrow songs were a reminder of their oppression.[257]

Furthermore, music and antislavery songs had an uncomfortable association with minstrelsy. Since Thomas D. Rice had created his Jim Crow character in 1832, minstrelsy corresponded with the rise of Garrisonian abolitionism in America, and initially both borrowed elements from each other (particularly the obsession with the Black body) to ensure success.[258] Hence there were occasions when the lines between abolition and minstrelsy were blurred. During Douglass's tour in 1846, a group named the Ethiopian Serenaders traveled to Britain and received rave reviews for its performances, and the group's popularity illustrated that racial stereotypes were still very much accepted into the national consciousness.[259] Douglass was unimpressed and lambasted their portrayal of Africans "as more akin to apes than to men." They were "the filthy scum of white society, who have stolen from us a complexion denied to them by nature, in which to make money, and pander to the corrupt taste" of white people.[260] The performers had tapped into and promulgated the existing stereotype of African American physical features; minstrel shows were damaging not only to African Americans, but also to society in general, as they had the potential to destroy and weaken race relations.[261]

However, during one meeting in 1845 Douglass mocked the enslaver's rhetoric that African Americans should be "grateful that God in his mercy brought [them] from Africa to this Christian land" and, in minstrelesque language, reiterated how "such is the ignorance in which the slaves are held that some of them go home and say 'me hear a good sermon to-day, de minister make ebery thing so clear, whiteman above a nigger any day'."[262] Douglass's use of minstrelsy here revealed a combina-

---

255   *The Limerick Reporter*, 25 November 1845, p. 2; Pettinger, *Frederick Douglass and Scotland*, p. 210.

256   Bradbury, "Frederick Douglass and the Chartists," pp. 169–87.

257   Ferreira, "All But 'A Black Skin and Wooly Hair,'" p. 77; Levine, *The Lives of Frederick Douglass*, pp. 53–55.

258   Nowatzki, *Representing African Americans*, pp. 1–12; 41–65.

259   Meer, "Competing Representations," pp. 141–46.

260   *The North Star*, 27 October 1848; Dickerson, *Dark Victorians*, pp. 62–64.

261   *The North Star*, 29 June 1849.

262   *The Leeds Times*, 15 November 1845, p. 7.

tion of assimilationist and subversive dissonant strategies to simultaneously appeal to Victorian audiences while he rejected white supremacy.[263] Douglass played on stereotypes of ignorant Black people and the superior Anglo-Saxon, and even if the enslaved figure was not educated by white standards, the minister who owned enslaved people and exploited his position of power over others was the real target of his rhetoric. He played on the trope of Black ignorance in order to mock the white racist ethos that enslaved people were unintelligent. This is one of the few examples in which he used plantation dialect to mass audiences, and there is little evidence to suggest he did so during the last six months of his trip.[264]

Following his refusal to exhibit instruments of torture, to sing songs or use plantation dialect, Douglass became conscious of the difficulties in embracing humor. During a speech in Leicester (reprinted in this volume), a newspaper correspondent commented that part of Douglass's speech was stated with "such irrestible humour, that the place rang again with applause and laughter."[265] In Belfast, Douglass read an advertisement from an American newspaper where he quoted a Baptist minister who "had asserted that the Scriptures warranted the holding of slaves" and therefore justified his own position as an enslaver. According to the local newspaper correspondent, "the reading of this advertisement created considerable merriment," but Douglass blisteringly reminded his audience that "instead of smiling and laughing at this, we should be sadly weeping to think that such a man ever lived . . . to think that Christianity should be so degraded by one of its professing ministers!"[266] Douglass once remarked to an American neighbor Jane Marsh Parker that "one of the hardest things I had to learn when I was fairly under way as a public speaker was to stop telling so many funny stories . . . I could keep my audience in a roar of laughter and they liked to laugh, and showed disappointment when I was not amusing." Significantly, he summarized: "I was convinced that I was in danger of becoming something of a clown, and that I must guard against it."[267] Douglass regularly employed humor in his speeches but had to navigate audience reaction: the situation was comical to his white spectators, who knew nothing of the soul-shattering realities of slavery, but to him the traumatic legacies of the prison house of bondage could never be interpreted as a joke. His audiences' laughter drowned out the lived reality of men such as the Baptist minister, who made the lives of his enslaved women, men, and children hell on earth on a daily basis.

When Douglass first began lecturing for the American Anti-Slavery Society, he was told to "give us the facts . . . we will take care of the philosophy." Rejecting such

---

263 Sweeney, *Frederick Douglass and the Atlantic World*, p. 130.
264 Blassingame, *Douglass Papers—Series One: Vol. 1*, pp. xlvii–xlviii.
265 *Leicestershire Mercury*, 6 March 1847, p. 2. See Ganter, "'He Made Us Laugh Some': Frederick Douglass's Humor."
266 *The Belfast Newsletter*, 26 December 1845, p. 1.
267 Douglass (ed. Bernier), *Narrative of the Life of Frederick Douglass*, p. 66.

racial paternalist thought, he vowed that it was unacceptable to simply "narrate wrongs; I felt like denouncing them."[268] Championing his own oratory instead, Douglass demonstrated to white abolitionists his creation of a new radical philosophy where Black men could become successful independent orators without proscribing to a white racist ethos. Thus, from the fall of 1846 to April 1847, Douglass refused to exhibit whips and chains, declined to sing abolitionist songs, and embraced opportunities to lecture away from the restrictions of his Garrisonian colleagues.

Between February and March 1847, Douglass held a series of final and farewell meetings in numerous cities across England, and his popularity with the public showed no signs of abating. The desire to hear him speak was so great throughout the latter part of his trip that in the last week of his journey alone he was forced to turn down thirty invitations to lecture across the country.[269] In particular, his hectic lecturing schedule in March 1847 meant he addressed new audiences nearly every night, speaking in Carlisle, Newcastle, Wrexham, Manchester, Sheffield, Northampton, Colchester, Warrington, Nottingham, Coventry, Leicester, Bridgwater, and London.[270] Thus far, the speeches in Leicester and Nottingham (reprinted in this volume for the first time) have been neglected by Douglass scholars, which presents a missed opportunity to show how his growing independence from the Garrisonian wing of the antislavery movement had manifested itself.

For example, Douglass's speech in Leicester in early March was a resounding success. The local newspaper correspondent was held spellbound by Douglass's rhetoric and covered his speech at length. After investing in racialized stereotypes to wax lyrical about Douglass's mixed heritage, the correspondent reported Douglass's firm rejection of the Garrisonian ideology to merely "give us the facts." Instead, he used the space on the platform to create his own philosophy: Douglass "purposely restrained from narrating tales of cruelties practised on the slaves because he wished rather to dwell on the principle involved in that system."[271] Refusing to compound his testimony with props, he chose instead to attack the immorality of slavery through the lens of religious hypocrisy. In doing so, he did not negate its horrors, but instead employed them beyond a mere recitation of its evils, connecting it with his denunciation of Southern enslavers:

> I have seen him rise from his prayers and take a female cousin of mine, tie her up, and flog her until the blood flowed down her; and while doing this he would quote the text, "He who knoweth his master's will and doeth it not shall be beaten with

---

268   Douglass, *My Bondage and My Freedom* (1855), pp. 359–62; Martin, Jr., *The Mind of Frederick Douglass*, pp. 22–23.

269   "Frederick Douglass's Last Appearance in England," *The Inquirer*, 10 April 1847.

270   *The Liberator*, 14 May 1847, p. 3.

271   *Leicestershire Mercury*, 6 March 1847, p. 2.

many stripes." (Loud cries of "Shame!") I have known him also take my brother, dash him to the floor, and kick him as he lay there. And I have known him take the same young woman my cousin, and have her tied up so (by the hands, with the wrists crossed), UNTIL HER FINGERS BECAME BLACKER THAN THE GOD WHO MADE HER PAINTED THEM. (Great sensation.) – Mr. Douglas proceeded still further, and in the same unsparing manner, to expose the hypocrisy of the religious supporters of slavery in America; to denounce every slave estate as neither more nor less than vast literal brothels; to give a specimen of the sermons preached to the slaves, in order to make them submit quietly to stripes.[272]

Demonstrating Douglass's brilliant conflation of spoken and printed pathways, the correspondent highlighted the brutal torture that was an everyday occurrence in the South. Douglass was "unsparing" in his attacks, and proceeded to share such testimony without fear of restraint; he shone a light on how religious ministers used the Bible as a sacred text to justify physical and sexual violence against young women, and how each plantation was a site of rape. His command of the visual left such an impression in the correspondent's mind as to dictate Douglass's speech as closely as possible; some reporters would leave out certain details, instead of graphically relaying the sound and imagery of the torture, but the correspondent above describes it with capitals and emphasis, noting the audience's shocked reaction. While Douglass does not rely on the cold and lifeless instruments of torture, he instead uses his own corporeal figure to visualize how the wrists were crossed, demonstrating with his own hands held high above him in full view of his entire audience. He compounds such violent statements and gestures with a religious quote, creating a glaring comparison between an enslaver whose text ran red with blood and a true Christian, who would refuse to pollute God's teachings with sin. The capitalized text implied Douglass's raised voice at the moment of extreme pain and suffering, to drive his point yet further at the hypocrisy of American enslavers. His blistering rhetoric evidently had a sensational impact on his audience, who cried, shouted, and gasped along with him, and no doubt Douglass paused deliberately and carefully after his shocking statement to let the horror sink in for his audience.

Later in this speech, Douglass refused to apologize for his uncompromising language. He attacked not only enslavers but the US nation as a whole, and challenged the sacred symbols associated with American freedom: under "the fluttering of their star-spangled banner, that assertion was contradicted by the fact, that there were THREE MILLIONS, or one-sixth of the whole population, rattling their fetters and clanking their chains in most abject Slavery." Refusing to say "our" or take any ownership over his American identity, he outrightly shrank from his association

---

272   Ibid.

with a nation that allowed him "no resting place." Worse still, in a direct reference to the Evangelical Alliance and the World's Temperance Convention, the British public associated with American enslavers or pro-slavery defenders and welcomed them with open arms into their institutions. He warned that slavery "morally and intellectually deadened all those who were brought within its influence." If one was to speak to an enslaver or those who came in close contact with slavery, "it was as though you spoke to the dead." By associating themselves with such men, the minds and souls of the British people were under threat, but more importantly, they were being hypnotized by the words of false prophets and ignored any "voice from the slave population" in reply. The enslaved "could hold no public meetings, pass no resolutions, tell no tale of their wrongs" – and Douglass used this to persuade his present audience to join the antislavery cause and renounce all fellowship with enslavers. If they did not do so, their fate would be moral and spiritual death by association.[273]

A few days later, in Nottingham, a local newspaper correspondent was similarly stirred by Douglass's words and wrote that his address was characterized by "correct pronunciation, breadth and force of thought, with occasionally the most potent and withering sarcasm, and now and then a burst of genuine eloquence." Once again, the correspondent exposed his racial paternalism, confused at Douglass's racial heritage and that he was "far from being a black man" in complete contrast to the "stock 'nigger' of the theatres." When Douglass began speaking, his voice must have been "inaudible" at the back of the hall, "but in a few minutes the volume of sound deepened and widened, and before long its clear tone and emphatic syllables were hurled most satisfactorily even beyond the rim of the most distant of his audience." In a rare insight into the aural effect of Douglass's oratory, we can comprehend his skill and experience where he fully understood how to orchestrate his voice according to the space in which he projected it. We can imagine here that his voice became louder with each passing statement against slavery, perhaps with audience members sitting at the back straining to listen before it resounded back to them.[274]

On this occasion, however, Douglass became frustrated at the chairman's interferences, once again illustrating his desire to control the structure and flow of his speech. When introducing Douglass to the platform, the chairman followed the arguments of the Free Church ministers who had suggested there should be a difference "between the individual and the system" in regard to enslavers and slavery. On rising, Douglass "was wholly unable to make any such distinction; and his reason was, that the American slave-holder was wholly without excuse in being such." These slaveholding Americans "were not what they professed to be; they were

---

273   Ibid.
274   *Nottingham Review*, 12 March 1847, p. 8.

hypocrites – a nation of hypocrites"; and he repeated his oft-quoted biblical phrase: "He that knoweth his master's will, and doeth it not, shall be beaten with many stripes." Exposing more than ever the uniqueness of a site-specific performance, some members of the Nottingham audience laughed and shouted "Shame! Shame!" The Mayor interrupted Douglass to convey to the audience that he had not meant to "seek an 'expression of mirth'"; in response to this unscheduled and paternalistic reaction, Douglass replied that he "was very glad to hear the explanation," but in a fury that burst from him, he continued "at great length, in a strain of fervid impassioned declamation, which was greeted at its pauses, sometimes with stamping of feet, sometimes with vocal applause, and always with expressions of deepest sympathy with the slave, and heartiest execration of his oppressors."[275] He was tired of disruptions from both audience members and his white supporters, particularly his brief lack of control over their reactions to his speech. In order to dispel their ignorance, his "impassioned" rhetoric was an example of unrestrained, raw emotion at the vast distance between himself, the white privilege of his audience, and all those who maintained a distinction between "slave-havers" and "slaveholders."

Finally, on 30 March, Douglass addressed a crowded audience in the London Tavern at a gathering in part organized by the father of his lifelong supporter Julia Griffiths. Charles Dickens sent apologies for his non-attendance, and thousands of eager listeners crammed into the venue to listen to Douglass's famed oratory one last time. At the commencement of his speech, he immediately rejected any patriotic or respectful feeling towards America. He had no "love for its churches or national institutions," for "the whole system, the entire network of American society, is one great falsehood, from beginning to end." He charged the whole nation as "one vast hunting-ground" where an enslaver could "set his well-trained bloodhounds upon the track of the poor fugitive; hunt him down like a wild beast, and hurl him back to the jaws of slavery." Despite "her broadest lakes and finest rivers," he could not praise America while the "tears and blood of my brethren are mingled and forgotten." The loud cries of freedom were designed to mask "a statute-book" where "every page is red with the blood of the American slave."[276] Douglass elaborated on this a few weeks after his return, in New York; in contrast to Garrison's argument that he had traveled home because of his patriotism, he reiterated that he had "no love for America . . . I have no patriotism. I have no country."[277] While he continued to defend Garrison publicly, Douglass ensured that his last speeches in England

---

275   Ibid.

276   *Farewell Speech of Mr. Frederick Douglass*, pp. 3–7; Douglas, "A Cherished Friendship," p. 267.

277   Frederick Douglass, Speech on 11 May 1847, in Blassingame, *Douglass Papers—Series One: Vol. 2*, p. 57. See also Wright, *Lecturing the Atlantic*, p. 65; McDaniel, *The Problem of Democracy in the Age of Slavery*, pp. 127–28.

reflected his radical expressions of his own authority, identity, and independence in other ways. He did not rely on tired abolitionist tropes and was free to use his own testimony and a fugitivity which he defined for himself, instead of it being imposed upon him.

Significantly, Douglass rejected his white abolitionist friends' decision to employ Henry Russell for introductory vocal music at this meeting.[278] Russell was a successful actor who toured Britain with his minstrel show. According to the press he had the ability to excite audiences through somber and comical songs but was most effective through his "accurate imitation of the voice, gestures, etc. of the American nigger," and his audiences laughed uproariously at his "droll stories in the negro dialect."[279] Incensed that the audience might have associated him with a racist portrayal of Blackness, Douglass condemned Russell's performance, which had "unjustly" painted Black people as "simple in [their] understanding." In doing so, he subverted Russell's introduction to the evening: Douglass did not want his audience to invest in minstrel stereotypes when instead they could refer to a real African American, as opposed to the clownish and distorted caricatures Russell presented on stage.[280] Here, Douglass challenged racist stereotypes in person and criticized Russell for his espousal of negative stereotypes of Black people. In doing so, he also subtly attacked white abolitionists for their decision to employ Russell in the first place.[281]

Over the course of his trip, Douglass created a unique performance that, publicly, left little room for fatigue. Part of his celebrated and also racialized persona – particularly in the press – meant he could not show any signs of exhaustion. There were cracks in this façade, however, and through such cracks we can begin to understand the toll his tour must have taken upon him. Challenging racism, defending himself against charges of fraud, and convincing thousands of people about the true nature of slavery, together with the repetition of his traumatic stories, was a heavy burden to bear. In Cork in 1845, Douglass declared that while he bore the scars of the whip, "which he would carry with him to the grave . . . they were not the most degrading marks of his bondage, for he bore them on his soul, debasing his humanity, and often crushing down his spirit to the very darkest depths of shame and degradation."[282] This was something no white abolitionist could feel or experience, and the loneliness of conducting such a tour caused him much weariness.

---

278   *Farewell Speech of Mr. Frederick Douglass*, p. 3.
279   *The Belfast Newsletter*, 30 September 1845, p. 2.
280   Frederick Douglass, Speech on 30 March 1847, in Blassingame, *Douglass Papers—Series One: Vol. 2*, pp. 19–52.
281   Nowatzki, *Representing African Americans*, pp. 13; 35–36. See also Smith, *Self-Discovery and Authority*, and Stepto, *From Behind the Veil*.
282   *The Cork Examiner*, 15 October 1845.

Douglass rarely admitted such wounding in public, but he did offer a glimpse into his trauma in some public speeches. In January 1842, he lamented: "I would I could make visible the wounds of this system upon my soul" and went on to write that "the grim horrors of slavery rise in all their ghastly terror before me, the wails of millions pierce my heart and chill my blood." Douglass underwent a terrible daily battle to reconcile his traumatic past with his antislavery activism, a union that in reality was impossible to manage. Instead, he relieved his feelings in part to his adopted sister Ruth Cox, alias Harriet Bailey, who stayed with the Douglasses in their Lynn, Massachusetts home. In a letter to Cox from England in May 1846, Douglass wrote: "I looked so ugly that I hated to see myself in a glass. There was no living for me . . ." Unlikely and unwilling to confess such trauma to white abolitionists, in January 1847, he said "there are many things I should like to write about – but I am not in a state of mind to write – I am miserable – unhappy – and it seems I must so live and die." As Celeste-Marie Bernier summarizes, his "traumatized confession[s] regarding his personal turmoil establishes the full extent of his emotional and physical wounding as a survivor of slavery" and "he suffered from repeated bouts of psychological illness that threatened his existence."[283]

The loneliness of such an exhausting lecturing tour, together with the absence of Harriet and his family, no doubt contributed to his mental burden. Struggling with the constant repetition of his trauma, with few outlets, he was also blindsided by certain revelations or milestones while in Britain. When Thomas Auld broke his silence in the wake of Douglass's growing celebrity, Douglass wrote that he must feel "keenly my exposures, and nothing would afford him more pleasure than to have me in his power." However, Auld's denial that he had never beaten him "rather staggered me at the first." Such a public retraction jarred with his sharp and painful memories testifying to the contrary, and his trauma response was one of shock and bitterness. After all, he said, "my memory, in such matters, is better than his."[284] Similarly in Bristol, he noted that the previous time he had lectured there "was on the eighth anniversary of the evening preceding his freedom from bondage." Furthermore, a decade beforehand, "he had passed in the woods, planning with four of his friends the escape which proved unsuccessful." Such traumatizing memories were significant milestones that could never be forgotten, together with the friends he left behind. Important dates in the struggle for his liberty were no doubt compounded by the stark contrast from that moment of running through the woods to his present position on a platform in Bristol.[285]

---

283   Douglass (ed. Bernier), *Narrative of the Life of Frederick Douglass*, pp. 50–65.
284   Frederick Douglass to William Lloyd Garrison, 16 April 1846, in McKivigan, *Douglass Papers— Series Three, Vol. 1*, pp. 108–10.
285   *The Liberator*, 14 May 1846, p. 3.

Douglass suffered yet further with his physically demanding schedule. In the first month of his trip, he confessed that one of his initial objectives in visiting Britain was "to get a little repose, [so] that I might return home refreshed and strengthened," but if "the labor of the last two weeks be a fair sample of what awaits me, I have certainly sought repose in the wrong place." He had to turn down several invitations to speak, something which was such a difference "from my treatment at home!"[286] The curiosity and interest in Douglass continued unabated, and in the spring of 1846, Thompson described Douglass's busy lecturing schedule. He had "crammed a year's sensations into the last five days" and spoke at an antislavery meeting on Monday, a peace society meeting on Tuesday, a suffrage meeting on Wednesday, a temperance meeting on Thursday, and another antislavery meeting on Friday in a speech that lasted three hours to around 2,500 people.[287]

As a result of the constant string of lectures, Douglass suffered from frequent bouts of illness that threatened his performance on the British stage. During April 1846, he complained of poor eyesight and in particular a "difficulty with my right eye which has troubled me very much."[288] The exhausting traveling schedule meant Douglass had to cope with illness after spending hours on trains or carriages, followed by speaking for one or sometimes two hours a night on a traumatic subject. After an Exeter Hall meeting in 1846, Garrison noted he was "quite weary in body and Frederick was still more so" and noticed Douglass was "naturally enough sighing to see his wife and children."[289] This was unsurprising given all the important birthdays and other milestones he was sacrificing while in England. When reminiscing about Douglass's first visit, Mary Carpenter later wrote that,

> I remember your telling some of us who travelled with you from Bridgewater to Bristol ... between 40 & 50 years ago, that you had had a letter from Rosetta with the news of her having had a tooth out! She was a small child then & of course the loss of a tooth was an event.[290]

---

286   Frederick Douglass to William Lloyd Garrison, 29 September 1845, in Foner, *Life and Writings of Frederick Douglass*, Vol. 1, p. 120.

287   George Thompson to Henry C. Wright, 23 May 1846, BPLAC, MS.A.1.2 V.16, p. 51.

288   Frederick Douglass to Richard D. Webb, 25 April 1846, BPLAC, identifier: lettertodearfrieoodoug_6. and Frederick Douglass to Richard D. Webb, 26 April 1846, BPLAC, M.S.A.1.2 V.16, 38.

289   William Lloyd Garrison to Richard D. Webb, 12 September 1846, BPLAC, identifier: lettertomydearweoogarr5. William Lloyd Garrison to Helen Garrison, 17 September 1846, BPLAC, identifier: lettertomydearwioogarr21.

290   Mary Carpenter to Frederick Douglass, 7 May 1894, FDP Digital Collection, Library of Congress. Thank you to Celeste-Marie Bernier for pointing this out to me. See also Bernier, *The Anna Murray and Frederick Douglass Family Papers, Volumes 1–3* (forthcoming, 2021).

With his exhausting traveling schedule thousands of miles from home, missing such an event was a heartbreaking casualty of his unrelenting activism. These letters may have been a lifeline between himself and his loved ones, but they were also stark reminders of what he gave up while on the road. He wrote in a letter to Rosetta that he was terrified she would forget him, despite her assurance that this was impossible because the family "talk about you every hour in the day."[291]

By the end of 1846, Douglass had become ill as a result of his relentless lecturing schedule.[292] He canceled a meeting in Leeds because of a "fit of sickness" which sapped his "usual strength," according to local abolitionist Mary Brady.[293] When he finally attended the rescheduled meeting, however, even the newspaper correspondent noticed that "he was evidently labouring under [a] severe disposition"; and halfway through his speech his "strength failed him, and he was compelled to resume his seat, requesting that some one might address the meeting until he had in some measure recovered."[294] The exhausting lecturing tour impacted Douglass's performance, and near the end of his journey caused one correspondent in Warrington to note how his speeches were "suffering from great debility owing to the large amount of fatigue he has lately endured."[295] Even at the end of March 1847, Brady noticed again in Sheffield that Douglass was "too ill, from long continued exertion, to do full justice to himself," but was forced to face the throngs who waited "to give him the parting shake by the hand."[296] Ultimately, the infrequency with which he let his exhaustion show on a public stage was symbolic of his well-orchestrated performance. Despite personal trauma and bodily exhaustion, he was able to rely on his brilliant oratory to rouse hundreds of people in numerous towns and cities across Britain and Ireland.

The Journey Home (April 1847)

In early April 1847 Douglass boarded the Cunard steamship *Cambria* with a first-class ticket, but as soon as he stepped aboard, he was "smitten with the pestilential breath of her slave system!" His berth had been given to someone else, as the "American public demanded my exclusion from the saloon of the steamship, and the company owning the steamer had not the virtue to resist the demand."

---

291   Douglass (ed. Bernier), *Narrative of the Life of Frederick Douglass*, p. 62.

292   Fulkerson, "Exile as Emergence," pp. 81–82.

293   Mary Brady to Maria Weston Chapman, 30 December 1846, BPLAC, MS.A.9.2.22, p. 139.

294   *The Leeds Times*, 26 December 1846, p. 7.

295   Foner, *Life and Writings of Frederick Douglass, Vol. 1*, pp. 73–75.

296   Fulkerson, "Frederick Douglass and the Anti-Slavery Crusade," pp. 138–39. See *The Liberator*, 23 April 1847, p. 2.

Outraged, he wrote a letter to *The Times* and questioned how he had managed to travel across Britain for nineteen months without encountering prejudice (a performative exaggeration, of course), only to face it on his return to the United States.[297] Behind the scenes, Douglass worked with local abolitionists to exploit the incident; before he sailed, he dictated a letter to William Short, as he hoped "to have the facts in his own language as a reference after the *Cambria* was gone."[298] William Logan copied Douglass's letter, distributed it to fifty newspapers around the country, and sent it to numerous friends of the cause in the hope they would further exploit their own connections. As a result, Logan stated, the news was printed in "every influential paper in Britain." When he traveled to Manchester, Edinburgh, and Glasgow a week later, he deliberately visited libraries and reading rooms. Articles had appeared in over one hundred newspapers about the incident; he collected examples and immediately sent them to *The Liberator*.[299]

In response to Douglass's letter, *The Times*, a conservative paper, declared that the incident was "wholly repugnant to our English notions of justice and humanity."[300] *The Times* had a daily circulation of 40,000 at this point, and Douglass knew it was regularly quoted by other publications in Britain. The incident highlighted a dilemma for Britain: a transatlantic individual had exposed, on a national scale, the difference between how the country wanted to be seen and its reality. Wounding British pride was a skillful method of attracting British attention, and signified Douglass's bold exploitation of British racism as well as print culture in general.[301] Ignoring the nation's blatant bigotry and imperialism, the newspapers reported that racism was a distinctly *American* problem and, while the sea was a difficult geographical place to negotiate in terms of social attitudes, the customs were clear: Douglass's experience jarred with the image of Britain as a nation of freedom and tolerance. Under the headline "AMERICAN SLAVERY IN ENGLAND," *The Bradford and Wakefield Observer* reported:

> Here is an attempt to resuscitate the foul spirit of slavery . . . Here, in the land of equal laws and liberty, is an act of gross injustice perpetuated upon a man, *because he has a black skin!* . . . But mark – it does not involve more of injustice to Mr Douglass than of insult and cool contempt of the British people. It is an

---

297 Frederick Douglass to William Lloyd Garrison, 21 April 1847, in McKivigan, *Douglass Papers—Series Three, Vol. 1*, pp. 203–05. For more on the *Cambria*'s return to the US, see Chaffin, *Giant's Causeway*; Fenton, *"I was Transformed"*; Pryor, *Colored Travelers*.

298 William Short to William Lloyd Garrison, 17 April 1847, BPLAC, MS.A.1.2, V.17, P. 29.

299 Pettinger, *Frederick Douglass and Scotland*, pp. 246–48.

300 *The Examiner*, 10 April 1847, p. 3.

301 Barker, *Newspapers and English Society*, pp. 32–33.

attempt to set up in the second port in the empire the worst spirit of American slavery. This must not be tolerated. In vain shall we attempt to shame the Americans out of their national vice and their national reproach if we suffer the unclean spirit to set up a temple in our own country.[302]

Interpreting Douglass's visit along racial and class lines, he had been treated abominably in contradiction to Britain's self-professed aggrandizements of freedom. His class, stature, celebrity, and savvy decision to call out the Cunard Company all played a part in the controversy. Slavery was dead in the British Empire, but it had the potential to rise again, ghostlike, if the British public was not roused to defend itself. The newspapers argued that a man such as Douglass, whose "eloquent lectures" had "made his name and history familiar throughout the length and breadth of the land" should not suffer racial discrimination while under the protection of the British flag.[303] British antislavery had become inexorably tied to patriotism, and for an "anti-slavery" nation that prided itself on being a beacon of hope and freedom to the rest of the world, this insult trumped any lingering racism toward Douglass.[304] Hence, if that global mission was thwarted then it was as though Britain itself was under attack. Britain itself represented liberty and equality, where enslaved people would instantly walk free on British soil. Slavery or social injustice was not tolerated, so the patriotic narrative went, and the self-erasure of Britain's role in the slave trade was essential to this xenophobic outrage at Douglass's treatment.

It was no surprise at least to abolitionists, then, that the Cunard Company's conduct was "noticed with strong and well deserved censure in our leading newspapers."[305] Mary Estlin remarked on how letters poured in from all corners of Britain, "overflowing with the commotion thus aroused."[306] The controversy reached such a height that the Cunard Company was forced to respond. Charles McIver, its Liverpool agent, replied to Douglass publicly through the press. He denied the charge of racism, and declared that the main reason Douglass had been refused his berth was the trouble he had caused on his journey to Britain nearly two years earlier. His presence and subsequent lectures had led to such a "serious disturbance on board" that the captain had been forced to intervene, and McIver did not

---

302   *The Bradford and Wakefield Observer, and Halifax, Huddersfield, and Keighley Reporter*, 8 April 1847, p. 8.

303   *The Leeds Times*, 10 April 1847, p. 4; *Leicestershire Mercury*, 10 April 1847, p. 1; *Manchester Times*, 10 April 1847, pp. 2; 7; *Norfolk News*, 10 April 1847, p. 3.

304   Turley, *The Culture of English Antislavery*, pp. 153–56.

305   Lucy Browne to Maria Weston Chapman, 1847, BPLAC, identifier:lettertomydearmroobrow2.

306   Mary A. Estlin to Maria Weston Chapman, 1847, BPLAC, identifier: lettertomydearmrooestl9.

want a repeat, regardless of how famous Douglass had become.[307] In McIver's eyes, it was a prudent business decision to separate Douglass just in case he threatened future patrons. Although McIver claimed he would have made the same decision even if Douglass were white, he denied him a ticket because he was concerned his race would offend others.

Not long after this, a letter appeared from one Charles Burrop, a Cunard Company representative from Virginia. He defended the actions of McIver and accepted no blame for the persistent racial prejudices of his customers, adding that as a business, Cunard was only doing what was best for the majority. Cunard was at risk of losing money, and so this policy would only change when racism ended. Again, newspapers widely printed this correspondence – but the plot thickened yet further when a letter signed by Mr. Samuel Cunard himself appeared very quickly and denied the existence of an individual named Charles Burrop. Significantly, Cunard promised that such discrimination would no longer have a place on his ships.[308]

In a transatlantic circulation of print culture, numerous editions of *The Liberator* overflowed with condemnation from the British press. All of the correspondence between Douglass, *The Times*, McIver, Burrop, and Cunard was printed verbatim, alongside countless outraged articles on the conduct of McIver and the company across the British Isles. *The London Morning Chronicle* wrote with surprise of how Cunard had imported "the infamous transatlantic doctrine" of racism, and recommended immediate legal action. *The Glasgow Times* simply said: "Do we live in the middle of the nineteenth century, or in the darkest of the dark ages?" Garrison was delighted at the response and was convinced that it had "resulted in a glorious triumph of justice over the foul spirit of complexional caste."[309] For a formerly enslaved African American to receive a public apology from a transatlantic businessman, and for his story of discrimination to be discussed in the press for weeks and even months afterwards, suggests how strong an impact Douglass had made on British society. According to Douglass himself, the *Cambria* incident was a "crowning chapter" in Britain's history, and the transatlantic flurry created by the press was "of the greatest importance to my down-trodden and long-abused race."[310]

The impact of Douglass's British trip was extraordinary. He enlightened hundreds of thousands of British and Irish citizens about the brutality of slavery, and as a result, donations poured in from antislavery societies and supportive individuals alike. Songs, poems, and sonnets were published in the local press; many of these are

---

307 *Carlisle Patriot*, 16 April 1847, p. 3.
308 *Hampshire Telegraph*, 17 April 1847, p. 7.
309 *The Liberator*, 14 May 1847, pp. 1–4.
310 *North Star*, 14 April 1848, p. 2.

republished here for the first time. He created and sustained controversies around the Free Church of Scotland, the Evangelical Alliance, and the World's Temperance Convention; and the furore over the *Cambria* incident indicated a savvy understanding of the relationship between performance and print culture, which he exploited to great advantage. The legal purchase of his freedom meant he could return to his family in (relative) safety and continue to share his testimony against slavery; and his *Narrative* had sold hundreds of copies, giving him a certain degree of financial freedom. He had honed and perfected his oratory and, especially in the last few months of his trip, exercised an independence away from Garrisonian control.[311]

Most newspaper reports, too, made reference to the "tremendous" or "deafening" applause that resounded down the aisles of churches, town halls, or assembly rooms, bursting forth as Douglass repeated charge after charge against American enslavers, the Free Church, or religious ministers who spurned non-fellowship.[312] Correspondents waxed lyrical about his "soul-stirring eloquence," his ability to draw "a heart-rending picture" of slavery, and the packed lecture halls which came to symbolize his tour. Discussions of slavery erupted even in places Douglass had never visited.[313] One reporter asked "who could listen to his heart-rending description of the horrors of slavery, and not heartily hate the institution? His picture of its evils and cruelties, how dark! How black! How affecting!"[314] Douglass had also inspired and created Black networks of kinship whenever he could speak alongside a fellow survivor; although, in a reverse incident outside of his control, one enterprising Black man attempted to exploit his celebrity by impersonating him in lectures across northern England.[315]

Aside from all this, the friends he had made in the British Isles would financially and sometimes emotionally sustain him for the rest of his life. Jane Wigham wrote that Douglass had "gained many warmly attached friends on this side of the Atlantic" and promised to "watch with deep interest his fortune career whenever he may be settled."[316] In Bridgwater, Lucy Browne wrote that "he left behind him in our

---

311   *The Liberator*, 29 January 1847. See also Blackett, *Building an Antislavery Wall*; Murray, *Advocates of Freedom*, pp. 211–13; Fenton, *"I was Transformed,"* pp. 87–91; Whyte, *Send Back the Money!*, pp. 105–06.

312   *Northampton Mercury*, 3 April 1847, p. 3; *The Freeman's Journal*, 24 September 1845, p. 4; *Leicestershire Mercury*, 6 March 1847, p. 2.

313   *The Liberator*, 4 June 1847, p. 4. Frederick Douglass, Speech on 2 February 1847, in Blassingame, *Douglass Papers—Series One: Vol. 2*, pp. 3–8. Douglass did not visit Cornwall or Cambridge, but articles appeared in the *Cornwall Royal Gazette*, 11 December 1846, p. 4; *Cambridge Independent Press*, 12 December 1846, p. 1. The correspondent from *The Worcestershire Chronicle and Provincial Railway Gazette*, 24 February 1847, p. 7, described Douglass's speech as "heart-rending."

314   *The Liberator*, 27 February 1846.

315   *Dundee, Perth and Cupar Advertiser*, 5 September 1846, p. 1.

316   Jane Wigham to Maria Weston Chapman, 1847, BPLAC, identifier: lettertomydear47wigh1.

little circle as I doubt not he has done in many other circles in England, warm feelings of friendship and attachment."[317] Mary Carpenter declared that "the wronged Africans could not have had a more noble champion" and his "satire [and] pathos" together with "his rich deep tone of voice" would surely "rouse the guilty nations of the new world."[318] Responding to Douglass's visit and specifically the wide distribution of his slave narrative in Belfast, Anglican minister Thomas Drew declared Douglass was to be "the stone in the sling to over-throw the Goliath of slavery."[319] Such religious iconography illuminated Douglass's charisma on a public stage but also in private; his personality and strength of mission towards ending slavery combined. He was regarded as no ordinary man or African American, and evidently his perceived exceptionalism was not confined to intimate conversations or public lectures.

Such memories were long-lasting and deeply cherished. Thomas Yule Miller, a newspaper correspondent for the *Dundee Courier*, wrote years later that he remembered as a small child "passing along the streets with my father one Sunday on his way to Gilfillan's Church . . . and seeing on the walls large posters bearing the words 'Send Back the Money.' What these words meant puzzled me, and in reply to my query my father said the Free Kirk ministers had run away with money which did not belong to them."[320] Colchester native Henry Clubb, who later emigrated to the U.S., recalled a lecture Douglass had given at Exeter Hall in 1846. Despite being "surrounded by the most eloquent preachers of Great Britain", the "impression he produced and the enthusiasm he aroused far exceeded the effect of any other speeches at the same meeting."[321]

And after hearing Douglass speak in Kilmarnock, one listener wrote forty years later that the hall had been "densely crowded" and "when the chairman rhetorically asked his audience 'is this a chattel, is this a thing to be bought and sold?' the loud 'No!' with which the vast audience answered the interrogation, seems still to reverberate over the waste of years which separate this day from that memorable night."[322]

As a physical token of their esteem, British and Irish friends orchestrated the "Douglass Testimonial," a subscription designed to raise money for Douglass to purchase a printing press, which unwittingly provided a stepping stone to further estrangement from the Garrisonians. In November, Douglass received a cheque for £445 17s.6d, transferred into $2,175.00 – "a much larger sum than I expected." He was grateful for the contributions toward a press, which he had already purchased along with "all the necessary printing materials." In publishing such a paper, he was free from "party or society" and would "advocate the slave's cause in that way which,

---

317   Lucy Browne to Maria Weston Chapman, 15 October 1846, BPLAC, identifier: lettertomydearm-a00brow.

318   Mary Carpenter to Maria Weston Chapman, 1 April 1846 (?), BPLAC, identifier: letter-tomrschapmoocarp2.

319   Ritchie, "'The Stone in the Sling,'" pp. 245, 256.

320   Fenton, "*I was Transformed*," p. 91.

321   Ottawa (Michigan) Clarion, 11 June 1857, 2. Thanks to Aaron Barnhart for this reference.

322   *The Newcastle Daily Chronicle*, 20 June 1887, p. 4.

in my judgment, will be the best suited to the advancement of the cause."[323] Douglass relished the opportunity to exercise control over his own literary and oratorical testimony, but also to maintain power over his own lecturing schedule, one that allowed him to spend more time with his family.[324]

American Garrisonians labored for over a year to persuade Douglass that his talents were more suited to oratorical rather than journalistic work. He wrote more regularly for abolitionist periodicals and African American journals, but the desire to launch his own vehicle never died. With the undiminished support of his international friends, Douglass launched *The North Star* in Rochester, New York, in December 1847. That location was, in part, selected to establish more independence from the largely East Coast Garrisonian centers, where several activists had tried to prevent him from doing so. In the first edition, Douglass demanded that only the "man STRUCK is the man to CRY OUT – and that he who has *endured the cruel pangs of Slavery* is the man to *advocate Liberty*." African Americans must lead the antislavery movement, "in connection with our white friends," as long as they recognized and respected their ignorance concerning the realities of slavery, racism, and their own white privilege. Douglass sent a national gesture of solidarity to all African Americans who had "writhed beneath the bloody lash" and bore scars "indelibly marked in our living flesh," and promised to fight alongside them on equal terms, free from the victimization and racial paternalism Douglass was still experiencing within the largely white abolitionist movement.[325]

Maintaining *The North Star*, however, was a constant struggle. Douglass noted with "considerable surprise and much regret" the backlash against his decision to start a newspaper; Garrison himself doubted Douglass's success and recommended he "give himself unreservedly to the great and successful work of addressing the multitudes instead." It was impossible to be both orator and editor without one profession suffering.[326] Douglass admitted to Elizabeth Pease that the newspaper suffered numerous difficulties, and he sensed that his Garrisonian friends wanted the paper to fail in order to prove his inability to manage it. The significance of his undertaking went far beyond their jealousy and paternalism; he established the paper to provide African Americans with a voice, considering they often felt hesitant about speaking to or with white people. The newspaper would be "a means to bring out their power – in such a manner as to silence hurtful misrepresentations."[327] However, friends such as

---

323   Frederick Douglass to Jonathan D. Carr, 1 November 1847, in McKivigan, *Douglass Papers— Series Three*, Vol. 1, pp. 266–67.

324   Sekora, "'Mr. Editor, If You Please,'" pp. 613–16.

325   *The North Star*, 3 December 1847, p. 2.

326   *The Liberator*, 23 July 1847, p. 2.

327   Frederick Douglass to Elizabeth Pease, 8 November 1849, in McKivigan, *Douglass Papers—Series Three*, Vol. 1, pp. 403–04.

Julia Griffiths were unrelenting supporters of Douglass's paper from the beginning. As well as raising money for the Testimonial, she encouraged antislavery bazaars and financial donations, used the columns of *The North Star* to advertise where such gifts could be sent, and reached out to friends in London, Birmingham, Coventry, Leicester, Leeds, Sunderland, Bristol, Manchester, and Carlisle to send aid to Rochester.[328]

In his farewell speech in London, Douglass declared: "I came a slave; I go back a free man. I came here a thing – I go back a human being. I came here despised and maligned – I go back with reputation and celebrity." While he had used such comparisons as performative techniques, he nevertheless returned to the US well aware of the stark differences between lecturing on platforms 3,000 miles apart. Despite his relative safety and security in Britain, however, he had never seriously entertained a life there, and preferred instead to work "in the service of my brethren." With a renewed strength in his oratory, a printing press paid for and supported by British friends, and a growing independence away from his Garrisonian friends, he resolved to use his testimony on behalf of African Americans everywhere, "to speak and write in their vindication."[329] On reaching the safety of home, he reflected fondly on his memories and wrote that all "England is dear to me; and, though long in her borders, and absent from home, and anxious to be at home, I left her with a heaviness of heart that words cannot express."[330]

328   *The North Star*, 21 September 1849; Fought, *Women in the World of Frederick Douglass*, pp. 112–15.

329   *Farewell Speech of Mr. Frederick Douglass*, p. 21.

330   Frederick Douglass to Anna Richardson, 29 April 1847, in McKivigan, *Douglass Papers—Series Three, Vol. 1*, pp. 208–09.

Chapter 2

"Blast Not the Budding Hopes of Millions": 1850–1865

Arm in arm with Julia and Eliza Griffiths, who had recently sailed to America, Frederick Douglass walked alongside New York's Battery in 1850 and was met with insult and physical assault. Fed by Douglass's own anglophilia when he crossed the Atlantic, several British publications reprinted American newspaper accounts of the incident.[1] The ensuing furore led Douglass to write to *The Times* of London and comment on this transatlantic storm of protest, thanking the paper for its "animadversions on the brutal assault made upon me by a mob." Douglass wrote:

> My offence was that I walked down Broadway in company with white persons on terms of equality. Had I been with those persons simply as a servant and not as a friend, I should have been regarded with complacency by the refined and with respect by the vulgar class of white persons who throng that great thoroughfare. The clamour here about human equality is meaningless. We have here an aristocracy of skin, with which if a man be covered, and can keep out of the state prisons, he possesses the high privilege of insulting a coloured man with the most perfect impunity. This class of aristocrats are never more displeased than when they meet with an intelligent coloured man. They recognise in him a contradiction to their ungenerous and unsound theories respecting the negro race, and not being able to reason him down to a level with the brute, they use brute force to knock him down to the desired level.[2]

---

1 *The Worcestershire Chronicle and Provincial Railway Gazette*, 19 June 1850, p. 3; *Coventry Herald and Observer*, 14 June 1850, pp. 3–4; *Sheffield and Rotherham Independent*, 15 June 1850, p. 7; *The Dundee Courier*, 19 June 1850, p. 2; *Dumfries and Galloway Standard and Advertiser*, 19 June 1850, p. 3.

2 The story was covered in: *Hereford Times*, 6 July 1850, p. 11; *The Dundee Courier*, 10 July 1850, p. 2; *Dundee, Perth and Cupar Advertiser*, 23 July 1850, p. 3; *The Fife Herald, and Kinross, Strathearn and Clackmannan Advertiser*, 25 July 1850, p. 2; *The Stirling Observer*, 25 July 1850, p. 2. See also Blackett, "Cracks in the Antislavery Wall."

Douglass used this violent assault as an opportunity – as he had with the *Cambria* – to illustrate British freedom versus the racial injustice he faced in the United States. He had conversed and dined with the aristocracy of England but in America, the "aristocracy" of skin prevented such harmless relations. The letter demonstrated his genuine belief that the circulation of such stories and the subsequent chatter from the transatlantic press would be a further nail in the coffin of slavery, and he used his international platform to denounce Black inferiority and champion racial justice. His own testimony was designed to correct any miscommunication or errors in the reports: it was not enough for editorials to state that he was walking with two white women, rather the most essential part of the story which American newspapers neglected to mention was that he walked alongside them "on terms of equality." The resulting clamor was partly due to this, with the notion that an "intelligent coloured man" had exercised his physical right to walk down a street as an equal with his companions and then eloquently defended himself through the press. The ugly stain of racism meant that Americans, when confronted with such a man, resorted to violence to silence him.

Between 1849 and 1855, Julia Griffiths, unrelenting activist and fierce friend, lived with the Douglass family in Rochester to support his activism, *The North Star*, and its successor *Frederick Douglass' Paper*. A large proportion of Douglass's subscribers lived in Britain and Ireland, which meant expensive postage, greater possibility of lost mail, and a higher chance the paper would be passed around among friends instead of each taking an individual subscription. In 1849, Douglass reported he was $2,000 in debt, but within a year this had been completely paid off and Griffiths' indefatigable efforts meant that the circulation increased from 2,000 to 4,000. She organized donations, edited *Autographs for Freedom*, which was published on both sides of the Atlantic, and reached out to British friends to raise money for the paper.[3] Using her detailed and skillful knowledge of the printing industry, Griffiths saved the newspaper from debt and cultivated friends including Mary Howitt, members of the BFASS, William Henry Seward, and Gerrit Smith to invest in the paper's longevity.[4]

Griffiths' presence did little to mend the growing tension between Douglass and Garrison, which eventually cracked in 1851. Douglass declared that the Constitution was in fact antislavery in nature, and embraced politics as an arena to forge forward with abolition. Garrison and his followers were outraged, as these principles were two of the central pillars of Garrisonian abolitionism. Douglass had never completely agreed with every piece of the ideological framework, but by 1853 Garrison had written that Douglass was "scornful and defiant, his language bitter as wormwood," with

---

3 Frank E. Fee, Jr., "To No One More Indebted: Frederick Douglass and Julia Griffiths, 1849–1863," *Journalism History*, 37:1 (2011), pp. 14–16; Fought, *Women in the World of Frederick Douglass*, p. 142; Meer, "Douglass as Orator and Editor," pp. 51–56.
4 Fought, *Women in the World of Frederick Douglass*, pp. 113–14.

"his pen dipped in poison."[5] Douglass defended his actions, exposed the racial paternalism of the abolitionist movement, and pointed out that "too often the cause of
the slave had been compelled to give place to the cause of a society." When Harriet
Beecher Stowe visited England in 1853, Douglass praised the fact that she traveled
"untrammeled and free" and would "not make Lewis Tappan a saint, and William
Lloyd Garrison a Satan, but will see in both these men, honest and devoted friends
of emancipation." Such petulant squabbles between abolitionist societies came at the
expense of the cause, and he was tired of the sectarian strife that had deeply racist
undertones surrounding his own position in the movement.[6]

Throughout the 1850s in Britain, divisions within groups over ideals and sometimes even between Black individuals themselves had caused serious rifts among
abolitionist societies. While some Black men and women remained independent
of abolitionist divisions through choice or circumstance, others aligned themselves
with Garrisonian activists or the BFASS, which had varying degrees of success.
Often, the British and Irish public were confused at the various allegiances and thus
most people lent their support to an individual after a lecturing tour, or via religious
groups who supported or criticized a particular antislavery society. Hence, the networks Griffiths forged and nurtured were essential to Douglass's success.[7]

Upon her return to England in 1855, Griffiths was determined to find a printer
for Douglass's second autobiography, *My Bondage and My Freedom*; on top of this,
she compiled lists of supporters, posted Douglass's newspaper to people across the
country, mailed British goods to be sold at the Rochester Bazaar, and wrote "Letters
from the Old World," which recounted her lecturing tours, travels, and interactions with abolitionists.[8] As Griffiths traveled around the British Isles, she created
or reawakened antislavery societies, lectured on the Underground Railroad, and
amplified Douglass's testimony. By circulating Douglass's various forms of print culture, Griffiths educated transatlantic audiences on his abolitionist crusades but also
the cruelty of slavery itself.[9] She wrote thousands of letters and covered "hundreds
of miles, in weather of all kinds – been present at more than one hundred and fifty
anti-slavery committee meetings, at diverse times and places – besides having had
the gratification of . . . narrating to my kind friends something of what I saw, heard

5   Selby, "The Limits of Accommodation," pp. 52–60.
6   Mary Estlin, 29 April 1853?, in Taylor, *British and American Abolitionists*, pp. 398–99; John R. McKivigan
    and Rebecca A. Pattillo, "*Autographs for Freedom* and Reaching a New Abolitionist Audience," *Journal
    of African American History*, 102:1 (Winter 2017), pp. 35–51.
7   Temperley, *British Antislavery*, pp. 246–47. See also Murray, *Advocates of Freedom*.
8   Meer, "Public and Personal Letters," pp. 252–55; 260–61; Fought, *Women in the World of Frederick
    Douglass*, pp. 112–15; 141–42.
9   *The Aberdeen Journal*, 23 December 1857, p. 6; *The Huddersfield Chronicle*, 6 March 1858, p. 5; Janet
    Douglas, "A Cherished Friendship," pp. 267–70.

and *felt* about American slavery while in the United States."[10] Douglass thanked Griffiths for her constant letters, financial assistance, and support, and wrote that "few hearts [were] more keenly alive to the wrongs and miseries of the American bondman than hers."[11]

In the US, Douglass's *My Bondage and My Freedom* sold 5,000 copies in the first two days of publication, and 15,000 were sold in the first two months; as he had done on both sides of the Atlantic with his *Narrative*, Douglass often took copies of the book to sell at his lectures.[12] In a callous act of protest, Garrisonian newspapers dismissed or ignored the book completely. When English abolitionist George Thompson wrote favorably of the autobiography in the British press, he hastily retracted it after incurring the wrath of Garrison himself, who wrote that the book was "reeking with the virus of personal malignity towards Wendell Phillips, myself . . . and full of ingratitude and

Frederick Douglass

Figure 2.1 Frederick Douglass, Frontispiece to *My Bondage and My Freedom* (New York: Miller, Orton & Mulligan, 1855). British Library, as digitized by Google.

10 *Douglass' Monthly*, 11 April 1859, pp. 54–55. Griffiths (by this point married to Henry Crofts) talks about her letters, in Crofts to Frederick Douglass, 27 January (Undated), FDP Digital Collection, Library of Congress.

11 *Douglass' Monthly*, January 1859, p. 2; *Douglass' Monthly*, February 1859, p. 1.

12 Frederick Douglass' Paper 7 December 1855, p. 4. See also Fought, *Women in the World of Frederick Douglass*, pp. 142–43; Douglass (ed. Bernier), *My Bondage and My Freedom*, pp. xiv–xv; Blassingame and McKivigan, *Douglass Papers—Autobiographical Writings*, Vol. 2, pp. xxxi–xxxii.

baseness towards as true and disinterested friends as any man ever yet had on earth." Thompson apologized, but still noted that the book was a valuable addition to the abolitionist cause because Douglass had experienced bondage himself.[13]

Douglass had exposed the paternalist actions of many Garrisonian abolitionists, and the decision to include a preface by James McCune Smith only further highlighted his desire to be an independent activist, to have full literary and editorial control over his work and celebrate the tradition of Black radicalism. He also inserted a long chapter on his travels to the British Isles, together with a letter he had written to William Lloyd Garrison in 1846 and his Finsbury Chapel speech. A deliberate decision to spurn his former Garrisonian colleagues – this had been a meeting which he had organized himself, speaking to a broad audience not strictly Garrisonian in its setting – it also symbolized the impact of his English travels. Neglecting to choose a speech from Scotland or Ireland, the London speech contained his blistering definition of slavery, his charges of hypocrisy against the US surrounding Independence Day, and the pollution of American Christianity.

Across the Atlantic, *The Scotsman* produced one of the lengthier and overwhelmingly positive commentaries of the book (included here in Part 4). The work was one of "deep interest and of great ability . . . a precious literary curiosity," considering his birth in enslavement. The reviewer may have heard Douglass speak during his journey in Scotland, for he wrote that his audiences "listened to an address singularly devoid of figures of rhetoric or flowers of oratory, without a paragraph or sentence of mere useless adornment"; and while other orators may have been congratulated on their language or speech in general terms, when "Frederick Douglass made his appeal to humanity in the cause of humanity, the people said, 'Arise, let us march to the overthrow of slavery!'" Unlike any other orator, Douglass had the brilliant and inspiring ability to turn his audiences into footsoldiers for social justice.[14]

However, fueled by Douglass's exposure of their racial paternalism, Garrisonian abolitionists continued to attack him and his relationship with Griffiths. Douglass wrote in 1857 that "evil minded persons, I learn, have insinuated that Miss G is receiving donations in my name for her own benefit. There is no truth in this insinuation or charge." Douglass blamed transatlantic Garrisonians for "the war against me," and reported that "they regard my repudiation of their religious or irreligious teaching to her influence."[15] According to them, Griffiths had poisoned Douglass against the Garrisonians and made him less effective in the antislavery movement. In distinctly racialist language, Douglass was "slumbering in the lap of a prejudiced,

---

13 Blassingame and McKivigan, *Douglass Papers—Autobiographical Writings, Vol. 2*, pp. xxxi–xxxii; xl–xli.
14 *The Scotsman*, 13 February 1856, p. 3.
15 Frederick Douglass to the Edinburgh New Anti-Slavery Association, 9 July 1857, FDP Digital Collection, Library of Congress.

sectarian Delilah."[16] John Estlin believed she only acknowledged "Antislavery with him [Douglass] alone" and had "no ideas upon the subject beyond rendering herself useful to Douglass." Estlin's dislike was no doubt based on Griffiths' activism, intelligence, and expertise, which were crucial to the survival of Douglass's paper and his antislavery mission, including her connections with the rival BFASS.[17] Undaunted, Griffiths persevered with her efforts, but she never forgot the damage the Garrisonians had done. Almost two decades later, she lambasted Garrison for his criticism of President Rutherford B. Hayes; he "<u>must attack someone!</u>" she wrote, adding "it's so mean of him . . . I never <u>did like</u> any of that lot of folks & <u>never shall!</u>"[18]

Frederick Douglass's Second Visit to Britain (1859–1860)

In the autumn of 1859, radical white abolitionist John Brown launched an assault on Harpers Ferry, Virginia in an attempt to spark an uprising of the enslaved population. Brown had visited Douglass for nearly two weeks while planning his raid, so Douglass was deeply knowledgable about the violent conspiracy. Virginian authorities were quick to involve Douglass, whose letters they had found in Brown's possession after his capture. Thus implicated in the failed insurrection, Douglass was forced to flee the country. He had been planning a visit to England for some time, but the insurrection was a catalyst in cementing his plans. Barely escaping arrest by US marshals, he hastily fled to Canada. From there, he boarded the steamer *Nova Scotian* and landed at Liverpool on 24 November. He was welcomed by Julia Griffiths and her new husband Henry Crofts, a Methodist minister; the family had settled in Staffordshire, where she continued her antislavery work on top of her new role as mother to Crofts' children. When Douglass arrived, she immediately organized speaking engagements around the country.[19] A restless Douglass feared for his family's safety and the possibility that he "was going into exile, perhaps for life," and thus began his journey "with feelings far from cheerful."[20]

While Douglass did have numerous friends in Britain and held very successful meetings, his severed Garrisonian connections hampered opportunities for further

---

16   Fought, *Women in the World of Frederick Douglass*, p. 96; McKivigan and Pattillo, *"Autographs for Freedom."*

17   Fought, *Women in the World of Frederick Douglass*, pp. 108–14; 142–44.

18   Julia Griffiths Crofts to Frederick Douglass, 5 July (undated, c. 1877), FDP Digital Collection, Library of Congress.

19   *Newcastle Courant*, 24 February 1860, p. 8. For Douglass's second visit to Britain, see Fought, *Women in the World of Frederick Douglass*; Blassingame, *Douglass Papers—Series One: Vol. 3*; Blackett, "Cracks in the Antislavery Wall"; Murray, *Advocates of Freedom*.

20   Douglass, *Life and Times* (1892), p. 392.

Figure 2.2 Frederick Douglass, *c.* 1862, J. W. Hurn (Library of Congress, Prints and Photographs Division).

controversy on British soil.[21] Even before Douglass's arrival in the British Isles, he was targeted by Mary Estlin, who tried to understand his motives for returning. She believed he would "succeed in promoting his own interests, whether by assured friendship, or avowed hostility, to the cause's true friends." Showing the supercilious strain within white antislavery politics, Estlin thought Douglass selfish and an enemy to the antislavery movement.[22] Samuel J. May also contributed to this racist dialogue, and remarked to Richard D. Webb that Frederick Douglass "will do mischief." He will "avoid anything beyond insinuation and implication" in regard to the American Anti-Slavery Society, "at which he is a master; but in private his malice will have full swing, I do not doubt. You will have an eye upon him, unquestionably."[23]

Due to these tensions, many Garrisonian networks – for example, that in Bristol, of which the Estlin family was a part – prevented him from lecturing in certain cities

21 Blackett, "Cracks in the Antislavery Wall," pp. 190–91.

22 Mary Anne Estlin to Maria Weston Chapman, 20 October 1859, BPLAC, identifier: lettertomydearmrooestl2.

23 Samuel May to Richard D. Webb, 13 September 1859, in Taylor, *British and American Abolitionists*, p. 441.

or other Garrison-supported hubs. However, there were some British abolitionists who were encouraged by Douglass's plans to return and hoped he could unite or at least inspire new waves of abolitionist sentiment. As the most famous African American of the nineteenth century, his name alone could draw crowds, but his association with John Brown and the Harpers Ferry rebellion secured a high interest. After hearing Douglass speak, for instance, James Walker, a member of the Leeds Young Men's Anti-Slavery Society, was confident that his influence would lead "us more actively and devotedly into anti-slavery work than ever."[24] Several newspapers also expressed their excitement at hearing him once again, since "the eloquence of his addresses during his former visit is still fresh in the remembrance of the public."[25] *The Daily Post* wrote that Douglass "is too well known as an eloquent advocate for the freedom of the slave to need any eulogy from us," but those "who had the privilege of hearing him on his former visit to England, about twelve years ago, cannot have forgotten his burning eloquence, his great powers as a lecturer."[26] Considering Douglass was an international celebrity by this point, his arrival in the British Isles was certainly newsworthy.

In an echo of his former visit, newspaper correspondents also pointed to Douglass's physiognomy, described him as a "negro Demosthenes," and clamored to write racialized descriptions:

> That head, with its keen caustic humour and luminous intelligence, must needs be, in every sense, a terrible witness to the injustice of a system which once made its owner labour under the lash along with the beasts of the field. Sharply cut and proudly set, as the head of an Arab Chief, is that head, for which brutal men of fairer complexion, but very inferior intellectual powers, offer a price. In Douglass the people see, wherever he goes, a man noble planned and noble endowed; and they hear from his lips that in America men as gifted, as industrious, as high-minded as himself are born to bondage, whipped to their toil, and taunted with the darkness and degradation in which they are intentionally reared.[27]

Tapping into racial stereotypes, the correspondent echoed earlier descriptions of nobility, intelligence, and eloquence from the 1840s, and expressed surprise that a man so "endowed" could ever have been enslaved. The romantic description

---

24 Foner, *Frederick Douglass*, pp. 182–83.
25 See *The Belfast Newsletter*, 29 November 1859, p. 4; *The Elgin and Morayshire Courier*, 2 December 1859, p. 2; *The Saturday Press*, 3 December 1859, p. 3; *Leicester Chronicle*, 24 December 1859, p. 4.
26 *The Daily Post*, 19 January 1860, p. 5.
27 *Dundee, Perth and Cupar Advertiser*, 3 February 1860, p. 2; *Dundee, Perth and Cupar Advertiser*, 14 February 1860, p. 2.

of an "Arab Chief" reflected a noble savage archetype that implied Douglass – as a chief – would lead his race to victory, imbuing him with a sense of importance and the exotic. It was a description designed to increase racial curiosity; Victorian audiences expected a foreign prince, or even an indigenous American from afar. Douglass possessed a noble mind, heart, and spirit, a form of exalted moral excellence to which few white and fewer Black people could aspire. He was naturally gifted and nobility radiated from his body and voice, in stark contrast to the racist and "comic" images of Black Americans in the press or in minstrel shows.

During the first few weeks of his trip, Douglass stayed with the Crofts family in Huddersfield; Russell and Mary Carpenter in Halifax; William Howard Forster in Leeds; and the Richardson family in Newcastle, who organized lectures across northern England and Scotland.[28] Throughout his journey, he argued that only the strength of the international community could end slavery, "a system so well calculated to blind and darken the moral sense of those who were brought immediately in contact with it – so paralyzing to the arm uplifted to strike it down – so corrupting to all the institutions in its vicinity, that the power to overthrow it did not exist in its more immediate locality."[29] While Douglass was no longer a Garrisonian in the strictest sense, he did employ elements of moral suasion in order to awaken British audiences to their antislavery duty. In the years since 1845, slavery had entrenched itself into the heart of the American nation yet further, and Douglass needed the help of his audiences to overthrow it.[30] Thus, he employed strategic anglophilia once again to wax lyrical about British freedom and recalled his first trip, where "he never saw the first look, or heard the first word which reminded him of his colour." Although he admitted that "England had sinned against his poor perishing race," Britain had "struck off the chain from eight hundred thousand of the oppressed"; he was content to praise British abolition and use the past as a tool to reawaken antislavery activity and encourage audiences to challenge United States slavery. His tactics were successful, particularly in Halifax, where his presence stimulated more gifts to an antislavery bazaar that raised over £300.[31]

As the speeches in our volume indicate, examining Douglass's rhetoric thematically reveals a multitude of subjects from the definition of slavery, John Brown, his criticism of British apathy regarding antislavery, self-made men, and Black radicalism.[32] More

---

28 Fenton, "I was Transformed," pp. 200–01; Fulkerson, "Frederick Douglass and the Anti-Slavery Crusade," pp. 383–84.

29 Frederick Douglass, Speech in Newcastle, 23 February 1860, in Blassingame and McKivigan, Douglass Papers—Autobiographical Writings, Vol. 2, pp. 334–40.

30 Fulkerson, "Frederick Douglass and the Anti-Slavery Crusade," p. 385.

31 Douglass' Monthly, April 1860, pp. 248–49. See also Third Annual Report of the Halifax Ladies' Anti-Slavery Society (Halifax Ladies' Anti-Slavery Society, 1860).

32 Frederick Douglass, Speech on 4 January 1860, in Blassingame, Douglass Papers—Series One: Vol. 3, pp. 289–300.

so than ever before, however, Douglass chastised the British public for their "non-intervention" toward American slavery. In a speech given in Sheffield and reprinted in this volume, Douglass directly connected the British people through the consumption of their slave-produced goods with the torture of enslaved people in America: he laid blame for slavery at their feet, urging them to pick up the gauntlet he had placed before them and aid his quest for abolition. The British public should resist the "corruption" through their economic relationships with America so that "when they met an American, they might be able to lay upon him an anti-slavery mustard plaster."[33] Shortly afterwards, in Dundee, he elaborated on this and "strongly condemned the pro-slavery feeling" that had begun to poison parts of British society. He criticized the portrayal of African Americans through minstrel shows specifically, condemning such performances as corrupt and inconsistent with fact; the rise in their popularity made it clear to Douglass at least why his second visit did not attract the same attention as his first.[34] In a complete contrast to 1845, he went so far as to say that Britain's "proud boast" of liberty could not be made at the present moment because "American prejudice might be found in the streets" of British cities. He blamed "pro-slavery ministers" and "that pestiferous nuisance, Ethiopian minstrels," who had "brought here the slang phrases, the contemptuous sneers all originating in the spirit of slavery."[35] These sentiments were echoed in 1861 by Henry Highland Garnet, who struggled to win support in front of a large audience in Liverpool. Americans, he said, had poured "pro-slavery poison into the ears and hearts of the British people."[36] For both men, the popularity of minstrel shows, the influence of pro-slavery Americans in Britain, and the nation's abandonment of antislavery principles threatened its proud history of abolition. Douglass feared that unless the public acted immediately, the toxic influence of racism would pollute society and make international abolition impossible.

In the first few speeches of his British sojourn, Julia Griffiths Crofts had urged Douglass to avoid mentioning John Brown for fear of alienating audiences in England and Scotland. Despite this, Douglass could bear the silence no longer after reading erroneous reports of Brown in the British press.[37] At the annual meeting of the Leeds Young Men's Anti-Slavery Society in December 1859 (coverage of which is reprinted in this volume), Douglass spoke alongside Black Garrisonian abolitionist Sarah Parker

---

33 *Supplement to the Sheffield and Rotherham Independent*, 21 January 1860, p. 10.

34 *Dundee, Perth and Cupar Advertiser*, 14 February 1860, pp. 2–3. Blackett, "Cracks in the Antislavery Wall," pp. 201–03.

35 Frederick Douglass, Speech on 23 February 1860, in Blassingame, *Douglass Papers—Series One: Vol. 3*, pp. 334–40. Blight, *Frederick Douglass: Prophet of Freedom* and Blackett, *Building an Antislavery Wall* discuss this briefly.

36 Blackett, "African Americans, the British Working Class and the American Civil War," pp. 55–56.

37 McFeely, *Frederick Douglass*, p. 203.

Remond; a radical advocate for social justice, feminism, and equality, Remond was leading her own speaking tour around the British Isles and made use of numerous Garrisonian networks to promote her lectures. Both Remond and Douglass defended Brown's rebellion, and Douglass remarked here that:

> It might be a crime for a man on the deck of a pirate ship to strike down the captain and take her into the nearest port, where the victims of piracy might be set at liberty, and in no other sense was Brown's act a crime. English people were apt to look upon Brown as one who had gone into a peaceable neighbourhood and had there created a deep-seated discontent and disturbance, but this was simply a picture of fancy. (Hear). John Brown disturbed no such neighbourhood as this. (Hear). He entered Virginia not when she was in a state of peace but when she was in a state of war . . . for if a state of war existed anywhere on the face of the globe, it did at this moment on the soil of the southern states. (Hear). Slavery was itself an insurrection, and the slave holders were an armed band of insurgents against the just rights and liberties of their fellow-men.[38]

Turning the arguments against Brown upside down, he accused enslavers of permanently committing an insurrection against the liberties of enslaved women, men, and children. Brown was no rebel who had disturbed the peace with malice and murderous intentions, because slavery by its very existence represented war. Blood was spilled through torture, violence, and rape on a daily basis "at the touch of the slaveholder's scourge," and as Brown sacrificed himself on the altar of freedom, he exposed the enslavers' war crimes against Black people to the international community. Douglass compared Brown to the prophet Moses, framing his insurrection as "an exodus of liberty . . . to the land of freedom." He did not expect his audience to fight slavery with arms, but "when they found a man disinterested enough to lay down his life for his fellow-men, he hoped the memory of that man would not be tarnished." He compared him to George Washington, who was only celebrated because he had successfully established a new republic, though he was a traitor to the British government.[39]

Douglass noted during another meeting that Brown was charged in the *Leeds Mercury* "as criminally interfering with the laws of Virginia." Waving the newspaper performatively in his hand, he declared that Brown "would have been glad to see the result of his labour, glad to have seen the slaves free; but he went to the scaffold

---

38   *The Leeds Times*, 24 December 1859, p. 3. Douglass also spoke alongside Remond here; see *The Barnsley Chronicle*, 14 January 1860, p. 8.
39   *The Leeds Times*, 24 December 1859, p. 3.

with the consciousness of having only discharged his duty to his God and his fellow man."[40] Douglass reiterated that he was a "peace man," but his

> theory of peace was this: the man who did most to establish justice on this earth was the true man of peace. There could be no real peace where there was injustice . . . Let [enslavers] dream of death when they sleep, let them suspect death in their dish and in their drink – for when a man reduces his fellow man to slavery, when he takes from him the right of speech, when he blots out from him the word of god, when he darkens his soul, when he takes that name that might be inscribed in the lamb's book of life and sacrilegiously inscribes it in his ledger, and when he declares that he shall have no means of escape, but that his children and his children's children after him shall linger in hopeless bondage, then he (Mr Douglass) should say that if the slaveholder did welter in his blood he had his own crimes to thank for it.[41]

Here, Douglass described his abhorrence of war, but since slavery was a *state* of war, then it should be immediately overthrown, with arms if necessary. Enslavers were currently at war against the bodies and souls of African Americans, and Douglass understood that true peace and liberty could never be achieved in the US while there was "injustice." In the meantime, let enslavers sleep uneasily, for righteous and divine vengeance would be delivered against them. With his blistering rhetoric, he also condemned the plantation "ledger" – a document that symbolized the very dehumanization and brutalization of slavery, where women and men were listed like animals sold at the marketplace, with their children often signed away in blood before they were born.[42]

Through his defense of Brown, Douglass was forced once again to share his definition of slavery and educate his audiences on its true horrors. Those who had never suffered the eradication of their own identity and liberty, he argued, could never know what it felt like to be enslaved. During a speech in Paisley in January 1860 (reprinted in this volume), Douglass declared:

> You know what the highway robber is. He meets you at midnight, in a lonely place, and with a pistol at your head demands your purse or your life. That is highway robbery. What is slavery? Precisely the same. There is not a shadow of difference between the principle of highway robbery and the principle of slavery. Much as you value your purse, you value your life more. And what is the language

---

40 *Supplement to the Sheffield and Rotherham Independent*, 24 December 1859, p. 10.
41 *The Leeds Times*, 24 December 1859, p. 3.
42 *The Caledonian Mercury and Daily Express*, 31 January 1860, p. 3.

of every slaveholder to his slave? "You shall give up your liberty or your life." The chain, the whip, the bowie knife, the revolver, the rifle – all these instruments are used to keep the slave. He must give up his liberty or die.[43]

In order for his audience to fully grasp the meaning of slavery and liberty, Douglass used a comparison they would be familiar with to illustrate that the structure of slavery rested on the erosion of freedom, sustained by brutal violence. To rebuke pro-slavery arguments, he denied the racist and false belief that enslaved people were "well-treated" and happy on the plantation. Because "men naturally love liberty," it was impossible for the millions of enslaved people to be content in their condition. The "whip" and "bowie knife" were essential to slavery, or else the enslaved would simply walk free. They faced no choice in their oppression; they valued their life, and always fought to attain the liberty that had been stolen from them.[44]

Recounting such brutalities once again in front of a British audience, Douglass revealed his impatience and frustration with the slow progress of the antislavery movement. At the start of his career,

> he went out, addressing meetings, showing his brands and wounds, for he carried on his back to this day the marks of the slave driver's lash, and they would go to his grave with him. Deep and clear as these marks were, deeper and clearer were the marks of slavery on his soul; for he had felt its debasing influence robbing him of his manhood; degrading in heaviness his darkening soul; and sending him from time to eternity in the dark. He knew what slavery was by bitter experience; for before he was made part of this breathing world, fetters were forged for his hands and the irons for his ankles; and the lash was platted for his back. He thought it would be sufficient for men to know all of the dark recesses of the slave's experience, to call forth a sentiment so powerful as to have sent slavery staggering to its grave, as if smitten by a bolt from heaven. But he was mistaken. Slavery still existed, and the slaveholder tightened his grasp with every effort to rescue his victim. He thought it only wanted light; but he found it needed fire.[45]

In a rare acknowledgment of his exhibition of physical scars, Douglass pointed to the traumatic wounds upon his soul and how his spirit had been crushed by the brutal reality of slavery. His largely white audience would never understand his pain and loss, where millions of African Americans suffered the same fate at that very moment, marked for violence and torture before birth. As he reiterated during another speech, the dehumanizing nature of slavery meant that before "I knew my

---

43 *The Paisley Herald and Renfrewshire Advertiser*, 28 January 1860, p. 4.
44 Ibid.
45 Frederick Douglass, Speech on 7 December 1859, in Blassingame, *Douglass Papers—Series One: Vol. 3*, pp. 276–88.

own name it was inscribed in a book along with horses, oxen, sheep, and swine. I bear yet on my back the marks of the scourge of the surveyor."[46] He had believed that to share such blistering and painful eyewitness testimony – including his own scarred back, at the behest of white abolitionists – would surely be enough to spark a greater zeal for abolition. However, his words, infused with divine power, could not strike down the power of enslavers, and it was no longer enough to shine a light and remove the veil of ignorance surrounding slavery. Instead, fire was the only weapon capable of scorching the South and forcing enslavers to surrender Black women, men, and children. Firmly re-establishing his commitment to the "wall of anti-slavery fire" he had pronounced so early during the period 1845–47, he added a further shade of violent retribution to his argument: instead of surrounding the South in a circle of fire to shame or smoke out the enslavers, here he implied the necessity of burning everything to the ground.[47]

Despite several successful meetings in the north of England and parts of Scotland, when Douglass reiterated his position on the American Constitution as an antislavery document, he raised the ire of Garrisonians on both sides of the Atlantic and prompted George Thompson to challenge him to a public debate.[48] In Glasgow, he gave an entire lecture on the antislavery nature of the Constitution: he was deliberate in this site-specific criticism, for Glasgow was still a Garrisonian hotbed. Thompson organized a series of lectures to denounce him, and read some of his former speeches from 1846 in order to highlight Douglass's differing opinions. In effect, he wanted to make it clear that Garrison had never wavered in his beliefs or devotion to the antislavery cause, in comparison to Douglass, who had completely changed his mind on several pillars of Garrisonian thought. Incensed, Douglass refused to meet him on the platform and declared that he was "under the fire of both platform and press," charging Thompson with *dealing out blows upon me as if I had been savagely attacking him . . . I do not hesitate to pronounce that speech false in statement, false in its assumptions, false in its inferences, false in its quotations even, and in its arguments, and false in all its leading conclusions."* The dissolution of the Union would not abolish slavery, and as for his previous remarks in 1846: "I cannot pretend that I have never altered my opinion both in respect to men and things."[49]

---

46 Frederick Douglass, Speech on 14 February 1860, in Blassingame, *Douglass Papers—Series One: Vol. 3*, pp. 323–33.

47 Frederick Douglass, Speech on 7 December 1859, in Blassingame, *Douglass Papers—Series One: Vol. 3*, pp. 276–88.

48 Griffin, "George Thompson, Transatlantic Abolitionism and Britain," pp. 564–65.

49 Frederick Douglass, Speech on 26 March 1860, in Blassingame, *Douglass Papers—Series One: Vol. 3*, pp. 340–66. See also Fulkerson, "Frederick Douglass and the Anti-Slavery Crusade," pp. 387–91. Garrison covered both Douglass and Thompson's speeches in *The Liberator*: see 23 March 1860 and 30 March 1860.

Tragically, Douglass's visit to Britain was cut short when he received the heart-breaking news that his daughter Annie had died three weeks previously. An article in *Douglass' Monthly* mentioned that at her funeral, "frequent allusions were made to the father of little ANNIE so far away, who would be so sad to be present, and yet still *more* sad to be absent."[50] Throughout his life, Douglass constantly struggled to find a balance between his public activism and his role as a private father and husband, but never was this more apparent than after the catastrophic event of Annie's death. Being thousands of miles away from home, and knowing that his family had been grief-stricken for weeks, only added to his sorrow. When the family finally received a letter from him, his daughter Rosetta described that there was no "composure of mind."[51] Publicly, Douglass wrote of his grief in a measured and orchestrated fashion: as he explained in his third autobiography, *Life and Times* (1881), the news "of the death of my beloved daughter Annie, the light and life of my house" reached him in Scotland, and, "deeply distressed by this bereavement, and acting upon the impulse of the moment, regardless of the peril, I at once resolved to return home, and took the first outgoing steamer."[52] Douglass's account gave the impression that he immediately left for America, but newspaper reports of the time suggest otherwise. Douglass certainly arranged passage back to the United States as soon as possible, but he did not cancel his antislavery meetings. He continued his hectic lecturing schedule despite the news, even though in private he showed no "composure of mind."

Ever the virtuoso and public performer, he tried to hide the emotional strain behind his mask of performance. The trauma of maintaining this burden together with overwhelming sorrow eventually broke him. During a meeting in Ayr in March 1860, Douglass cracked under the pressure of maintaining his façade. The correspondent wrote that Douglass was "labouring under a depression" and, after speaking for an hour, "apologized to the audience" as he "had that morning received a letter from America bringing the melancholy tidings of the death of one of his family, a girl of ten years of age, the light of the family." The correspondent noted that the "meeting, which no doubt was disappointed a little in not bearing the address out, deeply sympathised with Mr Douglass in his bereavement." At a subsequent meeting in Paisley, another correspondent described his address as "a masterly piece of composition" despite the fact that he was "evidently undergoing a severe mental struggle, produced by the intelligence received within the last day or two, that one of his children had died." By the end of the evening, however, the correspondent noted that he made a speech "replete with the most thrilling passages of eloquence, and admirably shaded by a series of sparkling jokes." Douglass's private grief overflowed into a public performance he refused to reschedule, and the meeting was

---

50 *Douglass' Monthly*, April 1860, pp. 243–44.
51 Fought, *Women in the World of Frederick Douglass*, p. 173.
52 Douglass, *Life and Times* (1881), p. 328.

broken up early as a result. As he had done in the 1840s, Douglass tried to hide his "mental struggle" and construct a carefully orchestrated public performance. What "sparkling jokes" he told, despite the immense pain he must have then felt, we will never know. What was apparent, however, was that this soul-destroying tragedy threatened to expose the public/private divide in Douglass's life. Unwilling to avoid a situation like Ayr, Douglass resurrected his masked performance (perhaps even as a coping mechanism); the sheer mental anguish and energy this must have taken him is unimaginable.[53]

After his return to America, Douglass thanked his British friends "for all your kindness, hospitality, sympathy, aid and co-operation while a stranger and sojourner among you . . . Especially do I remember the many touching marks of sympathy with me in the loss of my dearly beloved daughter."[54] He neglected to mention, of course, the numerous friends who had tried to convince him to stay, in part worried for his safety in the wake of Brown's death, as well as others who were eager for him to continue his tour. While the concerns for his life were legitimate, the notion of Douglass staying and abandoning his family in their hour of need was at best unrealistic and, at worst, self-interested. To satisfy his benefactors, Douglass vowed to return in October that year.[55]

Few of Douglass's British friends had the chance to meet Annie, save Julia Griffiths Crofts, who had lived with the Douglasses at Rochester. In letters written months and even years afterwards, she mentioned or spoke warmly of her to comfort a grieving parent. On the first anniversary of her death, Crofts lamented in *Douglass' Monthly* "the vacant niche in your home circle, of the melancholy that must ever steal over you when looking back upon this (to you) sad year, and of the sweet little spirit that upward winged its flight, and left you to mourn its loss, my heart feels so sad, and I realize how vain are all human hopes and wishes."[56] The following year, she reminisced of the "the dear little companion of so many walks sweetly sleeps beneath the soil in Mount Hope Cemetery – 'She is not dead but sleepeth' 'not lost but gone before.' May this thought, my ever dear friend comfort your sorrowing heart & cause you to look upward, as well as onward."[57] To console him, Crofts made frequent reference to the land of "no more parting." In a letter to Douglass most likely written in 1869, she was heartbroken at "a vein of melancholy running through part of your letter that makes me sad. What I would not give for just a few hours conversation with you." Douglass's misery was likely a result of the devastating

---

53 *The Paisley Herald and Renfrewshire Advertiser*, 31 March 1860, p. 2.

54 *Douglass' Monthly*, June 1860, pp. 277–78.

55 Fulkerson, "Frederick Douglass and the Anti-Slavery Crusade," pp. 387–92.

56 *Douglass' Monthly*, February 1861, p. 407.

57 Julia Griffiths Crofts to Frederick Douglass, 1 September 1862, FDP Digital Collection, Library of Congress.

anniversary of Annie's birth. He had evidently confided in Crofts for support, as she wrote "how difficult it is to realize that your dear Annie would have been 20 now had she been spared!! I have never, <u>never</u> forgotten the darling child & how she used to run to meet us up that hill."[58] In another subsequent letter, she reminded Douglass once again of "our" Annie waiting in heaven; using "our" was a deliberate way of highlighting the familial connection between herself and Douglass, and how close she was to Annie herself.[59] Crofts shared cherished memories to reframe such grief into acts of love, and remembered such devastating milestones as an unspoken promise that Annie's short life was meaningful to so many and that she would never be forgotten. She wrote to acknowledge his grief and pain and to partially allay his deepest sorrow, as she recognized that such a loss could never fully heal.

The American Civil War (1861–1865)

As Black abolitionists had been predicting for years, the tumultuous conflict over slavery led to the American Civil War in 1861. In May, an editorial in *Douglass' Monthly* argued that *"The simple way, then, to put an end to the savage and disoluting war now waged by the slaveholders, is to strike down slavery itself,* the primal cause of that war."[60] The British Isles, meanwhile, was left with a dilemma of how to respond. The Union blockade disrupted Britain's supply of cotton, which caused a transatlantic crisis in which thousands of British men and women faced unemployment and poverty. Abraham Lincoln and the Union cause were slow to push antislavery as part of its agenda, fearing this would further antagonize its Border State allies and the Confederacy as a whole; this attitude did not impress antislavery critics in Britain.[61] Such conditions left many Britons susceptible to sympathizing with the aristocratic "Southrons," and numerous politicians and journalists used their position to influence the public even further. Many were swayed by romantic descriptions of a noble Confederate cause, which attempted to forge a new republic but faced oppression from the Union and threats abroad. Unsurprisingly, then, Britain came very close to recognizing the Confederacy.[62]

---

58 Julia Griffiths Crofts to Frederick Douglass, 10 December 1863, FDP Digital Collection, Library of Congress; Julia Griffiths Crofts to Frederick Douglass, 22 April (undated, but probably 1869), FDP Digital Collection, Library of Congress; Julia Griffiths Crofts to Frederick Douglass, 5 July (undated), FDP Digital Collection, Library of Congress. Thank you to Celeste-Marie Bernier for pointing this out to me. See also Bernier, *The Anna Murray and Frederick Douglass Family Papers, Volumes 1–3* (forthcoming, 2021).

59 Julia Griffiths Crofts to Frederick Douglass, 12 December 1873, FDP Digital Collection, Library of Congress.

60 *Douglass' Monthly*, May 1861, p. 451 (emphasis in original).

61 Doyle, "Slavery or Independence," pp. 107–09. See also Blight, "For Something Beyond the Battlefield."

62 Diffley, "Splendid Patriotism," pp. 385–93.

In *Divided Hearts: Britain and the American Civil War*, Richard Blackett argues that "no other international event . . . had such a profound effect on the economic and political life of Britain as did the war in America."[63] The war had a dramatic impact on the British political and economic landscape, particularly in counties such as Lancashire and Cheshire, which were dependent on slave-grown cotton. When stockpiles of cotton dried up, large numbers of people were unemployed; in Burnley, for example, 10,000 out of 13,000 were unable to work in 1862. President Lincoln eventually arranged several relief ships, including the *George Griswold*, which docked in Liverpool in early 1863 with food and money. These supplies were welcomed by working-class families who suffered from unemployment and lack of food, but there was certainly no unanimous support for the Union.[64]

Douglass was deeply concerned at Britain's wavering position toward the North. In the wake of the Battle of Antietam and Lincoln's draft Emancipation Proclamation, the October 1862 issue of *Douglass' Monthly* urged British friends to continue their antislavery efforts, as for years they had "steadily assisted us in speaking, writing, publishing and otherwise devoting our energies to the advancement of the antislavery cause. We shall need your continued sympathy, aid, and co-operation till the last fetter shall fall and the last chain shall be broken."[65] In response to a friend's request (most likely from Julia Griffiths Crofts), Douglass penned a literary masterpiece, "The Slave's Appeal to Great Britain," in 1862 (reprinted in this volume). It was designed to encourage British audiences to denounce slavery as the cornerstone of the Confederate republic.[66] Echoing previous themes he had espoused during his first visit in 1845, Douglass urged the transatlantic public to reject all fellowship with the South. Employing a distinct form of anglophilia, he proclaimed that the "inspiration of an enlightened Christianity" had led to the end of slavery in the British Empire, and the "tremendous crisis of American affairs" would lead to terrible suffering if Britain did not heed its humanitarian past.[67] He argued that Christian enslavers were the best soldiers in the Slave Power's army, but were also the Achilles' heel at which abolitionists could direct their attack. Douglass returned to the theme of the Slave Power in his rhetoric (that enslavers and what they stood for threatened white as well as Black freedom), and in his Appeal, argued it had spread its shadow over the Atlantic to infect the free soil of Britain too.[68]

---

63 Blackett, *Divided Hearts*, pp. 6–7; 25–26.

64 Rice, "The Cotton That Connects," pp. 295–99.

65 *Douglass' Monthly*, October 1862, p. 723.

66 In a letter to Theodore Tilton, Douglass mentions the request from a friend: 22 November 1862, Frederick Douglass Papers, University of Rochester Project, <https://rbscp. lib.rochester.edu/2496> (last accessed 11 October 2020). The Appeal was published in numerous newspapers, including the *Daily News*, 26 November 1862, p. 5; *The Saturday Press*, 29 November 1862, p. 4.

67 *London Daily News*, 26 November 1862, p. 5.

68 Blight, *Frederick Douglass's Civil War*, pp. 9–10; 39–40.

Douglass began by appealing to British patriotism and, as the representative of his enslaved brethren, declared that he was "fulfilling my appointed mission in making on the slave's behalf, this appeal to you." In dramatic and immediate language, he urged British audiences to resist the Confederacy's calls to recognize the new nation:

> Oh! I pray you, by all your highest and holiest memories, blast not the budding hopes of these millions by lending your countenance and extending your honoured and potent hand to the blood-stained fingers of the impious slaveholding Confederate States of America. For the honor of the British name, which has hitherto only carried light and hope to the slave, and rebuke and dismay to the slaveholder, do not in this great emergency be persuaded to abandon and contradict that policy of justice and mercy to the negro which has made your character revered, and your name illustrious, throughout the civilized world. Your enemies even have been compelled to respect the sincerity of your philanthropy. Would you retain this respect, welcome not those brazen human fleshmongers, those brokers in the bodies and souls of men, who have dared to knock at your doors for admission into the family of nations. Their pretended government is but a foul, haggard, and blighting conspiracy against the sacred rights of mankind, and does not deserve the name of government. Its foundation is laid in the impudent and heaven-insulting dogma that man may rightfully hold property in man, and flog him to toil like a beast of burden. Have no fellowship, I pray you, with these merciless men-stealers; but rather with whips of scorpions scourge them beyond the beneficent range of national brotherhood.[69]

Douglass praised the nation's history of abolition and argued that everything Britain stood for in law, morals, and customs represented the very opposite of slavery, "the vilest of all modern abominations." As he had done during previous West Indian Emancipation Day addresses, he made a deliberate political decision to ignore any form of hypocrisy in regard to British liberty or the Empire, and instead urged the nation not to form a brotherhood with the "blood-stained" hands of the Confederacy. Once again using the language of blood, as he had done in 1845, Douglass framed the war in Machiavellian terms as a gigantic struggle between good and evil, civilization and savagery, light and darkness.[70]

---

69   *London Daily News*, 26 November 1862, p. 5. The speech was printed several times—complete or in part—in northern England and Scotland, including in the *Dundee Advertiser*, 1 December 1862, p. 3; *The Elgin and Morayshire Courier*, 5 December 1862, p. 7; *The Hull Packet and East Riding Times*, 5 December 1862, p. 7; *The York Herald*, 13 December 1862, p. 5.

70   *London Daily News*, 26 November 1862, p. 5. See also McKivigan and Silverman, "Monarchical Liberty," pp. 7–18.

Anticipating the response of those Britons who wavered in their decision or pointed to the Union's lacklustre commitment to antislavery, Douglass attacked their hypocrisy, particularly in regard to Northern racism:

> Must you, because the loyal states have been guilty of complicity with slavery, espouse the cause of those who are still more guilty? Must you, while you reprobate the guilty agent, embrace in the arms of your friendship the still more guilty principal? Will you lash the loyal states for their want of a genuine detestation of slavery, and yet in open day form an alliance with a band of conspirators and thieves who have undertaken to destroy the loyal Government of this country, in order to make slavery perpetual and universal on this continent? Will you stand in the way of a righteous measure, because supported and urged by wrong and selfish motives? Will you prevent the slave from getting his due, because necessity and not a sense of moral obligation impels the payment?[71]

Using bold, repetitive statements, Douglass drove home British complicity with the Confederate republic and their shameful principles that allowed them to celebrate abolition while refusing to adhere to their professed ideas of liberty. In times of crisis, the British nation – when confronted with a stark reality of light and dark, abolition and slavery – should revoke its hypocrisy and support the Union in its effort to free the enslaved. He directly targeted politicians such as William Gladstone and influential newspapers like *The Times*, which acted as the "one grand source of the strength of our slaveholding rebellion," and loathed the nation's "early concession of belligerent rights to the rebels." Britain's "rebukes of the north" have "been construed as a renunciation of your former abhorrence of slavery, and you have thus kept these Confederate slave-masters in countenance from the beginning." He accused Gladstone again of remarking in a speech at Newcastle that "the interests of the negro were likely to be better cared for under the Southern Confederacy than in the Old Union." Such blatant racist falsehoods were not only shameful to Britain's moral principles and antislavery history, but fed the Confederacy's cause yet further.[72] Extending the jeremiad metaphor he had employed in the 1840s, Douglass reminded British audiences that they had a duty to support abolition because if they did not, the republic and millions of enslaved people were doomed. In concluding his Appeal, Douglass connected the war and suffering of Americans to the poverty of the English working classes, which could have been avoided if the nation had relied on free labour and had denounced the Confederacy from the beginning. Because of the nation's hubris, the only course of action that remained was to pursue the righteous path of

---

71   *London Daily News*, 26 November 1862, p. 5.
72   Ibid.

justice and openly revoke all fellowship with the Confederacy. If Britain intervened to help the South, all would be lost for the enslaved, the high moral principles of honor and freedom to which the nation aspired would be eternally unachievable, and the "stain" of their betrayal would never be wiped out from history.

Douglass exploited his transatlantic networks to publish the Appeal in as many newspapers as possible. Henry Richardson wrote that he had "forwarded [the Appeal] to the Editor of the 'Daily News,' with a note informing him that I sent it at your request." The Appeal was "inserted immediately, and the very next morning after its appearance, I observed about one half of it in our 'Daily Chronicle.'" Extracts were also published in the *Newcastle Guardian* and the *Leeds Mercury* and Richardson further remarked that there was a "turn of the tide [now] observable, and that the Northern States are beginning to be looked upon with more favour. Your appeal had doubtless helped on this change."[73] However, a somewhat exasperated Julia Griffiths Crofts expressed frustration with Richardson, as she hoped the *Leeds Mercury* would have "published the Appeal in full, and if she had had control of it, she would have "sent [it] at once to the Mercury." In an attempt to repair this mistake, Crofts corresponded with the proprietor of the *Mercury*, Frederick Baines, but he declared it "too late after the extract from the address was given, [and] they could not publish it whole." Instead, Crofts persuaded Baines to publish a private letter from Douglass, which she reminded him he had "thought might be published with advantage." Ever the astute activist, she provided further unique material to aid the antislavery cause; aware of the importance of timing, Crofts despaired at Richardson's actions, since any mistakes would limit the circulation and effectiveness of Douglass's message.[74]

Throughout the war, Crofts worked feverishly to amplify Douglass's speeches and writings concerning African Americans. In February 1863, Crofts and her husband held an antislavery meeting in Leeds and wrote to Douglass, "it would have done your heart good to have heard the thundering shouts for liberty, and the groans for slavery," but wished he could have been present to add "the weight of your testimony *to the guilty, the piratical Southern Confederacy*."[75] Crofts continued to hold meetings, circulated his speeches, read his letters aloud to provincial antislavery societies, and, in a transatlantic exchange, sent copies of British newspapers with his testimony in which she endeavored to show him "how serviceable to our cause I make your letters. I bought 2 dozen papers, & scattered them

---

73 Henry Richardson to Frederick Douglass, 4 December 1862, FDP Digital Collection, Library of Congress. See also McKivigan, *Douglass Papers—Series Three: Vol. 2*, pp. 373–75.

74 Julia Griffiths Crofts to Frederick Douglass, 5 December 1862, FDP Digital Collection, Library of Congress. See also McKivigan, *Douglass Papers—Series Three: Vol. 2*, pp. 377–79.

75 *Douglass' Monthly*, March 1863, pp. 803–04.

up & to our Glasgow friends."[76] In an attempt to rally the British people once again, both Crofts and Douglass exploited transatlantic mediums to challenge pro-Southern sympathy and encouraged the British not to abandon their antislavery principles. Thanks to Crofts' enterprising networks, Douglass's letters, either through extracts or printed in their entirety, were published across the nation in the service of the Union cause.

Such unexplored and forgotten testimony provides new insight into Douglass's activism and mental wellbeing during the Civil War. In May 1862, Douglass expressed frustration that "we could say that [the Confederacy] were fighting for slavery, but could not say that we were fighting against it," despite the devoted efforts of the Confederates to establish a constitution "in which slavery should be permanently secured against every political and moral shock."[77] In October, Douglass criticized those in the US and Britain who fell silent or ceased their antislavery efforts, despite the fact that "the moral sentiment of the country is still corrupt and deeply pro-slavery."[78] Hence, Douglass continued to urge friends to "circulate" his writings and speeches in England and in particular to "pass this copy around among your friends," fully aware of its importance to the antislavery cause and for dispelling any falsehoods regarding the Confederacy.[79]

Douglass and Crofts used the pages of *Douglass' Monthly* to spread support for the Union and to celebrate donations from British friends. In several editions, Reverend Jermaine W. Loguen thanked Crofts for their donations from, among others, societies in Birmingham, Dalkeith, Sheffield, Bradford, Halifax, Liverpool, Falkirk, Berwick-on-Tweed, and Derby.[80] In January 1862, Crofts sent Douglass £30 from regional antislavery societies in the north of England and Scotland, and two months later she enclosed another cheque for £20, half of which was for Douglass's lectures

---

76 Julia Griffiths Crofts to Frederick Douglass, 5 February 1864, FDP Digital Collection, Library of Congress. Crofts also discusses this here: Crofts to Frederick Douglass, 23 February (undated) and 19 May 1865, FDP Digital Collection, Library of Congress.

77 This letter was republished numerous times, including: *The Bury Times*, 3 May 3 1862, p. 4; *The Northampton Mercury*, 3 May 1862, p. 8; *The Rochdale Observer*, 3 May 1862, p. 7. Many of Douglass's speeches to white and Black audiences alike were published here: *The Daily News*, 30 December 1864, p. 3; *The Bradford Observer*, 5 January 1865, p. 3; *The Caledonian Mercury*, 9 January 1865, p. 2. Several British newspapers also published Douglass's "Call to Arms" to African American soldiers: "I urge you to fly to arms, and smite with death the power that would bury the government and your liberty in the same hopeless grave"—*The Dundee Courier and Argus*, 24 March 1863, p. 3; *The Saturday Press*, 28 March 1863, p. 4.

78 *The Dundee Courier and Argus*, 18 October 1862, p. 4.

79 *The Leeds Mercury*, 2 February 1865, p. 4.

80 Maria Webb to Frederick Douglass, 15 March 1862, FDP Digital Collection, Library of Congress; Julia Griffiths Crofts to Frederick Douglass, 23 November 1864, FDP Digital Collection, Library of Congress; *Douglass' Monthly*, September 1861, p. 517; *Douglass' Monthly*, May 1862, p. 655.

and his paper.[81] The Carpenters collected money and clothing to send to groups in the US, and organized lectures to stir public opinion.[82] Demonstrating the influence of *Douglass' Monthly* in transatlantic antislavery circles, an editorial in relation to a Dublin address in 1862 caused the Irish abolitionist John Elliot Cairnes to immediately write the periodical to explain that his remarks had been misconstrued.[83]

Therefore, Douglass's decision to cease publication of his newspaper during the war infuriated Crofts, who had advised against it. She wrote: "Our English friends have so much the notion that they now can do little or nothing more to aid the cause of the slave. Your paper kept them alive & placed yourself before them & your work also."[84] The distance, together with the lack of up-to-date news, threatened her efforts at raising support for Douglass and the antislavery cause as a whole. Similarly, when Mary Carpenter enclosed a cheque for Douglass, she indicated she had hoped for a larger sum but bluntly wrote that "since your paper has been given up I have not known exactly how to ask people for money! One wants something definite to ask for when we appeal to strangers, or those who don't know you personally . . . [they] cannot be expected to feel the same entire confidence that we do ourselves – that helping <u>you</u> in any way must be helping the cause of your people."[85]

Nevertheless, Crofts continued to send extracts of Douglass's letters to the local press, circulating them amongst her friends as a substitute for the paper. The close bonds of friendship meant he was perhaps more candid with her about the failures of the war and his own wavering strength: in August 1864, he wrote, "my patience and faith are not very strong now." Lincoln's criminal refusal to discuss Black suffrage, the treatment of African American soldiers, the lack of equal pay, the refusal to exchange prisoners, and lives "slaughtered in cold blood, although the president has repeatedly promised thus to protect the lives of his coloured soldiers, have worn my patience quite threadbare." Considering Douglass's unrelenting activism, together with the fact that two of his sons fought bravely for the Union, "you can easily imagine that my life during all this war has been an anxious one . . . there is no rest for my spirit amid this terrible strife."[86] Similarly, in a letter reprinted in this volume from February 1865, Douglass admitted that "time and toil begin (in spite

---

81   Julia Griffiths Crofts to Frederick Douglass, 16 January 1862 and 27 March 1862, FDP Digital Collection, Library of Congress.

82   Mary Carpenter to Frederick Douglass, 25? March 1865, FDP Digital Collection, Library of Congress.

83   McKivigan, *Douglass Papers—Series Three: Vol. 2*, pp. 379–81.

84   Julia Griffiths Crofts to Frederick Douglass, 19 August 1864, FDP Digital Collection, Library of Congress; McKivigan, *Douglass Papers—Series Three: Vol. 2*, pp. 447–52.

85   Mary Carpenter to Frederick Douglass, 19 February 1864, FDP Digital Collection, Library of Congress.

86   *The Caledonian Mercury*, 22 January 1864, p. 3; *Kendal Mercury*, 30 January 1864, p. 3. Other letters include *The Leeds Mercury*, 17 August 1864, p. 6; *The Derby Mercury*, 24 August 1864, p. 5.

of my determination to be young) to leave their marks upon me." The "constant traveling" was "enough to wear an iron constitution" and those who began speaking decades before the war had ceased altogether, or spoke only sporadically. Although he was resolved to "hold out until the jubilee," where he hoped "to spend what shall remain to me of life in a quiet equal to the storms through which I have passed," the harsh reality of segregation and lynching would force him to continue such exhausting activism beyond the Civil War.[87]

Concerned for his physical and mental wellbeing, Crofts wrote of her sadness that he could "rest so little" and "the perpetual wear & tear you must have."[88] She reassured Douglass of their friendship and was desperate to see him again, particularly after one letter which contained a "few words of despondency . . . I grieve for you & with you." She hoped her words gave him strength through the trials he suffered in the US and wanted to help as much as possible to share that burden with him: while she admitted that "my heart completely sickens when I think of past disappointment of [African American] hopes," she urged him to have faith in God to strengthen his resolve.[89] While others afforded their bodies rest with time or old age, Douglass pushed forward, ever sharing his testimony and sacrificing the ever elusive "rest" for his spirit.

---

87 *The Leeds Mercury*, 2 February 1865, p. 4.
88 Julia Griffiths Crofts to Frederick Douglass, 10 December 1866, FDP Digital Collection, Library of Congress.
89 Julia Griffiths Crofts to Frederick Douglass, 16 July 1866, FDP Digital Collection, Library of Congress.

Chapter 3

"For the Spiritual Emancipation of All": 1870–1895

Throughout the 1870s, the British press reported on Douglass's travels, his notable speeches, his political appointments, his support of President Grant's re-election in 1872, and his employment as Marshal of the District of Columbia in 1877.[1] Others published his opinions on events throughout the decade, with Julia Griffiths Crofts once again sharing his literary work with her contacts at *The Leeds Mercury*: such editorials included his controversial opposition to the "colored exodus," where he urged African Americans "to bide [their] time and wait, in the full assurance that time and events will sooner or later establish [their] rights in the South upon enduring foundations."[2]

In April 1881, Douglass signed a contract with the Park Publishing Company in Hartford, Connecticut for his third autobiography, *Life and Times*.[3] Douglass and other abolitionists who had spent decades of their life fighting for freedom and equality were devastated by rising racial violence, lynching, and the popularity of Lost Cause mythology, and wanted to issue a corrective to white supremacist narratives. William Still wrote that "the future looks very dark to me for the colored man both North + South" and used the publication of his book on the Underground Railroad to remind the public of the sacrifices African Americans had made for their country. The memories of abolition were fading with each passing generation and Douglass

---

1   For example, *The Dundee Courier and Argus*, 19 March 1871, p. 3; *The Standard*, 4 May 1871, p. 5; *The Luton Times and Dunstable Herald*, 18 May 1872, p. 4; *Lloyd's Weekly London Newspaper*, 11 August 1872, p. 12; *The Manchester Evening News*, 23 August 1872, p. 2; *The Liverpool Mercury*, 19 March 1877, p. 7; *The Morning Post*, 19 March 1877, p. 5; *The Birmingham Daily Post*, 23 March 1877, p. 8; and *The Leeds Mercury*, 23 March 1877, p. 4.

2   *The Leeds Mercury*, 3 June 1879, p. 6; Mary Carpenter to Frederick Douglass, 24 July 1879, FDP Digital Collection, Library of Congress.

3   McElrath and Crisler, "Note," in McKivigan, *Douglass Papers—Series Two: Vol. 3*, pp. 485–90.

wanted his autobiography to inspire younger generations and raise their aspirations; he was living proof of their capacity and capability to challenge racism. The book highlighted significant milestones in his life, encouraging others to follow in his footsteps and to bear the torch of freedom and progress. He made several editorial changes – particularly concerning previous descriptions of his mother, his escape from slavery, and the abolitionist movement – but struggled to reflect on decades of exhausting activism with the shattering reality that equality and social justice for African Americans had not yet been won.[4]

Unfortunately for Douglass, the editing and publishing process proved deeply frustrating, as the Park Company edited key sections, neglected to correct errors in the text, and included racist images he had not sanctioned. Later that year, he wrote that the Company had "marred and spoiled my work entirely" and pressed them to issue an edition "without illustrations, for Northern circulation." Their previous agreement did not give the Company a right to "load the book with all manner of coarse and shocking wood cuts, such as may be found in [the] news papers of the day." Some of these errors were corrected in later editions, but many of the illustrations remained.[5] Douglass detested them, as they jarred with his hopes for the book to act as a pillar of anti-racism. His life story represented a challenge to the struggles that had blighted his entire life, and the inclusion of such racist imagery alongside such trials and victories was contradictory and insulting. Regardless of Douglass's criticisms, the book sold 2,500 copies by April 1882, but soon the Company complained that "your book does not sell quite as well as expected, for the simple reason that the interest in the old days of slavery is not as great as we expected."[6] While Douglass and other survivors could not forget or relinquish their traumatic memories of slavery, the fight for abolition and the Civil War were fading memories for the majority of white Americans.

British social reformer John Lobb was keen to republish Douglass's book as a separate English edition. Lobb began his career as a lay preacher but swiftly recognized his talent for editorship; he worked with *The Christian Age* from 1872, and between 1880 and 1885 increased its circulation from 5,000 to 80,000 a week. He was instrumental in organizing Josiah Henson's visit to Britain in 1876 and republished his slave narrative; translated into twelve languages, the edition, together with a children's version of his story, sold a phenomenal 250,000 copies.[7] Lobb hoped to replicate this success. He had reportedly seen a copy of the autobiography and planned to publish

4 Jeffrey, *Abolitionists Remember*, pp. 65–67; 168–73; Bernier, "'His Complete History?'" See also Levine, *The Lives of Frederick Douglass*.
5 McElrath and Crisler, "Note."
6 Jeffrey, *Abolitionists Remember*, pp. 168–73.
7 Lobb, *Talks with the Dead*, p. 2. See Murray, *Advocates of Freedom*, pp. 350–51.

Figure 3.1 Frederick Douglass (ed. John Lobb), *Life and Times of Frederick Douglass* (London: Christian Age, 1882). British Library.

it without Douglass's immediate consent: in a somewhat hasty move, he must have informed a friendly newspaper correspondent, as an article appeared in the London *Morning Post* as early as December 1881 stating that Lobb "has in the press, 'The Life and Times of Frederick Douglass,' containing his early life as a slave, his escape from bondage, and his complete history to the present time . . . with many other interesting and important facts in his most eventful life."[8]

Perhaps Lobb finally decided to inform Douglass of his intentions, for it was not until February 1882 that he cabled him and wrote "permit me to republish your Life."[9] A month later, Lobb admitted in a private communication that he had not realized a Park Publishing Company edition existed on the market, which had reached out to other British publishers. Without asking their permission – or, more importantly, Douglass's – he continued with his own version: "in view of the advance stage of my work, which I commensed in December 1881 I resolved to complete it. Wishful also, that my edition should prove to be a success, the Rt Hon John Bright MP, kindly undertook to read the proof sheets." Considering Bright's introduction "and the power I may bring to bear from the influences of my two weekly journals, I largely trust, the work finding a sale." Somewhere along this protracted and restrictive process, Douglass must have acquiesced (which would have reminded him of the racial patronization and limiting nature of the white abolitionist movement), because Lobb thanked him for a list of corrections from the "American Edition." More alarmingly still, Lobb had apparently "anticipated a considerable number of them, when correcting my proofs. And, such as are 'too late' for correcting, are not at all likely to dishonour your work. I venture to believe, you will also be pleased, with the 'get-up.'" Whether all the corrections Douglass proposed aligned with Lobb's list of errors is unknown, but considering Lobb's heavy-handed editorial practice with Henson's work, it seems safe to say numerous changes were made according to Lobb's vision, where he reframed Douglass's literary testimony and tethered it to his, or a *British*, notion of reality. Lobb begged Douglass to come to England and promote the work: "It would do you good and my best services shall be at your call, in taking care of you!"[10] White reformers had performed paternalist acts in their capacity as amanuenses during the antebellum era, but Lobb extended this to the 1880s, and his editorship without Douglass's express permission reeked of white control over Black texts and also Black bodies on lecturing tours.[11] The alteration of Douglass's literary testimony smacked of racial paternalism, and was the antithesis of what he had originally wanted to achieve with his book. When

---

8   *The Morning Post*, 28 December 1881, p. 7.
9   John Lobb to Frederick Douglass, 20 February 1882, FDP Digital Collection, Library of Congress.
10 John Lobb to Frederick Douglass, 15 March 1882, FDP Digital Collection, Library of Congress.
11 McKivigan (ed.), *Douglass Papers—Series Two: Vol. 3*, p. 492.

the Lobb edition was eventually published in 1882, the Park Publishing Company raised the issue with Douglass, as they had hoped or already entered into a contract with a British publisher. This placed the Company in a difficult position wherein they had to grovel to the British publisher and ask for the books to be returned or request they sell them at a cheaper price.[12]

Lobb's book contained numerous changes, including the English spelling of certain words, altered punctuation, the removal of names Britons would find unfamiliar, and the deletion of an entire paragraph concerning a pro-slavery Englishman, as well as several uncorrected mistakes from the Park Publishing Company's edition.[13] Possibly the worst editorial crimes appeared on the front cover itself. Lobb changed the title completely and abbreviated the work to *Life and Times of Frederick Douglass: From 1817–1882*, but shortened the name to "Fredk." The image accompanying it would have incensed Douglass, too. The cover contained an illustration from the American version, of Douglass bowing his head over Colonel Lloyd's grave, depicted in gilded lines and lettering. The image proved representative of post-Civil War reunion romanticism, rather than the heroic radicalism present within the book's pages.[14] Considering Douglass's dislike of the reconciliation narrative so present after his meeting with Thomas Auld in 1877, it is no surprise that he detested it. As Robert S. Levine notes, the image was "deferential," and instead of "worshipping the former masters," Douglass wanted "to emphasize the enormous historical and social changes that undid the power of the masters," and he refused to sanction the image in further American printings.[15]

Additionally, Lobb made several changes to the illustrations within the main text itself. He included thirteen images, which differed significantly from those in its American counterpart. While he kept Douglass's frontispiece and nine other illustrations from the original, he added four new ones, including portraits of Harriet Beecher Stowe and Thomas Clarkson (two abolitionists well known in Britain), a portrait of President Garfield, and a view of Harpers Ferry in connection with John Brown's rebellion. He removed several illustrations from Douglass's early life, which included the "last time he saw his mother"; Sophia Auld teaching him to read; an illustration with Sandy Jenkins; "driven to jail for running away"; New Bedford; the mob in Indiana; portraits of Wendell Phillips and Charles Sumner, and of Douglass as commissioner to Santo Domingo. The concentration on political appointments

---

12 McElrath and Crisler, "Note," pp. 490–92.
13 Ibid.
14 Frederick Douglass, *The Life and Times of Frederick Douglass*, ed. John Lobb (London: Christian Age, 1882).
15 Levine, *The Lives of Frederick Douglass*, pp. 270–84; Bernier, "'His Complete History,'" pp. 595–610.

and known associates instead of a focus on Douglass's early enslaved life is significant in order to represent his transition from "slave" to elder statesman and "freeman."[16]

Lobb also restructured the appendix. In the American edition, the speech dedicated to President Lincoln at the Freedmen's Monument came before a West India Emancipation lecture from 1880, the latter designed as a transatlantic gesture to British friends and abolitionists. In Lobb's version, the Emancipation speech was presented first to further entice British readers, with the introduction from the American edition – written by Reverend George Ruffin – placed next, due to Bright's preface at the beginning. Lobb then added another appendix from a well-known and respected British minster, Reverend David Thomas, who had met Douglass in 1846 when the latter had spoken at the pulpit of his church in Stockwell, London. Thomas wrote that the book was symbolic of Douglass's legacy and acted as a living thing that transcended death and time: it "is a kind of incarnation of himself, a body in which he lives and works, long after the brain that thought it and the pen that wrote it have mouldered into dust. In it may be seen, not merely his passing opinions and floating feelings, but his thinking intellect and throbbing heart." The speech that Thomas had once witnessed at his church "gave me an impression which continues fresh to this hour, not only of his unique history, but of his extraordinary ability and genius. In memory I see him now as he appeared on the platform some thirty-six years ago." He continued:

> He was then a runaway slave. In stature tall, and somewhat attenuated, with a head indicative of large brain force, his dark countenance radiating with humour and genius, his large eyes, now flashing with the fire of indignation against tyranny, and now beaming with tender sympathy for his oppressed race . . . As an *orator* I have never heard his superior from that day to this. His voice was clear and strong, capable of every modulation, and of conveying all classes of sentiment, from the most terrific to the most gentle. His attitudes were natural, and therefore electrically commanding. He dramatised those awful memories of wrong that were at that time burning in his soul . . . To me, the book itself supplies the interest of "*Uncle Tom's Cabin*," and recalls tragic adventures equal to the boldest creations of romance.[17]

Thomas was inspired by Douglass's oratory, and had clearly never forgotten the experience. Tapping into old abolitionist and paternalistic stereotypes, he charted Douglass's journey from slave to free man, highlighting the eloquence and extraordinary "natural"

---

16 Douglass, *Life and Times* (1882).
17 Ibid. pp. 452–56.

abilities that he brought forth on both sides of the Atlantic. Phrenology was employed here to indicate Douglass's superior intellectual abilities, as well the engagement of minstrelesque language when pointing to his "dark countenance" alongside remarks of his humour. As most reformers were prone to do, he compared the work to Stowe's fictional book, and urged readers of antislavery inclination or those who were moved by her words to invest time in Douglass's own living memories. His life almost read like a romantic fiction, such were his achievements; and his testimony was supposed to authenticate Stowe's work, rather than the other way around.

As a last and final insult, Lobb commandeered the last two pages, where he placed adverts for *his* own books. This included the revised edition of Josiah Henson's *Uncle Tom's Story of His Slave Life* and a children's version of the book, *The Young People's Illustrated Edition of Uncle Tom's Story of His Life*. Further adverts also pointed to Lobb's journals, *The Christian Age* and *The Daisy*.[18]

Despite a transatlantic focus and readership, Lobb seemed to have some of the same problems as the Park Company did in publishing the book. In September 1882, Lobb wrote to Douglass and enclosed $72.52 from the sale of nine hundred copies out of a printed edition of one thousand. He stated he was only "able to effect the aforenamed sale, by extensive advertising," complicated by the fact that "your American edition has been extensively published through our London Booksellers." Despite this, he contemplated "binding up another thousand in a <u>cheaper form</u>. I have received some splendid reviews of the Life, from the sixty or seventy copies which were sent out."[19]

The majority of these reviews concentrated on Bright's preface and quoted how Douglass's life story would "stimulate the individual to noble effort and to virtue, whilst it will act as a lesson and a warning to every nation whose policy is based upon injustice and wrong."[20] In the *Paisley and Renfrewshire Gazette*, one correspondent pointed to the "effect produced" by Douglass in 1846, noting that "he was listened to with rapt attention by a crowded audience throughout the country, as in burning words he told the story of his wrongs and pleaded the cause of the coloured people."[21] Another noted that the book was "valuable" and required reading, but

> Had this deeply interesting and pathetic autobiography appeared twenty-five or thirty years ago it would perhaps have shared with "Uncle Tom's Cabin" almost exclusive popularity and been upon every library table throughout the length

---

18   Ibid. See Murray, *Advocates of Freedom*, pp. 350–51.

19   John Lobb to Frederick Douglass, 28 September 1882, FDP Digital Collection, Library of Congress.

20   *Lloyds Weekly London Newspaper*, 1 January 1882, p. 5; *The Western Daily Press*, 15 March 1882, p. 3; *Birmingham Daily Post*, 22 March 1882, p. 4.

21   *Paisley and Renfrewshire Gazette*, 13 May 1882, p. 5.

and breadth of the kingdom, in every hand, and the topic of every conversation. As it is, it seems almost to deal with "ancient history" and although not a single incident in it is exaggerated or invented, still its principal interest has for ever disappeared with the abolition of slavery. It is difficult now to realise that the awful events which Mr Douglas depicts so graphically really occurred but very recently, and that many who are still young can remember the time when men, women and children were sold.[22]

Completely dismissive of his earlier works – including My Bondage and My Freedom, which had been published three years after Stowe's novel – this assessment characterized Douglass as an elder statesman, someone to be trusted and revered despite the fact slavery was "ancient history." Barely twenty years had passed since abolition, but the subject was no longer relevant to the current generation as the era of such times had passed with, seemingly, no consequences. The review demonstrated how the memory of slavery and abolition had been corrupted in the British Isles, too, as well as highlighting the significant gap between those who experienced slavery, those who did not, and those who could easily romanticize it generations later as "the time when men, women and children were sold."[23]

Women and men who had been active agents in the transatlantic antislavery struggle, however, clamored to praise the work. Russell L. Carpenter suggested it to friends including the Quaker activist Catherine Impey,[24] and Henry Richardson recommended the book for his local subscription library in Newcastle and was pleased to see it there in September of that year.[25] Eliza Barlow read it with "the deepest interest" and ruminated on "how despicable those slaveholders were, & still more so the Overseers under them." Marveling at Douglass's meeting with Auld, she wrote "you little thought when in England that you wd ever go to see him or his Brother Hugh either!"[26]

When Mary Carpenter wrote to congratulate Douglass on the book, though, it was evident he had expressed his concerns to her. She assured him that even "if there are imperfections in the style of the 'get up' you may be sure that no one else will notice them as much as you do & the real value & interest of the book is not affected by them." She also dismissed concerns he had with the portrait: "But do you call the likeness on the frontispiece 'a miserable caricature' of your face? I wish

---

22   *The Morning Post*, 8 April 1882, p. 3.

23   Ibid. See Blight, *Race and Reunion*.

24   Russell L. Carpenter to Frederick Douglass, 19 May 1883, FDP Digital Collection, Library of Congress.

25   Henry Richardson to Frederick Douglass, 27 September 1882, FDP Digital Collection, Library of Congress.

26   Eliza Barlow to Frederick Douglass, 19 April (undated), FDP Digital Collection, Library of Congress.

you would let us see what your face is like, we cannot judge how far this is correct – without comparing it with the original. I call it a very refined thoughtful face." Oblivious to Douglass's hatred of any image that betrayed racialized characterization of his own physiognomy, together with his constant battles against it on both sides of the Atlantic, Carpenter pointed to the other illustrations in the book in an attempt to cheer him and wrote "the woodcuts on page 23 & 70, & those on p. 434 & 454, I like very much."[27]

Similarly, Ellen Richardson believed the book was "a succinct and <u>valuable</u> record of the stirring events connected with slavery," and, like Carpenter, could see no problems with the portrait save its association with age: "I must tell thee when I first opened the book and gazed on the frontispage I could but involuntarily exclaim 'Oh! such a change truly in Fredk Douglass . . . so venerable and <u>so aged</u>. No wonder after <u>such a life</u>.'" She, too, was insentient of the decades-long fight in which Douglass had been engaged to preserve his own imagery, memories, and testimony. Like numerous contemporary white reformers, she desired an illustration of his meeting with Thomas Auld, to capture a moment that symbolized no greater change than from the horrors of slavery to the present moment.[28] The book caused Richardson to reflect on her own "aged" appearance and her role within the movement. In previous letters, she had remarked on how even her own nephew had never heard of William Lloyd Garrison, and saw the book as a bridge between old and new generations: "for the <u>effects</u> of slavery must be felt for many generations to come especially in a land like yours." The book served as a memento, too, as Richardson herself knew what it was to have "our heartstrings wrung with the tales of horrors time after time and have <u>lived through</u> the events as they occurred."[29] Richardson would also praise Douglass's 1892 revised edition, for such a life as his, she wrote, "should have an ending as well as a beginning."[30]

Douglass's Third Visit to the British Isles (1886–1887)

Throughout the 1880s, British friends asked after Douglass's family, exchanged photographs of each other, and continued to send financial assistance to freedmen or

---

27 Mary Carpenter to Frederick Douglass, 27 February 1882, FDP Digital Collection, Library of Congress. See also Bernier, "'His Complete History?'"
28 Ellen Richardson to Frederick Douglass, 14 November 1882, FDP Digital Collection, Library of Congress.
29 Ellen Richardson to Frederick Douglass, 14 November 1882, FDP Digital Collection, Library of Congress. She also mentions this in an undated letter: Richardson to Douglass, FDP Digital Collection, Library of Congress.
30 Ellen Richardson to Frederick Douglass, 22 December 1892, FDP Digital Collection, Library of Congress.

"destitute colored people" in the United States.[31] Others reminisced about the past. In 1881, Eliza Barlow wrote of the "social & interesting times we had, & what exciting doings were then enacted . . . what noble meetings were held in the Music Hall!!"[32] Mary Carpenter invited Douglass to Bridport many times and wrote "I feel a longing to draw closer the ties that are still unbroken."[33] It is uncertain whether Carpenter extended the invitation to Anna Murray Douglass, as she is rarely (if ever) mentioned, but when tragedy struck the Douglass household with her death, British friends immediately penned letters to express their sympathy. Barlow wrote that "she will be much missed" and hoped "she did not much suffer."[34] Ellen Richardson sent her condolences and wrote that it "must be a great comfort" that Douglass had made her life so full with grandchildren after the trials of their earlier lives.[35] Briefly, Douglass considered traveling to Europe, but "felt it too late in life to break up my home and become a wanderer." He could not abandon his grandchildren, nor the cause he had served for decades.[36]

After Douglass's second marriage to Helen Pitts in 1884, an opportunity presented itself to visit Europe for an extended honeymoon. Ellen Richardson wrote she would be "glad to welcome thee once more in Newcastle and <u>with thy wife by thy side</u>. We have known thee in <u>sorrow</u> and <u>sadness</u> let us see the <u>lighter</u> side," while there was still time left.[37] Douglass and his wife planned a visit beyond the usual three-month tour that many Americans embarked upon, perhaps unsurprising given his absence of twenty-six years from warm and cherished friends.[38] As he later wrote: "My visit to England was in some respects sentimental. I wanted to see the

---

31 Russell L. Carpenter to Frederick Douglass, 27 January 1868, FDP Digital Collection, Library of Congress; Russell L. Carpenter to Frederick Douglass, 26 March 1877, FDP Digital Collection, Library of Congress; Mary Carpenter to Frederick Douglass, 12 April 1880, FDP Digital Collection, Library of Congress.

32 Eliza Barlow to Frederick Douglass, 7 June 1881, FDP Digital Collection, Library of Congress.

33 Mary Carpenter to Frederick Douglass, 5 June 1877, FDP Digital Collection, Library of Congress. See also Mary Carpenter to Frederick Douglass, 16 October 1875, FDP Digital Collection, Library of Congress; Mary Carpenter to Frederick Douglass, 29 April 1876, FDP Digital Collection, Library of Congress; Mary Carpenter to Frederick Douglass, 16 May 1879, FDP Digital Collection, Library of Congress.

34 Eliza Barlow to Frederick Douglass, 21 August 1882, FDP Digital Collection, Library of Congress.

35 Ellen Richardson to Frederick Douglass, May/August 1882 (?), FDP Digital Collection, Library of Congress.

36 Frederick Douglass to Sara Jane Lippincott, 9 October 1882. Frederick Douglass Papers, University of Rochester Project.

37 Ellen Richardson to Frederick Douglass, 2 November 1885, FDP Digital Collection, Library of Congress.

38 Fought, *Women in the World of Frederick Douglass*, p. 255.

faces and press the hands of some of the dear friends and acquaintances I met there over 40 years ago . . . Neither they nor I were as young and strong as when we met so long ago."[39]

On 14 September 1886, the couple boarded the *City of Rome* steamer for their "long desired and long meditated voyage at sea." Douglass had hoped to pass the voyage in relative quiet without being recognized, but he was instantly reintroduced to Reverend Herman Wayland, who had met him some years before, and to an American who had heard Douglass speak in Rochester "and had not forgotten the impression." He wrote in his diary with a hint of regret that the "voyage will thus evidently not be one of <u>solitude</u>."[40] Worse still, within a few days Douglass was asked to give an address, and Helen Pitts Douglass wrote in her diary that "there was a general desire to hear him," although it made her husband "uncomfortable as he fears imposing himself upon an audience. Nonsense! They need not come if they do not want to."[41]

In a marked change from the circumstances of his first voyage in 1845, Douglass was unanimously voted to speak, as no mob or death threats awaited him. Privately, he wrote that he had "hoped to escape this infliction but is easier in such cases to comply than to refuse so I am booked for an address on Monday." His hopes for a restful journey were cast aside; he was "dreading it," considering the "arrangement to do so was entirely unsought and even regretted by me. Yet I have found it impossible to say no to an invitation so polite and pressing. I hardly know what I shall manage to say to such an audience."[42] On 21 September, Douglass addressed the passengers and, according to Helen, it "was over before any one was ready for him to stop. He could have spoken an hour to their satisfaction but for himself he was saved that effort."[43] Unprepared and unwilling to give a speech, his celebrity had become almost a chore; this was an older Douglass, an activist whose impending trip would cause him to reflect on his own mortality, lost friends, and his desire to rest. In 1845, he had sailed to Britain in part for repose, although the trip provided exactly the opposite. Decades later, he desperately desired a temporary freedom from his lifelong activism, as he knew that however long the trip might be, he would return to an unrelenting toil of work.

---

39   Frederick Douglass, "A Sentimental Visit to England," *Commonwealth*, 1 October 1887, FDP Digital Collection, Library of Congress.

40   Frederick Douglass, 15 September 1886, in Douglass, *Diary of Europe and Africa 1886–1887*, FDP Digital Collection, Library of Congress. His 1880s visit is covered in Foner, *Frederick Douglass*; Quarles, *Frederick Douglass*; Chaffin, *Giant's Causeway*; Fought, *Women in the World of Frederick Douglass*; Fenton, *"I was Transformed"*; and Blight, *Frederick Douglass: Prophet of Freedom*.

41   Helen Pitts Douglass Diary, 1886, FDP Digital Collection, Library of Congress.

42   Frederick Douglass, 16–19 September 1886, in *Diary of Europe and Africa 1886–1887*.

43   Helen Pitts Douglass Diary, 1886, FDP Digital Collection, Library of Congress.

On 24 September, the Douglasses landed at Liverpool. Over the course of a week, the couple attended exhibitions, visited libraries and museums, and took day trips to its environs, including the Roman town of Chester. On the first of October, the couple left Liverpool to stay at the home of Julia Griffiths Crofts in St. Neots, and were met there "with open arms." Douglass visited Crofts' school, where he addressed the children "and a few invited friends," and gave a short lecture at the Corn Exchange. The stay with Julia was mainly a restful one, though. The trio visited Cambridge, traveled to London, relaxed on a boat belonging to Croft's neighbor, and toured local villages like Buckden.[44]

Crofts, as indefatigable and committed to the cause as always, likely helped organize the Corn Exchange meeting but was subsequently ignored in local press coverage. In anticipation of the lecture, the *St. Neots Advertiser* described Douglass as "fearless, eloquent and devoted" to antislavery and, amidst the previous conflict, as having leapt "to the front, and by voice and pen, by journalism and by powerful platform oratory,

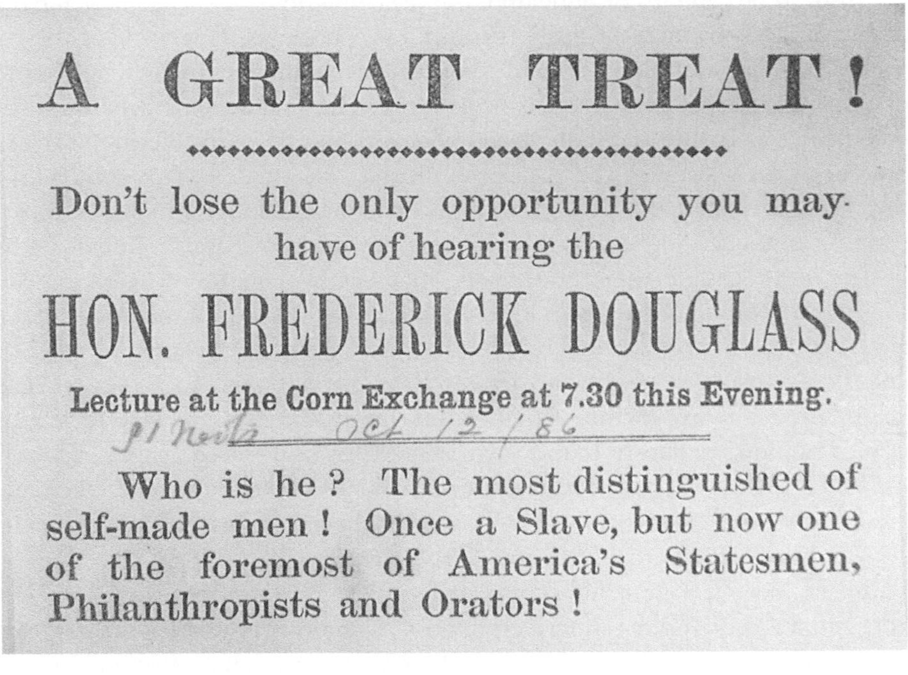
A GREAT TREAT!

Don't lose the only opportunity you may have of hearing the

HON. FREDERICK DOUGLASS

Lecture at the Corn Exchange at 7.30 this Evening.

St Neots Oct 12/86

Who is he? The most distinguished of self-made men! Once a Slave, but now one of the foremost of America's Statesmen, Philanthropists and Orators!

Figure 3.2 Ticket to Frederick Douglass's Lecture, St. Neots, Cambridgeshire (St Ives Museum, Huntingdon).

44 Helen Pitts Douglass Diary, 1886, FDP Digital Collection, Library of Congress; Fenton, "*I was Transformed,*" p. 222.

dragged into the light of day the vices and crimes of the abominable system of American slavery." Those who had heard of Douglass "will hail with unmixed pleasure this opportunity of heartily welcoming and hearing for themselves this celebrated veteran philanthropist, statesman and orator from America."[45]

Despite the poor weather on the night of the 12th, "an excellent company assembled" to hear Douglass speak and "give some of his 'Recollections of the Anti-Slavery Conflict in America'" with the proceeds going to the local Wesleyan church. Douglass spoke for an hour and a quarter, and while the local correspondent noted "he was suffering from a severe cold . . . his utterance was distinct and his language eloquent." He had clearly prepared some text to read but had to abandon this midway through the speech, as "the cold had affected his vision, and he should only give them a talk." Lecturing extemporaneously, unable to read his notes, he remarked that his enslavement, "terrible as it was, had now lost much of its horrors, and slept in his memory like the dim outlines of a half forgotten dream." He outlined his escape and his role in the antislavery movement; his enslaver "began to take steps to arrest him, so he came to old England, to Newcastle-on-Tyne." Douglass employed strategic anglophilia here to praise Britain and specifically Newcastle as the only legitimate safe haven for him, a fact he continued to reinforce throughout his trip as a scene of site-specific performance. Reflecting on his life, he remarked how he had visited first as a fugitive, secondly as an exile, and "thirdly by the blessing of God he had come as an acknowledged American citizen." He alluded to his political roles and to "an excellent lady" in St. Neots who had raised funds for fugitives. Most of the meeting, though, concerned the present condition of African Americans and how they were "emancipated under very unfavourable conditions." Committed to a full emancipation to the last, Douglass left his audience no room for refutation when he concluded that while slavery had been abolished, "its incidences, its consequences must follow it." As he had done in Britain and Ireland since 1845, Douglass educated predominantly white audiences on slavery and its brutal legacies. Despite his overwhelming exhaustion and the constant battle he faced against racism, he nourished a hope – expressed in his testimony here that "the Federal Government was not strong enough there to entirely protect them from persecution" – that one day it would be entirely removed from US soil.[46]

After St. Neots, the couple then traveled to Bridport to stay with Russell and Mary Carpenter, who organized a short lecture on 15 October. In the speech (reprinted in this volume), Douglass concentrated on the progress African Americans had made and the stark difference in his own life compared to the moment when, in 1846, he

---

45   *St. Neots Advertiser*, 9 October 1886, p. 1. Thank you to Liz Davies for sending me this.
46   *St. Neots Advertiser*, 16 October 1886, p. 3. Thank you to Liz Davies for sending me this.

had first addressed a Bridport audience. He recounted stories about his first visit to England, the purchase of his legal freedom, and his second visit in 1859.[47]

Douglass used a variety of mediums to share his testimony of rising racial violence. During a brief stop in London after his return from Bridport, he gave at least two interviews with the local press. A correspondent for *The Dundee Courier and Argus* wrote that he was "a heroic speciman of the coloured man, and although seventy years of age, he stands straight and stalwart" and "entertains high hopes of his race."[48] The longest and perhaps most revealing interview took place in London with a correspondent from the *Daily News*, published in this volume. It not only highlighted Douglass's special connection with Britain, but revealed a rare chink in his public performative armour: his melancholic depression at the entrenched racism in America threatened to overwhelm him. Ushered into the reading room of the Cannon Street Hotel, the correspondent was met with a man "whose name all England is familiar with." The correspondent noted that:

> Already the reverberations of the tremendous crash down of American slavery have died away in the far distance, and the chief actors in the terrible drama have become dim and distant figures in history . . . [However] To-day Frederick Douglass stands by universal consent the head and representative of his race in America. With a splendid physique, tall and powerfully built, the swarthy complexion of the mulatto, an abundant crop of negro hair white as snow, and features which, of the negro type, are nevertheless full of emotional fire and intellectual force, he looks every inch a man born for distinction . . . As the venerable negro chief sits and talks of this, and of the baronial splendour of the great slave-owner's establishment, one may almost fancy that even now his voice is tremulous, and that he is again imagining himself back in that Maryland plantation. It is strange, indeed to listen to such a voice, such words, to observe the gentle, dignified demeanour of the man, and to think of him as the slave who was beaten and starved, hired out like a horse and sold as chattel.[49]

The correspondent wrote about the encounter in a romantic and sentimental tone and painted Douglass as a hardened and battle-weary warrior, soldiering on against an overwhelming tide of racial prejudice. He was regarded as the "chief" or leader of the African American people: a physically and intellectually strong individual who did not have the supposedly typical "negro features" with which people might have become familiar through racialized imagery or minstrel shows. Aside from the

---

47 Fenton, "*I was Transformed*," pp. 222–24; *The Daily News*, 19 October 1886, p. 6.
48 *The Dundee Courier and Argus*, 20 October 1886, p. 3.
49 *The Daily News*, 21 October 1886, p. 3; Fenton, "*I was Transformed*," pp. 222–24.

physical description, which echoed those of the 1840s, the correspondent whimsically imagined Douglass dreaming of his plantation life, here without the violence or trauma about which he himself wrote. Instead, the correspondent referred to the "splendour" of the plantation, rather than the abuse that occurred within its walls. He displayed a sense of racially patronizing incredulity that a man such as Douglass could ever have been beaten and oppressed – as if he was too eloquent and dignified to ever "submit" to such cruel treatment.

Perhaps in anticipation of this, Douglass was at pains to highlight the difficult conditions Black Americans faced, considering "slavery is still a terrible reality" and emancipation had not yet been won. There was a melancholic tone to his attitude toward racism and segregation, and he could not "pretend to be satisfied" at the progress toward equality. While slavery had been abolished "in theory," racism was still "painfully manifest"; the rise of lynching and the convict lease system meant that "to the heart of a man like Frederick Douglass the process [of justice and progress] must no doubt appear painfully slow," for "his whole life is a battle with it." In an intimate moment, Helen Pitts Douglass gently reminded him of some of the progress made, particularly how he had been met with "kindness and courtesy" during their recent trip around the country. Both Pitts Douglass and Crofts were present at this interview, which indicated how their dedicated and unwavering support provided hope and positivity in a despairing moment.[50]

While in London, the couple explored the city through a tourist's eyes, visiting significant historical sites at a leisurely pace. They visited St. Paul's, the National Gallery, the British Museum, Madame Tussaud's, Westminster Abbey and the Tower of London.[51] While exploring the latter, Douglass made stinging rebukes against British imperialism: such a place, he noted, "with all its enginery of terror and death, stained by so many crimes" made it an odd choice for "the repository of the Crown Jewels" unless it was to "illustrate the motive, object and mainspring of many of the horrible crimes and the inhuman butcheries that have been there enacted, – for next to religion, nothing has given rise to more envy, ambition, treachery, cold-blooded crimes and brutal vengeance than the desire for these crowns, and the thirst for wealth and power represented by such crowns."[52] Although such comments were confined to his private diary, they revealed that Douglass was very much aware of the hypocrisy in Britain's conception of liberty – and that his speeches during the period 1845–47 represented a form of performative engagement which distinctly ignored such imperialist narratives to appeal to wider audiences.

---

50   *The Daily News*, 21 October 1886, p. 3.
51   Quarles, *Frederick Douglass*, p. 306.
52   Frederick Douglass, "My Trip Abroad," 1887, FDP Digital Collection, Library of Congress.

After spending some time in London, Bridport, and St. Neots, the Douglasses set off for the continent. As Leigh Fought notes, the couple "threw themselves into European culture and fashion" and crammed as many historic, religious, and cultural sites into their tour as possible. Pleased to report the absence of racism wherever he went, Douglass was keen to learn and witness the progress of other people of colour in Europe and in Egypt.[53] They traveled to Paris, visiting museums, art galleries, and monuments, including the National Bibliothèque, where Douglass enquired whether it contained any of his books, and "in a few minutes – it was a marvel how they could lay hands on it so soon – there was laid before me the book of my Bondage and My Freedom, and a little tract containing a letter of mine written in 1846 in reply to one by Dr. Samuel Hanson Cox." From there, they moved through France to Rome, where they visited St. Peter's Cathedral, the Forum, and the Coliseum, as well as calling on the sculptor Edmonia Lewis and the old Massachusetts sisters Sarah Parker Remond and Caroline Remond Putnam.[54]

The Douglasses moved on to Pompeii, the Amalfi Coast, and Naples. Douglass was invited to speak at a church where his "words of human brotherhood" were translated – a unique and site-specific performance where the barrier of language presented a completely different oratorical experience compared to his speeches at home or in the British Isles. Similarly, Douglass gave a short speech to the Sunday School of the United Presbyterian Church in Cairo and visited the Pyramids, Alexandria, and later, the Acropolis at Athens.[55] On 28 March, when the couple returned to Naples, a letter informed them that Helen Pitts Douglass's mother was ill. Both prepared to travel immediately, but upon learning that her mother's condition seemed to be stable the couple continued their trip, passing through Rome, Florence, and Venice.[56]

When they returned to England, however, Pitts Douglass was forced to travel to the US, as the condition of her mother had not improved. This left Douglass to visit friends alone. He wanted to see those who, "when I was a stranger, took me in; when I was an exile, sheltered me; when I was poor, helped me; and when I was a slave, ransomed me." Douglass met few of his original friends from the 1840s, many of whom had passed away, but instead met their children or grandchildren.[57] He was thankful to see the Richardson family in Newcastle, and those who had helped raise money for his ransom: "if I had no other compensation for my voyage across the sea, this would have been ample payment."[58]

---

53 Fought, *Women in the World of Frederick Douglass*, pp. 257–58.
54 Douglass, "My Trip Abroad"; Douglass, *Diary of Europe and Africa 1886–1887*.
55 Douglass, *Diary of Europe and Africa 1886–1887*.
56 Douglass, *Diary of Europe and Africa 1886–1887*.
57 Douglass, "My Trip Abroad."
58 Douglass, "A Sentimental Visit to England."

Despite his comparative lack of political engagements, Douglass's tour was somewhat exhausting. When in London, he had dinner with Margaret Bright Lucas, sister to John Bright; attended church to hear Charles H. Spurgeon speak; and met with Thomas Burt, who had arranged for him to see Prime Minister Gladstone in the House of Commons.[59] He visited Eliza Barlow in Carlisle, Eliza Wigham in Edinburgh, and Elizabeth Mawson in Newcastle, who would always cherish the memory of clasping his hand once again.[60] While in Edinburgh, Douglass visited the site of his former activism at Arthur's Seat, which had led to him nearly being arrested: "but the friendly grass of 40 years ago had obliterated all trace of the famous formula and my humiliation, as it has also happily blotted out all further need of that sentiment itself."[61]

In Newcastle, the local press reported that while he had been "quietly sojourning . . . among friends greatly beloved," he was invited to lay the foundation stone for the College of Science (coverage of the event is printed in this volume). For the few in the crowd who were old enough to remember, "his presence recalled a far-off time laden with controversies now settled for ever." According to the correspondent – who displayed an all-too-common ignorance of the legacies of slavery – "the foe he fought is vanquished, and peace now lies like a shaft of light across the sea."[62]

Douglass travelled once again briefly to St. Neots and Bridport and on his return stayed with the daughter of John Bright, Helen Priestman Bright Clark, in Street, where he was formally introduced to radical Quaker activist Catherine Impey. He made quite an impression on the young activist, whose powerful obituary printed in this volume gives an extraordinary insight into the "private" Douglass nearer the end of his life.[63] When he crossed over to Ireland, he stayed with the Wigham family in Dublin, but did not venture to Cork, Limerick, Waterford, or other towns where he had previously stayed, finding that for the most part his friends were now "all gone, and except some of their children, I was among strangers."[64] He did, however, visit Wilhelmina Webb in July 1887, timing his visit perfectly so the families would

59 Fenton, "I was Transformed," pp. 225–27.
60 Elizabeth Mawson to Frederick Douglass, 21 July 1887, FDP Digital Collection, Library of Congress; Fenton, "I was Transformed," pp. 225–27; Frederick Douglass to Helen Pitts Douglass, 28 June 1887, FDP Digital Collection, Library of Congress.
61 McKivigan, Douglass Papers—Series One: Vol. 5, pp. 268–73.
62 The Newcastle Daily Chronicle, 20 June 1887, p. 4; Fenton, "I was Transformed," pp. 225–27.
63 Fenton, "I was Transformed," pp. 229–31. Russell L. Carpenter arranged this meeting: see Carpenter to Frederick Douglass, 4 July 1887, FDP Digital Collection, Library of Congress; Catherine Impey to Frederick Douglass, 4 September 1888, FDP Digital Collection, Library of Congress; Catherine Impey to Frederick Douglass, 13 April 1889, FDP Digital Collection, Library of Congress.
64 Douglass, Life and Times (1892), pp. 674–80.

Figure 3.3 *Frederick Douglass in Ireland,* by Alice Shackleton. Maria Webb Scrapbook, Gilder Lehrman Collection, New York Historical Society.

not – as Webb described – "scatter for the holidays."[65] During his stay, he visited her sister Anna Webb Shackleton, Henry and Hannah Wigham, and Lydia Shackleton, and also reminisced with Susanna Fisher, who had previously lived in Limerick.[66] Reflecting on his trip, he marveled at the sights he had seen in Europe but regretfully wrote that "it has all come too late in life. I should have travelled thus when I was younger and my ambition for achievements was more vigorous." The melancholic tone implied an imagined alternative life, one in which he could have embarked upon such travels at leisure without pouring all his energies into an unceasing fight against slavery and its legacies.[67]

---

65 Wilhelmina Webb to Frederick Douglass 1887, 5 June (?), FDP Digital Collection, Library of Congress; Wilhelmina Webb to Frederick Douglass, 1 July 1887, FDP Digital Collection, Library of Congress.

66 Fenton, *Frederick Douglass In Ireland*, pp. 202–04.

67 Frederick Douglass to Amy Kirby Post, 10 June 1887, Post Family Papers, part of the Frederick Douglass Papers at the University of Rochester Project.

Douglass returned to the United States in early August 1887, and despite the short visit, Douglass's friends expressed their thanks and requested photographs of both him and Helen Pitts Douglass.[68] Deborah Webb wrote: "If you <u>can</u> spare a picture of yourself and Mrs Douglass, I shall let others see it besides our little household for instance our friends in Waterford and Cork who missed seeing you."[69] She wrote later to thank Douglass for the "beautiful picture . . . the photo is all that could be desired – I value it much." She noted he looked "a little sad," but was ultimately "pleased to see it, & many will be."[70] Alice Shackleton, too, enclosed copies of photographs she had taken when he visited: "I wish they were better especially the one of you by yourself but I can only hope you will some day let one have an opportunity of taking you again with Mrs Douglass and the violin too." She assured Douglass she thought of him often and hoped to see him once again.[71] When looking at an image of Douglass, Susanna Webb wondered that "sometimes it seems more like a dream than reality that you have been here – and that we have really and truly seen you again – and not very much changed at all. The hair white certainly and the figure stouter & less active but the same spirit of the man." Having a photograph of Douglass strengthened and sustained the bonds recently re-forged by his visit to Britain and Ireland, and Webb in particular treasured such a memento when combined with his own words on the back of the image, "truly yours always."[72]

Transatlantic abolitionists had always shared photographs of each other. Before 1865, activists had used photography as a weapon for reform, including images of scarred backs and Jonathan Walker's branded hand. Black abolitionists, too, shared daguerreotypes of Ellen Craft's disguise while escaping slavery, and Douglass himself orchestrated numerous photographs to counteract the racist portrayals of Black bodies in transatlantic society. Privately, abolitionists shared photographs of each other to reinforce social bonds, reflect on memories, or cherish friends and family members. In doing so, they built a transatlantic visual community where memories and past activism were archived in photographs.[73] Julia Griffiths Crofts cherished such bonds with her own family: some of the photographs she collected were for her stepchildren, for they were "starting books of their own for Cartes & I expect

---

68 Wilhelmina Webb to Frederick Douglass, 9? May 1887, FDP Digital Collection, Library of Congress; Ellen Richardson to Frederick Douglass, 14 September 1887, FDP Digital Collection, Library of Congress; Ellen Richardson had requested a photograph of Helen three years before: Richardson to Frederick Douglass, 2 November 1885, FDP Digital Collection, Library of Congress.

69 Deborah Webb to Frederick Douglass, 1 October 1887, FDP Digital Collection, Library of Congress.

70 Deborah Webb to Frederick Douglass, 30 June 1887, FDP Digital Collection, Library of Congress.

71 Alice Shackleton to Frederick Douglass, 8 August 1887, FDP Digital Collection, Library of Congress.

72 Susanna Webb to Frederick Douglass, 20 July 1888, FDP Digital Collection, Library of Congress.

73 Fox-Amato, *Exposing Slavery*, pp. 18–20; 165–75. See also Bernier, Trodd and Stauffer, *Picturing Frederick Douglass*; Bernier, "A Visual Call to Arms."

they will each want a likeness of the never forgotten 'Uncle Frederick.'"[74] In 1865, Mary Carpenter "was much pleased with the beautiful photograph of you wch you gave us, & wch hangs over the dining room chimney piece."[75] Carpenter refers here to a photograph taken in Glasgow, and potentially Douglass may also have had photographs taken in Edinburgh and Coventry, although none have yet been found.[76] Within these circles, photographs were used as mementos and tools to sustain the bonds of friendship over time. Their ownership and circulation were key to strengthening those ties: for those who missed Douglass in 1887, a photograph acted like a living object that served to help others imagine or re-enact shared scenes together. It was likely that Webb and her "friends" in the neighborhood used the photograph as a base to direct and focus their memories from his trip and keep his memory alive within family circles.

During the remaining eight years of Douglass's life, British correspondents wrote to share news of former abolitionists, their travels, political matters, family gossip, and recent meetings. Others expressed their sorrow at the death of grandchildren, illness, or difficult trials; they shared anxiety about the health of family members and the death of long-lasting friends. After Mary Carpenter lost her husband in 1892, a lifelong supporter of Douglass, she wrote of the depth of sorrow she experienced but promised to send a photograph in memory of him.[77]

British friends also entertained Douglass's friends and fellow activists. In 1893, Ida B. Wells visited Ellen Richardson, who marveled at her "unvarnished tale" of lynching.[78] Douglass himself corresponded with Wells during her visit to Britain in 1894, though the latter was deeply hurt by his coldness toward her journey in a

---

74 Julia Griffiths Crofts to Frederick Douglass, 10 December 1863, FDP Digital Collection, Library of Congress. See also Julia Griffiths Crofts to Frederick Douglass, 23 November 1864, FDP Digital Collection, Library of Congress.

75 Mary Carpenter to Frederick Douglass, 25? March 1865, FDP Digital Collection, Library of Congress.

76 William B. Hodgson to William Lloyd Garrison, 27 October 1846, BPLAC, identifier: lettertomy-fearfroohodg. Hodgson mentions a potential photograph with Douglass, Thompson, and Garrison in Scotland. Fenton, "I was Transformed" mentions one in Coventry (pp. 200–01) and Mary Carpenter discusses one in Glasgow (Carpenter to Frederick Douglass, 18 August 1871, FDP Digital Collection, Library of Congress).

77 Wilhelmina Webb to Frederick Douglass, 11 March 1888, FDP Digital Collection, Library of Congress; Ellen Richardson to Frederick Douglass, 7 August 1890, FDP Digital Collection, Library of Congress; Julia Griffiths Crofts to Frederick Douglass, 8 December 1892, FDP Digital Collection, Library of Congress; Mary Carpenter to Frederick Douglass, 18 March 1892, FDP Digital Collection, Library of Congress.

78 Ellen Richardson to Frederick Douglass, 29 May 1894, FDP Digital Collection, Library of Congress; Ellen Richardson to Frederick Douglass, 22 April 1893, FDP Digital Collection, Library of Congress.

rather lacklustre testimonial he wrote for her character.[79] Douglass had been suspicious of Wells's motives in traveling to the British Isles, but Wells demonstrated her radical and unceasing commitment to the cause in a series of stinging letters that betrayed the pain and anger she felt. In an attempt to repair some of the damage, Douglass sent letters to numerous friends and reformers in support of her mission.[80] In October that year, Douglass called on his British friends once again to welcome Hallie Quinn Brown from Wilberforce College, who – among other things – desired to organize a library named after him. Requesting help from the forty-years-strong friendship network, he was in no doubt that they would "gladly help in this effort to aid my people." Their continued service, together with their "effective testimony against the lawless violence and persecution to which our people have been subjected," reflected his sincerity and deep connection to his British friends and to the public.[81]

His friends were only too glad to oblige and flexed the muscles of transatlantic print culture once again. They copied extracts from his speeches or letters and sent them to friendly publications, circulated them amongst friends and family, and joined with him in support of fellow African Americans and in their horror toward lynching and racial violence. In 1888, Susanna Webb read one of Douglass's speeches that had been circulated around her friends and perused it "with deep interest and painful sympathy."[82] Ellen Richardson thanked Douglass for sending two speeches and noted that she had sent extracts to the local *Chronicle* newspaper. Although "it is not all I could have wished [it was] better than nothing," since "it seems to be that the very important information you give in that speech should have a wide range on both sides [of] the Atlantic."[83] Both women urged him to send more newspapers containing his speeches whenever he could, another link in the transatlantic chain that grew stronger the more such materials were exchanged.

The publication of Douglass's pamphlet *Lessons of the Hour* in 1894 also led to renewed correspondence. Mary Carpenter urged Douglass to send it to the English press and volunteered to contact certain editors around the country. She asked for

79 Ida B. Wells to Frederick Douglass, 6 April 1894, FDP Digital Collection, Library of Congress. See also Murray, *Advocates of Freedom*; Fought, *Women in the World of Frederick Douglass*.

80 Frederick Douglass to Ida B. Wells, 27 March 1894, FDP Digital Collection, Library of Congress; Ida B. Wells to Frederick Douglass, 6 April 1894, FDP Digital Collection, Library of Congress; Frederick Douglass to Helen P. B. Clark, 18 July 1894, FDP Digital Collection, Library of Congress; Frederick Douglass to Charles F. Aked, 22 May 1894, FDP Digital Collection, Library of Congress.

81 Frederick Douglass, "To my British Friends," 6 October 1894, FDP Digital Collection, Library of Congress.

82 Susanna Webb to Frederick Douglass, 20 July 1888, FDP Digital Collection, Library of Congress; Mary Carpenter to Frederick Douglass, 8 December 1892, FDP Digital Collection, Library of Congress.

83 Ellen Richardson to Frederick Douglass, 17 May 1888, FDP Digital Collection, Library of Congress.

at least six copies, and vowed to "try to get it noticed in as many as I can – & at all events I can make them useful." A family friend worked for *The Times*, and as a result she "may be able to get it noticed there – also I shall try the Spectator & Daily News & Graphic as it ought to be known in England."[84] Later in the year, she wrote to request more copies for a forthcoming Unitarian meeting in Lancashire, where she hoped to send it to as many ministers as possible, so they would have "no excuse for ignorance in the matter!"[85]

Of Douglass's friends, Ellen Richardson and Julia Griffiths Crofts were among the few who remained deeply concerned about Douglass's physical and mental well-being in the wake of such rising violence. Richardson bemoaned the pandemic of white terrorism and wrote "it is like stabbing you in the dark . . . I feel very sorry for you dear Frederick to have ever again to wield the cudgel, if indeed they have been even laid aside." It was the height of cruelty, she said, "after such life as you have had not to have some repose in old age," and she implored him to write honestly and "let me know how you are really in health and figure."[86] She tried to persuade him to stop, observing that "the evil is too gigantic for our lifetime to erase and seems even to increase as time rolls on."[87]

After receiving a pamphlet (probably on lynching), Crofts was so "upset by the terrible facts you have given that I feel I must send you a line of sympathy." Knowing the pain it must cost him, she wrote, "Dear friend, it is all so disappointing for you."[88] She was devastated by his misery and hoped that younger generations "must take up the work & carry it on . . . the sadness of your tone brings as I re-read yr letter tears, as the first reading did." Crofts bemoaned the lack – in her mind – of a suitable replacement to take up the torch he had held high for decades. Instead, she prayed to God to "give you much wisdom & strengthen you."[89] Douglass had clearly confided to her his exhaustion and war-weariness, together with the impossibility of accepting Richardson's advice, as there could be no rest for his soul while racism existed.

On 20 February 1895, Frederick Douglass died on the steps of Cedar Hill in Anacostia. The news was reported around the world and the British press clamored

---

84 Mary Carpenter to Frederick Douglass 4 April 1894, FDP Digital Collection, Library of Congress.

85 Mary Carpenter to Frederick Douglass, 7 May 1894, FDP Digital Collection, Library of Congress.

86 Ellen Richardson to Frederick Douglass, 1893, FDP Digital Collection, Library of Congress.

87 Ellen Richardson to Frederick Douglass, 22 April 1893, FDP Digital Collection, Library of Congress.

88 Julia Griffiths Crofts to Frederick Douglass, 12 February 1894, FDP Digital Collection, Library of Congress.

89 Julia Griffiths Crofts to Frederick Douglass, 24 August (undated), FDP Digital Collection, Library of Congress.

to write obituaries to the most famous African American, an activist who had made his mark on the British Isles. Their summaries mentioned his enslavement, his fame as an orator, his role in the antislavery movement, the American Civil War, and his journeys to Europe, including how British abolitionists had purchased his legal freedom. According to the *Western Daily Press*, Douglass had "paid two or three visits to England and created a deep impression by his oratorical fervour in the cause of freedom."[90] One newspaper contained a story regarding British Liberal politician Sir Andrew Fairbain, who had met Douglass during his travels in England. When Fairbain visited America, he unexpectedly encountered Douglass on a steamship and objected to the steamer's racial segregation of passengers. He declared that he had "received Mr Douglass at his own table in England, and he did not know that the dining room of an American hotel or lake steamer was any more sacred that his own home." Fairbain joined Douglass and the African American cook for dinner in protest.[91]

Some of the longer obituaries recounted Douglass's numerous political appointments and his published works, but it was in the *Daily News* and the *Dundee Courier* where the eulogies were most eloquent (both are published in this volume). The *Daily News* wrote of the "venerable Frederick Douglass, the famous coloured champion of the freedom of the slave." He was "regarded on both sides of the Atlantic as the representative of all that was best in his race," and

> the purity of his life and brilliancy of his talents as an orator and a man of letters were in themselves and without regard to the noble ends to which he made them subservient, among his highest services to the negro cause . . . as an orator, or as a writer for the press, his utterances reached to the farthest extremities not only of his own country but of ours . . . his own people have lost a father and a friend, and all good men a comrade in the fight, not only for the legal emancipation of one race, but for the spiritual emancipation of all.[92]

Such lavish praise for Douglass's achievements and his commitment to social justice were echoed by the *Dundee Courier*. One correspondent wrote that with his death, "the dark races have lost a warm and enthusiastic friend." He "produced a deep effect in this country, and many who before they heard him had but a dim

---

90   For example, see *Yorkshire Evening Post*, 22 February 1895, p. 2; *Western Daily Press*, 22 February 1895, p. 8; *The Leeds Mercury*, 21 and 22 February 1895, pp. 3–5; *The Manchester Evening News*, 21 February 1895, p. 2; *North-Eastern Daily Gazette*, 21 February 1895, p. 3; *The Birmingham Daily Post*, 22 February 1895, p. 8; *The Standard*, 22 February 1895, p. 3; *Berrow's Worcester Journal*, 23 February 1895, p. 5; *The Graphic*, 2 March 1895, p. 22.

91   *Yorkshire Evening Post*, 26 February 1895, p. 3.

92   *The London Daily News*, 22 February 1895, p. 4.

impression of the horrors and shamefulness of slavery were touched to the quick by his appeals and became the friends of the slaves, and used their influence to bring about their freedom."[93] According to these correspondents, among Douglass's many achievements was his brilliant ability to convey the truth of slavery, to inspire social justice, and to convert thousands to the antislavery cause using his oratorical, literary, and visual testimony.

British and transatlantic friends paid tribute to his legacy. Isabella Fyvie Mayo and the organizing committee of the Brotherhood of Man recognized "the great services" Douglass had rendered the cause of freedom, "which must increase a hundred-fold as years roll by." At the annual meeting of the Sturge Lodge Independent Order of Good Templars in Birmingham, African American activist Reverend Peter T. Stanford delivered a eulogy, and a resolution was passed to show how "his name will always be held in sacred keeping by us and by all lovers of liberty throughout the world."[94] Other remembrances highlighted the deep bonds of friendship and personal loss suffered. Helen Bright Clark wrote that Douglass was "the last of that band of remarkable men whom from children we have learned to admire and esteem." The visit he made in 1887 "will always be a great pleasure to look back on," and Clark was glad her children "could remember his venerable and noble figure" and hold his legacy aloft for future generations.[95] Caroline Richardson wrote that her grief was shared by the small community in Newcastle, and expressed that all who had spent time with him were enriched because of it.[96]

Finally, Ellen Richardson wrote to Helen Pitts Douglass that she shared "very deeply with you in the loss of our dear Frederick," and could barely express the pain she felt imagining him on his deathbed. Since 1845, Douglass had taken great care to sustain the bonds of fellowship with his British and Irish friends, as their support, together with his transformative experiences across the Atlantic as a whole, had dramatically changed his life in numerous ways. As he wrote in the spring of 1887, he remained thankful of the opportunity to visit the British Isles one last time, and to meet with those "loved long since but lost awhile."[97]

Today, the "lovers of liberty" continue to preserve Douglass's legacy across the globe and his life, testimony, and unrelenting fight against racism and white supremacy reinvigorates new waves of activists. In the wake of protests resulting from the deaths of Breonna Taylor and George Floyd in 2020, the transatlantic public looked

---

93 *Dundee Courier*, 22 February 1895, p. 2.

94 Douglass, *In Memoriam*, pp. 78–79; 86–87.

95 Ibid. pp. 83–84.

96 Ibid. pp. 87–88.

97 Ellen Richardson to Frederick Douglass, 30 September 1886, FDP Digital Collection, Library of Congress; Douglass, *In Memoriam*, p. 69; Quarles, *Frederick Douglass*, pp. 310–15.

to Douglass for guidance on how to destroy systemic racism and wrestle with the complexities of commemoration. On both sides of the Atlantic, calls to erect a monument to Douglass were reignited in the US and in the UK. In an uncertain and COVID-19-ravaged landscape, where people of color are still ruthlessly murdered despite international #BlackLivesMatter campaigns, Douglass's inspiring intellectual vision, his numerous sacrifices for the antislavery cause, the hundreds of thousands of miles he traveled, and the incalculable number of words written or spoken by him for social justice invite us to join in his hope that we will, one day, live in a more equal and just world.[98]

---

98   Jonathan W. White and Scott Sandage, "What Frederick Douglass Had to Say About Monuments," *Smithsonian Magazine*, 30 June 2020, <https://www.smithsonianmag.com/history/what-frederick-douglass-had-say-about-monuments-180975225/>; John Prideaux, "A Slavery Statue We Can All Agree On," *The Times*, 13 July 2020, <https://www.thetimes.co.uk/article/a-slavery-statue-we-can-all-agree-on-frederick-douglass-tvxxhb6px> (last accessed 11 October 2020).

Part II
"Men Naturally Love Liberty"

In this section, we reproduce eighteen reports of Douglass's lectures delivered in Britain and Ireland. The majority of these have never been published before and date from his first tour during the period 1845–47, while still a fugitive from slavery, but seven of them occurred during his less well-studied visit of 1859–60, as he fled possible prosecution as an accomplice to John Brown's Harpers Ferry raid. A final item, from 1886, records the reception shown Douglass in a speech made while he was honeymooning in England with his second wife, Helen Pitts Douglass.

The reports of these addresses provide great insight into British and Irish concern over the fate of African Americans. They reveal that from the 1840s to the 1880s, Douglass's lecturing in a community was treated as a major public event. Large halls were booked, and frequently described as filled to overflowing. In numerous communities, the mayor either presided or introduced Douglass; for example, in Dublin in September 1845, at the conclusion of Douglass's talk, the Lord Mayor was reported confessing to the audience that "He was at all times opposed to slavery (cheers); but after what he had heard that night he was a complete convert to abolitionist principles, and he would do all in his power to diffuse and support them."[1] Ministers were reported in large numbers on the dais at Douglass's lectures; their presence was probably calculated as a rebuttal to charges that he and fellow Garrisonians attacked the churches too indiscriminately, especially surrounding the controversy over the Evangelical Alliance. More than typical abolitionist society conventions, these public meetings convened to hear Douglass speak drew out a broad range of Irish and British community leaders who professed their disapproval of human chattel slavery.

Resolutions applauding Douglass, but also endorsing the abolition movement, were generally adopted at the conclusion of these meetings. They were regarded as an important affirmation of the community's commitment to the antislavery cause. When none had been drawn up for approval at a meeting in Sheffield in 1860, Douglass humorously chided that assemblage: "He was not sure whether the people of Sheffield had not sent too much crinoline to America, and had not too many good customers there whom they did not like to offend. If such was the case, they ought to be ashamed of themselves. (Laughter.)"[2] Several newspapers described

---

1   *The Freeman's Journal*, 24 September 1845, p. 4.
2   *Supplement to the Sheffield and Rotherham Independent*, 21 January 1860, p. 10.

question and answer sessions following Douglass's addresses. In a few cases, audience members attempted to rebut some of his claims. In Leicester in 1847, two questioners cited American denominations they contended should be spared from Douglass's sweeping denunciations of the pro-slavery character of religious institutions. Douglass generally handled such criticism effectively, and no reports survive of an audience solidly rejecting his message.

The principal contents of Douglass's remarks have been analyzed in Part 1, but a few more anecdotes seem timely. During an 1847 lecture in Northampton, the reporter noted that Douglass's "drollery was not less effective than his pathos." In particular, that reporter noted how the audience responded enthusiastically to the speaker's "spontaneous couplets," such as "Take away the cash,/and you would lose the lash" or *"Because their Mayor/Was in the chair."*[3] Frederick Douglass may not have been credited as a pioneer of hip-hop, but on that evening in England, he definitely seemed to be rapping. More seriously, in reports of several of his British addresses, Douglass employed rhetoric identical to the chants of modern-day civil rights and Black Lives Matter protestors; these similarities seemed particularly striking at the time this volume was being completed, when global demonstrations were taking place following the unprovoked deaths of George Floyd and Breonna Taylor at the hands of white law-enforcement officers. Douglass's relationship with Britain and Ireland offers a blueprint for modern activists to challenge racism, the legacies of slavery, and white supremacy from a transatlantic and international platform. During meetings in Leeds and Glasgow, for example, Douglass won applause for declaring that "there could be no real peace where there was injustice,"[4] demonstrating that his words remain relevant down to this day.

---

3 *Northampton Mercury*, 3 April 1847, p. 3.
4 *Leeds Mercury*, 24 December 1859, p. 3. See also *Daily Herald*, 1 February 1860, p. 3.

ANTI-SLAVERY SOCIETY

Dublin, Ireland, *The Freeman's Journal*, 24 September 1845, p. 4

Last night an anti-slavery meeting was held at the Music Hall, Abbey-street. The chair was taken by the Lord Mayor,[1] who on coming on the platform was greeted with loud and long continued cheers . . .

Mr. Douglas then came forward and was received in a very enthusiastic manner. He made a long and powerful speech on the evils of slavery, and was frequently applauded throughout. He shewed the fallacy of the argument so frequently resorted to by slave-holders, that the negro race were unfit for freedom, owing to their mental inferiority to the European nation. Admitting for sake of argument that the negroes were an inferior race, he would ask by what philosophy could any one justify himself for enslaving them? The Scriptures told the strong to endure the weak, not to oppress them; and no man, therefore, could obey the word of God and sanction slavery. It was objected that the negro was ignorant, and thereby incapable of participating in the advantages of social and political equality. But those who charged them with being ignorant and degraded condemned themselves in that charge, for they had made education penal, and darkened the understanding of the slave. The Americans generally had conspired against the negro, and they sought a justification for oppression in the results of that oppression. Even the Northern States sanctioned slavery, for they assented in congress to the enactment and continuance of those bloody laws by which three millions of the population of America were held in brutal bondage by men professing Christianity (hear, hear). The Society of Friends, with other sects, had conspired to keep them in degrading subjection, and had refused to admit them on equal terms into the house of that God who is no respecter of persons. But the Roman Catholics never denied to them the privileges of the Christian faith, and the offices of brotherly love, but had opened to them

---

1 John L. Arabin (1794–1863) assumed the role of Lord Mayor of Dublin in 1845. Kinealy, *Frederick Douglass and Ireland* includes this speech.

their churches without any distinction (tremendous cheering).[2] For fourteen years past there has been in America a strong opinion in favour of doing justice to the negro, and many of the grievances under which they had groaned were abolished, or but partially put in practice (hear, hear). But the slave was still a slave, submitted to the tyranny and caprice of his master, and no true justice could be extended to him till he was liberated (cheers). He would never ask of the white man to educate the black, or give him office – all he asked was to do the black man justice, and leave him to advance himself (cheers). Mr. Douglas then detailed many of the circumstances relating to his own captivity, which were given in a late number of the FREEMAN,[3] and after paying a high compliment to the Messrs. Hutchinsons[4] for their uniform resistance to slavery, concluded amid great cheering by thanking the Lord Mayor for the honourable part he had taken in the proceedings of the evening.

---

2 Douglass employed rhetorical techniques such as this to appeal to, in this case, his predominantly Catholic audience.
3 *The Freeman's Journal*, the oldest newspaper in Dublin and founded in 1763.
4 The Hutchinson Family was a US singing troupe composed of John, Asa, Jesse, and Judson Hutchinson, later joined by their sister Abby. They visited Britain alongside Douglass in 1845.

ANTI-SLAVERY SOIREE. MR. DOUGLAS, THE AMERICAN SLAVE

Limerick, Ireland, *The Limerick Reporter*, 25 November 1845, p. 2

Mr. Douglas then rose, and was received with loud cheers.[1] He said he felt grateful for the honour that had been done him, and gratified for the sake of the great and glorious cause which he came to advocate. He was frequently in the habit of meeting in such assemblies as this, and he assured them that he was never more delighted than at the present moment. – (cheers.) In the West Indies there had been 800,000 slaves, and the people of this country had done something for them. There were three millions and a-half of slaves in America that cried "come and help us." If he was now in America he would be his master's property, and be liable to be sold as a piece of merchandize. Thank GOD it was not so in this land – (cheers.) When he attempted to return gratitude for liberty he failed, for his heart rose to such a pitch of happiness, that he was rendered utterly unable to give utterance to his feelings. Seven years ago he was a slave – an object of merchandize – dragged and ranked with beasts to be sold in the market or auction mart. He was happy to see that not only the humble classes of Limerick recognised him, but its wealth and respectability. Oh, what a transition it was to be changed from the state of a slave to that of a freeman! Really, when he thought of his former condition and his present, he was puzzled to know whether Frederick Douglas then was the same Frederick Douglas now (laughter.) He could hardly believe how his proud spirit could be ever bound in chains. If he returned to the United States he would be taken and bound in slave chains. He must plant himself, therefore, under the protection of the Irish and British people. He was not there to denounce the American Government, but, indeed, he could not say much in favour of it – He would

---

1 Kinealy, *Frederick Douglass and Ireland*, includes this speech.

just relate an act of that government. In South Carolina the law goes so far as to take coloured seamen when they arrived there in different vessels, and put them in prison until the vessels are about to leave; and if the captain of the vessel does not go and pay jail fees, the unfortunate coloured seaman will be sold in the market to the highest bidder. This the British government denounced, and were by treaty promised that no coloured seaman in the employment of British vessels should be touched. The law of South Carolina was accordingly modified, but not changed. Some short time back a white gentleman had occasion to visit South Carolina, and was attended by a black servant. The authorities were about to enforce their law, but the gentleman remonstrated about his servant, and they told him the only way he could keep his servant was to place him in a British vessel which lay in the port. This was done and the American authorities dreaded to go near him, because he was under the British flag. The reason that this law was in force was, that they considered a free coloured man as an incendiary among the slaves, lest they should be struck with the thought of freedom – So that a colored freeman is liable in his own country, and under the American flag, to be dragged to prison, but not under the British flag (cheers). Again he said, he was not there to speak against the American government, but to bring under their notice American slavery, and to try to make America like any other Christian country in the world. It was the only nation on earth in which the African slave trade was allowed to be carried on. When this is washed away, the American escutcheon will be cleansed, and not till then (hear, hear). When England and France wanted to crush slavery on the high seas, America gave all the opposition in her power, and afforded every protection to the slavers. He then adverted to the annexation of Texas,[2] and denounced the conduct of America in wresting Texas from Mexico as that of a bully whose only right was that of the strongest. He then alluded to the various battles won for America by negro blood, and depicted in glowing colours the base ingratitude with which they were rewarded. He would not trespass further upon them. He found freedom and a welcome to spake against slavery in Dublin, Wexford, Waterford, and Cork, and though last not least in Limerick (cheers). Whether home or abroad he would never forget the very kind manner he was received in Limerick. Mr. Douglass resumed his seat amidst loud cheers.[3]

---

2   Originally part of Mexico, Texas was annexed by the US in 1845 and was a significant catalyst for the Mexican-American War (1846–48).

3   At the end of this meeting, the Mayor toasted Douglass's health and in response, Douglass sang an antislavery song.

LECTURES ON AMERICAN SLAVERY

Dundee, Scotland, *Dundee, Perth and Cupar Advertiser*, 30 January 1846, p. 3

Meetings were held relative to American Slavery, in School Wynd Chapel, on the evenings of Tuesday and Wednesday.[1] Both nights the Chapel was crowded to excess; the passages on the second night were all thronged, and many had to return home, being unable to obtain a hearing. Mr Frederick Douglass (lately a slave himself), in contrasting the atrocities of slavery with all other institutions permitted by civil laws to exist in any other country, said – He was not able to trace in any history which he had read such institutions as those of American slavery. The slave had intellect, conscience, and moral perception, prompting him to think and act one way. The slaveholder, so far as he was able, took these away; – he was not allowed to act for himself, to think for himself, or to decide for himself – all these the slave-holder does for him. He supplanted him of all these, and acted for him in every particular. He had assumed that right which God had forbidden man to assume – he had torn the husband from the wife. If more than seven slaves were found together without a White man, thirty-seven lashes were given; for a second offence, a greater number were inflicted; and for a third, a finger was cut off. For going off the regular path, thirty-seven lashes were given; for riding after hours on horseback, without a written permission, twenty-five lashes; and for riding in the day-time, a slave may be lashed, chained, cut, branded, with a little R, or have his ear cut away. He had seen a young woman caught in attempting to escape; she was overtaken and dragged back again, when her ear was nailed by her master against a post, and in this condition she was left for an indefinite period. The practice of branding slaves in America was as common as the custom of marking sheep was in this country. The slave was taken out

---

[1] Douglass had extraordinary success in Dundee and spoke three times at the School Wynd Chapel, 27–29 January 1846.

for the purpose, the furnace was heated, the branding-iron placed in the midst of the fire, and, when heated, taken sparkling from it, and applied to the ear. His cheek was scorched all over. These atrocities were not the doings of individual slave-holders, but were recognised in their full extent by the laws of an American Government. He had seen his own master tie up a young woman by the hands, and afterwards apply for fifteen minutes the bloody cowstick. He had seen his master's brother take up his own brother and throw him against the ground till blood gushed from his nose and cheek, for no other reason than another slave was absent who should have been present. They were very frequently cut and bruised. After enumerating other barbarities, he anticipated that many might question what purpose such atrocities could serve; and, in answer to this, he would say, that the slave had a love of liberty deeply impressed within him, which very often prompted him to evince, by symptoms, words, and sometimes deeds, that, were it in his power, he would regain his liberty; and hence their method of keeping him down. He had known a girl about seventeen years of age, who was held in slavery; her keepers came to her prison to feed her, along with other slaves; they let bread fall to her; she picked it up while they passed on to other slaves. The gate of the prison had been left open; she dropped the bread, and, before they were aware, she had cleared the gate; pursuit was made after her by the keeper; she gained a bridge; two Virginian slave-holders were coming up; meeting her, the poor girl stood; she saw slavery before her and worse than death behind; she clasped her hands, as if beseeching mercy, and then sprung over the parapet into the water, – at once preferring to appear before God, in all her sins, rather than again endure slavery. He was forbidden by the presence of the audience before him to tell all the secrets of his prison house; they could not endure to hear him, because these secrets were so horrible. A million of female slaves were left, to the lusts of the slave-holders. These might have their left hands cut off, – their heads severed from the trunk, – they might be quartered, and afterwards mutilated – yet such were the laws of Republican in America. He was himself a slave, if in the United States; in no portion of that immense country was he free; over its length and breadth slavery existed. The slave-holder could set the blood-hound on his track; and, wherever American republicanism held dominion, there was no valley so deep, no hill so high, as could save him from their search. After stating his reasons for visiting this country, and contrasting the usage which he had received since visiting it with what he had suffered in America, he regretted that his race was misrepresented by American travellers who came into this country, and the more so, that in many instances they were believed. On the free hills of Scotland he had heard strange apologies for the conduct of slave-holding Christians; but what were slave-holding Christians? There was no such anomaly as a slave-holding Christian in existence. Slave-holding religionists there were. The widow who bound herself on the funeral pyre of her husband was one, and the man who threw himself under the wheels of the car was another; but the slave-holder who professed Christianity, and made barter and oppression of human blood, was no Christian. If he understood what Christianity meant, he thought it was to be Christ-like. The slave-holder claimed for himself that adoration due only to the Deity; he wrested from the sacred page this devotion. "Thou shalt not steal" was violated by slavery; for what could be plainer than man was intended to be free; if not free, why was he given the desire to be so? Why was he given the liberty to think and reason? and he who could take those from him was a thief and a robber, though called a Christian. He had seen a husband and wife placed on the auction block – the wife was a strong, healthy, and fine-looking woman; her limbs were brutally exposed to the examination of the purchaser; she was first put up, and sold after a lengthened contest. The man followed, his eye resting upon his wife; from her it turned with an imploring look to him who had purchased her; and, so far was it understood, that he who had purchased the wife bade for him; but the price went too high, and he was sold to another, evincing the keenest symptoms of grief in being separated from her who had been till then his companion. He pleaded for permission to have one kiss, but was refused. Prompted by grief, he persisted in his aim, when he was violently struck by the butt-end of a whip. He stood a moment, gazing in stupefaction and grief, on the ground, and fell down dead, – and such was slavery. After referring to the influence which the attention of this country, when properly directed to the subject of slavery, would have upon America – to the fear and horror manifested by the United States when their deeds of blood and damnation done under the star-spangled banner were alluded to – he gave a geographical sketch of what were generally supposed to be the slave-holding States. But here he stated an error existed: The whole States of America were one on the subject of slavery – they had entered into mutual agreement to return the slave who had escaped to his former holder; they had pledged their word that the Black population should remain slaves; and should they attempt to gain freedom they will shoulder musket and say to the slave – be a slave or die. America as a whole might at present be said to be on a mission of plunder and aggrandizement. They were seizing Mexico with one hand, with the other they pointed to Oregon; and staining wherever conquest led them, with the damning mark of slavery.[2] There were in America at present three millions of slaves, and one million of these were eagerly waiting an opportunity for revolt – they would rise at the sound of the first

---

2   Oregon had been divided in 1818 between America and Great Britain, and was equally claimed by Spain and Russia. Increasing settlement by pioneers led to disputes over territorial control, which led to the Oregon Treaty of 1846; the territory was split between the US and UK at the 49th parallel.

trumpet. He did not wish to foster a spirit of war; but let England, in her claim of Oregon, decry slavery, and their slaves would flock to her banner[.] Were this done, there would be no war. America had enough on hand in governing her own population. Mr Douglass, after a long and eloquent speech, sat down amidst great cheering.

AMERICAN SLAVERY &
THE FREE CHURCH

Edinburgh, Scotland, *Caledonian Mercury*, 11 May 1846, p. 3

On Thursday night, another meeting was held in Mr M'Gilchrist's[1] Church, Rose Street, on the subject of the connection of the Free Church with American slavery. Admission was by tickets issued at a small charge, and the attendance was exceedingly numerous.

Mr Douglas addressed the audience at great length. He commenced by stating, that the meeting was suggested by various ministers of the United Secession. They desired him to express his views on the character of American slavery, together with the means which are adopted for sustaining the system. He would endeavour to put them in possession of as many facts as their time would allow. The principle of slavery is defended by the laws of the United States. The principal point is that the slave is a thing, a chattel personal, under the entire dominion and control of his master. He may not decide for himself; the master is the sole disposer of his time, his strength, his power of body and mind. The master decides for him as to what is right and what is wrong. The slave may not decide in his affections. The master decides for him even in marriage. Let them but reflect on that state of society where the marriage vow is not respected. That state of things is in the Southern States of America; there, the slave has been forced to put in practice the abominable doctrines of Socialism. There are to be found three millions of human beings compelled by law to live practically in a state of absolute concubinage; and he here could not forbear saying, that Christians have gone into the midst of that pollution without raising a word against it – (shame.) The duty of the slave, then, is unlimited submission to his master; the will of God is set entirely aside when that of his master comes

---

1   The Reverend John M'Gilchrist, minister at Rose Street Chapel.

in competition with it; no matter at what sacrifice of conscience – no matter how bad the master may be – the slave is bound to obey in all things. The moral evils that result from slavery are incomparably greater than are the physical. The slave's mind is either darkened or enlightened just in so far as his master thinks proper. But a word about the cruelties. He would not speak of those he endured himself. He would not show them the stripes on his own back; but he would read them a number of advertisements daily inserted in the newspapers by the masters themselves, which may lead to the detection of the runaway slaves. Mr Douglass then read a great number of these, from which it appeared that the runaway slaves, when recovered, are branded and mutilated in a horrible manner. Some had pieces of chains on their legs, attached to which were heavy bars of iron to prevent them from escaping, while others (and these were chiefly women) were decorated with iron collars. Mr Douglass next gave a detail of the punishments that were inflicted upon the slaves, for the slightest offence, or (as more frequently happened) for no offence at all. Lashing, of course, was general, while some of the slaves had their ears cropped off, others were branded on the skin with hot irons, and numerous other mutilations were inflicted. Outlawry, he said, was very general amongst the slaves, and in these cases people, if they were so disposed, might shoot them at pleasure without any fear of punishment. Blood-hounds are trained to run after slaves. He described a Baptist clergyman who had whipped his slave to death, unpunished; so horrible was the fatal punishment that the slave was beat to jelly, so that no one, when they saw the man after death, could recognise him. Women at auction stalls, when being sold, are there exposed and examined by the slaveholders in the most indelicate way. He described the case of a man and wife who were thus exposed to sale. His wife was sold first; the man beseeched that he should also be bought by the same party in order that he might not be severed from the wife he loved. Unfortunately, however, he was sold to another. After he saw his fate, he rushed forward to take one last embrace from his wife, but this he was prevented from doing by the hard-hearted slave holder. In the struggle that ensued, the poor slave fell down a corpse. His heart was broken – (great sensation.) No woman slave was allowed to defend her person against the evil wishes of her master, for the moment she did so her master had the power to strike her dead. There was another case of extreme cruelty which Mr Douglass depicted, namely, that of a young man who had previously met with much ill usage, and who wished to escape; in his endeavours he ran into a creek up to the neck. He was told immediately to come out; but he had counted the cost – he refused, and for his refusal he was immediately shot dead by his master.[2] Mr Douglass

---

2   Douglass is referring to the case of Bill Denby the story of which he retells in *Narrative* (1845), p. 20, and *My Bondage and My Freedom* (1855), pp. 122–23.

stated another case, which, from its barbarous details, created a feeling of horror amongst the audience. It was the case of Mackintosh, who defended himself against the assaults of a white man; in this attempt he was caught by the mob, taken by them to a wood, and burnt. When the lower half of his body was burnt away, and his murderers thought he was dead, he shrieked out "shoot me." "No," said his murderers, "we shall lower the intensity of the fire in order that you may be slowly consumed." Mr Douglass detailed a great many cases of a like nature. You ask me, continued Mr Douglass, is there no religion in the United States? Yes, there never was a more professing people on the face of the globe – but it is a slaveholding religion – (cheers.) The people there take up the ground that their slaveholding, with all its cruelties, is sanctioned by God Almighty. They take it for granted, like the Free Church, that it is of Divine origin. They say if it is a moral evil, why does it exist? man did not create it, therefore he cannot destroy it. Now, said Mr Douglass, if stealing is a crime, so is slaveholding, for it is the highest species of stealing. The liberty of the human being is stolen, not to speak of his energies and labour – (cheers.) All religion there was interwoven with slaveholding. But they might ask him, was there no Christianity there at all? This was best known to the Searcher of Hearts. As for himself, he would say that so far as he understood Christianity, it was not preached there. If the gospel in its native purity and freeness was preached as liberty to the captive, then slavery would cease. But its supporters take care of that. The slaveholder and the minister are combined in one and the same individual, and thus they make the whole religion of Christianity to sanction slavery. But are there no revivals there? Yes! but they go hand in hand with slavery. The slave-prison and meeting-house stand side by side with each other; in short, the enormities of slavery are all covered with the holy garb of religion. But it is asked, what do the abolitionists want? They want to establish the principles of the meek and lowly Jesus. We do not believe that his followers exist there. We do not say, like some, that the slaveholders may be Christians; we deny that they can be so. But some say, "Mr Douglass, the crime is in the United States, not here; here we all remonstrate against it." He admitted all that. He was there to thank them for the exertions they had already made; but although they had thus spoken, they must speak again. If they had whispered before, they must now speak aloud. Let their voice be carried across the blue waves of the Atlantic to cheer the depressed heart of the slave and fill with alarm and dread the heart of the slaveholder. Public opinion in this country was against slavery, and what he wanted was that all denominations should combine in pronouncing that the slaveholders should be excommunicated from the privileges of Christians. The slaveholders do not wish enlightenment on the subject, they know it in its true bearings with Christianity; all they want is the support of the Christians in this country in their horrid traffic. To say that a slaveholder can be a Christian is a contradiction, an anomaly. We might as well say, that a man may be a Christian who does not believe the fundamental principles of the gospel. If a man preaches and prays well here, and cheats in Liverpool, will we exclude him? Yes, says any one – (cheers.) Let us apply this rule to the slaveholder; he cheats and steals every day from his poor slaves, and therefore, although he may preach and profess as he may, he could not be fellowshipped with as a Christian. After detailing the heavy punishments (in some cases death) inflicted for attempting to teach negroes to read and write, or even to instruct them in the Christian religion in the Southern States, Mr Douglass gave a very interesting detail of the manner in which he stole his education.

SECOND LECTURE ON AMERICAN SLAVERY

Newcastle, England, *Newcastle Guardian*, 15 August 1846, p. 5

On Thursday evening, a numerous and highly respectable audience assembled in Salem Chapel, Hood Street, for the purpose of hearing Mr Frederick Douglass, deliver a second lecture, on his personal history during his enslavement in the United States. John Fenwick,[1] Esq., occupied the chair, and after a few introductory remarks, introduced

Mr DOUGLASS, who said he was born a slave, the property of Mr Anthony,[2] of Talbot county, Maryland. His mother was a black woman; his father was a white man; and he had heard his master was his father. This was frequently the case, for slaveholders often sustain to their slaves the double relation of master and father. He was separated from his parents at an early age. He never saw his mother until he was about five years of age, and then only for a short time, for she soon afterwards died. He was brought up in the most degraded society, and without any degree of knowledge. He was literally ranked among the brutes; and regarded in the same light as horses, sheep, and swine, are regarded by their owners. He was fed from a trough, not unlike that used in a pig-sty; and for his bed he had the cold damp ground. Clothing he had scarcely any, until he was about seven or eight years of age; all that he could remember to have worn during that time was a little linen shirt, which he wore winter and summer. He would have been frozen to death several times had he not contrived to steal a bag into which he used to crawl, and sleep during the winter nights; but he always took care to put the bag in its place again in the morning. Such was the state of the weather that, at one time, it was possible to put a finger into the

---

1 John Ralph Fenwick (1761–1855), physician, reformer, and abolitionist based in Newcastle.
2 Aaron Anthony (1767–1827) was head overseer for the wealthy Lloyd family of Maryland's Eastern Shore.

gashes in his knees, made by the frost. Surrounded by these degrading influences – hearing nothing but the most degrading conversation among the slaves, and the cursings and swearings of a hard overseer, he, of course, made very little intellectual, moral, or religious progress at that time. He saw slavery then as he had ever seen it since; and, even at the weary age of seven, he was fully impressed with the sinfulness of making slaves of human beings. He regarded his master, at that age, as nothing but a systematic robber. The first view of the cruelty of slavery that he had occasion to witness was, the whipping, by his old master, of his aunt, who had committed an offence by leaving the house when she was wanted at home. Early one morning he was awakened by the sound of the whip, and dreadful shrieks. When he drew out of his little closet, he saw the horrible spectacle of a young woman about seventeen years of age, with her back laid bare, her hands tied to the joists, and her master, with a long cow-skin, beating her unmercifully, – the blood dripping at her feet.[3] This was the first instance of the kind that he had ever seen; and it made an impression upon his mind that could never be erased. He saw then what he himself must come to; he looked forward to the day when he himself would have to be subjected to the same torture, and to experience the same cruelties as others. But when he was about seven years of age, a brighter prospect dawned. He was given over by his master to one of his relatives, residing in Baltimore; in whose wife he found a very kind mistress.[4] She had never held any slaves herself, nor had any of her family. When he had been in this family a short time, his mistress very kindly commenced to teach him the alphabet, which was an act sel[d]om done by any master or mistress in any of the slave states, it being diametrically opposed to laws enacted for the purpose of depriving slaves of education. By the assistance of his mistress, he was soon taught to spell words of three or four letters; but his progress was arrested in consequence of his master forbidding his wife to teach him any more for, he said, "If you give a nigger an inch, he will take an ell; if you teach him to read, he will want to know how to write, and going on thus, he will not be contented until he runs away." He (Mr Douglass) happened to over-hear this conversation. He was then about nine years of age, and hearing that this learning to read and write was to make such a change in his temper and disposition, and to render him entirely unfit for slavery, he resolved immediately to learn as much as possible. He did this in various ways. While in this situation he was very kindly treated, and had always sufficient to eat, and sometimes more than necessary. Whenever it happened that he had more bread than he wanted, he would take the first opportunity of going into the streets, among

---

3 Douglass refers to the beating of Aunt Hester as the "blood-stained gate, the entrance to the hell of slavery" in his *Narrative* (1845), p. 6.
4 Sophia Auld (1797–1880), wife of Hugh Auld.

a number of hungry urchins, and proposed to them to give him a lesson, in exchange for which he would give them some bread. By this means he was soon enabled to read tolerably well; and then he had a desire to write. He was now placed to work in a ship-yard amongst ship-carpenters, and his first idea of learning to write was by seeing one of them, after he had hewn a piece of timber, made a letter with chalk on the wood to denote what part of the ship it was intended for. On inquiry, he found it was the letter L, which denoted that the piece of wood was intended for the larboard side; then he saw him make the letter S, which meant the starboard side, and it was by this and similar means that he at length learned to write. Mr Douglass then gave a detailed account of his escape from slavery, and concluded his eloquent lecture by exhorting the Christian denominations of this country to withhold their fellowship from the slaveholders of the United States. At the close of the lecture, a collection was made in aid of the anti-slavery society, after which a vote of thanks was given to Mr Douglass, on the motion of James Finlay,[5] Esq., and the meeting separated.

---

5   Joseph Finlay was a member of the British and Foreign Anti-Slavery Society and the National Peace Society.

MR FRED DOUGLAS'S LECTURE ON AMERICAN SLAVERY

Carlisle, England, *Carlisle Journal*, 22 August 1846, p. 4

Mr. FREDERICK DOUGLAS, the American Slave who, having escaped from bondage in the "land of liberty," has come over to England to get up an agitation against slavery, delivered a lecture on the subject, on Friday night last, in the Athenaeum in this city, to a numerous audience. The lecturer entered the room soon after eight o'clock. For a negro, he has an intelligent and even a pleasing face, and he had not been long before the meeting until he gave unmistakeable signs of extraordinary talent, – his impassioned eloquence taking the majority of his hearers, to whom he was a stranger, by surprise. His voice is deep-toned and powerful, and his style of speaking much resembles that of George Thompson.[1] With the pronunciation of the English language and with its grammar he displayed an intimate acquaintance; and when warmed with his subject he spoke with great force, as well as propriety. The great length of his discourse precludes the possibility of our giving a full report of it; but the rapid sketch of the chief points of it, which we subjoin, will serve to indicate the topics upon which he dwelt.

JOSEPH FERGUSON,[2] Esq., of Fisher Street, who presided, having introduced him to the meeting,

Mr. FREDERICK DOUGLAS came forward and said he made no pretensions to learning, never having had a day's schooling. All the knowledge he possessed had been "stolen," as it were, during his enslavement. The question of American slavery was becoming well understood throughout England: and it would soon

---

1 George Thompson (1804–1879), English M.P., abolitionist, and friend of Douglass and William Lloyd Garrison.
2 Joseph Ferguson (1788–1863) was a mayor and M.P. of Carlisle.

become the all-engrossing topic throughout Christendom – arousing the attention of the wise and good of every nation, as a foul blot upon common humanity. There were fifteen slave states, and thirteen free states in America. Each state had its own constitution, and made its own laws, being considered sovereign in itself, so far as all within its own boundary were concerned. But all the states were parties to the Federal Government, which regulated commerce, declared war and peace, levied taxes, and provided for the common safety. The individual states, however, had the power to create and abolish institutions – slavery, for instance – peculiar to their own locality, the Federal Government having no power over them. Now, slavery had been represented as an institution peculiar to the south; but the crime connected with its support was shared in by the whole country: for there was a clause in the Federal constitution by which the slave-holder could summon the whole physical force of his district to suppress revolt among the negro population; and fugitives were, by another clause, doomed to slavery wherever they went the whole land being literally made hunting ground for the foul kidnappers of the south, who found an unerring detective police in well trained blood-hounds.[3] He (the lecturer) when in America was liable to be dragged back into slavery, for wherever he went – whether to Bunker's Hill,[4] or to this or that place where the battle of freedom had been fought, he was amenable, under the star-spangled banner, to the state regulations by which man-stealing was legalised. The extent of the execrable institution of slavery in the United States was astounding. There were 300,000 slave-holders, and 3,000,000 slaves. These slaves were men equally powerful, physically speaking, with their masters, – if anything, more powerful than they; and they *could*, under certain circumstances, gain their freedom by force. He was not there, however, to encourage insurrection amongst them; but it was notorious that the power of redemption was with them, if they had nothing to contend with but their masters, who confessed that such was the fact. In the event of a foreign invader in the north, it was openly confessed in congress, the slave would rally round the flag of emancipation; and without the northern states the slave-holders of the south would not hold their slaves in bondage. For how could one man make slaves of ten men? And there were ten slaves to every slave-holder. They could run away and take their freedom, and they would butcher their masters if it were merely

---

3   Douglass refers to the Fugitive Slave Acts, first passed in Congress in 1793, and Article 1, Section 8 of the Constitution, which stated that Congress had the power "to provide for calling forth the Militia to execute the Laws of the Union, suppress insurrections and repel invasions."

4   The site of one of the first battles in the American Revolution in June 1775, Bunker Hill became synonymous with the fight for freedom, and Douglass frequently referred to the monument there (completed in 1843).

a contention between the slaves and the slave-holders; but public opinion was in favour of slavery, which received a moral support from the people, a civil support from the government, and a physical support under the constitution of the country – and that was the secret of its prolonged existence. And what was slavery? it was that by which one man enforced a right in the body and soul of another man. It was the reducing a human being, by another human being, to the condition of a brute; compelling him to find companionship with the ox and the horse; making him a marketable commodity; driving him before the lash; withdrawing him from the natural relation with his God and his brethren; and making him a thing to be governed, guided, and directed just as his master wished, in eating, working, and thinking. That was slavery as it existed in the United States, – as it was, had been, and would always be. It was sin in its conception, sin in its progress, and sin [in] its ultimate results. Well, it might be asked, what could be done in England to operate against an evil existing in a land three thousand miles distant? He was there to tell the audience. England was but fourteen days sail from America, and any word written or spoken against slavery was heard and appreciated in Boston and in New York in a fortnight. So much for the achievements of science, which gave Englishmen the power, by means of public opinion, rapidly conveyed through the medium of steam and the press, to alarm the consciences of the slaveholders and to cheer the hopes of those who were now living in bondage, and kept in subjection by the whip, the scourge, the thumb-screw, and the manacle. The lecturer next warned the meeting to beware of the plausible sophistries of forty-five gentlemen who had come over to this country from the United States, as delegates to the Temperance Convention in London, and who in advocating the cause of temperance, were insidiously using their eloquence for the purpose of perpetuating slavery. With an apparent ingenuousness that would appear to spring from true philanthropy, these persons advocated principles which enthralled mankind. It had become his duty lately, in Covent Garden Theatre,[5] boldly to condemn their opinions and to denounce their conduct; and should they visit Carlisle he warned the audience to take heed of them. It was just in proportion to the effect of the exposures of the system abroad that America yielded; and he instanced the case of John L. Brown,[6] who was sentenced to be hanged for assisting the escape of a slave: the discussions on the circumstance in the British Parliament had the effect of commuting his

---

5 The World's Temperance Convention, held at the Covent Garden Theatre in August 1845. Douglass was a registered delegate from Newcastle and was invited to speak one evening on his own experience with temperance and the cause.

6 John L. Brown was a South Carolina native who was condemned to death for helping fugitives escape. His trial began in 1843 but his sentence was commuted after immense pressure from American and British abolitionists.

punishment to public whipping; and even that commuted punishment was not carried into effect, in consequence of a petition, numerously signed, from ministers of the Church of Scotland, and others. He also instanced the case of Jonathan Walker, whose sentence for a like offence was remitted in consequence of a demonstration of public opinion in England.[7] The moral influence of England, he believed, was necessary for abolitionising the United States, and that once enlisted in favour of the slave, slavery could no longer exist. Physical means of attaining this consummation he repudiated: he relied upon the force of truth, which would prove all potent, for so long as one voice was raised against the system, and the finger of scorn was pointed against its upholders, their consciences would be touched, and their minds be ill at ease. After a graphic description of slavery as it exists in the southern States of America, and after reading a number of advertisements from the American newspapers, detailing the scars and disfigurements of runaway slaves by the lash, he said that those descriptions revealed the utmost apathy to horrors – such as the branding by hot irons, the cutting off of ears, and the stripes of the scourge – the bare revelation of which caused a shudder in lands where liberty existed. And this abominable system found supporters and advocates – ay, the strongest of its supporters and advocates – in the clergy of the United States. Religion and slavery in America went hand in hand; and his object was to excite such an interest in the subject as to induce Christians in England to speak out against so disgraceful a state of things. Children were sold to buy communion service, women to buy bibles, and men to send the gospel to the heathen! The lecturer then proceeded to denounce the connection between the Free Church of Scotland and slavery in the United States;[8] describing the visit of the deputation who collected the contributions, and who accepted the "blood-stained money" in spite of the remonstrances of the Abolitionists, who met them when they landed on the shores of America, and protested against their mixing themselves up with the sins of slaveholders and slavery. But, notwithstanding these remonstrances, they visited the slave-holding districts, slept in slaveholders' houses, preached in their pulpits, pocketed their money, took it to Scotland, and carried it into their "Sustentation Fund." They had thus proclaimed fellowship with man-stealers, men to whom the

---

7   Jonathan Walker (1799–1878) was an American abolitionist, famously known as "The Man with the Branded Hand" after he was caught helping enslaved people to escape in 1844. The infamous 'SS' (slave stealer) branded into his right hand became a visual tool for the transatlantic abolitionist campaign.

8   Controversy surrounded the Free Church of Scotland after several ministers accepted donations from enslavers in the South in 1844. Douglass, William Lloyd Garrison, George Thompson, and Henry Clarke Wright led transatlantic abolitionists in decrying the Church's actions and exhorting it to "send back the money."

titles of thieves and robbers applied equally with highwaymen and pirates, for they lived and had their being, and amassed their wealth by plunder – by the unpaid toil of the slave. And the Free Churchmen proclaimed their fellowship knowingly – styling those who traded in the bodies and souls of men, "brethren," "Christians." He condemned them for justifying their conduct by appeals to the Gospel of Christ. What, then, must the Free Church do? (Several voices – "Send back the money.") Ay, let them send back the money – (applause) – because by sending it back an agitation might be produced in the United States which would give slavery a blow that would send it reeling to its grave. (Cheers.) Would the Free Church do this? That depended upon the people of England. They, and especially the Dissenters, should speak out, and din into her ears, "Send back the money": saying, in the language of Dr. Campbell,[9] of London, that their honestly-gotten money and the money of the American slaveholders should not clink in the same treasury – and that if the Free Church did not cut the connection with slavery, they would cut the connection with her. (Applause.) That was the plan to be pursued – the only effectual plan. Dr. Chalmers[10] endeavoured to draw a distinction between the system and its upholders – he had discovered a *free* mode of upholding the system by making a distinction between the character of the sin and the character of the sinner; and this was the last heresy of the Free Church of Scotland. (Cheers and laughter.) It was really lamentable that Drs. Chalmers, Candlish,[11] and Cunningham[12] should have stultified themselves by becoming the apologists of so heinous a system. Dr. Cunningham defended it on the plea that the laws of the country legalised the thing, and made the legislators of the country, and not the slaveholders, the parties responsible for it. "The sum of all villainies, the compendium of all crimes," as John Wesley[13] had called slavery, had thus found upholders in the Free Church men of Scotland. But the alliance must be undone, and it was only to be undone by the instrumentality of the people of England. The reputation of the slaveholder, as given to him by these men, must be undone. (Applause.) Here, continued the lecturer, he might speak thus boldly in safety but for uttering these principles in Scotland he had been condemned as an "infidel." (Laughter.) Now, to the slave-

---

9   Reverend John Campbell (1795–1867) was a London-based Congregationalist minister. He later attended Douglass's speech at Finsbury Chapel in May 1846.

10 Thomas Chalmers (1780–1847) was a Scottish minister and leader of the Free Church of Scotland.

11 Along with Chalmers, Scottish minister Robert Smith Candlish (1806–1873) played a central role in the establishment of the Free Church of Scotland.

12 William Cunningham (1805–1861) was a minister, theologian, and leading figure in the creation of the Free Church of Scotland.

13 John Wesley (1703–1791) was a theologian and leading figure in the creation of Methodist thought in England.

holding, woman-whipping, cradle-robbing religion of slavery he did boldly proclaim himself an infidel – for such a religion had no principles in common with the beautiful precepts of Christianity. The lecturer, after dilating eloquently on this head of his discourse, announced that he was connected with the Old Abolition Society of the United States, which held annually, in Boston, a bazaar, the proceeds of which were used for the purpose of publishing pamphlets and sending out lecturers to inform and influence public opinion on the slavery question. He then referred to the efforts of Maria M. Chapman,[14] who is at the head of the anti-slavery ladies in America, and by whose indomitable perseverance the greater part of the funds are collected, by which the anti-slavery agitation is carried on; and he indicated the progress of the agitation by stating that whilst in 1830 there were no lecturers or newspapers in favour of it, they were now most numerous, and those who were formerly treated with scorn and contumely, were now respected and countenanced and applauded in many of the northern states of America. He concluded by inviting contributions to the bazaar from the ladies of Carlisle.

---

14 Douglass refers to the American Anti-Slavery Society, founded in 1833, led by William Lloyd Garrison. Maria Weston Chapman (1806–1885) was a US-based abolitionist, writer, and feminist, and an ardent supporter of Garrison's party.

ANTI-SLAVERY MEETING.
WILLIAM LLOYD GARRISON
AND FREDERICK DOUGLASS

Dundee, Scotland, *Dundee Courier*,
29 September 1846, p. 3

Last night a public meeting was held in Bell Street Hall, to listen to addresses by Messrs William Lloyd Garrison[1] and Frederick Douglass, on the subject of American Slavery, the present position of the Free Church, and the recent proceedings of the Evangelical Alliance[2] in regard to the slavery question . . .[3]

Mr Douglass said, he was glad to be again in Dundee, and he was glad to find that the feeling on the subject of American slavery which pervaded the town six months ago had not departed from it, – that they were here to cheer the heart of the anti-slavery advocate, and strike terror into the hearts of the pro-slavery portion of the community. Since he last addressed an assembly in this town, the subject of slavery had assumed a somewhat new phase. The General Assembly of the Free Church of Scotland had held its session since that.[4] The Evangelical Alliance has held meetings for a considerable length of time, and has dissolved and gone back to its original elements since that time. The subject of slavery has been presented in various forms to the people of England, Ireland, and Scotland since that time. The Synod of the

---

1 William Lloyd Garrison (1805–1879), US-based writer, abolitionist, and editor of *The Liberator*, who hired Douglass to speak on behalf of his organization, the American Anti-Slavery Society, in 1841.

2 Despite a rise in tensions as to whether enslavers should be members, the newly formed Evangelical Alliance met in August 1846 in London. During the week of discussion, debates about slavery threatened its success and an international approach was eventually abandoned as a direct result of Douglass's agitation against it.

3 Garrison began this meeting by reading anti-abolitionist articles from the *Northern Warder*, a Free Church-supporting newspaper, and discussed the relationship between slavery, religion, and the Bible.

4 Douglass had attended the General Assembly at the end of May 1846, alongside George Thompson.

Secession Church has declared "no union with slaveholders" since that time. (Applause.) The Relief Synod has declared "no union with slaveholders" since that time. (Applause.) The Presbyterian General Assembly in Ireland has declared "no union with slaveholders" since that time. (Continued applause.) He wished to direct attention for a moment to the proceedings of the Evangelical Alliance. That body met in London a few weeks ago, and one of its first acts, after having assembled, was to declare that it would not be prudent to let it be known what they were going to do, or what they did. One of the first acts was to shut out the reporters. It was dangerous to admit them. What would the Protestant people of this country think if a body of Papists meeting together for supporting Popery, were, the very first thing they did, to shut out all reporters? The Evangelical Alliance come together for the support of pure and undefiled Christianity, yet they keep the world uninformed of what they are about to do. Mr Douglass then shortly narrated the proceedings of the preliminary meeting of the Alliance at Birmingham, and the resolution proposed by Dr Candlish to exclude slave-holding ministers, and agreed to. That resolution was looked upon as an insult by the slaveholders in the United States, more especially as coming from one in the position of Dr Candlish; and they resisted it on the ground that the body who passed it had no right to decide what complexion the Alliance should be of. He then mentioned that great numbers of American divines came over – men of talent and professors of theology, &c. – about 70 of them, and among the number Dr Smyth[5] of South Carolina, a man who marries slaves and leaves out the most important part of the ceremony, "Whom God hath joined let no man put asunder."[6] This man is now in this country, and preached in Edinburgh for Dr Chalmers. This miserable creature creeped into the Evangelical Alliance, and left the mark of his slime behind him. (Hear, hear.) The first thing to be settled after the meeting was to determine the basis. They called together the Alliance, and when they met they found they were without a basis. (Laughter.) They were in an unhappy predicament. Dr Hinton[7] then proposed that all assenting to the basis, not being slaveholders, should be admitted. Up to this time things had gone on delightfully. They had prayed – they had said how much they loved each other. The most unbounded love, in fact, was manifested towards each other; but the introduction of the proposal to exclude slaveholders

---

5   Irish-born Thomas Smyth (1808–1873) emigrated to the US and served as a Presbyterian minister in Charleston. He had returned to Britain and Ireland in 1846 on personal business, but was incensed at Douglass's success; he issued a slanderous letter against him, but was later forced to apologize.

6   A quote from the Bible, "Therefore they are no more two, but one flesh. What therefore God hath joined together, let not man put asunder" (Matthew 19:6).

7   John Howard Hinton (1791–1873) was a Baptist minister, author, and member of the British and Foreign Anti-Slavery Society. He attended the World's Anti-Slavery Convention in 1840 and delivered a speech on slavery at the Evangelical Alliance.

raised a most exciting scene all at once. The proposal to keep out men-stealers from the Evangelical Alliance because they were men-stealers was a most important and difficult point. (Hear, hear.) Dr Wardlaw[8] and Dr Hinton stood by the statement for a time, that there should be no Christian fellowship with slave-holders. Rev. Mr Pringle stood firm to the last.[9] The Rev. Mr Nelson of Belfast,[10] Mr Stanfield of Belfast,[11] also stood up. The great number of the American delegation, stood up as strongly on the other side, and threatened the Alliance, that they who had come 3000 miles, such was their love, would abandon them if a resolution like that of Dr Hinton was agreed to. Such was their firmness that Dr Hinton's resolution was with-drawn and the whole matter referred to a committee, who sat for a week, the subject was such a difficult one. During this time the Rev. Dr Smyth, this violator of mar-riage, a man who has been guilty of the greatest slanders, according to his own con-fession, this Rev. gentleman very piously rose up, and proposed that they should engage in prayer, so difficult was it for the committee to arrive at a decision. Nay, they even went without their breakfast. (Mr Robertson[12] – "Dinner.") They went without their dinner, so great was their anxiety about the committee coming to a decision. Think of that – what fasting. (Great laughter.) How often have the poor slaves not only gone without their dinners and their suppers, but been afterwards driven out to the field, without an expression of sympathy. Mr Douglass then went on to narrate the farther proceedings of the Alliance on the slavery question – that even the reso-lution which they did adopt at one time had to be wiped off their books to please the American brethren. How could Dr Wardlaw, or the other English and Scotch divines who had expressed sound views, thus give up their judgments? He held that the deci-sion to which the Alliance had come was the greatest support to Atheism. They had thunders against the Pope of Rome for discouraging the reading of the Bible by the laity; but they had not a word to say in regard to the three millions of human beings who were denied the privilege of learning to read the name of their Creator. They sat in Christian fellowship with their oppressors. Mr Douglass continued to animadvert for some time on the doings of the Alliance, exposing the glaring inconsistency of their conduct. He then came to the doings of the Free Church Assembly, exciting

8   Ralph Wardlaw (1779–1853) was a Scottish Presbyterian minister and theologian who, along with Hinton, attended the Evangelical Alliance. He later broke with the Garrisonians to support their American abolitionist rivals led by Lewis Tappan.

9   Reverend James Pringle (1782–1866) was a Scottish minister and theologian.

10   Isaac Nelson (1809–1888) was an M.P. and Presbyterian minister of a chapel in Donegall Street, Belfast, where Douglass spoke several times in 1845–46.

11   James Standfield (c. 1809–c. 1861) was an abolitionist based in Belfast, and one of the secretaries of the Belfast Anti-Slavery Society.

12   James Robertson was a Scottish abolitionist based in Edinburgh, and secretary of the Scottish Anti-Slavery Society.

much laughter by the admirable manner in which he imitated various of the leaders, and carrying the meeting along with him in his comments upon their speeches. On Dr Duncan's[13] distinction betwixt slave-holding and slave-having, he said he enjoyed the ingenuity of the thing, although he pitied the man. In America they had also fine distinctions. It was the "peculiar institution," the "domestic institution," the "social institution," more recently, "the impediment," more recently still, "unenlightened labour," and more recently still, Dr Duncan calls it "slave-having." What would they think if he was to say, concubine having was not concubine-holding? How would that sound? Would it not sound as offensive to their sense of morality? There was great joy in the Assembly at the discovery of Dr Duncan – great clapping of hands when Brother Duncan made the notable discovery; Dr Candlish shook him warmly by the hand, and Dr Cunningham congratulated him on his success. Mr Douglass then referred to Dr Cunningham's speech. He was what he would call a straightforward man. He not only said that Christ and his apostles had held fellowship with slaveholders, but with slaveholders who had a right to kill their slaves; and Mr George Thompson, for crying hear, hear, to this, and drawing attention to it, was immediately surrounded by a number of the Free Church people; and a cry got up of "put him out." Mr Douglass then took up Dr Cunningham's defence of slaveholders on the ground that if an Act of Parliament was passed declaring all servants slaves, their masters would be guiltless; and asked would the Free Church say so if polygamy, concubinage, or the worship of Juggernaut was thus enjoined, although he could not discover from Dr Cunningham's speech that he would offer resistance? Was it not the duty of all parties to petition and protest against all iniquitous laws; and had the Americans ever done this? Were not the slaveholders the lawmakers themselves? He then took up the defence that was set up on the ground of the laws enjoining slavery, and said he would reply in the words of an eloquent statesman of this country (Lord Brougham)[14] – "In vain you tell me of the rights of the planters. I deny their rights. To the principles and feelings of our common nature I appeal. In vain you tell me of laws and statutes that sanction such a claim. There is a law above all the enactments of human codes – the same throughout the world – the same in all ages – such as it was before the daring genius of Columbus[15] pierced the night of ages, and opened up to one world the sources of power, wealth, and knowledge, and to another all unutterable woes. It is the law written by the finger of God on the heart of man; and by

---

13   Reverend John Duncan (1796–1870) was a theologian and minister of the Free Church of Scotland.

14   Lord Henry Brougham (1778–1868) was an M.P., abolitionist, and member of the British and Foreign Anti-Slavery Society. He served as Lord High Chancellor and supported reformist causes such as free trade and the 1832 Reform Act.

15   Born in Italy, Christopher Columbus (1451–1506) was a sailor, explorer, and colonizer who is credited with "discovering" the Americas.

that law, unchangeable and eternal, while men loathe rapine and abhor blood, they will reject with indignation the wild and guilty phantasy that man can hold property in man." (Great cheering.) Mr Douglass then referred to the sentiments he at one time entertained towards the Free Church, and how much these were changed since he knew the conduct of her leaders. He called on the party who had got up a movement within her on this subject to continue their exertions, and concluded by mentioning that an Anti-Slavery Society[16] had been formed by some of her members, which showed they were in earnest. (He sat down amidst long continued cheering.)

---

16 A reference to the short-lived Free Church Anti-Slavery Society, founded in 1846.

SLAVERY IN AMERICA: FREDERICK DOUGLASS IN WAKEFIELD

Bradford, England, *Bradford and Wakefield Observer, and Halifax, Huddersfield, and Keighley Reporter*, 21 January 1847, p. 8

On Friday last, Mr. Frederick Douglass, and a deputation from the Anti Slavery Society, paid a visit to the town of Wakefield, and on the evening of that day, they addressed a most numerous and highly respectable gathering, of the inhabitants, in the Corn Exchange, on the subject of American slavery.

Mr. DOUGLASS then arose, and was hailed with a hearty welcome from the vast assembly. After the cheering and clapping of hands, which continued for some minutes, had subsided, he commenced by telling his audience, that within fourteen days sail of the shores of Britain, there was at the present moment no fewer than three millions of our coloured fellow-beings under the yoke of bondage and undergoing all the hardships which slavery in its most direful and hideous forms could inflict upon them. He and his companions of the Anti-Slavery League appeared before the inhabitants of Wakefield, to arouse their feelings and to excite their influence in behalf of this immense multitude of the human family, who are daily undergoing hardships almost past enduring, and he said that a reward of glory was in store for every one who would exert himself for the freedom of these poor coloured prisoners from a set of the most tyrannical and inhuman monsters beneath the skies. A slave was no more thought of by his holder than an animal of the brute creation, and he humbly asked the sons of Britain to unite themselves for the purpose of sending a powerful voice across the Atlantic, demanding a speedy annihilation of that infernal and unjust system which makes one human being the property of another. The poor slave would give up his liberty rather than give up his life. They were the heroes of the human race, who endured the real hardships; but there were others of the human family, who would suffer death rather than yield to the bondage of slavery, and upon these he called to aid in securing the emancipation of our unfortunate and too long neglected kindred in slavery. He then proceeded to inform his hearers that he himself was a runaway slave, and although he was through the kindness of providence possessed of his freedom in the British domains, yet he was still in the eye of the American law, a piece of property and nothing more. He had served and had suffered in the bonds of slavery, and as he knew more of it, than those who had fortunately not experienced it, he would tell his hearers what it was. Although certain parties had laboured to show that slavery was confined to a few small tracts of country, yet it was a fact notorious as the sun at noontide, that the horrid system was carried on extensively throughout the lengths and breadths of the "far west," and although there were certain states distinguished as free, yet still the law makers of the latter had joined in union with those of the former, to perpetuate the system. The law makers had everything to do with slavery. If the slave holders were left alone in their infernal traffic they would have but little power to keep up the abominable system, but they were aided not only by the law makers, but also by those who elected them, and the cruel holders had the command of the military, if the poor slave dared to revolt. If such was not the case, the poor slaves would rise and snap their fetters. The slave holder was a thief and nothing else, let him be a doctor in divinity or what he may, because he takes that liberty which rightfully belongs to another. God gave man his hands for his own especial use and for nothing else, otherwise they would have been formed in a different way. Mr. Douglass then asked the audience whether they were of the same opinion with him, in calling that person a thief who robs another of liberty without any just cause for so doing, and after they had testified their opinion in the affirmative, he said, "why then there are in America, Bishops and church ministers, doctors in divinity, and class leaders, who are thieves!" There are whole churches composed of thieves, who meet to preach, sing and pray together, and some of these had come over to England on a recent occasion, as wolves in sheep's clothing, and why did not Englishmen detect them? If ever they dare approach the shores of Britain again, he hoped the people would not stick at telling them what they were, and what was their opinion respecting them. Slavery had been misrepresented by interested parties, and it was well that at least one slave had effected his escape, to tell the people of this country the cruel practices which were then imposed upon his brethren in bondage. He knew slavery by experience, and although the friends of slavery did not like it, he would give his hearers a faint likeness of it, though he did not wish to harrow up their feelings, by exhibiting their cruelties before the public. He then proceeded to give a brief narrative of the horrors he had witnessed, while he was under the yoke of tyranny. He belonged to one Thomas Hall,[1]

---

1   A reference to Douglass's enslaver, Thomas Auld (1795–1880). The misspelling is indicative of the mistakes found in Victorian press coverage, forcing us to tread carefully with these sources; it could also result from the correspondent's position and how the acoustics of the venue, or his position in the crowd, had an impact on the accuracy of the piece.

a *class leader*, and who was represented in his own country as a good sort of a man, and he had seen this said Thomas Hall, the *good man*, tie up a young female slave by the hands, for some alleged trifling offence, and flog her with the cat until the blood trickled down on all sides, brine was then poured on her wounds, and the poor woman was sent to resume her work in the midst of her agonies. He had also seen mothers served out in like manner, in the presence of their children, and the latter had also been flogged most unmercifully because they cried to see their mothers so cruelly dealt with. Sales by auction of human beings were of frequent occurrence, and on one occasion he saw a man and his wife sold to different masters, who lived at a great distance from each other. The poor man wished to speak to his wife previous to their parting, but this was denied him, and on his making an attempt to get to her without leave, the horrid barbarians set to work and actually beat him to death before her eyes. He had likewise seen his own brother and many others beat in the most savage and ferocious manner, and he cited several other cases at which humanity could not help to shudder. The speaker then mentioned various other revolting practices to which the poor slaves were subjected, and he said that there were no fewer than seventy-one crimes for which a coloured man was punishable with death, but the cruelties inflicted upon the poor creatures were always cloaked under religion, and that was the worst of all. Children were sold to buy bibles, and men and women were sold to build churches. He then briefly alluded to the blot which the Free Kirk of Scotland had entailed upon itself in respect to slavery, and concluded his long and powerful speech, by exhorting his numerous hearers to raise their voices in favour of an emancipation of slavery throughout the world. Mr. Douglass sat down amidst much applause.[2]

---

2 Henry Clarke Wright was also present at the meeting and, according to the local correspondent, "made some rather severe cuts both at the Free Kirk of Scotland and the Evangelical Alliance."

FREDERICK DOUGLASS IN LEICESTER: THE ANTI-SLAVERY MEETING IN THE NEW HALL

Leicester, England, *Leicestershire Mercury*,
6 March 1847, p. 2

On Tuesday evening the New Hall was filled literally to overflowing (for hundreds, after strenuously endeavouring to find an entrance into the spacious room, were obliged to give up the attempt as hopeless,) by an audience composed of all sects and parties, who came to hear this truly eloquent "Runaway Slave" speak of the grievous and appalling wrongs endured by his brethren in the professedly democratic and religious United States of America. And well were they repaid; for rarely, if ever, has it been our good fortune to listen to a more heart-stirring appeal on behalf of the oppressed, of whatever colour, clime, or creed – never have we heard a more uncompromising yet more dignified denunciation of the oppressor and of those who gloss over and strive to palliate the crimes which he daily perpetrates in the sacred name of the law, and even of religion. It is a source of deep regret to us that, owing to the many other calls upon our space this week, we can do no more than give a bare outline of Mr. Douglas's address and the other proceedings of the evening . . .

Mr. DOUGLAS then stood forward; and his open, intelligent, and cheerful countenance, most expressively spoke the thanks his tongue would have uttered, for the hearty welcome with which he was greeted, if he could have made himself heard above the cheering which burst simultaneously from all parts of the vast assembly. – Mr. Douglas, we may observe *en passant*, is tall and straight, though somewhat spare in figure; his features are striking, – they would be considered handsome even in a white man; – and we should think there were few who listened to his harrowing description of the enormities practised upon his own relatives, or his manly assertion of the claims of his race to be free and looked upon as equal in the sight of God, or to his narration of his escape from bondage, but must have recalled to mind the scene where the Moor of Venice[1] tells how, "his story being done," the fair Venetian lady

> "Gave me for my pains a world of sighs:
> She swore, in faith 'twas strange, 'twas passing strange;
> 'Twas pitiful, 'twas wondrous pitiful.
> She wished she had not heard it; yet she wished
> That Heaven had made her SUCH A MAN!"

Nor could they longer wonder that she, who had doubtless been brought up to share her father's prejudices against "coloured people," save as slaves or vassals, should have been led to recant her heresy, and to proclaim to the world of Venice that she now disregarded such poor and petty prejudices, and

> "Saw Othello's *visage in his mind.*"

But we must proceed. Mr. Douglas began by expressing the great pleasure it gave him to meet so large an audience, assembled to hear him urge the claims of his so long abused and deeply-injured race. He had nothing in the way of learning, or in the score of experience in addressing public assemblies, to recommend him to their notice: he had nothing which could entitle him to their attention but A LONG EXPERIENCE OF SLAVERY, and a heart devoted to the redress of the wrongs of his brethren. The crowded assembly he saw before him, gave him additional pleasure, because it afforded another proof, that however many forms Slavery might assume to itself, there was a deep-seated conviction in the heart of every community, that it was a grievous wrong which ought to meet with the reprobation of every honest man. (Applause.) It might, perhaps, have struck many of them, that it was strange he should have to come from a country like America – professing such large and liberal views of the equality of all men – to a country like this possessing monarchical institutions, to rouse up a feeling against the continuance of Slavery in the former country. The only explanation he could give was that the United States were not a republic. (Hear, hear.) Their Declaration of Independence asserted the equal rights of all men; while, under the very eaves-droppings of their Senate-house, and the fluttering of their star-spangled banner, that assertion was contradicted by the fact, that there were THREE MILLIONS, or one-sixth of the whole population,

---

1 The Moor of Venice is a reference to Shakespeare's *Othello*. The correspondent subsequently goes on to quote Act 1, scene 3.

rattling their fetters and clanking their chains in most abject Slavery. (Hear, hear.) The meeting must bear in mind that the northern were the *free* and the southern the *Slave* States; that each state had its own constitution; and that yet, by the general constitution of the United States, the maintenance of Slavery was guaranteed, – because, often when persons came over from the United States and were spoken to on the subject of Slavery, they replied, "Oh, they came from the free States, and were in no way responsible for what took place elsewhere." Thus it was that these parties attempted to shirk all the responsibility. (Hear.) But while this was certainly the case – and while it was true the general government had no right to interfere with the Slave States, – yet that general government actually bound every citizen to aid the slave-holder to keep his slaves in bondage. (Shame!) Slavery *was*, therefore, an American "institution;" indeed, the slave-holders themselves confessed that, without the aid of the other states, they could not keep their slaves in bondage. This must be the case when, while there were 3,000,000 slaves, there were only 300,000 slave-holders; for, but for these other states, those 3,000,000 slaves could easily walk off, or if they wished to be cruel, kill their masters and take possession of the soil. A celebrated political orator[2] of the Southern States, had confessed this – that they were in a very dangerous position there – that they were living in the midst of an ignorant and enslaved population; who, if they were not conscious that the whole force of the other states would gather together to repress them, would doubtless rise and assert their natural feeling for independence – that, but for the certainty of the aid of the northern states, those of the south could not repress that feeling. The fact was, Slavery was one of the national institutions; every man who dropped his vote into the ballot-box was thereby understood to say, "The slave shall be still a slave, or he shall die," notwithstanding the declaration of Jefferson,[3] that opposition to a tyrant was justified in the sight of God. (Hear.) Let no man, then, tell them when he came from the Northern States, that he had nothing to do with the existence of Slavery. He had. The constitution of the United States was such, that it made the whole of the country one vast hunting-soil for the recapture of slaves. (Hear.) There was not one single rood of earth, in all that vast continent, where, six months ago, he could have said he was safe from pursuit – where he could feel he was secure from the talons of the American Eagle. (Hear.) A slave was looked upon in that free country as a piece of property, to be bought and sold, and to be hunted down by blood-hounds if he made his escape. – I have myself (said the speaker, after a momentary pause,) experienced the anxiety and trepidation

---

2   Kentuckian Joseph Rogers Underwood (1791–1876), a gradual emancipationist, made those remarks while serving as a Whig in the House of Representatives.

3   Thomas Jefferson (1743–1826) was a founding father of the United States, author of the 1776 Declaration of Independence, third US President, and a slaveholder.

consequent on this state of things; for I am, as I believe most of you are aware, A RUNAWAY SLAVE. (Hear, hear, and enthusiastic applause.) I have found no resting place for the sole of my foot there – in that "free country." You have heard of our wide-spread lakes, our lofty mountains, our boundless prairies, and of the spirit of freedom which dwells throughout our land? I am here to tell you that there is no mountain so high, no valley so low, no forest so vast, no place so sacred, as to have secured to me the right to my own person! (Hear.) – It was to this fact (Mr. Douglas proceeded) that his presence in that hall that evening was owing. He had managed to make his escape from slavery, and after living, in obscurity for three years, he was brought into notice by some friends of the Abolition Cause,[4] and at their request made some statements respecting the system at a public meeting. It might perhaps be asked how he could do this, if there was no security for the slave in America? The fact was, he was living under an assumed name – and surely he had a right to assume a name if he chose? (Hear, and laughter.) Whatever right other men might have, he thought the man who had had no sponsor to give him a name, might be allowed the small privilege of taking a name for himself? (This was said with such irrestible humour, that the place rang again with applause and laughter.) When, therefore, (the speaker continued,) he found himself in a state where he was regarded as free until he was claimed, he assumed the name under which he now appeared before them, and by this means he succeeded in keeping his master in ignorance of his whereabouts. His master had doubtless heard of Frederick Douglas, a black, who was going about exposing the iniquity of the slave holders; but until recently he had no idea that it was the veritable "Fred" whom he had so often kicked and cuffed over his estate! Well, going about the States in this manner, he (Frederick Douglas) acquired some considerable amount of information – "for a slave," (hear, and applause,) and this excited a suspicion in the minds of the Pro-Slavery party, that he was not actually what he professed to be, a runaway slave: if he had been, he could not speak as he did, and so on – "he must be some free black whom the Abolitionists had got hold of, instructed what to say, and then sent him forth to speak, in order to prop up their tottering cause. Yes, it must be so, for you will observe that the man only speaks generally upon the system, and keeps us in ignorance of where he came from." This was the way in which they talked; and at last he found it necessary, if he wished to exert any influence on behalf of the slave, that he should give this information. He therefore set about the matter, wrote a narrative of his life,[5] and published it some twenty months ago – giving in this his name, the name of his master, where he came from, besides exposing a great deal of the wickedness which was carried on in that vicinity. He thus proved that he was indeed a fugitive slave,

---

4   Douglass refers to William Lloyd Garrison and the American Anti-Slavery Society.
5   Douglass's *Narrative of the Life of Frederick Douglass, An American Slave* (1845)

but he thus also incurred the risk of being recaptured. Acting, therefore, on the advice of his friends, he had felt it best to leave America for a time until the excitement consequent upon the publication of his narrative should have subsided. He had heard of a land where he might be free, and that England was that land: he therefore embraced the first opportunity which presented itself, and came over here. He was prepared for a kind and generous reception at the hands of the British public; but he must say that the reception he had everywhere met with, from his first landing eighteen months ago, had been more kind, more benevolent, and more enthusiastic, than his warmest hopes had led him to anticipate. (Loud cheers.) Never, indeed, from the moment he had landed on British soil, had he met with a single person, boasting the name of a Briton, who had given the slightest cause for suspecting that he disliked him (the speaker) because God had given him a different coloured skin. (Applause.) Very different was his treatment in the United States! The contrast between the two was so great, that he could scarcely realize his identity after he got to this country. (Applause). He had not known at one time that he should ever be able to return to the United States; but now he should go back – yes! he should go back, although it would be to be kicked and cuffed as he had been before. (Loud cheers.) He should return there with the conviction, however, that for eighteen months he had enjoyed a state of uninterrupted manhood and liberty, and that while he had been in safety himself, he had also been able to make his mission useful to his brethren who were still in bondage. (Cheers.) But he might be asked – as he had been asked – what good was to be accomplished by bringing the question of American Slavery before the British public? "Three thousand miles of ocean are between us and them," it might be said; "we are not slave-holders; why not go to them and discuss the question there?" He would answer that question. Besides a number of smaller reasons, there was one that he thought would at once carry conviction with it: – American Slavery was upheld by the force of public opinion in those States, depended for its stability very much on the public opinion of other countries – especially on that of England. (Hear.) Both spoke the same language – each professed the same religion; and England was united to the United States by social, commercial, and ecclesiastical ties. There was a constant influx of English literature into the States, and a constant interchange of religious association between the two countries: so that the one greatly depended upon the other for its public opinion. (Hear.) But, in addition to this, there had been an attempt on the part of the American slave-holder and his friends, to sap and undermine the Anti-Slavery cause in England. (Hear, hear.) There had been a deep-laid scheme to get the religious public of England implicated in the crime of upholding Slavery; and it was therefore necessary that scheme should be exposed. Without at present going into details, he would now merely advert to this fact: that no less than seventy American ministers – Methodist, Congregationalist, Baptist, and others – came over to this country last year; and for what purpose? For no other than to bring the religious public of England into Christian fellowship with the American men-stealers.

(Hear.)[6] He would name some of these men – Dr. Cox,[7] of Brooklyn, Dr. Emery,[8] Dr. Pratten,[9] and others, the sum and substance of all whose proceedings in the Ecumenical–Evangelical Alliance, which met in London in May last, was to effect a union with the Christians of this country which should for ever keep down-trodden the slaves of America – for ever silence the voice of this country on their behalf. This was the real object of their visit; and to some extent, he was sorry to say, they succeeded. They did hoodwink, they did deceive, some of the most learned, the most philanthropic ministers of whom England could boast, into the belief that it was their duty to remain silent upon the subject of American Slavery – to lift up no protest against that foul damning blot upon the American constitution. (Hear, hear.) And if there were no other reason than this, this alone was a sufficient reason that he should come here – that one slave at least should break his chains and expose the shameful hypocrisy of the slave-owner and his friends. (Loud cheers.) If Slavery had no other cause for condemnation – if they could not speak of whips, and thumb-screws, and bloodhounds, and manacles – this one simple fact ought to be enough to rouse this nation to raise its voice against American Slavery – that it morally and intellectually deadened all those who were brought within its influence. If you spoke to them, it was as though you spoke to the dead. The slave-holder came over there, and, in canting tone, spoke of the kindness with which the slaves were treated; – but there was no voice from the slave population heard in reply. *They* could hold no public meetings, pass no resolutions, tell no tale of their wrongs; – but could the English, dare they, stand by silent and motionless, while there were millions of their fellow creatures, within fourteen days' sail of them, virtually shut up in prison all their lives – having tongues like other men, yet not allowed to speak – intellect, yet not allowed to use it? Yes, strange as it might seem to some in this country, the slave was a man like all other men. He was as readily touched by a tale of woe, his moral nature was as susceptible of kindly impressions, as his white brethren: one nature was common to them all. As the poet Cowper had said –

> "Fleecy locks and black complexion
> Cannot forfeit nature's claim;
> Skins may differ, but affection
> Dwells in white and black the same."[10]

6   A reference to the US ministers at the Evangelical Alliance.

7   Samuel Hanson Cox (1793–1880) was a Presbyterian minister and apostate abolitionist from New York. He began a public exchange with Douglass after the World's Temperance Convention in 1846.

8   Possibly a reference to Robert Emory (1814–1848), president of Dickinson College.

9   William Patton (1798–1879) was a US preacher, abolitionist, and leading figure in the creation of the Evangelical Alliance.

10 Douglass slightly misquotes the last four lines of the second verse of the poem "The Negro's Complaint" by English poet William Cowper (1731–1800).

(Loud cheering.) Let them remember, then, that the slaves had rights as well as the slave-holder, whose rights were so much talked about; and that they ought to be as much respected as his. (Hear, hear.) – Mr. Douglas then proceeded to observe that he had purposely restrained from narrating tales of cruelties practised on the slaves because he wished rather to dwell on the principle involved in the system. He wished to shew them that Slavery was upheld in the United States because the slaveholder was not looked upon out of the States as so disreputable as he ought to be. And why was this? because his character was not so well known as it ought to be. (Hear.) He ought to be classed as a man-stealer – as an abuser of men and women – and ought to be as much shunned and avoided as a horse-stealer, a sheep-stealer, or any other thief. (Applause.) But he came over here with a fine coat, and as a gentleman – sometimes as a diplomatist at the Court of St. James's,[11] sometimes as an author or a man of science, sometimes as a lecturer or delegate to a temperance convention, sometimes (and more frequently of late) in the character of a minister of religion, a D.D.,[12] a friend to religious and Bible Societies, "was deeply interested in the cause": in a word, he came over as an "evangelical man-stealer." (Hear, hear, and applause.) Now, what he (Mr. D.) wanted to see was, that, whatever were these men's pretensions, whatever the character in which they came, they should be branded as enemies to the truth, as men stealers, as thieves. (Hear, hear.) What was a thief? One who took that which belonged to another. Well, did not the slave belong to himself? Did not God give him his hands as well as the slave-holder? did not God intend him to use those hands for his own benefit? and did He not declare, amidst thunder and lightning, "Thou shalt not steal, thou shalt not covet they neighbour's goods?" But the slave-holder became covetous, and then he became a man-stealer. All those who thought he had made out a case, let them hold up their hands. (This was at once complied with.) It was carried unanimously; and when he went back, he would tell the slave-holders that the people of Leicester called them men-stealers and thieves. (Hear, and laughter.) Mr. Douglas went on to compare slave-holding with sheep-stealing and other crimes, and proved it to be of far deeper die. The attempt which had been in the Ecumenical Evangelical Alliance to palliate its enormities had utterly failed. Slavery was still slavery. It was of infernal, not of celestial origin. He then quoted with admirable effect, the following eloquent passage from Lord Brougham's celebrated speech on slavery delivered in 1830: –

"Tell me not of rights – talk not of the property of the planter in his slave. I deny the right – I acknowledge not the property. The principles, the feelings of our common nature, rise in rebellion against it. Be the appeal made to the understanding or

---

11   The royal court for the British monarch.
12   Doctor of Divinity.

the heart, the sentence is the same that rejects it. In vain you tell me of laws which sanction such a claim! There is a law above all the enactments of human order – the same throughout the world, the same in all times – such as it was before the daring genius of Columbus pierced the night of ages, and opened to one world the sources of power, wealth, and knowledge; to another, all unutterable woes; – such as it is at this day: it is the law written by the finger of God on the heart of man; and by that law, unchangeable and eternal, while men despise fraud, and loathe rapine, and abhor blood, they will reject with indignation the wild and guilty phantom, that man can hold property in man!"

Mr. Douglas then exposed the fallacy of the pleas, that the slave would be worse off, if he were liberated, and that, if liberated, he had nowhere to go and dwell in freedom. This was grossly false: – the United States were bounded on three sides by the British power; and, if the slave population were only to be told that "conscience" (how long it had slept!) would no longer suffer their owners to steep them in bondage, but that, as it was not safe for them to remain there, they must leave the United States, there would not be a slave in the whole country who would not immediately decide for himself. These sophistries, however, had had their effect on the Evangelical Alliance, which had thus been induced to erase every word from their resolutions condemnatory of slavery! (Shame, shame.) It was this religious countenance given to slavery in America which was its strongest support – this was its darkest feature; and it was this which had led to the advocates of the abolition of slavery being called "infidels" because they had had to expose the inconsistencies of professing Christians who upheld so foul an institution. (Hear, hear.) Oh, what a contrast between this state of things and that in the West India islands, where the Missionaries and slave owners waged incessant war (hear, hear, hear) – where the Knibbs and other well-known missionaries had struck terror to the hearts of the slave-holders.[13] (Cheers.) Deacons, and ministers, and even bishops were often slave-holders in America; and men, women, and children were actually sold to support Bible Societies and build churches and chapels. ("Shame, shame.") – The very master who owned, or claimed to hold him (the speaker) was a class-leader in the Methodist church; and (said Mr. Douglas) I have seen him rise from his prayers and take a female cousin of mine, tie her up, and flog her until the blood flowed down her; and while doing this he would quote the text, "He who knoweth his master's will and doeth it not shall be beaten with many stripes."[14] (Loud cries

---

13 William Knibb (1803–1845), English Baptist minister, activist, and missionary in Jamaica. He was a leading figure in the campaign to abolish slavery in the British Empire. In this paragraph, Douglass makes reference to the ongoing unrest in Jamaica between enslavers, the enslaved, and British missionaries; the Great Jamaican Slave Revolt (1831–32) being just one example.

14 Douglass quotes from Luke 12:47.

of "Shame!") I have known him also take my brother, dash him to the floor, and kick him as he lay there. And I have known him take the same young woman my cousin, and have her tied up so (by the hands, with the wrists crossed), UNTIL HER FINGERS BECAME BLACKER THAN THE GOD WHO MADE HER PAINTED THEM. (Great sensation.) – Mr. Douglas proceeded still further, and in the same unsparing manner, to expose the hypocrisy of the religious supporters of slavery in America; to denounce every slave estate as neither more nor less than vast literal brothels; to give a specimen of the sermons preached to the slaves, in order to make them submit quietly to stripes; – but here we are with regret compelled to draw our report of his speech to a close.

SLAVERY IN AMERICA

Nottingham, England, *Nottingham Review*, 12 March 1847, p. 8

The Exchange Hall was most densely occupied on Monday evening last, by a highly respectable and most enthusiastic auditory, assembled to receive Mr. Frederick Douglass, a liberated slave, who after escaping from the hands of American man-stealers, has been recently exciting the utmost interest in the minds of the inhabitants of this free country with respect to the detestable slave system of the United States. The spacious hall was crowded in an extraordinary degree, the ante-room being thrown open to accommodate the numbers who were unable to obtain seats, which were all occupied some time before seven o'clock, the hour when Mr. Douglass was expected to make his appearance . . . [1]

Mr. Frederick Douglass hereupon walked to the front of the platform, and commenced an address which would not have disgraced any orator we have ever had occasion to hear, and which was characterised by correct pronunciation, breadth and force of thought, with occasionally the most potent and withering sarcasm, and now and then a burst of genuine eloquence. Mr. Douglass is far from being a black man; true, he has a nose not exactly Roman, and his complexion is far from being closely allied to the driven snow, and he has moreover a famous bushy wig of his own: but still, no one could look at his intelligent and animated, and in some respects handsome face, and witness his quiet, dignified, and gentlemanly demeanour without feeling that between such a man and the stock "nigger" of the theatres, there was a very wide distinction. At the commencement of his address, his voice

---

1 In this long account of Douglass's meeting, the chairman (and mayor) of Nottingham, William Cripps (1798–1884), spoke and welcomed Douglass to the platform. We have left the long preamble in to demonstrate how Douglass was racialized by newspaper correspondents, but also to show his oratorical techniques. The audience were evidently impressed by his speech, as numerous copies of his narrative were sold and afterwards large numbers of men "walked up to the platform, for the purpose of shaking him by the hand."

was not well filled out, and must have been inaudible at the far end of the hall; but in a few minutes the volume of sound deepened and widened, and before long its clear tone and emphatic syllables were hurled most satisfactorily even beyond the rim of the most distant of his audience. To give an adequate report of his speech would be impossible, within any limits we are able to assign it: therefore we shall content ourselves with making a few disjointed extracts.[2] He coincided heartily in the sentiments of their excellent chairman, in asserting that this question was one of universal concern – (applause) – for the enslavement of any member of the human family was a matter of just concern to every member of that family: and slavery in any part of the world was a matter of concern to the people of all parts of the world. (Hear, hear.) This was no question of geography, of opinion, of municipal or internal regulations of states; it was an outrage deep, dark, and damning, committed upon their common humanity; and humanity had a right in its own name to denounce it. (Great applause.) Their chairman[3] had distinguished between the individual and the system; but he (the speaker) was wholly unable to make any such distinction; and his reason was, that the American slave-holder was wholly without excuse in being such; if he were surrounded by circumstances which compelled him to hold a slave; if he were driven by dire necessity, and could not help himself, such a necessity would be a legitimate excuse; but who were these American slave-holders? They were Christian professors; – men who seventy years ago, rushed to battle under these stirring words – "*Resistance to tyranny, is obedience to God!*" (Hear, hear.) They were the men who emblazoned on their banners, "*We hold these truths to be self-evident, that all men are created equal, and are endowed by their Creator with certain inalienable rights, among which are life, liberty, and the pursuit of happiness.*" (Immense cheering.)[4] They were the men who on every 4th of July, assembled together for the purpose of reading a declaration of independence, every third line of which was redolent of sentiments of freedom. They were the men who stamped liberty upon their coins, from the cent to the dollar, and from the dollar to the eagle: – the men who were making more profession of love of freedom and regard for humanity than probably all the nations of the earth together. But the truth was, the Americans were not what they professed to be; they were hypocrites – a nation of hypocrites; he did not

---

2   A clear reminder that Victorian newspaper reports should not be interpreted as accurate representations of Douglass's speeches, particularly when correspondents could not capture the lecture in its entirety (as admitted here) or edited his testimony in regard to column space.

3   In his preamble, the chairman had agreed with Free Church ministers that a distinction should be made between individual enslavers and slavery itself, which angered Douglass and shaped the rest of his speech.

4   Douglass refers to a notorious phrase from Scottish Presbyterian minister John Knox, used frequently by Thomas Jefferson: "Resistance to tyrants is obedience to God"—and then quotes directly from the Declaration of Independence.

mean to say that every individual was a hypocrite; but he did say that the ruling parties in that country – both the Whigs and Democrats, in the Church and in the State, were profound hypocrites. (Great sensation.) At this very moment there were three millions of the people of the United States, stripped of every right – herded with the beasts of the field – doomed to be sold like brutes in the market, and herded together in concubinage; and for a black woman to raise her hand against a white man, no matter how foul his purpose, was legally death upon the spot. (Expressions of horror.) There were three millions of people who were forbid by statutory enactments to learn to read the name of the God who made them; and for a mother to teach her child to read the Bible, was death on the second or third offence. He knew something about slavery: he had felt the cruel lash; he bore upon his back the marks of the slave-driver's whip. And for his part, he made no professions of any great sympathy for the slaveholders. Seventeen millions of people in the United States were at that moment standing with all their might upon the quivering heart-strings of three millions of people. He did not exempt any state in the union; for while slavery was not legal in any of the New England states, still, New England was the bodyguard of slavery, and with all her professions of freedom, stood behind the man-stealer to work his slaves into sugar, tobacco, rice, and cotton: and if the slaves should at any moment become tired of their chains, and adopt the watchword of the American revolution – that resistance to tyrants was obedience to God – those states would say to the slave-holder, Our arms, ammunition, and force are at your service, to crush them into obedience again – (much stamping of feet). And if they made their escape into the New England states, they were returned to their master; for in the eye of the constitution, a slave was as much a slave among the hills of New Hampshire, and in the glades of Florida, as in the slave-holding states. Three months ago, he could not have remained in safety in any part of the United States: and why could he do so now? Why, because some benevolent persons in England knew that he was here as an exile, while his family was in the United States; and unsolicited, they had entered into correspondence with the man who had the audacity to claim him as his property; and now he stood indebted for his freedom to the humanity of a British lady who was willing, in connexion with her friends, to be robbed of £150, in order that he might go home to his family unmolested by his African owners.[5] This master of his was a *religious* slave-holder; a class leader in the Methodist Episcopal church: and he had seen that man rise up deliberately from his knees in the morning, after an apparently very feeling prayer, and walking into the kitchen, seize a young woman, tie her two hands together with a strong cord, until it was half buried in her flesh, and then, fastening her to a hook in the joist, made for

---

5 A reference to Ellen and Anna Richardson of Newcastle, who secured Douglass's legal freedom.

the purpose, cause her to stand upon the ends of her toes for five hours at a time, and at intervals, with a heavy cow-skin, lash her back till the warm blood would drip to her feet, – (looks and cries of horror and execration), and in justification he would quote this scripture, "He that knoweth his master's will, and doeth it not, shall be beaten with many stripes." – (Laughter, and cries of "Shame! shame!") – The absurdity of thus quoting scripture might well excite a sense of the ridiculous, but the profanity and blasphemy he thought ought to inspire any other feeling.

The Mayor hereupon rose to explain, that the manifestation alluded to by Mr. D., was intended simply as a laughing to scorn of the hypocrisy of the wretch, and not as an expression of mirth, or mere ridicule. – (Loud applause.)[6]

Mr. Douglas was very glad to hear the explanation, and still more glad to hear the response to it. The truth was, however, that the quoting of Scripture was often done in such a way as to make them lose sight of the cruelty, and excite only feelings of contempt and mirth. The relation of master and slave was such as could only exist where there was cruelty. If slavery much be maintained, cruelty must be maintained also. The coloured people would work for money, but they would not work otherwise, unless in the presence of the whip. The lash was indispensible in the absence of the cash. And all the talk about getting rid of the cruelties of slavery, while the relation existed of master and slave, was absurd. (Applause.) He would tell them by what means this slave system was upheld. It was by public opinion. This was indebted for its support mostly to the clergy and the press. The slave was looked upon as a slave by the press and the pulpit of America. This was one of the darkest features of the system. Slave holding and the religion of America went hand in hand. They had in the same newspaper, long eulogies on ministers of the gospel, and rejoicings over the spread of religion, side by side with advertisements offering human beings for sale. The blood-stained gold resulting from the sale of man's flesh went to support the pulpit. (Shame! shame!) Men were sold to buy Bibles and communion-services. Professed ministers of Him who came to preach deliverance to the captive, and the opening of the prison to those in bonds, trafficked in the bodies and souls of their fellow-creatures. They denounced the Pope, and hurled their anathemas at his followers, and yet American Protestants, by the sale of members of their own churches, condemned them to grope their way from time to eternity without God and without hope – (Shame) – Methodist sold Methodist – Baptist, Baptist – Congregationalist, Congregationalist – Episcopalian, Episcopalian. He declared to the slave-holder, truly this was the house of God, but you have made it a den of thieves. (Great sensation.) He would state facts. In 1836, the all-absorbing question

---

6 Much to Douglass's annoyance, the mayor interrupts him here, and later, prevents an audience member from asking a question about slave-grown sugar.

of the day, was slavery. The Methodist Episcopal Church was the largest in America, and that church then considered this question at its Conference, and passed the following resolution: – "Resolved, that we are decidedly opposed to abolitionism, and disclaim any right, wish, or intention to interfere with the relation of master and slave as it exists in the slave-holding states of this union." (Cries of "Shame.") They were no better in 1840; for they then "Resolved, that it is unjustifiable for any minister of our conference to admit coloured persons to testify against white persons in church trials." What was this for? These ministers knew that if the slave were permitted to tell what took place at home, by day and by night, the slave-holder could not but appear a disreputable person. And the result of this was, that any member of that church could commit whatever cruelty or crime he chose upon a coloured male or female, and none could be heard in accusation of him. The slave-holder came to England as a minister, a temperance man – (laughter), – and attended the world's temperance convention; and spoke of the comfort of the slaves, – but the slaves were not allowed to speak for themselves. The slave-holder pretended that the Bible sanctioned slavery, but he never allowed the slave to read it. (Hear, hear.) He knew better. But if he really believed it did so, he would be anxious his slave should read it there. The fact was, he did not believe any such thing: *he was like his father.* (Laughter and applause.) The Episcopalians, or Church of England men were worse than any. They preached in support of this abominable crime. And yet they would say in their prayers, "O Lord, we thank thee that we live in a land of civil and religious liberty!" He would read them an extract from a sermon preached by Bishop Mead,[7] which we must own, of all the jesuitical and hypocritical compositions we ever heard, was one of the most horrible. And thus Mr. Douglass continued, at great length, in a strain of fervid impassioned declamation, which was greeted at its pauses, sometimes with stamping of feet, sometimes with vocal applause, and always with expressions of deepest sympathy with the slave, and heartiest execration of his oppressors.

---

7 William Meade (1789–1862) was a US Episcopal bishop, the third Bishop of Virginia. He supported colonization but ultimately did not regard slavery as inherently sinful.

MR. FREDERICK DOUGLASS, THE ESCAPED SLAVE, AT NORTHAMPTON

Northampton, England, *Northampton Mercury*, 3 April 1847, p. 3

A very interesting and important meeting (to which we regret our inability to do justice), was held on Monday evening, at the New-hall, Newland.[1] The two-fold object of this gathering was to introduce to the people of Northampton, the individual known for some months in this country as the "run-away slave," and to elicit such an expression of feeling as may aid public opinion in putting down the detestable system of which Mr. Douglass has been the victim, and the iniquities of which he has so eloquently and successfully exposed. When we entered the hall we found it well filled with a respectable and attentive auditory, to whom the Mayor (Thomas Sharp, Esq.)[2] who had been called to the chair, was lucidly and impressively explaining the object of the meeting, adding a very appropriate allusion to the moral influence which Nations may exert upon each other, showing how the decided and strong expression of the feelings entertained on the subject of American Slavery in this country would affect the public mind, and ultimately the social institutions of the United States. At the conclusion of his address he introduced Mr. Douglass, who rose amidst the warmest greetings. His lecture was of exceeding length and interest, and to the effect of its sterling truth and unexaggerated manner, the tears of human sympathy trickling down the cheeks of many of the listeners, bore conclusive evidence. As was well observed by one of the speakers who followed him, his drollery was not less effective than his pathos, and assuredly the easy transition from one to the other might have been more amusing than impressive

---

1   Once again, at the end of this meeting crowds of people ran to the platform "to get a good look at, or shake hands with the gifted and intrepid enemy of slavery."

2   Thomas Sharp served as Northampton's mayor in 1839 and again in 1847.

had he ever compromised by this facility the intense feeling and entire devotion which make him so distinguished and triumphant an advocate of his enslaved race. One of the highest compliments to Mr. Douglass's style of oratory was a comparison with that of Mr. O'Connell,[3] which we heard made on the night of his lecture, and which would be mainly supported, we think, by that graceful and simple interweaving and relieving of gay and grave, to which we have just referred. Apart, however, from his oratorical attractions (and these must not be quitted without advertence to his copious vocabulary, his tasteful selection of phraseology, his appropriate imagery, his acquaintance with the poets, and other classical writers, and his altogether refined elocution) Mr. Douglass possesses personal advantages which are no mean auxiliaries to the effect which he produces. His figure is commanding, his eyes and entire countenance animated and expressive, his voice at once sonorous and musical; and with perfect self-possession he united equal modesty of manner. His address consisted of the thousand times told tale of the horrors of the Slave traffic, illustrated by his personal experiences, and relieved by those inimitable *morceaux* of humour which give to his oratory so distinctive a character. Whilst contending with so much earnestness for the creation of a moral power which should be irrestible in its action upon the accursed system, he did not affect to consider that there were not other gigantic wrongs to be wrestled with – other slaveries to be extirpated; but this he said, "*towered above ordinary crimes – a solitary horror.*" He dwelt strongly on the sordid passion which is the mainspring of slave-dealing propensities, coming to the obvious conclusion that were the *trade* rendered unprofitable it would cease altogether, here introducing one of his extemporaneous couplets: –

"Take away the cash,
and you would lose the lash."

Alluding to his own sufferings as a slave, he stated that he had been whipped for *looks* – whipped because robbed of all his rights as a human being, proscribed every social privilege, a trampled and contemned nonentity, he could not *look* as he *ought*, resigned and happy. His master was a Methodist class leader, and probably as good as most slave-holders, but his cruelties were of the most atrocious description. Very harrowing indeed were the details into which Mr. Douglass proceeded: he had seen the blood pouring over the back and bosom of a female; and such gratuitous tortures inflicted when the sufferers have been fainting in their agony, as humanity shudders to think of, and demons alone could perpetrate. "I would put down so demoralizing a system," exclaimed Mr. Douglass, "for the sake of the slave-master himself."

---

3 Daniel O'Connell (1775–1847), nicknamed "The Emancipator," was an Irish nationalist and supporter of Home Rule. Douglass shared a platform with him in Dublin in 1845, and O'Connell referred to him as the "Black O'Connell."

These men, he urged, had no particular prepossession as to the *colour* of the article in which they dealt; it was the abstract love of slavery for the sake of its gains which influenced them, and care should be taken that the unholy traffic did not ultimately extend to *white* men. They who would steal black men would steal white ones. Among other startling facts, Mr. Douglass stated that the grand-children of President Jefferson are at this moment slaves in the Southern States! Adverting to the sensation occasioned here and in America by his lectures and proceedings, Mr. Douglass said, "I come here because the slave-holders don't want me to come; and I shall go back because they will be equally unwilling to see me there. My freedom has been purchased for £150, and I can now go back to Hugh Auld, my master – my *uncle* Hugh – for they tell me he is a bit of a relation of mine![4] I have got all the documents of my manumission, and with these in my hand I depart for America next Sunday." Loud applause followed the announcement of this heroic resolution. Mr. Douglass went on to state that he knew and did not under-rate the perils which he would have to encounter, but no apprehension of these would deter him from the performance of his duty. Alluding to the Evangelical Alliance, and its unprincipled shrinking from all denunciation of the crime of slavery, Mr. Douglass forcibly exposed the complete undermining and destruction of all manliness of character and true piety which is the inevitable consequence of the traffic in human beings, and unsparingly castigated "those *White-blackbirds* – the Evangelical Man-eaters." Reverting to the proceedings of the "Evangelical Alliance," he took occasion to do justice to, and pass a high eulogium on Messrs. Nelson and Stanfield, of Belfast, who spiritedly protested against the conduct of the Alliance in this particular. His portrait of a religious defender of slavery in the person of Dr. Cox, "a very dear, nice man," was exceedingly piquant. It appears that whilst the Doctor was cordially shaking hands and exchanging unctuous amenities with his reverend and religious brethren in this country, he was writing letters about them to the American newspapers, full of satirical condemnation and grotesque caricature. The Doctor hoped and expected to be safely returned to America, or at least on his way thither, before any account of those epistolary sincerities should appear in judgment against him in this country. But driven by stress of weather into Dundrum Bay,[5] and detained there by the merciless winds, back came the letters to shame the candid preacher, and proclaim to his associates what manner of animal they had been dealing with.

---

4   Throughout his life, Douglass never knew his father's identity: here he implies Thomas Auld, but he also refers to Aaron Anthony as a possible candidate. All Douglass ever knew was that his father was white. See Blight, *Frederick Douglass: Prophet of Freedom*, pp. 13–14, and Bernier in Douglass (ed. Bernier), *Narrative*, pp. 30–31, who suggests that Edward Lloyd VI, a son of Colonel Edward Lloyd V, may be Douglass's father.
5   Located on the coast of Ireland, Cox was stranded on the SS *Great Britain* at Dundrum Bay on his return to the United States.

"Imagine," exclaimed Mr. Douglass, "the Doctor's state of mind!" – Towards the conclusion of his lecture, Mr. Douglass took occasion, with admirable effect, to introduce Campbell's lines "To the United States of North America":[6] –

> "United States, your banner wears
> Two emblems – one of fame;
> Alas, the other that it bears
> Reminds us of your shame.
> Your standard's constellation types
> White freedom by its stars;
> But what's the meaning of the stripes? –
> They mean your negroes' scars."

(Loud applause.) The lecturer concluded with a glowing contrast between *his* treatment during his sojourn of nineteen months in this country, and that to which his unfortunate brethren are subjected in America. One of these in America approaching a public conveyance would be rudely repulsed with, "we don't carry niggers!" To *him* (Mr. Douglass) every public establishment had been cordially opened, from places of amusement or instruction, up to the Houses of Parliament themselves. He amused the meeting by adding that the very asses of Old England were more kindly disposed towards men of his colour than were the people of America. He had never met with one of these creatures which did not look at him sociably and shake his ears with a sort of friendly greeting. "I will go back," he said, "and I'll use English donkeys to shame the American Republicans!" (Loud laughter and applause). He was grateful, he continued, to Englishmen, – he loved England; and he had been offered the means of remaining here, but this could not be, as he had *work to do in America*. (Much cheering). Among the most pleasant and sustaining recollections which he should carry back to that country, would be that of this large and unanimous Northampton meeting, which he should not fail to make much of, and which would not be the less influential in America,

> Because their Mayor
> Was in the chair –

(laughter) – for the Americans, considering their Republican pretensions, had an extraordinary fondness for titles, dignities, and authorities. (Hear, hear).

---

6 Douglass and other Black abolitionists frequently quoted these lines from Thomas Campbell (1777–1844), a Scottish poet.

MR. FREDERICK DOUGLASS ON THE HARPER'S FERRY INSURRECTION

Leeds, England, *Leeds Mercury*, 24 December 1859, p. 3

The annual meeting of the Leeds Young Men's Anti-Slavery Society was held on Thursday evening, in the Music Hall, Edward Baines,[1] Esq., M.P., in the chair.[2] There was a numerous attendance. After the Chairman had opened the proceedings in a pertinent speech, in which he alluded to the recent insurrection at Harper's Ferry,[3] the report was read by one of the secretaries . . . The speakers included Mr. Frederick Douglass, the distinguished Anti-Slavery advocate, who is now in this country to protect himself from the violence of the Southern slaveholders, and Miss Sarah Remond,[4] also of colour, from Boston, U.S.

Mr. DOUGLASS was very warmly received. After some prefatory denunciations of slavery, Mr. Douglass addressed himself to the explanation of his supposed connection with John Brown,[5] of the Harpers Ferry rebellion notoriety. He said he was exceedingly glad that the chairman had alluded to that dear old departed saint, John Brown. (Hear.) He had just read an account of the execution, in which poor old Brown was spoken of as having entered upon a criminal career and as having met a criminal's doom. He was spoken of as having met the merited doom of the gallows. He (Mr. Douglass) had been glad to hear the chairman say that Brown's crime was

---

1 Edward Baines (1800–1890), English M.P. for Leeds and editor of the *Leeds Mercury*.
2 Most of Douglass's lectures were organized by Julia Griffiths Crofts (1811–1895), activist, editor, and long-term friend of Douglass and his family.
3 A reference to John Brown's rebellion at Harpers Ferry, Virginia.
4 Sarah Parker Remond (1824–1894) was a radical feminist and advocate of social justice who led an extensive speaking tour of Britain and Ireland in the late 1850s.
5 John Brown (1800–1859), US abolitionist and leader of the failed insurrection against slavery at Harpers Ferry, Virginia. He was captured and executed in December 1859.

simply a technical crime – that it was a crime according to form but not according to substance. (Hear.) It might be a crime for a man on the deck of a pirate ship to strike down the captain, and take her into the nearest port, where the victims of piracy might be set at liberty; and in no other sense was Brown's act a crime. (Hear.) English people were apt to look upon Brown as one who had gone into a peaceable neighbourhood and had there created a deep-seated discontent and disturbance; but this was simply a picture of fancy. (Hear.) John Brown disturbed no such neighbourhood as this. (Hear.) He entered Virginia not when she was in a state of peace but when she was in a state of war – that he (Mr. Douglass) undertook to say – for if a state of war existed anywhere on the face of the globe, it did at this moment on the soil of the Southern States. (Hear.) Slavery was itself an insurrection, and the slave holders were an armed band of insurgents against the just rights and liberties of their fellow-men. (Loud applause.) They appealed to their laws to prove their lawful right to traffic in the souls and bodies of men; they said their laws allowed them to have property in men; but this he indignantly denied. There was a higher law than that of man, and John Brown held to that higher law. (Loud applause.) When Lord Brougham, then Henry Brougham, was appealed to on the subject of "the claims" of the West Indian planters, he indignantly replied, "Tell me not of rights in men; I deny such a right; I acknowledge no such property; the feelings of our common nature rise in rebellion against such a claim. (Hear.) There is a law above every enactment of man's, and that is God's law, a law written by the finger of God to the world, and by that law – unchanged and eternal – it is impossible for man to hold property in man." (Hear.) John Brown, the Southerners said, had violated the laws of Virginia, or rather violated his honour and his duty as a citizen of the United States. In answer to this he (Mr. Douglass) had to say that he believed in a heaven, and he would also say, in reference to old John Brown, that "with such as he, where'er he be, might he be saved and lost." John Brown was a man of as devout and pious character as any man he (Mr. Douglass) knew in the world, and he always thought of his duty as a man before he considered his duty as a citizen of the United States. (Hear.) Brown did not enter Maryland or Virginia with any purpose of carnage or bloodshed. (Hear.) He did not enter those States for the purpose of murdering slaveholders and carrying off property – that was not his aim. His motive was as pure as that of Moses when he entered Egypt to conduct an exodus of liberty. Brown went to conduct an exodus to a land of freedom. In conducting his army of men out of the Southern States he meant to defend himself, if necessary, even unto blood; and although he (Mr. Douglass) was not here in England to ask the Young Men's Anti-Slavery Societies to countenance or support any armed opposition to slavery in the United States, yet when they found a man disinterested enough to lay down his life for his fellow-men, he hoped the memory of that man would not be tarnished. (Hear.) Brown was not an insurgent, but as a man against an armed band of insurgents, because in the South there was not a moment in which the blood of negroes was not being let forth at the touch of the slaveholders' scourge. (Hear.) Brown interfered; he saw the strong man beating out the brains of his fellow-man; and he interposed himself between. (Hear.) It might be said that his act was an imprudent one; but on this subject he (Mr. Douglass) had a few words to say. Prudence had seldom made heroes. Imprudent John Brown was, in one sense, because he did not succeed. If George Washington,[6] when he unsheathed the American sword of independence, had been hanged by the neck for his act, he would have been the veriest criminal imaginable, but he succeeded, and therefore he became the saviour of his country, and he was at the present time so much admired in England that his portrait might be seen in many English homes. John Brown was imprudent because, like Louis Kossuth,[7] he failed. Since he (Mr. Douglass) arrived in England on this visit he had received many letters from warm friends advising him to be at peace. He might again state that he was a peace man, but his theory of peace was this: the man who did most to establish justice on this earth was the true man of peace. There could be no real peace where there was injustice. But if there was any peace which he detested, it was the peace of death, and not of life. (Hear.) He (Mr. Douglass) was denounced as being implicated in Brown's scheme of emancipation. In all countries there were two distinct periods of history, the one in which lawless men had the ascendancy, and the other in which law and order were maintained by the sovereign people. It was so in California, and in all new countries it would be so. And the slaveholders of the South could not understand the true doctrine of peace. They wished to be let alone; they wished to enjoy the false peace of the wicked. "Shut out the light, and then, shut out the light." (Hear.) There could be no millennium for slaveholders. Let them dream of death when they sleep; let them suspect death in their dish and in their drink – for when a man reduces his fellow man to slavery, when he takes from him the right of speech, when he blots out from him the word of God, when he darkens his soul, when he takes that name that might be inscribed in the lamb's book of life and sacrilegiously inscribes it in his ledger; and when he declares that he shall have no means of escape, but that his children and his children's children after him shall linger in hopeless bondage; then he (Mr. Douglass) should say that if the slaveholder did welter in his blood he had his own crimes to thank for it. He hoped he should be able on some future occasion to have an opportunity of speaking more at length to the people of Leeds.

---

6   George Washington (1732–1799) was a military general, founding father, the first president of the United States, and an enslaver at Mount Vernon, Virginia, his family home.

7   Louis Kossuth (1802–1894) was a Hungarian lawyer, politician, and short-lived governor of Hungary. Abolitionists on both sides of the Atlantic regarded him as a freedom fighter and attended his lectures in Britain and the United States.

In conclusion, Mr. Douglass said he entertained no fears of the dissolution of the union. The Southern slaveholders dare not separate themselves from the Northern States, for it was these latter provinces which gave to the union all that it boasted in literature, science, learning, and national character. The slave States dare not dissolve the union. Which State would consent to be the breakwater between slavery and freedom? Maryland would not, neither would North Carolina, Virginia, or Kentucky. Missouri was not going to dissolve the union, and why? Because she could not. (Laughter). And while the mouth of the Mississippi was where it was, while it reached in its extensive range the important States in the North-West, which must have an outlet for their trade and commerce, these States would never consent to that outlet being in the hands of a foreign power. (Hear.)[8]

---

8 Sarah Parker Remond's speech was ignored in local newspaper reports, and the correspondent here erases her radical contribution to the meeting.

MR. DOUGLASS ON AMERICAN SLAVERY

Sheffield, England, *Supplement to the Sheffield and Rotherham Independent*, 21 January 1860, p. 10

Mr. DOUGLASS said that he wished to make his audience acquainted with the struggle at present going on between liberty and slavery. The question was an all absorbing one, and was felt to be the question of questions for the age, and for the American nation to solve. And well it might, for there were four millions of human beings in slavery in the United States. Slavery was as old as the foundation of the American nation. It dated back to the time of the Pilgrim Fathers, for at the time when the Mayflower was on her way to Plymouth Rock, a Dutch galliot was on its way from Africa to James River, with a cargo of slaves, to be sold in Virginia, and from this one cargo the system called slavery had spread through 15 States of the American Union, whilst liberty had spread from the Mayflower through 18 States.[1] Thus the two ships, the one with its cargo of slaves and the other with its liberty loving passengers, represented the contest of ideas and systems now going on in the United States. At the time of the declaration of American independence, slavery was perfectly insignificant as a power in the Southern States, or any other part of the country. At that time the right of speech on this subject generally prevailed, and the religious organizations of the land were decidedly and actively opposed to the system of slavery. What then had produced the great change in the public mind of America on this question? Cotton had done it, and the same influence which had produced a change in the public mind of America in favour of slavery, was silently doing a work in England at the present moment. It would perhaps shock their anti-slavery feelings, but he felt perfectly sure that in some manufacturing towns in

---

1 Douglass refers here to the *Mayflower* voyage in 1620 to the US, contrasting this so-called journey of freedom with one of the first journeys of enslaved people to Virginia in 1619.

England there was a sympathy springing up with the slaveholders, arising from the intimacy caused by trade. The cotton gin had increased the wealth of the slavehold-ers, for it had raised the value of the slave from $200 to $700 or $800. The price of human flesh on the Mississip[p]i was regulated by the price of cotton in Manchester. The slave power, which was estimated at twenty hundred million of dollars, had completely made itself master of the legislature of the slave states, and silenced everything adverse to the system. Having completely annihilated everything opposed to itself in the slave states, of late years the slave power had set itself to work to make itself a national system, aiming to attain power in the whole of the United States. Hence had arisen the conflict between the republican and the demo-cratic parties. By a change in the use of words, the democratic party in the states was the despotic pro slavery party. They had succeeded to a considerable extent in nationalising slavery, and there was not a spot of earth, from the St. Lawrence to the Rio Grande, where a black man could be protected in his rights. Many ministers and doctors of divinity in the States upheld slavery, and held it to be perfectly right to take escaped negroes back to bondage. Among these were Drs. Stuart,[2] Latham,[3] Blagden,[4] "South Side" Adams,[5] and others. Slavery looked strong at present, because it was organised and had the symbols of power round it, but, notwithstand-ing this, he (Mr. Douglass) was prepared to look forward hopefully to its downfal[l] and overthrow. (Cheers.) He would give them some idea of the present position of slavery in America. The abolitionists were divided into different sects; unhappily they were not united among themselves, and did not hold the same theory, nor adopt the same modes of action. They agreed, however, in this, that immediate, unconditional emancipation was the right of the slave and the duty of the master. (Cheers.) There were the Free Labour Abolitionists, who abstained from the con-sumption of the produce of slave labour. There were also the Compensationists, represented by Elihu Burritt,[6] who proposed the sale of the public land of the coun-try, and the purchase of the slaves with the produce. Another class were the Disunion, or Garrisonian Abolitionists,[7] who took the ground that abolition was to

---

2   The Reverend Moses Stuart (1780–1852) was a Yale University professor faulted by abolitionists for biblical studies that exonerated American slaveholders of moral guilt.
3   Probably Methodist Minister Henry D. Latham of Brooklyn, who defended enforcement of the Fugitive Slave Law.
4   George Washington Blagden (1802–1884), US minister and author of *Remarks, and a Discourse on Slavery* (1854).
5   Nehemiah Adams (1806–1878), US theologian, minister, and author of A *South-Side View of Slavery* (1854).
6   Elihu Burritt (1810–1879) was an editor, journalist, author, and social reformer.
7   Followers of US abolitionist William Lloyd Garrison.

be accomplished by the dissolution of the Union. This class held that the constitution of the States was a slave-holding instrument, but, in his (Mr. Douglass') judgment, it was not so. There was not a line, not a sentence, not a word, which gave countenance or sanction to slavery. (Cheers.) Slavery could not exist if the constitution were carried out. He (the lecturer) did not agree with the modes of action of any of the parties named. Instead of being in favour of disunion, he was for making the union more and more firm, for grappling with slave owners nearer and nearer, and for bringing the system as much as possible under the flashing light of northern civilization and Christianity. The objection to the disunion plan was that it left the slave in chains. It merely freed the north from responsibility, but at the same time it deprived it of its influence in abolishing the system. He belonged to that class of abolitionists who denied that there was any law for slavery in the universe, and held that no constitutions nor anything else could establish the right of property in man, and who regarded all laws which enslaved men as null and void. Besides these classes there was the republican party of anti-slavery men. It was a powerful party, numbering 107 members in the House of Representatives, and was at present struggling with the democratic party as to who should be Speaker. This was not strictly an abolition party, but it was anti-slavery, and opposed to the plans and purposes of the slave power. In 1844, this party had only 60,000 votes, while in 1856 it registered two millions, and it was probable that in 1860 it would cast a sufficient number of votes to elect a President of the United States (Loud cheers.) Although he did not look to this party to abolish slavery, still he looked to it to lead to its abolition; it would at least check the growth of the system, and give strength to the anti-slavery feeling of the country. It would give the black man an opportunity of being a man in the Northern States. If the republican candidate should be elected, the fugitive slave law would receive a staggering blow; and the Dred Scott[8] decision would be disregarded; instead of anti-slavery advocates being under a ban, they would be free to utter their sentiments and would have a fair hand-to-hand fight with slavery. He had been requested to state what the people in England could do, and asked why he brought the question before the British people at all? Because the slave-holder was largely under the influence of the people of England through trade, through the power of ideas and through the power of civilization. It was important that England should not only be on the right side, but remain on that side of the question. No man could read the *Times* without feeling that Englishmen were growing cold on the subject of slavery. That paper openly, and shamelessly as it seemed to him, went to the aid of the slaveholder in denouncing that noble patriot and Christian martyr,

---

8   The Dred Scott decision (1857) was a ruling by the Supreme Court that Black Americans were not citizens of the United States.

John Brown. (Loud cheers.) Englishmen were liable to corruption by their constant contact with America. It was therefore necessary that they should have their sympathies and sensibilities keenly alive to the question, that when they met an American, they might be able to lay upon him an anti-slavery mustard plaster. (Laughter.) In conclusion, the lecturer said he was sorry that a number of resolutions had not been drawn up to be presented to the meeting condemnatory of slavery, as had been done at other towns he had visited. He was surprised that all the trouble of getting up that meeting had devolved on ladies. He was not sure whether the people of Sheffield had not sent too much crinoline to America, and had not too many good customers there whom they did not like to offend. If such was the case, they ought to be ashamed of themselves. (Laughter.) He intended to come again, however, when he hoped some resolutions would be prepared.

AMERICAN SLAVERY – ADDRESS BY MR F. DOUGLAS

Paisley, Scotland, *Paisley Herald and Renfrewshire Advertiser*, 28 January 1860, p. 4

A lecture was delivered in the Abbey Close U.P. Church, on Thursday night, by Mr Frederick Douglas, a gentleman of colour, from the United States, on slavery in that country, to a very large and respectable audience. Indeed, although the night was both cold and stormy, there was not a vacant seat in the church, the interest attaching to Mr Douglass's alleged complicity in the outbreak in Virginia, at Harper's Ferry, and his well remembered ability as a lecturer on American slavery, proving irrisistable attractions on the occasion . . .

Mr DOUGLAS, who, on rising, was loudly cheered, said – I experience great pleasure in once more being privileged to stand before an audience in Paisley. There are pleasant associations about this place. I have pleasant recollections of the town in which I now am, and of the people to whom I am speaking. It is now nearly four-teen years since I stood before a Paisley audience, so the little boys and girls who were seven years of age then are twenty-one now, and I speak in some respects to another generation, although I am glad to see some here to-night who welcomed me here fourteen years ago. (Applause.) Although their locks may have become white, their hearts are still warm towards the oppressed and enslaved in another land, and they are here again to give me once more a welcome to Paisley – a welcome which not only gives joy to my heart, but which will give joy to the hearts of the downtrod-den on the other side of the Atlantic, with the hope of "the good time" when the opinion of mankind will snap their fetters and allow them to go free. (Applause.)[1] I have not the vanity to suppose that I can instruct a Paisley audience, or any other audience in Great Britain, on the principles of civil and religious liberty. I know

---

1 Potentially a reference to the Scottish poet Charles Mackay (1814–1889) and his poem "The Good Time Coming."

where I am, and I know to whom I speak, and if there is any place more than another where freedom has found a home, it is in the kingdom of Great Britain and Ireland. I first came here as a fugitive. I was then in danger of being captured and sent back to bondage. I am here again – although purchased by British gold I am here again as a fugitive – flying not from one master, but from many masters – from a Government, which, although boasting of its liberty, would stretch forth its bony arm to snatch me into the jaws not of slavery, but of death. You are aware that my name has been associated with that of a man who has gone to the scaffold and suffered as a martyr for my enslaved people. In the United States I am charged with acquiescence or complicity in John Brown's great scheme to deliver the slaves of Virginia and Maryland out of their bondage. I do not think it necessary to try to enlighten you on the abstract principles of liberty. With those abstract principles you are fully acquainted. I have no vain purpose of bringing you here to-night to disclose anything novel, and perhaps very little that is startling; I am here rather to stir up your minds to the remembrance of what you have already learned than to throw before you any new truths on the subject. Properly speaking there is no such thing as new and old truths. Error may be new or old – it had a beginning and must have an end – but truth is neither old nor new, like the great God from whose bosom it emanates, it is from everlasting to everlasting, and can never pass away. Man is born with a right to liberty. It entered into the very idea of his creation. It was his before he wanted it. The title-deed is inscribed upon all the powers and faculties of the human soul, and the record of it is with God; and until tyrants can scale the eternal throne and remove the Almighty, no agreement, no combination into which tyrants may enter can abrogate or destroy that right. It belongs to every man. The wonder is that there ever could have been two opinions about it. It is amazing men ever could have differed as to the rightfulness of liberty on the one hand, and as to the wrongfulness – the stupendous iniquity – of slavery on the other. As to complexion, one is none the more a man for being white, and another is none the less a man for being black. All possess the same elements of manhood – a head to think, and a heart to feel, and to be touched with the tale of a brother's woe; and the blacks, like the whites, can rise through all the gradations of human condition, and of human progress, upwards from sublunary things to Heaven, from the earth to the skies, until they grasp the glorious idea of a God, in common with the rest of mankind. And thus is his right established. Is it not a wonder there ever were two opinions as to the rightfulness of liberty on the one hand, and of the wrongfulness and hell-black iniquity of slavery on the other? Slavery is directly contrary to every man's sense of right and wrong. Now, we hold the American people are divided into two classes – anti-slavery men and pro-slavery men; and it has been well remarked it is fire which is wanted and not light. It is not so much an intelligent appreciation of principles as a disposition to be just and honest that we need to overthrow slavery. What is there in this question that it should be called a difficult one? The very dogs in old

Scotland are capable of understanding the principles involved in it. (Laughter.) The ground of the anti-slavery movement is simply this, that every man is himself. That is all (Cheers.) That he belongs to himself. That his hands, and head, and legs are his own, and belong to nobody else, and that if he runs away on his own legs, nobody else has a right to find fault with him. Now, I think this is so simple, that any respectable Newfoundland dog might understand it. But this is taking the human view of the subject, while some of the American defenders of slavery tell us not to look at it from this human stand-point. The negro, they tell us has a black skin, woolly hair, flat nose, thick lips, and dull intellect, and that this is not applicable to him. Many Doctors of Divinity holding these ethics think slavery too bad to be human, but good enough to be divine. I have been accustomed to look up to God as the source of all excellence, and I reply to this, if there be anything good, if there be anything noble, if there be anything benevolent, and if there be anything of good report in us, it comes from the centre and source of all goodness alone, and it is, therefore, impossible that slavery can be divine. In order to ascertain whether slavery is divine, we have only to ascertain what slavery is, and what God says are his attributes. God never approves and sanctions anything unlike himself. Then if slavery be divine, it must be like God – it must correspond with his attributes. What then is slavery? You know what highway robbery is. You know what the highway robber is. He meets you at midnight, in a lonely place, and with a pistol at your head demands your purse or your life. That is highway robbery. What is slavery? Precisely the same. There is not a shadow of difference between the principle of highway robbery and the principle of slavery. Much as you value your purse, you value your life more. And what is the language of every slaveholder to his slave? "You shall give up your liberty or your life." The chain, the whip, the bowie knife, the revolver, the rifle – all these instruments are used to keep the slave. He must give up his liberty or die. Every man has in his soul the love of liberty, ever urging him upwards and onwards, and when anything trammels him, he cries out for elbow room. No amount of food and clothing, or any other earthly good, will compensate for the want of liberty. Man loves liberty, and he can only be a responsible being when he has liberty. (Cheers.) It is said by some people, that the American slave is well treated, well fed, well clothed, and well taken care of, better even than the working men and working women of this country. That is the boast. What have I to say to this? In the first place, I have to say that it is impossible, on any large scale, that they can be contented and happy in the slave states. Men naturally love liberty, and loving liberty, they cannot but act, and move, and give evidence of discontent at being slaves. However treated, let them take away the chain, the whip, the blood-hound, the revolver, and the rifle, and the slave will walk out of his house of bondage at once. These are all needed to keep him in bondage, because he loves liberty. Mr Douglas then went on to show that the British travellers who formed such favourable opinions of slavery, only saw what the slaveholders pleased to exhibit to them, while they were dining at their tables, and dancing with their daughters, and that it was not likely they would be fools enough to call up their slaves to be whipped for the entertainment of their guests. In such circumstances, the slaveholders were put upon their good behaviour. It was maintained that the cruelties practised on the slave, were only the abuses of the system, but the slave had a right to liberty by virtue of his manhood, and was restless and discounted in proportion, as he was kindly treated. That was human nature. He became taller with every improvement of his condition, and the only way to produce a kind of contentment was to crush the slave and put out his intellectual eye. He next discussed the question how some of the planters got work out of their slaves without the use of the lash, and showed that it was by operating upon their affections, and threatening to sell them to others who would use them worse. He likewise replied to the argument, that a man would not use his slave badly, because it would lessen his value, by showing that the reasoning faculty of the slave, and his love of liberty, made him worse to manage than the horse. The man must be crushed, broken down, extinguished before he would be contented. When they showed him a contented slave, they would show him a man with the image and superscription of his Maker effaced from his soul, and the man gone. The whole aim of the slaveholders was to make the slaves work to them for nothing, and find themselves. He then made a severe attack upon the American clergymen who came over to this country, and made themselves the defenders and apologists of slavery, and urged that such men should not meet with the countenance which they received. As a specimen of this class he mentioned a Dr Pomroy,[2] who being questioned as to how it happened amidst so much liberty, and religion, and revivals in the United States, there were four millions of slaves in the land, replied in the following strain: – "Well brother that is a very deplorable circumstance. (Laughter in consequence of the canting tone in which the words were uttered.) We do deplore slavery very much, but it is a question surrounded with very embarrassing difficulties and we must be pardoned if we say to you our transatlantic friends, that you do not understand this question. We should be left to deal with it ourselves." (Cheers and laughter.) Although Americans talked in this way, they knew that the people of this country understood the question too well. After again urging that they should do all in their power to make slavery disreputable, he gave a long list of passages of Scripture, which were completely ignored in the Southern States, as bearing against slavery, while any number of sermons might be preached on the text, "servants obey your masters." He cleverly and eloquently touched on a number of collateral topics, and concluded this part of his address, by saying, that as they loved all the elements of Christianity, they were bound to oppose slavery as an

---

2   A reference to the Congregational minister S. L. Pomeroy (?–1869?) of Bangor, Maine, who had objected to discussion of slavery at the Evangelical Alliance.

enemy to their christian name – as an enemy to religion – as an enemy to liberty – as an enemy to humanity – and as an enemy to the whole universe – which the whole universe should take arms to put down. (Loud applause.) Mr Douglas then gave an account of the insurrection at Harper's Ferry. On the 15th of October, he said, John Brown and a handful of followers entered the place, containing about 3,000 inhabitants, and captured the arsenal which contained 80,000 stand of arms. He opened the prisons, and liberated for the time some three hundred slaves. They kept possession of the arsenal for thirty-six hours, when it was surrounded and captured by the United States troops, when John Brown had two sons shot, and his son-in-law and himself taken prisoners. He had since been tried, found guilty, and hanged, for having committed high treason against the state of Virginia. He did not regard what John Brown did as wrong in itself. The district of country in which the occurrence happened, was in a state of chronic insurrection. Slavery itself was an insurrection. Slaveholders were an armed band of insurgents, arrayed against the rights and liberties of their brother men. (Cheers.) John Brown only stepped in to put an end to that insurrection, and to show them that blows in such a state were to be taken as well as given – that the crushed worm might turn and sting them. He then argued that it was not as some said a mad enterprise, but that if John Brown had succeeded he would have ranked with Washington as a patriot, but as he failed, he was hanged as a rebel. He made a blunder in remaining several hours too long in the arsenal. His intention was to take to the chains of mountains which runs from Virginia down through North Carolina, South Carolina, Alabama, and Mississippi. These mountains which contained a hundred Thermopylae's[3] were to form the base line of John Brown's operations, and they were well suited for that purpose. After referring to the constancy and fortitude displayed by Brown; he maintained that in reality his sacrifice might lead to success greater than would have been accomplished, had his project for raising the slaves succeeded. He then narrated the circumstances of his own purchase for £150, by a subscription raised in this country, and alluded facetiously to the rise which must have taken place in his value, since Governor Wise,[4] of Virginia, had offered a reward for him of 50,000 dollars. (A laugh.) He then mentioned a few facts, as proving, that the anti-slavery cause in America, was steadily, and rapidly progressing, and concluded by intimating, that he intended delivering an address on that part of his subject, in the same place, on Friday, next week. The lecturer spoke for two hours and a quarter, in a pleasing and sometimes eloquent manner, and was frequently loudly applauded.

---

3   Douglass refers to the Battle of Thermopylae, c. AD 480, where a small force of Spartans led by King Leonidas held off against a larger Persian force through a mountain pass in Greece.
4   Henry Alexander Wise (1806–1876), US lawyer and governor of Virginia, who sentenced John Brown to death.

RECEPTION SOIREE TO MR. FREDERICK DOUGLASS

Glasgow, Scotland, *Glasgow Herald*, 1 February 1860, p. 3

Last night, in the City Hall, a reception soiree was given to Mr. Frederick Douglass, a gentleman of colour, who has recently arrived in this country from the United States, and is alleged to have been implicated in the outbreak at Harper's Ferry. The hall was nearly filled . . .

Mr. DOUGLASS, on rising, was received with loud and renewed applause. His address was, to a great extent, a repetition of the lecture which he delivered in Paisley, and which appeared in our impression of Saturday. In addition, Mr. Douglass, when speaking of the outbreak at Harper's Ferry, said that John Brown's object was to free the slaves of Virginia and Maryland. His purpose was not to shed blood, not to destroy property, not to inaugurate the dreadful scenes which marked the career of insurrection in India, but simply to inaugurate a great exodus of slaves from their masters, a grand exodus from the plains to the mountains of Virginia, which were a grand highway from slavery to freedom. According to his (Mr. Douglass's) knowledge, John Brown, by his original plan, only aimed at a grand exodus of the slaves of Virginia into the Free States, and from the Free States up into Canada, where the British lion, with its shaggy mane, welcomed the bondman, and where he could lay his head free from the fierce talons and bloody beak of the American eagle. They might be assured, however, that in case his march had been interrupted, he would not have hesitated to use arms. He had no conscientious scruples on that point. He was perfectly willing to use arms in self-defence. Insurrection was not his first aim, and the question now arose would the course pursued by John Brown be defended? It was said that he did wrong in going into a peaceful community and raising a standard of insurrection, but was a slave-holding community to be regarded as a peaceful community at all? To his mind a slave-holding community was in a state of insurrection. He looked upon every slaveholder as an armed insurgent against the just rights of his fellow-men. The whole system was one grand, one wholesale insurrection and uprising on the part of the strong to enslave the weak and trample on the helpless. Peaceful community! There was no peace there. There was not an hour in any day, there was not a minute in any hour, there was not a moment in any speck of time, in which the blood of his people was not called forth by the scourge. John Brown had stepped into the community where men were beating and scouring their fellow-men, and cried, "Hold, we are men." This was John Brown's mission: it was not to interrupt the peace of a community. There was no peace in slavery. But it was said, "You are not to resort to force." He himself had been shown the cold shoulder since he came to this country by some old-fashioned abolitionists, because of his supposed complicity with this Harper's Ferry outbreak. He did not mean to state to this audience that he was or was not implicated in the affair. Perhaps it was proper that he should say nothing on the subject; but one thing he asserted that no man had been able to prove that he was at all implicated in the affair. (Laughter and applause.) But because of his supposed implication, he was supposed to be a man of war, of blood, and so forth; but he was a peace man, and his peace principles were those which he derived from the Bible. The first mode of establishing peace, according to the Bible, was to establish justice. It was so in California, where men were brought together under an impulse – love of gain. There it became necessary first to establish justice. There could be no peace where there was oppression: there could be no peace where there was injustice. There could be no peace between one man standing on the neck of his brother, and the man who was under his heel. He was not for maintaining peace between these parties, and the reason was that the very submission of the slave for 200 years to his bondage, in the United States, without resistance, without resorting to force to break his chains, was one of the strongest arguments in the mouths of the tyrants themselves for perpetuating the tyranny. He was for submitting to injury when submission could be construed into a Christian grace, but when it was construed into a want of courage, then he said – It is time, forebearance has ceased to be a virtue. He wished to throw in a few exculpatory circumstances for his poor friend – he would not say poor, for he believed John Brown was rich – far richer to-night than any of those tyrants whose chambers were built by fraud in Virginia. The principle on which he acted ought to be held up. It would be a proclamation of a millennium to tyrants to let them say, that hereafter they need not fear these worms. The day was coming when the slave would be free; whether by peace or by war he knew not. Slavery could not much longer exist in the United States. There were four millions of them, and God did not permit four millions of people to exist in any quarter of his globe without His eye being on them. He (Mr. Douglass) did not, of course, ask them to unite in any effort at forcible emancipation, but he did ask them to say that the man who was unjustly deprived of his liberty had a right to get his liberty – peaceably if he could, forcibly if he must. And if a man had a right to get his liberty, he had a right to be helped to get it. He thought it about the first thing that a man had to do in this world in order to be a man, was to be free. No man in a state of slavery was in a condition to honour his Maker; the man was extinguished, the soul crushed out of him, when the haughty master arrogantly assumed towards his brother man the position which God alone could claim. He was thus for peace, but no peace to the wicked – no peace to those who robbed and enslaved their fellow-men. But it was said that John Brown's raid was a failure. He was not so sure of that. He was not sure that John Brown had not succeeded much better for the cause – though not for himself – by the failure than he would have done if he had been able to hold out till this time. John Brown had dropped an idea in connection with slavery in the right place, where no railroad could carry it – where no electric wires could convey it – where no man could bear it in any way. They would see, by glancing at the map of the United States, the Alleghany chain of mountains running into the very heart of Pennsylvania. These mountains run through the very heart of the slave states, and seemed to have been planted there for the very purpose to which John Brown intended to put them, and so they might yet be used. John Brown had suggested that idea. There were dens, caves, and ravines among them: there were ten thousand hiding-places, ten thousand Sebastopols built by the hand of God, stronger than any Sebastopol, stronger than any fortress built by man, where the slaves might flee and hide, and defend themselves, and defy all the armies of the United States in any attempt to dislodge them. No one, it seemed, had ever thought of it until John Brown dropped the idea among them. Mr. Douglass then mentioned the fact that in Congress 105 members were in favour of the abolition of slavery, and that 25 had dared to tell the slaveholders that they regarded slavery as a crime. He referred also to the support which many clergymen in the United States gave to slavery, and particularised Dr. Southside Adams, Dr. Blayden, Dr. Latham, and Mr. Spencer.[1] After an eloquent appeal in favour of some degree of interference by Britain in this question, he concluded by saying that he certainly hoped to go back to America notwithstanding – (Mr. Douglass filled up his sentence by a significant nod in allusion to the reward of $50,000 which Governor Wyse of Virginia had offered for him, and resumed his seat amid laughter and long-continued applause.)

---

1 Possibly a reference to US Presbyterian minister and author Ichabod Spencer (1798–1854).

FREDERICK DOUGLASS ON AMERICAN SLAVERY

Falkirk, Scotland, *Falkirk Herald*,
Thursday 9 February 1860, p. 3

This well known and popular advocate for the abolition of slavery, and who has recently arrived in this country on a mission tour in behalf of the cause to which he is so zealously and earnestly devoted, appeared before a Falkirk audience for the first time, in the Free Church, on Monday evening.[1]

Mr DOUGLASS, who, on rising, was received with great applause, said that he never stood up to address a public audience on the subject which was to engage their attention that night, without feeling extremely inadequate to come up to the expectations which may have been previously entertained in his favour. He would, however, humbly and unostentatiously lay the claims of his enslaved brethren before them, and craved a patient and indulgent hearing. Before doing so, however, he would remark, with regard to himself, that he was born a slave, and passed 21 years of his life in that degrading capacity; he had never enjoyed the benefits of a scholastic education. These disadvantages would plead his excuse when he appeared with his tale of woe before an intelligent and refined community. Mr Douglass then contrasted the system of slavery as it existed in Brazil, and other places, with that at present enforced in the Southern States of America, and fully proved that to the latter the comparison was anything but favourable. In the former, the slave, if

---

1 Douglass was introduced by the chairman after a long preamble; nearer the end of his speech, Douglass replied to other speeches on the platform and stated "he had not spoken that evening with perhaps the same animation which actuated him as when addressing an American audience. There he had prejudice and obstinacy to contend against, and had therefore to proceed with more warmth. On the present occasion he was aware his audience were even in advance of him in his ideas on the subject, and he had therefore little farther exertion to use than to state his case in a familiar and somewhat conversational style."

enabled at any time, could purchase his freedom in terms of the law of the country – not so in the slave states of America without the consent of his master – whatever money or goods the slave possessed there at any time was not his own, but by the iniquitous slave law belonged to his master, and could be taken from him. Little prospect dawned for the poor negro there but to attempt to effect his escape to British soil, and this was attended with extraordinary risk and danger. There were, he noticed, 350,000 slaveholders in the United States, who owned about four millions of slaves, and these were liable at any time to be sold and resold at the slave markets like cattle to the highest bidder. Such an atrocious and debasing system called for its immediate abolition. The highway robber demands of the traveller "your money or your life"; in the same manner the slaveholder demands from the slave "your labour or your life." Mr Douglass depicted a few instances which he witnessed of the cruel manner in which the slave was treated by his master for the most trivial offences; and an instance occurred on the plantation where he wrought of a poor negro, who, instead of coming as he was ordered by the slave-driver to the whipping post to be lashed, fled to the nearest river, and stood in the water up to the chin. He was, however, shot like a water fowl because he would not succumb. The lecturer afterwards entered upon the principle of slavery, which he characterised as a system which undermined the chief purpose of man's creation, was contrary to divine law, and abhorrent to the best feelings of humanity. In referring to the present aspects of slavery, Mr Douglass compared the work which had been achieved during the last fifteen years by the abolitionists with what yet remained to be done. The question was at present engrossing public attention throughout all the States. A contest was going on in the House of Representatives regarding the election of a Speaker.[2] The democratic party, strange to say, were not only for upholding slavery as it at present existed, but were for nationalising it, so that in the Northern States it might be respected with the view subsequently of being actually introduced. The Republican party, though holding anti-slavery views, were not abolitionists, and from the latest accounts could muster 105 votes, being within three of the required number to return their man. He had no doubt at the first election of a President, which would take place within eighteen months, that one holding anti-slavery views would be elected, and he had no fear but in a short time they would have an abolitionist President of their own choosing. Some doubts had been expressed as to a Speaker being elected at all; he had no fear of this, because each representative was paid at the rate of 3000 dollars a year, and not a single dollar could any representative draw until a Speaker was elected. The people of this country were too well acquainted with the

---

2 Forty-four ballots were required to elect conservative New Jersey Republican William Pennington as speaker over the US House of Representatives in February 1860.

wide-awake disposition of the Americans when they had anything to gain, to imagine that a Speaker would be long before being elected. In alluding to several doctors of divinity who had written in support of slavery, and in quoting their names, Mr Douglass, in pointed irony, observed that the system required considerable "doctoring," and which certainly told against it in unmistakeable terms. (Cheers.) The promulgation of pro-slavery views by these doctors of divinity had done much in retarding the emancipation of the slave, and, he was of opinion, was more dangerous to the spread and growth of genuine Christianity than infidelity itself. Mr Douglass, after giving a few statistics with regard to slavery, from 1844 downwards, closed his thrilling address by referring to the assistance to the cause which had been given by the different anti-slavery associations in this country, and trusted that his mission would meet with that sympathy and support to which it was entitled. It need scarcely be stated, he said, that the money so contributed was applied for the purposes of supplying with clothing and money such fugitives as had effected their escape to Canada. The audience were also aware that he had established a paper several years ago, and which in his absence was conducted by his son,[3] for the purpose of disseminating anti-slavery and abolitionist views. In doing so, he had almost insurmountable difficulties to contend against, and at times he was subjected to great inconvenience by post-office espionage. He was frequently grieved to find upon inquiry at the post-office that after all the other papers and letters were despatched for the day, his own papers were piled up as entire as when they were posted. Mr Douglass resumed his seat amid great applause.

---

3   Lewis Henry Douglass (1840–1908), with the assistance of veteran abolitionist journalist Abram Pryne, managed the *Douglass' Monthly* while Douglass was in Britain.

ANTI-SLAVERY MEETING IN MONTROSE

Montrose, Scotland, *Montrose, Arbroath, and Brechin Review*, 17 February 1860, p. 4

Mr Douglass then rose to address the meeting on "The Present Aspects of the Anti-Slavery Struggle in America." He commenced a very able, eloquent, and stirring address by expressing the satisfaction it afforded him to see so many of the citizens of Montrose present that evening to hear what he had to say on the subject of slavery, and it also afforded him great pleasure to think that they had been able to come with their own consent – able to come without being driven by the task-master, and in the exercise and enjoyment of that freedom which belonged to them more than to any other people in the earth. He did not come before them with the intention of making them acquainted with any new principles in connection with this great question. It would possibly be enough for him, instead of going in search of new principles with the view of enlisting their sympathies, to confine himself to the exposition of principles long ago admitted as those which should regulate mankind generally. Properly speaking, there was not such a thing as new truth, it was old truth; man's opinions might change, but not so with it. Like the great God from whom it sprung, it was from everlasting to everlasting, and could never fade away. As with truth so with man's right to liberty. Man was born with it, it entered into the very idea of his creation. Man knew by his own conscious manhood that his right to liberty was inalienable, and was not the gift of his fellowman, but the bestowment of his Creator. He (Mr Douglass) did not require to argue the question before the British people, at least; it was strange, indeed, that he should have to argue it anywhere – strange that there should be any diversity of opinion in regard to slavery. Why, there was not a child in Scotland that did not know something about the first principles of liberty. Even the very dogs, it appeared to him, understood as much about the question of slavery as the doctors in America – (laughter) – for there was not a dog in Scotland that did not know the great fact which the promoters of this movement wished to impress upon the public mind and to which they laboured to direct attention. It was simply that every man was himself – that his body was his own body and nobody else's body – that he was born, lived, and died singly. Slavery, he said, broke down individuality, denied him his rights and liberties, was opposed to the very principles of justice and religion, and snapped asunder the ties that bound man to his brother man. (Applause.) He then proceeded to refer, in glowing terms, to the great conflict which was at present going on in America in regard to the slave question, and pointed out its cause. So long ago as 240 years, this conflict began in America. In 1620, during the cold bleak winds of December, two vessels crossed the Atlantic Ocean – the one being the Mayflower which sailed from Plymouth with a company of liberty-loving passengers who spread the right ideas of those times in favour of freedom; the other a Dutch galliot which landed on the banks of the James' River, Virginia, a company of twenty slaves, imported by men too indolent to work and too proud to beg. The Mayflower and the Dutch galliot were the types of two opposite phases of humanity, and the explanation of the present collision between the North and the South. He contrasted the feeble hold which slavery at first had in the States, but its evil influence gradually spread and is now very powerful. At the present time, the slave-holders possess all the power in the South, and do not allow a word to be said against that institution. And the secret of the present conflict at Washington was that the slave power sought to assimilate to itself everything with which it came in contact. The Democratic party in the States was held by the slave-holding power; the Republicans expressed opinions of a freer tendency. He very strongly denounced the conduct of a certain portion of the clergy in America. The blood-stained gold, he said, resulting from the selling of human flesh went to support the pulpit, and the pulpit in return for this favour covered the infernal business with the garb of Christianity. Through time slavery, once despised by them, became respectable – when it became respectable the slave-holders joined the church, and when they joined the church there were very excellent reasons why the ministers should teach the necessity of that abominable traffic from the pulpit. But the anti-slavery principle was making progress in America. Fourteen years ago, they had not two members of Congress who dared to say they belonged to the anti-slavery movement; now there were 109 voting plump every day for anti-slavery speakers. At that time, they had but one man in the Senate who dared to call himself an anti-slavery man, and he said it so jocosely that the slave-holders liked it rather than otherwise; now they had got twenty-five in that body, which consisted only of sixty-six members, while they would have had ten more at this moment if the people could only get at them as at members to the other House. In 1844, they cast 60,000 votes for an anti-slavery man; in 1848, a million of votes; in 1856, they carried eleven States of the North for an anti-slavery man; and in 1860, they expected to have an anti-slavery man in the Presidential chair. He then denounced the idea of the negro character, which was professed to be given by minstrels who appear in various parts of the country, as being quite inconsistent with the fact; and the terms in which he spoke of the revivals in some parts of America where the religious movement had been joined in by persons who, notwithstanding, continued to hold slaves and endeavoured to apologise for slave-holding, were very pointed and condemnatory. In conclusion, he impressed upon the British people the necessity of maintaining a moral feeling in this country against slavery, and strongly condemned the pro-slavery opinions which were, in a manner, insinuated by many visitors to this country from America, and by some of our own country-men who take up their abode in the "far west." Slavery was apparently very strong just now and indeed was so; but like many other nefarious institutions, he believed it would continue to flourish till the very day of its fall, when all at once it would go down with a tremendous crash. Some slave-holders entertained very intelligent and clear views on the subject and had emancipated their bondmen; and he firmly believed that day was coming when the whole system of American slavery would be shaken to its foundation. Mr Douglass concluded his splendid oration by thanking the Montrose Ladies' Anti-Slavery Society for their valued sympathy and co-operation, and sat down amid loud applause.

FREDERICK DOUGLASS

Bridport, England, *Daily News,*
19 October 1886, p. 6

Mr. Douglass was appointed U.S. Marshal of (Washington) the District of Columbia, and President Garfield transferred him to the post of Registrar of Deeds in that District. Though he strongly opposed the election of a Democratic President, Mr. Cleveland[1] kept him in office, till a few weeks ago, when he appointed a Democrat of the same complexion.[2] Mr. Douglass told his hearers that 41 years ago he had visited England as a fugitive slave, and his free papers were purchased by ladies in this country; in 1859, he came as an exile, to escape the pro-slavery fury after John Brown's attack on Harper's Ferry: now he came as an American citizen, who had received the recognition of the American Government. Speaking of the present condition of his people, he regarded it as hopeful, considering the circumstances of emancipation. No provision was made for them in the war which set them free; they were left landless and destitute – not, as in Russia, where the emancipated serfs had been given land; and their old masters were naturally hostile to them, as the witnesses to their humiliation. They have, however, rapidly increased in numbers; they are acquiring education and property; and their social position is improving, in spite of many serious obstacles. Mr. Douglass had been in England about a month, but came for refreshment, not for public work. He is going on the Continent with Mrs. Douglass this week, and hopes to return here in the early summer.

---

1 Grover Cleveland (1837–1908), US lawyer, statesman and 22nd and 24th president of the United States.
2 Douglass's successor as Recorder of Deeds was James Campbell Matthews (1844–1930), but the US Senate later refused to confirm his appointment.

Part III

"A Sunbeam into the Darkness of the Hour": The Responses to Great Britain

Douglass's three visits to Britain and Ireland had a transformational impact upon him. Each time he returned to the United States, he continued to draw inspiration from the positive treatment and encouragement he had received from transatlantic reformers. For the remainder of his public career, he recalled his uplifting experiences across the Atlantic repeatedly in the rhetorical arguments he advanced on behalf of the cause of African Americans.

We have selected a representative sampling of the hundreds of references Douglass made to his British and Irish travels. In this portion of the book we include the texts of three editorials penned for his own newspapers; two articles written for other American periodicals; three speeches delivered before American audiences; a chapter from each of Douglass's later two autobiographies; and two letters he sent to British friends, and then published in the press there. Except for the last group, these documents were aimed at influencing American opinion. This might account for the near total absence of the complaints about British racial paternalism or efforts to control his message that are present in his other speeches and letters, especially on his first visit. Most likely, Douglass minimized such incidents in order to emphasize to fellow Americans, including white abolitionists, that the British were enviable role models for race relations.

Douglass was lavish in his praise of British institutions and practices when addressing his fellow Americans. In a *North Star* editorial, he enthused: "Under no government in the wide world is there more respect shown, or encouragement offered to reform, than under that of England. During the last thirty years, some of the most important reforms ever achieved under any form of government have taken place in Great Britain."[1] He reproached Americans for their pervasive racial discrimination by reporting in his second autobiography, *My Bondage and My Freedom* (1855), that he had no problem in England "obtaining admission into any place of worship, instruction, or amusement, on equal terms with people as white as any I ever saw in the United States."[2] Douglass contrasted the positive reception he had experienced in Ireland to the racism commonly directed against antebellum African Americans: "The truth is, the people [of Ireland] know nothing of the republican negro hate prevalent in our glorious land. They measure and esteem men according to their moral and intellectual worth, and not according to the color of their skin."[3]

---

1   *North Star*, 5 May 1848, p. 2.
2   Douglass, *My Bondage and My Freedom* (1855), p. 371.
3   Ibid. p. 372.

In a reminiscence written in the 1880s, Douglass summarized the rhetorical strategy he had employed during his pre-Civil War tours of Britain: "The going away of a man from a republic in search of liberty in a monarchy was a striking commentary upon the institutions of both countries and the inappropriateness of names signifying things at that time the republic meant slavery and the monarchy freedom, at least so it was in my case."[4] He noted how pro-slavery Americans had berated him for criticizing the United States while overseas and claimed that those attacks had only enhanced his effectiveness. Again, in *My Bondage and My Freedom*, he recalled: "A man is sometimes made great, by the greatness of the abuse a portion of mankind may think proper to heap upon him. Whether I was of as much consequence as the English papers made me out to be, or not, it was easily seen, in England, that I could not be the ignorant and worthless creature, some of the American papers would have them believe I was."[5]

When addressing other Americans, Douglass voiced his admiration not only for British institutions but for the many individual Britons and Irish who had assisted him in his anti-slavery struggles and continued to aid him in his postbellum battle against racism. His last autobiography effusively praised those old allies. Once again, he thanked the British abolitionists, especially Anna and Ellen Richardson, who had purchased him out of slavery. His resentment against patronizing treatment by some British Garrisonians melted away after the Civil War. Even Richard Webb and George Thompson received warm compliments in Douglass's postwar speeches and writings for their dedication to the cause of human freedom. Not forgetting all feuds, Douglass contrasted Daniel O'Connell's rejection of contributions from American enslavers with the behavior of the Free Church of Scotland.

Douglass's enduring admiration for the British was put to the test during the Civil War. He antagonized over evidence of sympathy for the Confederate cause by some portions of the British public. His "Slave's Appeal," which sought to reverse such sentiment, has already received ample analysis, but we also present *Douglass' Monthly* editorials that wrestled with the issue. Douglass explained to American readers that it was the failure of the Union government leaders to make emancipation the war's goal in 1861 and 1862 that allowed some British to defend the Confederate cause. Britons, he wrote, see "that ABRAHAM LINCOLN at Washington is sternly opposed to emancipation, as JEFF. DAVIS is sternly in favor of slavery, and that the cause of civilization has nothing to hope from either."[6] When the Trent Affair raised the unwanted prospect of a Union–British confrontation,

---

4 A.M.E. *Church Review* 3 (October 1886), pp. 136–45.
5 Douglass, *My Bondage and My Freedom* (1855), p. 381.
6 *Douglass' Monthly*, January 1862, pp. 578–79.

Douglass condemned the action of the US Navy in seizing that British ship, but also encouraged the British to demonstrate respect to neutral vessels on the high seas in future conflicts.

There were other occasions when Douglass spoke negatively about the actions of the British government. In the *North Star*, he gave his endorsement to the Chartist movement as long as it pursued its goals in line with Garrisonian pacifist tactics. In the late 1860s, during debate over the Second Reform Bill, Douglass observed the equivalent right of the British worker and the African American freedman to full suffrage, but contended that the former group was still better treated: "In your country a man is protected whether he has a vote or not; because, though not now a voter, he may be one to-morrow, – and there is nothing in his race or past position to mark him out for abuse or insult. This is not so here. The best work I can do, therefore, for the freed-people, is to promote the passing of just and equal laws towards them. They must have the cartridge box, the jury box, and the ballot box, to protect them."[7]

The issue that most severely tested Douglass's warm regard for the British people was that of Irish Home Rule. In addressing this divisive political question, Douglass reminisced about the friendly support that both nations had given him during the abolitionist crusade. He acknowledged that some of his British friends, such as John Bright, opposed Home Rule for Ireland, and admitted that: "The spirit of the age does not favor small nationalities."[8] Nevertheless, in both speeches and writings, Douglass threw his support behind Irish Home Rule. He reversed his assessment of William Gladstone, whom he had harshly denounced during the Civil War for sympathizing with Confederate independence. Following his third visit to Britain in the midst of the Home Rule debate, Douglass applauded Gladstone for favoring "the rule of justice instead of the rule of the bayonet, the rule of love instead of the rule of hate, the rule of trust and confidence instead of the rule of doubt and suspicion."[9] In an article for the *Baltimore Commonwealth*, Douglass endorsed the passage of Home Rule because: "The glory of England will cease to be soiled with shame for the grievances of Ireland, and Ireland will be put upon her good behavior before the world, and made responsible for her own good or ill condition."[10] In his advocacy for the Irish, Douglass found ways to simultaneously advance the cause of his own race, proclaiming that "The right that I am claiming for Ireland I claim for every man here – North and South."[11] As he had

---

7   *Manchester Times*, 20 May 1865, p. 5.
8   *Commonwealth*, 1 October 1887, p. 1.
9   Ibid.
10 Ibid.
11 *Grand Reception to Arthur O'Connor, Esq., M.P. and Sir. Thomas H. Grattan Esmonde, Bart., M.P., at Masonic Temple, Washington, D.C.* (Washington, DC: William H. Moore, 1887), pp. 21–23.

done his entire public career, Douglass tied the Irish cause to universal principles of human rights: "I am for the fair play for the Irishman, the negro, the Chinaman, and for all men of whatever country or clime, and for allowing them to work out their own destiny without outside interference."[12]

---

12 A.M.E. *Church Review* 3, pp. 136–45.

CHARTISTS OF ENGLAND

Rochester, NY, *North Star*, 5 May 1848, p. 2

When we first learned that this class of reformers had resolved upon a resort to brute force, to overcome the government of that country, we were satisfied that the wild and wicked measure would be defeated.[1] It was therefore as expected as it was gratifying, to learn by our last advices, that they had wisely abandoned the mischievous and useless project. In all circumstances, we are inflexibly opposed to a resort to violence, as a means of effecting reform; and of all violence, we regard none with more absolute horror, than that attending civil war. Whatever may be the evils, and however inveterate the forms of oppression and t[y]ranny in continental Europe, and whatever pretexts may exist there for assailing those forms of oppression with brute force, we are confident that no such causes or pretexts can be properly cited in Great Britain, as justifying a resort to violence. While the liberty of speech is allowed – while the freedom of the press is permitted, and the right of petition is respected, and while men are left free to originate reforms without, and Members are left free to propose and advocate them within the walls of Parliament, – no excuse can be valid for resorting to the fearful use of brute force and bloodshed. When words will accomplish, as they certainly will, all righteous measures, it is wild, irrational and wicked to resort to blows.

Under no government in the wide world is there more respect shown, or encouragement offered to reform, than under that of England. During the last thirty years, some of the most important reforms ever achieved under any form of government, have taken place in Great Britain; so that now, that country may be justly regarded as far in advance of all other European governments, and in some, and very important particulars, far in advance of our own. The passage of the Reform Bill in '32, the Emancipation Act in '34, and the repeal of the Corn Laws in '46,[2] are reforms

---

1   Douglass wrote this in response to Chartist unrest during May 1848.

2   Three key pieces of British reform legislation: the Reform Bill of 1832 broadened suffrage and abolished many "rotten" boroughs; the Catholic Emancipation Act of 1834 removed religious tests against Roman Catholics in British politics; and the repeal of the Corn Laws in 1846 was a major step toward free trade.

which are still fresh in the memory of all, and afford ample proof that that country may be as effectually ruled by opinion as our own. No reform need fail there with patient, earnest and persevering efforts for its success. Within the walls of the House of Commons – aye, the Commons, the clearly expressed will of the people, through that body, whatever the lords spiritual and temporal may be pleased to say of it at the first, is as certain to become the law of the realm, as that manhood follows infancy. On the floor of that House, may be seen Richard Cobden,[3] John Bright,[4] Dr. Bowring,[5] Sharman Crawford,[6] W. J. Fox,[7] and the peerless orator and philanthropist, George Thompson, ready to advocate and defend justice and liberty, encouraged or assailed by whom they may be. With such advocates in Parliament, how absurd, monstrous and wicked it is for Chartists or any other class of reformers in that country, to dream of bloodshed as a means of furthering their cause! To do so is to deserve defeat. We are, if we understand Chartism, a Chartist; and we are even in favor of more radical reforms than they have yet proposed; and still, for the time being, we rejoice that they have failed in their 10th of April demonstration. A victory gained by such means would be far worse in the sequel than all the pain and mortification they must have experienced in their present signal failure. Away with all mobs and all violence as a means of reform! We have experienced too much of this species of tyranny already. There is a more excellent way. With free speech, and unshackled press, and the right of petition, we can defy error, whether in the church or in the state – whether sustained by prescription, or defended by the sword – in any case truth shall triumph. War, slavery, monopoly, and the whole train of inequalities that spring from the demon selfishness, must fall and expire in the presence of those mighty agents.

> "The pen shall supersede the sword,
> And right not might shall be adored,
> In the good time coming."[8]

---

3   Richard Cobden (1804–1865), M.P. and founder of the Anti-Corn Law League.
4   A prominent Liberal M.P., John Bright (1811–1889), broke with his party leadership late in life over Irish Home Rule.
5   Sir John Bowring (1792–1872) was a free-trade M.P. who later held diplomatic posts in China.
6   William Sharman Crawford (1781–1851) was a supporter of Irish rights in Parliament.
7   Unitarian minister William Johnson Fox (1786–1864) was a Liberal M.P.
8   Douglass quotes from Charles Mackay, "The Good Time Coming."

ON ROBERT BURNS AND SCOTLAND

Rochester, NY, *North Star*, 2 February 1849, p. 2

I regard it as a pleasure, not less than a privilege, to mingle my humble voice with the festivities of this occasion.[1] Although I am not a Scotchman, nor the son of a Scotchman, (perhaps you will say "it needs no ghost to tell us that") (a laugh), but if a warm love of Scotch character – a high appreciation of Scotch genius – constitute any of the qualities of a true Scotch heart, then indeed does a Scotch heart throb beneath these ribs. From my earliest acquaintance with Scotland, I have held that country in the highest admiration. As I travelled through that land two years since, and became acquainted with its people, and realized their warmth of heart, steadiness of purpose, and learned that every stream, hill, glen, and valley have been rendered classic by the heroic deeds in behalf of Freedom, that admiration was increased. That you may know that I have some appreciation of the genius of the bard whose birth-day you have met to celebrate, I went [on] a pilgrimage to see the cottage in which he was born; and had the pleasure of seeing and conversing with a sister of the noble poet whose memory we have met to do honor. I can truly say that it was one of the most gratifying visits I made during my stay in Scotland. I saw, or thought I saw, some lingering sparks in the eyes of this sister, that called to mind the fire that ever warmed the bosom of Burns. But, ladies and gentlemen, this is not a time for long speeches. I do not wish to detain you from the social pleasures that await you. I repeat again, that though I am not a Scotchman, and have a colored skin, I am proud to be among you this evening. And if any think me out of place on this occasion (pointing to the picture of Burns), I beg that the blame may be laid at the door of him who taught me that "a man's a man for a' that."[2] (Mr. D[ouglass] sat down amid loud cries of "go on!" from the audience.)

---

1 Douglass was an invited speaker at the Robert Burns Festival held in Rochester, New York, on 25 January 1849.

2 Douglass paraphrases Robert Burns' poem "For A' That and A' That."

TWENTY-ONE MONTHS IN GREAT BRITAIN

Frederick Douglass, *My Bondage and My Freedom*
(New York and Auburn: Miller,
Orton & Mulligan, 1855)

GOOD ARISING OUT OF UNPROPITIOUS EVENTS – DENIED CABIN PASSAGE – PROSCRIPTION TURNED TO GOOD ACCOUNT – THE HUTCHINSON FAMILY – THE MOB ON BOARD THE CAMBRIA – HAPPY INTRODUCTION TO THE BRITISH PUBLIC – LETTER ADDRESSED TO WILLIAM LLOYD GARRISON – TIME AND LABORS WHILE ABROAD – FREEDOM PURCHASED – MRS. HENRY RICHARDSON – FREE PAPERS – ABOLITIONISTS DISPLEASED WITH THE RANSOM – HOW THE AUTHOR'S ENERGIES WERE DIRECTED – RECEPTION SPEECH IN LONDON – CHARACTER OF THE SPEECH DEFENDED – CIRCUMSTANCES EXPLAINED – CAUSES CONTRIBUTING TO THE SUCCESS OF HIS MISSION – FREE CHURCH OF SCOTLAND – TESTIMONIAL.

THE allotments of Providence, when coupled with trouble and anxiety, often conceal from finite vision the wisdom and goodness in which they are sent; and, frequently, what seemed a harsh and invidious dispensation, is converted by after experience into a happy and beneficial arrangement. Thus, the painful liability to be returned again to slavery, which haunted me by day, and troubled my dreams by night, proved to be a necessary step in the path of knowledge and usefulness. The writing of my pamphlet[1] in the spring of 1845, endangered my liberty, and led me to seek a refuge from republican slavery in monarchical England. A rude, uncultivated fugitive slave was driven, by stern necessity, to that country to which young

---

1   Douglass's *Narrative of the Life of Frederick Douglass* (1845).

American gentlemen go to increase their stock of knowledge, to seek pleasure, to have their rough, democratic manners softened by contact with English aristocratic refinement. On applying for a passage to England, on board the Cambria, of the Cunard line, my friend, James N. Buffum[2] of Lynn, Massachusetts, was informed that I could not be received on board as a cabin passenger. American prejudice against color triumphed over British liberality and civilization, and erected a color test and condition for crossing the sea in the cabin of a British vessel. The insult was keenly felt by my white friends, but to me, it was common, expected, and therefore, a thing of no great consequence, whether I went in the cabin or in the steerage. Moreover, I felt that if I could not go into the first cabin, first-cabin passengers could come into the second cabin, and the result justified my anticipations to the fullest extent. Indeed, I soon found myself an object of more general interest than I wished to be; and so far from being degraded by being placed in the second cabin, that part of the ship became the scene of as much pleasure and refinement, during the voyage, as the cabin itself. The Hutchinson Family, celebrated vocalists – fellow-passengers – often came to my rude forecastle deck, and sung their sweetest songs, enlivening the place with eloquent music, as well as spirited conversation, during the voyage. In two days after leaving Boston, one part of the ship was about as free to me as another. My fellow-passengers not only visited me, but invited me to visit them, on the saloon deck. My visits there, however, were but seldom. I preferred to live within my privileges, and keep upon my own premises. I found this quite as much in accordance with good policy, as with my own feelings. The effect was, that with the majority of the passengers, all color distinctions were flung to the winds, and I found myself treated with every mark of respect, from the beginning to the end of the voyage, except in a single instance; and in that, I came near being mobbed, for complying with an invitation given me by the passengers, and the captain of the "Cambria,"[3] to deliver a lecture on slavery. Our New Orleans and Georgia passengers were pleased to regard my lecture as an insult offered to them, and swore I should not speak. They went so far as to threaten to throw me overboard, and but for the firmness of Captain Judkins,[4] probably would have (under the inspiration of *slavery* and *brandy*) attempted to put their threats into execution. I have no space to describe this scene, although its tragic and comic peculiarities are well worth describing. An end was put to the *melee*, by the captain's calling the ship's company to put the salt water mobocrats in irons. At this determined order, the gentlemen of

---

2 James N. Buffum (1807–1887), US politician, abolitionist, and mayor of Lynn, Massachusetts. Buffum had traveled to Britain and Ireland with Frederick Douglass in 1845.

3 The *Cambria* steamship, where Douglass's lecture descended into chaos created by proslavery men on board.

4 Charles H. E. Judkins (1811–1876), captain of the *Cambria* steamship.

the lash scampered, and for the rest of the voyage conducted themselves very decorously. This incident of the voyage, in two days after landing at Liverpool, brought me at once before the British public, and that by no act of my own. The gentlemen so promptly snubbed in their meditated violence, flew to the press to justify their conduct, and to denounce me as a worthless and insolent negro. This course was even less wise than the conduct it was intended to sustain; for, besides awakening something like a national interest in me, and securing me an audience, it brought out counter statements, and threw the blame upon themselves, which they had sought to fasten upon me and the gallant captain of the ship. Some notion may be formed of the difference in my feelings and circumstances, while abroad, from the following extract from one of a series of letters addressed by me to Mr. Garrison, and published in the Liberator. It was written on the first day of January, 1846,

"MY DEAR FRIEND GARRISON: Up to this time, I have given no direct expression of the views, feelings, and opinions which I have formed, respecting the character and condition of the people of this land. I have refrained thus, purposely. I wish to speak advisedly, and in order to do this, I have waited till, I trust, experience has brought my opinions to an intelligent maturity. I have been thus careful, not because I think what I say will have much effect in shaping the opinions of the world, but because whatever of influence I may possess, whether little or much, I wish it to go in the right direction, and according to truth. I hardly need say that, in speaking of Ireland, I shall be influenced by no prejudices in favor of America. I think my circumstances all forbid that. I have no end to serve, no creed to uphold, no government to defend; and as to nation, I belong to none. I have no protection at home, or resting-place abroad. The land of my birth welcomes me to her shores only as a slave, and spurns with contempt the idea of treating me differently; so that I am an outcast from the society of my childhood, and an outlaw in the land of my birth. 'I am a stranger with thee, and a sojourner, as all my fathers were.' That men should be patriotic, is to me perfectly natural; and as a philosophical fact, I am able to give it an *intellectual* recognition. But no further can I go. If ever I had any patriotism, or any capacity for the feeling, it was whipped out of me long since, by the lash of the American soul-drivers.

"In thinking of America, I sometimes find myself admiring her bright blue sky, her grand old woods, her fertile fields, her beautiful rivers, her mighty lakes, and star-crowned mountains. But my rapture is soon checked, my joy is soon turned to mourning. When I remember that all is cursed with the infernal spirit of slaveholding, robbery, and wrong; when I remember that with the waters of her noblest rivers, the tears of my brethren are borne to the ocean, disregarded and forgotten, and that her most fertile fields drink daily of the warm blood of my outraged sisters; I am filled with unutterable loathing, and led to reproach myself that anything could fall from my lips in praise of such a land. America will not allow her children to love her. She seems bent on compelling those who would be her warmest friends, to be her worst enemies. May God give her repentance, before it is too late, is the ardent prayer of my heart. I will continue to pray, labor, and wait, believing that she cannot always be insensible to the dictates of justice, or deaf to the voice of humanity.

"My opportunities for learning the character and condition of the people of this land have been very great. I have traveled almost from the Hill of Howth to the Giant's Causeway, and from the Giant's Causeway to Cape Clear.[5] During these travels, I have met with much in the character and condition of the people to approve, and much to condemn; much that has thrilled me with pleasure, and very much that has filled me with pain. I will not, in this letter, attempt to give any description of those scenes which have given me pain. This I will do hereafter. I have enough, and more than your subscribers will be disposed to read at one time, of the bright side of the picture. I can truly say, I have spent some of the happiest moments of my life since landing in this country. I seem to have undergone a transformation. I live a new life. The warm and generous coöperation extended to me by the friends of my despised race; the prompt and liberal manner with which the press has rendered me its aid; the glorious enthusiasm with which thousands have flocked to hear the cruel wrongs of my down-trodden and long-enslaved fellow-countrymen portrayed; the deep sympathy for the slave, and the strong abhorrence of the slaveholder, everywhere evinced; the cordiality with which members and ministers of various religious bodies, and of various shades of religious opinion, have embraced me, and lent me their aid; the kind hospitality constantly proffered to me by persons of the highest rank in society; the spirit of freedom that seems to animate all with whom I come in contact, and the entire absence of everything that looked like prejudice against me, on account of the color of my skin – contrasted so strongly with my long and bitter experience in the United States, that I look with wonder and amazement on the transition. In the southern part of the United States, I was a slave, thought of and spoken of as property; in the language of the LAW, *'held, taken, reputed, and adjudged to be a chattel in the hands of my owners and possessors, and their executors, administrators, and assigns, to all intents, constructions, and purposes whatsoever.'* (Brev. Digest, 224.) In the northern states, a fugitive slave, liable to be hunted at any moment, like a felon, and to be hurled into the terrible jaws of slavery – doomed by an inveterate prejudice against color to insult and outrage on every hand, (Massachusetts out of the question) – denied the privileges and courtesies common to others in the use of the most humble means of conveyance – shut out from the cabins on steamboats – refused admission to respectable hotels – caricatured, scorned, scoffed, mocked, and

---

5 Prominent geographical locations on the eastern, northern, and southern coasts of Ireland.

maltreated with impunity by any one, (no matter how black his heart,) so he has a white skin. But now behold the change! Eleven days and a half gone, and I have crossed three thousand miles of the perilous deep. Instead of a democratic government, I am under a monarchical government. Instead of the bright, blue sky of America, I am covered with the soft, grey fog of the Emerald Isle. I breathe, and lo! the chattel becomes a man. I gaze around in vain for one who will question my equal humanity, claim me as his slave, or offer me an insult. I employ a cab – I am seated beside white people – I reach the hotel – I enter the same door – I am shown into the same parlor – I dine at the same table – and no one is offended. No delicate nose grows deformed in my presence. I find no difficulty here in obtaining admission into any place of worship, instruction, or amusement, on equal terms with people as white as any I ever saw in the United States. I meet nothing to remind me of my complexion. I find myself regarded and treated at every turn with the kindness and deference paid to white people. When I go to church, I am met by no upturned nose and scornful lip to tell me, 'We don't allow niggers in here!'

"I remember, about two years ago, there was in Boston, near the south-west corner of Boston Common, a menagerie. I had long desired to see such a collection as I understood was being exhibited there. Never having had an opportunity while a slave, I resolved to seize this, my first, since my escape. I went, and as I approached the entrance to gain admission, I was met and told by the door-keeper, in a harsh and contemptuous tone, 'We don't allow niggers in here.' I also remember attending a revival meeting in the Rev. Henry Jackson's meeting-house, at New Bedford,[6] and going up the broad aisle to find a seat, I was met by a good deacon, who told me, in a pious tone, 'We don't allow niggers in here!' Soon after my arrival in New Bedford, from the south, I had a strong desire to attend the Lyceum, but was told, 'They don't allow niggers in here!' While passing from New York to Boston, on the steamer Massachusetts, on the night of the 9th of December, 1843, when chilled almost through with the cold, I went into the cabin to get a little warm. I was soon touched upon the shoulder, and told, 'We don't allow niggers in here!' On arriving in Boston, from an anti-slavery tour, hungry and tired, I went into an eating-house, near my friend, Mr. Campbell's,[7] to get some refreshments. I was met by a lad in a white apron, 'We don't allow niggers in here!' A week or two before leaving the United States, I had a meeting appointed at Weymouth, the home of that glorious band of true abolitionists, the Weston family, and others.[8] On attempting to take a seat in the omnibus to that place, I was told by the driver, (and I never shall forget his fiendish hate,)

---

6   Henry Jackson (1798–1863), US Baptist minister and abolitionist.

7   Probably John Reid Campbell, a Boston shoe merchant and ally of William Lloyd Garrison in the abolitionist movement.

8   The Weston family were stalwart Garrisonian abolitionists and Maria, Caroline, Anne, and Deborah in particular were active in the antislavery cause.

'*I don't allow niggers in here!*' Thank heaven for the respite I now enjoy! I had been in Dublin but a few days, when a gentleman of great respectability kindly offered to conduct me through all the public buildings of that beautiful city; and a little afterward, I found myself dining with the lord mayor of Dublin.[9] What a pity there was not some American democratic christian at the door of his splendid mansion, to bark out at my approach, '*They don't allow niggers in here!*' The truth is, the people here know nothing of the republican negro hate prevalent in our glorious land. They measure and esteem men according to their moral and intellectual worth, and not according to the color of their skin. Whatever may be said of the aristocracies here, there is none based on the color of a man's skin. This species of aristocracy belongs preëminently to 'the land of the free, and the home of the brave.' I have never found it abroad, in any but Americans. It sticks to them wherever they go. They find it almost as hard to get rid of, as to get rid of their skins.

"The second day after my arrival at Liverpool, in company with my friend, Buffum, and several other friends, I went to Eaton Hall, the residence of the Marquis of Westminster,[10] one of the most splendid buildings in England. On approaching the door, I found several of our American passengers, who came out with us in the Cambria, waiting for admission, as but one party was allowed in the house at a time. We all had to wait till the company within came out. And of all the faces, expressive of chagrin, those of the Americans were preeminent. They looked as sour as vinegar, and as bitter as gall, when they found I was to be admitted on equal terms with themselves. When the door was opened, I walked in, on an equal footing with my white fellow-citizens, and from all I could see, I had as much attention paid me by the servants that showed us through the house, as any with a paler skin. As I walked through the building, the statuary did not fall down, the pictures did not leap from their places, the doors did not refuse to open, and the servants did not say, '*We don't allow niggers in here!*'

"A happy new-year to you, and all the friends of freedom."

My time and labors, while abroad, were divided between England, Ireland, Scotland, and Wales. Upon this experience alone, I might write a book twice the size of this, "My *Bondage and my Freedom.*" I visited and lectured in nearly all the large towns and cities in the United Kingdom, and enjoyed many favorable opportunities for observation and information. But books on England are abundant, and the public may, therefore, dismiss any fear that I am meditating another infliction in that line; though, in truth, I should like much to write a book on those countries, if for nothing else, to make grateful mention of the many dear friends, whose benevolent actions toward me are ineffaceably stamped upon my memory, and warmly treasured

---

9   John L. Arabin (1794–1863) assumed the role of Lord Mayor of Dublin in 1845.
10 The Cheshire home of Richard Grosvenor (1795–1869), 2nd Marquess of Westminster.

in my heart. To these friends I owe my freedom in the United States. On their own motion, without any solicitation from me, (Mrs. Henry Richardson, a clever lady, remarkable for her devotion to every good work, taking the lead,) they raised a fund sufficient to purchase my freedom, and actually paid it over, and placed the papers of my manumission in my hands, before they would tolerate the idea of my returning to this, my native country.[11] To this commercial transaction I owe my exemption from the democratic operation of the fugitive slave bill of 1850. But for this, I might at any time become a victim of this most cruel and scandalous enactment, and be doomed to end my life, as I began it, a slave. The sum paid for my freedom was one hundred and fifty pounds sterling. Some of my uncompromising anti-slavery friends in this country failed to see the wisdom of this arrangement, and were not pleased that I consented to it, even by my silence. They thought it a violation of anti-slavery principles – conceding a right of property in man – and a wasteful expenditure of money. On the other hand, viewing it simply in the light of a ransom, or as money extorted by a robber, and my liberty of more value than one hundred and fifty pounds sterling, I could not see either a violation of the laws of morality, or those of economy, in the transaction.

It is true, I was not in the possession of my claimants, and could have easily remained in England, for the same friends who had so generously purchased my freedom, would have assisted me in establishing myself in that country. To this, however, I could not consent. I felt that I had a duty to perform – and that was, to labor and suffer with the oppressed in my native land. Considering, therefore, all the circumstances – the fugitive slave bill included – I think the very best thing was done in letting Master Hugh have the hundred and fifty pounds sterling, and leaving me free to return to my appropriate field of labor. Had I been a private person, having no other relations or duties than those of a personal and family nature, I should never have consented to the payment of so large a sum for the privilege of living securely under our glorious republican form of government. I could have remained in England, or have gone to some other country; and perhaps I could even have lived unobserved in this. But to this I could not consent. I had already become somewhat notorious, and withal quite as unpopular as notorious; and I was, therefore, much exposed to arrest and recapture.

The main object to which my labors in Great Britain were directed, was the concentration of the moral and religious sentiment of its people against American slavery. England is often charged with having established slavery in the United States, and if there were no other justification than this, for appealing to her people to lend their moral aid for the abolition of slavery, I should be justified. My speeches

---

11   Newcastle abolitionist Anna Atkins Richardson (1806–1892) joined her sister-in-law Ellen Richardson in arranging Douglass's legal purchase from Hugh Auld in 1846.

in Great Britain were wholly extemporaneous, and I may not always have been so guarded in my expressions, as I otherwise should have been. I was ten years younger then than now, and only seven years from slavery. I cannot give the reader a better idea of the nature of my discourses, than by republishing one of them, delivered in Finsbury chapel, London, to an audience of about two thousand persons, and which was published in the "London Universe," at the time.

Those in the United States who may regard this speech as being harsh in its spirit and unjust in its statements, because delivered before an audience supposed to be anti-republican in their principles and feelings, may view the matter differently, when they learn that the case supposed did not exist. It so happened that the great mass of the people in England who attended and patronized my anti-slavery meetings, were, in truth, about as good republicans as the mass of Americans, and with this decided advantage over the latter – they are lovers of republicanism for all men, for black men as well as for white men. They are the people who sympathize with Louis Kossuth and Mazzini,[12] and with the oppressed and enslaved, of every color and nation, the world over. They constitute the democratic element in British politics, and are as much opposed to the union of church and state as we, in America, are to such a union. At the meeting where this speech was delivered, Joseph Sturge[13] – a world-wide philanthropist, and a member of the society of Friends – presided, and addressed the meeting. George William Alexander,[14] another Friend, who has spent more than an American fortune in promoting the anti-slavery cause in different sections of the world, was on the platform; and also Dr. Campbell, (now of the "British Banner,") who combines all the humane tenderness of Melancthon, with the directness and boldness of Luther.[15] He is in the very front ranks of nonconformists, and looks with no unfriendly eye upon America. George Thompson, too, was there; and America will yet own that he did a true man's work in relighting the rapidly dying-out fire of true republicanism in the American heart, and be ashamed of the treatment he met at her hands. Coming generations in this country will applaud the spirit of this much abused republican friend of freedom. There were others of note seated on the platform, who would gladly ingraft upon English

---

12 Giuseppe Mazzini (1805–1872), Italian politician, editor, activist, and advocate for the unification of Italy.

13 Joseph Sturge (1793–1859), British reformer, abolitionist, and founder of the British and Foreign Anti-Slavery Society.

14 George William Alexander (1802–1890), British philanthropist, abolitionist, and co-founder of the British and Foreign Anti-Slavery Society.

15 Philip Melanchthon (1497–1560) and Martin Luther (1483–1546) were German theologians and prominent figures in the Protestant Reformation.

institutions all that is purely republican in the institutions of America. Nothing, therefore, must be set down against this speech on the score that it was delivered in the presence of those who cannot appreciate the many excellent things belonging to our system of government, and with a view to stir up prejudice against republican institutions.

Again, let it also be remembered – for it is the simple truth – that neither in this speech, nor in any other which I delivered in England, did I ever allow myself to address Englishmen as against Americans. I took my stand on the high ground of human brotherhood, and spoke to Englishmen as men, in behalf of men. Slavery is a crime, not against Englishmen, but against God, and all the members of the human family; and it belongs to the whole human family to seek its suppression. In a letter to Mr. Greeley,[16] of the New York Tribune, written while abroad, I said:

> "I am, nevertheless, aware that the wisdom of exposing the sins of one nation in the ear of another, has been seriously questioned by good and clear-sighted people, both on this and on your side of the Atlantic. And the thought is not without weight on my own mind. I am satisfied that there are many evils which can be best removed by confining our efforts to the immediate locality where such evils exist. This, however, is by no means the case with the system of slavery. It is such a giant sin – such a monstrous aggregation of iniquity – so hardening to the human heart – so destructive to the moral sense, and so well calculated to beget a character, in every one around it, favorable to its own continuance, – that I feel not only at liberty, but abundantly justified, in appealing to the whole world to aid in its removal."

But, even if I had – as has been often charged – labored to bring American institutions generally into disrepute, and had not confined my labors strictly within the limits of humanity and morality, I should not have been without illustrious examples to support me. Driven into semi-exile by civil and barbarous laws, and by a system which cannot be thought of without a shudder, I was fully justified in turning, if possible, the tide of the moral universe against the heaven-daring outrage.

Four circumstances greatly assisted me in getting the question of American slavery before the British public. First, the mob on board the Cambria, already referred to, which was a sort of national announcement of my arrival in England. Secondly, the highly reprehensible course pursued by the Free Church of Scotland, in soliciting, receiving, and retaining money in its sustentation fund for supporting the gospel in Scotland, which was evidently the ill-gotten gain of slaveholders and slave-traders. Third, the great Evangelical Alliance – or rather the attempt to form

---

16   Horace Greeley (1811–1872), US journalist and editor of the *New York Tribune*.

such an alliance, which should include slaveholders of a certain description – added immensely to the interest felt in the slavery question. About the same time, there was the World's Temperance Convention, where I had the misfortune to come in collision with sundry American doctors of divinity – Dr. Cox among the number – with whom I had a small controversy.

It has happened to me – as it has happened to most other men engaged in a good cause – often to be more indebted to my enemies than to my own skill or to the assistance of my friends, for whatever success has attended my labors. Great surprise was expressed by American newspapers, north and south, during my stay in Great Britain, that a person so illiterate and insignificant as myself could awaken an interest so marked in England. These papers were not the only parties surprised. I was myself not far behind them in surprise. But the very contempt and scorn, the systematic and extravagant disparagement of which I was the object, served, perhaps, to magnify my few merits, and to render me of some account, whether deserving or not. A man is sometimes made great, by the greatness of the abuse a portion of mankind may think proper to heap upon him. Whether I was of as much consequence as the English papers made me out to be, or not, it was easily seen, in England, that I could not be the ignorant and worthless creature, some of the American papers would have them believe I was. Men, in their senses, do not take bowie-knives to kill mosquitoes, nor pistols to shoot flies; and the American passengers who thought proper to get up a mob to silence me, on board the Cambria, took the most effective method of telling the British public that I had something to say.

But to the second circumstance, namely, the position of the Free Church of Scotland, with the great Doctors Chalmers, Cunningham, and Candlish at its head. That church, with its leaders, put it out of the power of the Scotch people to ask the old question, which we in the north have often most wickedly asked – "*What have we to do with slavery?*" That church had taken the price of blood into its treasury, with which to build *free* churches, and to pay *free* church ministers for preaching the gospel; and, worse still, when honest John Murray, of Bowlien Bay[17] – now gone to his reward in heaven – with William Smeal,[18] Andrew Paton,[19] Frederick Card,[20] and other sterling anti-slavery men in Glasgow, denounced the transaction as disgraceful and shocking to the religious sentiment of Scotland, this church, through its leading divines, instead of repenting and seeking to mend the mistake into which it had fallen, made it a flagrant sin, by undertaking to defend, in the name of God

17 Scottish abolitionist John Murray (?–1849) was a founder of the Glasgow Emancipation Society in 1833.

18 A Quaker and Garrisonian abolitionist, William Smeal (1793–1877) was co-secretary of the Glasgow Emancipation Society.

19 Andrew Paton (1805–1884) was a Glasgow merchant and Garrisonian abolitionist.

20 Possibly a reference to Frederick Cash, from Glasgow.

and the bible, the principle not only of taking the money of slave-dealers to build churches, but of holding fellowship with the holders and traffickers in human flesh. This, the reader will see, brought up the whole question of slavery, and opened the way to its full discussion, without any agency of mine. I have never seen a people more deeply moved than were the people of Scotland, on this very question. Public meeting succeeded public meeting. Speech after speech, pamphlet after pamphlet, editorial after editorial, sermon after sermon, soon lashed the conscientious Scotch people into a perfect *furore*. "SEND BACK THE MONEY!" was indignantly cried out, from Greenock to Edinburgh, and from Edinburgh to Aberdeen. George Thompson, of London, Henry C. Wright,[21] of the United States, James N. Buffum, of Lynn, Massachusetts, and myself were on the anti-slavery side; and Doctors Chalmers, Cunningham, and Candlish on the other. In a conflict where the latter could have had even the show of right, the truth, in our hands as against them, must have been driven to the wall; and while I believe we were able to carry the conscience of the country against the action of the Free Church, the battle, it must be confessed, was a hard-fought one. Abler defenders of the doctrine of fellowshiping slaveholders as christians, have not been met with. In defending this doctrine, it was necessary to deny that slavery is a sin. If driven from this position, they were compelled to deny that slaveholders were responsible for the sin; and if driven from both these positions, they must deny that it is a sin in such a sense, and that slaveholders are sinners in such a sense, as to make it wrong, in the circumstances in which they were placed, to recognize them as christians. Dr. Cunningham was the most powerful debater on the slavery side of the question; Mr. Thompson was the ablest on the anti-slavery side. A scene occurred between these two men, a parallel to which I think I never witnessed before, and I know I never have since. The scene was caused by a single exclamation on the part of Mr. Thompson.

The general assembly of the Free Church was in progress at Cannon Mills, Edinburgh. The building would hold about twenty-five hundred persons; and on this occasion it was densely packed, notice having been given that Doctors Cunningham and Candlish would speak, that day, in defense of the relations of the Free Church of Scotland to slavery in America. Messrs. Thompson, Buffum, myself, and a few anti-slavery friends, attended, but sat at such a distance, and in such a position, that, perhaps, we were not observed from the platform. The excitement was intense, having been greatly increased by a series of meetings held by Messrs. Thompson, Wright, Buffum, and myself, in the most splendid hall in that most beautiful city, just previous to the meetings of the general assembly. "SEND BACK THE MONEY!" stared

---

21 Henry Clarke Wright (1797–1870), radical abolitionist, journalist, and Garrisonian, who occasionally lectured beside Douglass during his first visit to Britain.

at us from every street corner; "SEND BACK THE MONEY!" in large capitals, adorned the broad flags of the pavement; "SEND BACK THE MONEY!" was the chorus of the popular street songs; "SEND BACK THE MONEY!" was the heading of leading editorials in the daily newspapers. This day, at Cannon Mills, the great doctors of the church were to give an answer to this loud and stern demand. Men of all parties and all sects were most eager to hear. Something great was expected. The occasion was great, the men great, and great speeches were expected from them.

In addition to the outside pressure upon Doctors Cunningham and Candlish, there was wavering in their own ranks. The conscience of the church itself was not at ease. A dissatisfaction with the position of the church touching slavery, was sensibly manifest among the members, and something must be done to counteract this untoward influence. The great Dr. Chalmers was in feeble health, at the time. His most potent eloquence could not now be summoned to Cannon Mills, as formerly. He whose voice was able to rend asunder and dash down the granite walls of the established church of Scotland, and to lead a host in solemn procession from it, as from a doomed city, was now old and enfeebled. Besides, he had said his word on this very question; and his word had not silenced the clamor without, nor stilled the anxious heavings within. The occasion was momentous, and felt to be so. The church was in a perilous condition. A change of some sort must take place in her condition, or she must go to pieces. To stand where she did, was impossible. The whole weight of the matter fell on Cunningham and Candlish. No shoulders in the church were broader than theirs; and I must say, badly as I detest the principles laid down and defended by them, I was compelled to acknowledge the vast mental endowments of the men. Cunningham rose; and his rising was the signal for almost tumultuous applause. You will say this was scarcely in keeping with the solemnity of the occasion, but to me it served to increase its grandeur and gravity. The applause, though tumultuous, was not joyous. It seemed to me, as it thundered up from the vast audience, like the fall of an immense shaft, flung from shoulders already galled by its crushing weight. It was like saying, "Doctor, we have borne this burden long enough, and willingly fling it upon you. Since it was you who brought it upon us, take it now, and do what you will with it, for we are too weary to bear it."

Doctor Cunningham proceeded with his speech, abounding in logic, learning, and eloquence, and apparently bearing down all opposition; but at the moment — the fatal moment – when he was just bringing all his arguments to a point, and that point being, that neither Jesus Christ nor his holy apostles regarded slaveholding as a sin, George Thompson, in a clear, sonorous, but rebuking voice, broke the deep stillness of the audience, exclaiming, "HEAR! HEAR! HEAR!" The effect of this simple and common exclamation is almost incredible. It was as if a granite wall had been suddenly flung up against the advancing current of a mighty river. For a moment, speaker and audience were brought to a dead silence. Both the doctor and his hearers seemed appalled by the audacity, as well as the fitness of the rebuke. At length a shout went up to the cry of *"Put him out!"* Happily, no one attempted to execute this cowardly order, and the doctor proceeded with his discourse. Not, however, as before, did the learned doctor proceed. The exclamation of Thompson must have reëchoed itself a thousand times in his memory, during the remainder of his speech, for the doctor never recovered from the blow.

The deed was done, however; the pillars of the church – *the proud, Free Church of Scotland* – were committed, and the humility of repentance was absent. The Free Church held on to the blood-stained money, and continued to justify itself in its position – and of course to apologize for slavery – and does so till this day. She lost a glorious opportunity for giving her voice, her vote, and her example to the cause of humanity; and to-day she is staggering under the curse of the enslaved, whose blood is in her skirts. The people of Scotland are, to this day, deeply grieved at the course pursued by the Free Church, and would hail, as a relief from a deep and blighting shame, the "sending back the money" to the slaveholders from whom it was gathered.

One good result followed the conduct of the Free Church; it furnished an occasion for making the people of Scotland thoroughly acquainted with the character of slavery, and for arraying against the system the moral and religious sentiment of that country. Therefore, while we did not succeed in accomplishing the specific object of our mission, namely – procure the sending back of the money – we were amply justified by the good which really did result from our labors.

Next comes the Evangelical Alliance. This was an attempt to form a union of all evangelical christians throughout the world. Sixty or seventy American divines attended, and some of them went there merely to weave a world-wide garment with which to clothe evangelical slaveholders. Foremost among these divines, was the Rev. Samuel Hanson Cox, moderator of the New School Presbyterian General Assembly. He and his friends spared no pains to secure a platform broad enough to hold American slaveholders, and in this they partly succeeded. But the question of slavery is too large a question to be finally disposed of, even by the Evangelical Alliance. We appealed from the judgment of the Alliance, to the judgment of the people of Great Britain, and with the happiest effect. This controversy with the Alliance might be made the subject of extended remark, but I must forbear, except to say, that this effort to shield the christian character of slaveholders greatly served to open a way to the British ear for anti-slavery discussion, and that it was well improved.

The fourth and last circumstance that assisted me in getting before the British public, was an attempt on the part of certain doctors of divinity to silence me on the platform of the World's Temperance Convention. Here I was brought into point blank collision with Rev. Dr. Cox, who made me the subject not only of bitter remark in the convention, but also of a long denunciatory letter published in the New York Evangelist and other American papers. I replied to the doctor as well as I could, and was successful in getting a respectful hearing before the British public, who are by nature and practice ardent lovers of fair play, especially in a conflict between the weak and the strong.

Thus did circumstances favor me, and favor the cause of which I strove to be the advocate. After such distinguished notice, the public in both countries was compelled to attach some importance to my labors. By the very ill usage I received at the hands of Dr. Cox and his party, by the mob on board the Cambria, by the attacks made upon me in the American newspapers, and by the aspersions cast upon me through the organs of the Free Church of Scotland, I became one of that class of men, who, for the moment, at least, "have greatness forced upon them." People became the more anxious to hear for themselves, and to judge for themselves, of the truth which I had to unfold. While, therefore, it is by no means easy for a stranger to get fairly before the British public, it was my lot to accomplish it in the easiest manner possible.

Having continued in Great Britain and Ireland nearly two years, and being about to return to America – not as I left it, a slave, but a freeman – leading friends of the cause of emancipation in that country intimated their intention to make me a testimonial, not only on grounds of personal regard to myself, but also to the cause to which they were so ardently devoted. How far any such thing could have succeeded, I do not know; but many reasons led me to prefer that my friends should simply give me the means of obtaining a printing press and printing materials, to enable me to start a paper, devoted to the interests of my enslaved and oppressed people. I told them that perhaps the greatest hindrance to the adoption of abolition principles by the people of the United States, was the low estimate, everywhere in that country, placed upon the negro, as a man; that because of his assumed natural inferiority, people reconciled themselves to his enslavement and oppression, as things inevitable, if not desirable. The grand thing to be done, therefore, was to change the estimation in which the colored people of the United States were held; to remove the prejudice which depreciated and depressed them; to prove them worthy of a higher consideration; to disprove their alleged inferiority, and demonstrate their capacity for a more exalted civilization than slavery and prejudice had assigned to them. I further stated, that, in my judgment, a tolerably well conducted press, in the hands of persons of the despised race, by calling out the mental energies of the race itself; by making them acquainted with their own latent powers; by enkindling among them the hope that for them there is a future; by developing their moral power; by combining and reflecting their talents – would prove a most powerful means of removing prejudice, and of awakening an interest in them. I further informed them – and at that time the statement was true – that there was not, in the United States, a single newspaper regularly published by the colored people; that many attempts had been made to establish such papers; but that, up to that time, they had all failed. These views I laid before my friends. The result was, nearly two thousand five hundred dollars were speedily raised toward starting my paper. For this prompt and generous assistance, rendered upon my bare suggestion, without any personal efforts on my part, I shall never cease to feel deeply grateful; and the thought of fulfilling the noble expectations of the dear friends who gave me this evidence of their confidence, will never cease to be a motive for persevering exertion.

Proposing to leave England, and turning my face toward America, in the spring of 1847, I was met, on the threshold, with something which painfully reminded me of the kind of life which awaited me in my native land. For the first time in the many months spent abroad, I was met with proscription on account of my color. A few weeks before departing from England, while in London, I was careful to purchase a ticket, and secure a berth for returning home, in the Cambria – the steamer in which I left the United States – paying therefor the round sum of forty pounds and nineteen shillings sterling. This was first cabin fare. But on going aboard the Cambria, I found that the Liverpool agent had ordered my berth to be given to another, and had forbidden my entering the saloon! This contemptible conduct met with stern rebuke from the British press. For, upon the point of leaving England, I took occasion to expose the disgusting tyranny, in the columns of the London Times. That journal, and other leading journals throughout the United Kingdom, held up the outrage to unmitigated condemnation. So good an opportunity for calling out a full expression of British sentiment on the subject, had not before occurred, and it was most fully embraced. The result was, that Mr. Cunard[22] came out in a letter to the public journals, assuring them of his regret at the outrage, and promising that the like should never occur again on board his steamers; and the like, we believe, has never since occurred on board the steam-ships of the Cunard line.

It is not very pleasant to be made the subject of such insults; but if all such necessarily resulted as this one did, I should be very happy to bear, patiently, many more than I have borne, of the same sort. Albeit, the lash of proscription, to a man accustomed to equal social position, even for a time, as I was, has a sting for the soul hardly less severe than that which bites the flesh and draws the blood from the back of the plantation slave. It was rather hard, after having enjoyed nearly two years of equal social privileges in England, often dining with gentlemen of great literary, social, political, and religious eminence – never, during the whole time, having met with a single word, look, or gesture, which gave me the slightest reason to think my color was an offense to anybody – now to be cooped up in the stern of the Cambria, and denied the right to enter the saloon, lest my dark presence should be deemed an offense to some of my democratic fellow passengers. The reader will easily imagine what must have been my feelings.

---

22 Samuel Cunard (1787–1865), an Anglo-Canadian who founded the Cunard Line; Douglass sailed on the Cunard ship *Cambria* in 1845 and 1847.

WAR WITH ENGLAND

Rochester, NY, *Douglass' Monthly*, January 1862, pp. 578–79

Troubles seldom come singly, either to individuals or to nations. They are usually encountered in groups. A mysterious chain, invisible but strong, seems to link one misfortune closely to another, so that when once within the iron girdle, we may well look for a succession of calamities till the circuit is finished. To what a fate have we as a nation been already doomed! We seem to be drinking the cup of wrath to its very dregs. Possessing men and money without end, valor and skill in abundance, mental activity and general knowledge, such as no other nation on the globe can boast; yet we have confusion and contradiction in the Cabinet, and doubt, uncertainty and hesitation on the field. No grand effort has been made to strike at the heart of this slaveholding rebellion since the Bull Run battle;[1] and to-day the rebel hosts are within a few miles of Washington, as fierce, determined and defiant as ever. In this state of facts, war with England looms upon the political horizon as a more than possible event. There are, it is true, good men both in England and America, who are exerting all their influence to prevent a disaster so ruinous to both parties, as such a war would prove; but we cannot shut our eyes to what is passing before us. Both countries are studded with the materials by which nations are hurled from peaceful security into the boiling abyss and fierce tumults of war. England is suffering at this moment untold calamities from the rebellion in this country. She sees that ABRAHAM LINCOLN[2] at Washington is sternly opposed to emancipation,

---

1 On 21 July 1861, the first major Union campaign in the East was turned back by Confederates at Bull Run near Manassas Junction, Virginia.

2 Republican Abraham Lincoln (1809–1865) of Illinois was president of the United States during the Civil War.

as JEFF. DAVIS[3] is sternly in favor of slavery, and that the cause of civilization has nothing to hope from either. She sees nothing like a vigorous prosecution of the war for the suppression of rebellion, and to all human seeming our war is to go on for long years, poisoning the moral sentiment of the world, and dealing out stagnation and death to the world's industry. These, aside from the Trent affair[4] are well calculated to breed bad blood towards us in England. While, on our side, hesitating, doubting, shrinking on the Potomac before our rebellious foe, sending brigades to look for the enemy where it is known he is not, but carefully avoiding all the places where he is known to be, we, nevertheless, with true Celtic bravado, deal in fiery talk about a war with England. We are vain, boastful and haughty, the very qualities favorable to bringing on war, though not of victory. As to the affair of the Trent, with which our readers are already familiar, the public mind has, we think, hardly been treated with candor. Our newspapers and orators have kept back part of the truth, and allowed the masses to suppose that we are all right, while, in truth, taking our own past versions of international law, we are all wrong. Up to this writing, it is not known what views will control our National Cabinet, concerning the conduct of Capt. WILKES,[5] but in the street, and in the newspapers, his conduct is everywhere commended. By the same authority, no doubt WILKES would have been sustained if he had made the capture in a British port, instead of the deck of a British steamer.

To our mind, the capture was wrong and inexcusable on general principles, and especially so on American principles. No nation has maintained a more steady position against the right of search in all its forms, and exacted a greater deference to our national flag than have the American Government and people.

We have seen our national flag the last refuge of pirates and slave-traders, and have contended that even this abuse could not justify even the right of visit. While all the great powers have been ready these twenty-five years to unite in a treaty by which slave-traders could not shelter their hell-black traffic under their respective flags, the United States, with her usual tenderness towards slavery in all its forms, and her sensitive regard for the sacredness of our flag, have sternly refused to unite with the world in the honorable concession for the promotion of honesty on the ocean. We have contended, over and over again, that the deck of an American ship is as sacred as any part of the national domain. But what a commentary on this doctrine is the conduct of Captain WILKES. He hails a British mail steamer, on her way from one neutral port to another – sends a cannon ball a few yards from

---

3   The Confederate States of America selected veteran Democratic Party politician Jefferson Davis (1808–1889) of Mississippi as their president.

4   In November 1861, a US Navy cruiser halted the British ship *Trent* in mid-Atlantic waters to capture two Confederate diplomats en route to Europe, touching off an international crisis that briefly seemed to threaten war between the United States and Britain.

5   Charles Wilkes (1798–1877) captained the USS *San Jacinto* in the Trent Affair.

her bow – boards her with armed men – demands her passenger list, and captures by force four of her passengers. We are not skilled in the law of nations, and know not what may be brought from that source to sustain this conduct; but we know enough to know that whatever sustains such conduct is a point blank condemnation of all our pretensions at this point hitherto. We have contended that free ships make free goods, and the same of passengers. The practice of boarding American ships, and capturing so-called British subjects, led to the war of 1812.[6] We were not deterred from declaring war either by any sentiment of magnanimity, considering that England had then a grand European war on her hands, and had enough to attend to without fighting us. We mention this, not to justify England in her present position – for she is just about as inconsistent as ourselves – but simply to induce men to look at this affair more calmly and candidly than they have been wont to do.

But MASON and SLIDELL[7] were belligerent ambassadors. That is a character which, from the first, we have denied them. We have complained that other nations should look upon them as belligerents, and felt affronted when England and France so recognized them.

Well, they were rebels; yes, they are rebels; but not rebels against any other than the American Government, and no other Government or people under heaven has any right to make any discrimination against them on this account. Whatever these men might be to us, we hold that they were passengers to the Captain of the Trent, and that as such they were under the protection of the British flag. Wo[e] to the world when Governments can pursue rebels beyond their own territories, and where there shall no longer be asylum for those political offenders! Had the Trent run the blockade – escaped from one of our ports – the case would have been different. These so-called Commissioners were out of American waters before the British flag covered them, and Captain WILKES had no more right to capture them there than he would have had to capture them crossing from Dublin to Liverpool. Against all bravado, against all inflated talk about national honor, while we hate with all the hate one man can feel, the conduct of these guilty rebels, we say, if England demands them, GIVE THEM UP. Our honor can not require England's dishonor, and we should certainly regard the deed done to her as done unto ourselves.

Wisdom has triumphed over folly, common sense over false pride, the sober second thought over violence and passion. The foregoing article was written before the news of the release of the rebels MASON and SLIDELL had reached us, and when the

---

6   The War of 1812 (1812–15), fought between the US and Great Britain.
7   James Murray Mason (1798–1871) and John Slidell (1793–1871) were the two Confederate politicians and diplomats seized by Union forces on the Trent.

terrible issue of peace and war trembled in the balance. – Thank God that this calamity no longer hangs over us, and that the nation may now go forward in suppressing the rebels and traitors marshalled against it, without apprehension of foreign interference! The Cabinet at Washington has done its duty, and shown itself deaf to all vulgar and senseless clamor. Putting itself right on American principles, it has saved both the nation's honor and the nation's welfare. Our duty is done.

If England can afford to preach one doctrine and practice another – to claim for herself a right which she does not grant to an other – she will hereafter simply appear before the world as a bully, and the world will find some way of protecting itself from her bold assumptions of power. There is, however, good reason to believe that she will never again assert for herself a right, or exercise a power which she has now denied as under the loud menace of war. The seizure of MASON and SLIDELL was done upon English, not American principles. Examples of such seizures are a part of the history of English naval exploits. By demanding the release of the arch traitors and rebels, MASON and SLIDELL, she can never again claim the right to seize English subjects on the high seas, and under whatever flag she may find them, without the most brazen and scandalous contradiction to her present position. Thus, out of this unauthorized and dangerous proceeding of the San Jacinto in stopping the Trent, may come a great advantage to the cause of justice and freedom on the high seas to America and to other nations, besides making the danger of a conflict with England upon any other point far less than previously – for seeing the moderation and justice of the American Government in this matter, will disarm English violence in the immediate future.

We have done our duty, and done it under circumstances severely trying to our national pride, under a liability to be misconstrued, and having the act attributed to our sense of fear, rather than our sense of justice. We have done it promptly and gracefully. Now, let England do hers. Not by uttering complaints of the inefficiency of our blockade; not by decrying our army and navy; not by grumbling about our tariff, which the war has made necessary; not by holding out hopes of recognition to the Confederate States; not by proclaiming the inability of the North to suppress this most foul and unnatural rebellion; not by magnifying the victories of the rebel arms, and disparaging those of the loyal people; not by hints of a purpose to raise the blockade to obtain cotton for her mills; but by a whole-soul sympathy, such as one friendly nation should gladly show to a sister nation undergoing the perils of a formidable and terrible rebellion. Let the ties of friendship between the two countries, now weakened to almost dissolution, become strong. – Let her not now talk and act as if she had wrung concession from cowardice, and humility from helplessness; for from such base motives, to wring concessions and humility would be as dishonorable to her as discreditable to us. Already, her ready menace of war against us is set down to her knowledge of our present weakness, rather then to her sense of honor, or her knowledge of her own strength. – that is not true valor which offers battle to a man when his hands are tied, or assails one when fighting another; and it will add little honor to British diplomacy or to the British flag, if hereafter it shall appear that she has been moved to menace us with war, less from a sense of the sacredness of the laws of nations, than from apprehension of our inability to cope with her while passing the trying ordeal of civil war. If America is in any measure disgraced by surrendering MASON and SLIDELL, England must share equally with America that disgrace. Of the two governments, looking at all the circumstances of the case, our Government stands at this moment in a vastly more enviable position than that of England. But the subject is disposed of. – Let us have done with it, and now attend earnestly to the rebellion, and to slavery, its cause.

THE SLAVE'S APPEAL TO GREAT BRITAIN

London Daily News, 26 November 1862, p. 5.
Other texts in New York *Independent*,
20 November 1862, p. 1; San Francisco
Pacific Appeal, 27 December 1862, p. 3

Hear this, my humble appeal; and grant this, my most earnest request. I know your power; I know your justice; and, better still, I know your mercy; and with the more confidence, I, in my imperfect speech, venture to appeal to you. Your benevolent sons and daughters, at great sacrifice of time, of labor, and treasure, more than a quarter of a century ago, under the inspiration of enlightened Christianity, removed the yoke of cruel bondage from the bowed down necks of eight hundred thousand of my race, in your West India Islands; and later, a few of them, in their generosity, unasked, with silver and gold, ransomed me from him who claimed me as his slave, in the United States, and bade me speak in the cause of the dumb millions of my countrymen still in slavery. I am now fulfilling my appointed mission in making on the slaves' behalf this appeal to you.

I am grateful for your benevolence, jealous for your honor, but chiefly now I am concerned, lest, in the present tremendous crisis of American affairs, you should be led to adopt a policy which may defeat the now proposed emancipation of my people, and forge new fetters of slavery for unborn millions of their posterity. You are now more than ever urged, both from within and from without your borders, to recognize the independence of the so-called Confederate States of America. I beseech and implore you, resist this urgency. You have nobly resisted it thus long. You can, and I ardently hope you will, resist it still longer. The proclamation of emancipation by President Lincoln will become operative on the first day of January, 1863.[1] The

---

[1] Issued by Abraham Lincoln on 22 September 1862, the Emancipation Proclamation promised that unless Confederates had abandoned their rebellion as of 1 January 1863, all enslaved people in areas still in arms against the Union would be free.

hopes of millions, long trodden down, now rise with every advancing hour. Oh! I pray you, by all your highest and holiest memories, blast not the budding hopes of these millions by lending your countenance and extending your potent and honored hand to the blood-stained fingers of the impious slaveholding Confederate States of America.

For the honor of the British name, which has hitherto carried only light and hope to the slave, and rebuke and dismay to the slaveholder, do not in this great emergency be persuaded to abandon and contradict that policy of justice and mercy to the negro which has made your character revered, and your name illustrious, throughout the civilized world. Your enemies even have been compelled to respect the sincerity of your philanthropy. Would you retain this respect, welcome not those brazen human fleshmongers, those brokers in the bodies and souls of men, who have dared to knock at your doors for admission into the family of nations. Their pretended government is but a foul, haggard, and blighting conspiracy against the sacred rights of mankind, and does not deserve the name of government. Its foundation is laid in the impudent and heaven-insulting dogma that man may rightfully hold property in man, and flog him to toil like a beast of burden. Have no fellowship, I pray you, with these merciless men-stealers; but rather with whips of scorpions scourge them beyond the beneficent range of national brotherhood.

You long ago fixed the burning brand of your reprobation upon the guilty brow of the whole slave system. Your philanthropy, religion, and law – your noblest sons, living and dead – have taught the world to loathe and abhor slavery as the vilest of modern abominations. You have sacrificed millions of pounds and thousands of lives to arrest and put an end to the piratical slave-traffic on the coast of Africa; and will you now, when the light of your best teachings is finding its way to the darkest corners of the earth, and men are beginning to adopt and practically carry out your benevolent ideas, – will you now, in such a time, utterly dishonor your high example and your long cherished principles? Can you, at the bidding of importunity of those negro-driving lords of the lash, Mason and Morehead,[2] whose wealth is composed of the wages of laborers which they have kept back by fraud and force, take upon you and your children the dreadful responsibility of arresting the arm now outstretched to break the chains of the American slave?

Ah! but I know the plea. The North as well as the South has wronged the negro. But must you, because the loyal states have been guilty of complicity with slavery, espouse the cause of these who are still more guilty? Must you, while you reprobate the guilty agent, embrace in the arms of your friendship the still more guilty principal?

---

2   The Confederacy sent former US Senator James Murray Mason (1798–1871) of Virginia as their diplomatic representative to the UK. Charles Slaughter Morehead (1802–1868), a former governor of Kentucky, made pro-Confederate speeches in Great Britain during the Civil War.

Will you lash the loyal states for their want of genuine detestation of slavery, and yet in open day form an alliance with a band of conspirators and thieves who have undertaken to destroy the loyal Government of this country, perpetual and universal on this continent? Will you stand in the way of a righteous measure, because supported and urged by wrong and selfish motives? Will you prevent the slave from getting his due, because a sense of necessity and not a sense of moral obligation impels the payment? Oh! again, Great Britain, let me implore you, by all things high and sacred, fling away all false and selfish reasoning, and bear aloft higher than ever that standard of justice and humanity which has justly exalted you to the head of civilized nations.

That the loyal states have grievously wronged the black man – slave and free – is, alas! too true. That these states, even now, for the sake of an empty peace – there can be none other while slavery continues – might be induced to receive the rebels, slavery and all, into the Union, cannot well be disproved. And that their immeasurable blood-guiltiness is drawing down upon them the fierce judgments they now suffer, is a most solemn and instructive truth, for your edification as well as ours. There is no more exemption for nations than for individuals from the just retribution due to flagrant and persistent transgression. For the time being, America is the blazing illustration of this solemn truth. But yesterday she sat as a queen among the nations of the earth, knowing no sorrow and fearing none. She killed some of her prophets, and stoned those who were sent unto her, and who pointed to her great prosperity as a proof of her honesty. But now the evil day is upon her, and she is making one grand effort, through blood and tears, through fire and death, to return to the ways of righteousness and peace. In the name of the slave – whose fate for weal or for woe trembles in the balance – and for the sake of a war-smitten country, now struggling to save itself by doing right, I entreat you, beware what you do concerning us!

Can it be doubted that the hope so persistently kept alive by such organs of British public opinion as *The London Times*, and by such eminent statesmen as Mr. Gladstone,[3] that recognition of the independence of the Confederate States is only a question of time, – that this hope is one grand source of the strength of our slaveholding rebellion? Your early concession of belligerent rights to the rebels – the adoption of neutrality as between the loyal and the rebel governments – the oft-repeated assertion in high places that the rebels can never be subdued – the ill-concealed exultation sometimes witnessed over disasters to our arms – the prompt action of your Government in the Trent affair, now happily settled by a ready and friendly compliance with your demand, although coupled with irritating menace – with much else which it can do no good and might do harm to mention here, have evidently served the bad purpose of keeping life and spirit in this horrible rebellion.

---

3   William E. Gladstone (1809–1898), Liberal politician and prime minister of Great Britain.

I have no hesitation in saying that if you, Great Britain, had, at the outset of this terrible war, sternly frowned upon the conspirators, and had given your earnest and unanimous sympathy and moral support to the loyal cause, to-day might have seen America enjoying peace and security, and you would not have been the sufferer in all your commercial and manufacturing interests you now are. The misfortune is that your rebukes of the North have been construed into sympathy and approval at the South. Your good opinion of the slaveholders has been taken as a renunciation of your former abhorrence of slavery; and you have thus kept these confederate slave-masters in countenance from the beginning. But I will not deal in language of recrimination. There has been far too much of this already on both sides. Nor will I argue the question of difference between us. I can only appeal and entreat. Nevertheless, I will say that the issue between the North and the South is seldom fairly stated in Great Britain by those who take the Southern side. The Federal Government is held to be fighting utterly apart from any connection with the welfare of the four million slaves of the South. Theoretically the statement has a show of truth, but practically it is entirely false. This sophistry found its way where little expected, in the speech of Mr. Gladstone at Newcastle-upon-Tyne, when he argued that the interests of the negro were likely to be better cared for under the Southern Confederacy than in the old Union.

An intelligent answer to the inquiry, Why did the South rebel against the Federal Government? will exhibit the unsoundness of that pretense. The whole history of the rebellion will show that the slaveholding rebels revolted, not because of any violation of the United States Constitution, or of any proposed violation of it, but from pure and simple opposition to the Constitution itself, and because, in their judgment, that Constitution does not sufficiently guard and protect slavery. The first serious objection to the Constitution dates back to 1789, and was raised in the Virginia Convention met to ratify that Constitution. Patrick Henry,[4] one of the leaders of the struggle for severing the colonies from the British crown, declared himself against the Constitution, on the ground, as he said, that it gave power to the Federal Government to abolish slavery in all states, and that, with a strong anti-slavery sentiment, that power would surely be exercised. The answer to this objection by Mr. Madison[5] is significant of the state of public opinion concerning slavery at that time, and shows that the objection of Mr. Henry could not be met by positive refutation; for Mr. Madison simply said, he hoped that no gentleman would vote against the Constitution upon an objection so discreditable to Virginia. The

---

4   Patrick Henry (1736–1799), US lawyer, politician, and orator, famous for his expression "Give me liberty, or give me death."
5   James Madison (1751–1836), founding father, enslaver, and fourth president of the United States.

Constitution was too anti-slavery for Mr. Henry. The anti-slavery sentiment which he anticipated three-quarters of a century ago, asserted itself in the election of Mr. Lincoln.

Near the close of the late inglorious administration, Mr. Buchanan[6] proposed several amendments to the Constitution, giving full and explicit guarantees for the better protection of slavery. The proposition as embodied by him – happily for the interests of freedom and humanity – found but little favor North or South; the former evidently opposed to the measure in itself; and the latter, believing it impossible to carry it, proceeded with the rebellion already determined upon. In this simple, brief statement may be clearly discerned the real cause of the rebellion. Wanting a slave-holding constitution, from which all hope of emancipation should be excluded, the Southern states have undertaken to make one, and to establish it upon the ruins of the old one, under which slavery could be discouraged, crippled, and abolished. The war, therefore, to maintain the old against the new Constitution is essentially an anti-slavery war, and ought to command the ardent sympathy and support of good men in all countries.

What though our timid Administration at Washington, shrinking from the logical result of their own natural position as the defenders of an anti-slavery constitution against a radical slave-holding one, did, at the first, refuse to admit the real character of the war, and vainly attempt to conciliate by walking backward and casting a mantle over the revolting origin of the rebellion? What though they instructed their foreign agents to conceal the moral deformity of the rebels? You could not fail to know that the primal causes of this war rested in the selfishness and wickedness of slavery, and a determination on the part of the slaveholders to make their stupendous crime and curse all-controlling and perpetual in America.

But I will not weary you by statement or argument. The case is plain. The North is fighting on the side of liberty and civilization, and the South on the side of slavery and barbarism.

You are suffering in your commerce and in your manufactures. Industry languishes, and the children of your poor cry for bread. God pity them! The calamity is great. But would any interference with us bring relief to those sufferers? You have shared with the American slaveholders the unhallowed gains of the blood-stained products of slave-labor, preferring Carolina slave to India free, making Manchester a party to the slave plantation, and largely in sympathy with the slaveholding spirit of America. What else in the world could have come of all this but participation with us in the common retribution? Must the world stand still, humanity make no progress, and slavery remain for ever, lest your cotton-mills should stop and your poor cry for bread? You are unable to obtain your usual supply of American cotton.

---

6   James Buchanan (1791–1868), lawyer, secretary of state, and 15th president of the United States.

Would this be made better by plunging yourselves into the hardships, expenses, horrors, and perils of a war, which would in any event shed no luster on your arms, and only feed the fires of national hate for a century to come – and just in this your time of need greatly diminish your American supply of corn? Can any thinking man doubt for one moment that intervention would be an aggravation rather than a mitigation of the evils under which your laborers mourn? It is insisted that you ought, from considerations of humanity towards both sections, intervene, and put an end to the fratricidal strife. Ah! but there's the rub! Could you put an end to it? Never did wilder delusions beset a human brain. I say it in no menacing spirit, the United States, though wounded and bleeding, is yet powerful. Heavy as have been her losses, in life and treasure, her weaknesses from these causes offer no temptation to foreign assault, even supposing you could be influenced by such motives.

But I have no taste for this view of the subject, and will not dwell upon it. The lesson of our civil war to you is the cultivation of cotton by free labor. It tells you that you should base your industry and prosperity on the natural foundations of justice and liberty. These are permanent. All else, transient – hay, wood, and stubble. A house built upon the sand can as well resist the winds and floods, as slavery can resist enlightenment and progress. The moral laws of the universe must be suspended, or slavery will go down. Look, therefore, to India, where your laws have carried liberty. Look to the West Indies, where your philanthropy has planted Christianity. Your resources are great and ample. You have the islands to the west of you, India to the east of you, and Africa with her perennial cotton-plant to the south of you. Intervene there, not with swords and guns and other warlike implements, but by means of peaceful industry. Convert a calamity into prosperity, a curse into a blessing. I fully believe in the general rectitude of the British heart. The poorest of all the sufferers in Lancashire would hardly be willing to purchase even life itself by replunging a liberated slave into hopeless slavery. Much less would they do so were another door open for relief. Abraham might have slain his son but for the appearance of a more appropriate sacrifice – and you have a far better alternative than war with us.

I will not weary you. The case is before you. No excuses, however plausible – no distances of time, however remote – no line of conduct hereafter pursued, however excellent, will erase the deep stain upon your honor and truth, if, at this hour of dreadful trial, you interpose in a manner to defeat or embarrass the emancipation of the slaves of America. If at any time you could have honorably intervened in American affairs, it was when the Federal Government was vainly striving to put down the rebellion without hurting slavery – when our army and generals wore the brass collars of slave dogs, and hunted negroes for their rebel masters. That gloomy and disgusting period ended on the 22d Sept, 1862[7][.] From that day our war has

---

7   The date that President Lincoln issued his Preliminary Emancipation Proclamation.

been invested with a sanctity which will smite as with death even the mailed hand of Britain, if outstretched to arrest it. Let the conflict go on! There is no doubt of the final result, and though the war is a dreadful scourge, it will make justice, liberty, and humanity permanently possible in this country.

MR. FREDERICK DOUGLASS ON THE PROSPECTS OF SLAVERY

Leeds, England, *Leeds Mercury*, 2 February 1865, p. 4

The following interesting extract is from a letter of Frederick Douglass to a friend:[1] –

"Rochester, U.S., January 4th, 1865.

"I long to be able to report all chains broken, and the slaves free; the end, however, is not yet, though I believe the long prayed-for event is at hand, and that I shall live to see it, and to tell you that the work is done. The dreadful war in our country is drawing to a close; the rebellion will be suppressed, and I now have high hopes that slavery will go down with it. My reasons are, first the re-election of Mr. Lincoln, who was mainly opposed on the ground of his alleged abolition designs; secondly, the elevation of your old friend and correspondent, Solman P. Chase,[2] to the Chief-Justiceship of the Republic, in place of Judge Taney[3] deceased; thirdly, the general tone of public opinion, demanding the entire abolition of slavery and the unification of the nation on the basis of universal freedom. Any other end of the war must brand it as murderous and useless, for the country can never be united while slavery exists. The signs of the times are nearly all indicative of Abolition[;] the Constitution will be changed, if not by this congress, certainly by the next, so that no slave State can ever be a member of the Union. I have recently

---

1 Likely to be Julia Griffiths Crofts.

2 Ohio politician Salmon Portland Chase (1808–1873) had been a leader of the Liberty, Free Soil, and Republican parties in succession. He served Lincoln as secretary of the treasury before accepting an appointment as chief justice of the US Supreme Court in 1864.

3 Maryland lawyer Roger Brooke Taney (1777–1864) had been appointed chief justice in 1836 by President Andrew Jackson as a reward for faithful service, first as attorney general and then secretary of the treasury. His historical memory has centered on his infamous 1857 ruling in Dred Scott vs. Sandford, which denied any rights of citizenship to African Americans, enslaved or free.

been on a lecturing tour – where do you suppose? In the State of Maryland and in Virginia – in Maryland, the State of my birth and my bondage. I gave six lectures in Baltimore (where three years ago I should have been murdered at sight) without molestation. The papers here have been full of my sayings and doings during my visit. Among the most interesting incidents was meeting my dear sister Eliza, whom I had not seen for nearly thirty years, and with whom, under the slave laws, I could not correspond, and did not know but that she was dead. She heard of my coming to Baltimore, and at once left her home, travelling sixty miles to see me.[4] Our meeting can be better imagined than described. She had (before the Act of Emancipation in the State) bought and paid for herself by her own toil, has nine children, most of them men and women, and she is still quite straight and vigorous. From her I got some facts concerning other members of our family, most of them painful, for they have been sold and scattered through the rebellious slave States . . .

For my own part, time and toil begin (in spite of my determination to be young) to leave their marks upon me. The constant travelling from place to place, changing my bed and board every twenty-four hours – are of themselves enough to wear an iron constitution. Most of the anti-slavery lecturers who began when I did have withdrawn from the field, or at least speak only occasionally. I want to hold out until the jubilee. When that comes I hope to be able to return to the soil for my bread; to spend what shall remain to me of life in a quiet equal to the storms through which I have passed. Before doing this, however, you may yet see me editing a paper in Baltimore, for there is a serious effort to have me start one in that city. I have told my friends there that if they get me one thousand paying subscribers in that city, all paying in advance, I will come. You will see that there is something poetic in the idea of my returning to Maryland for such a purpose. Think of my going into that State from which I escaped as from a doomed city; and after an absence of more than twenty-six years, starting a paper to promote the elevation of my people! I do not say, mark you, that I shall be able to do this, but only that the thing is in contemplation. Should I go forward, I know I may rely on your hearty cooperation; for whatever you may hear or read to the contrary, I am now as ever earnestly and actively at work in the righteous cause to which I have pledged the best energies and years of life. I shall send you the proceedings of the Coloured National Convention held at Syracuse in Oct. last,[5] by this mail. It might be well to circulate that paper

---

4 While speaking in Baltimore in 1865, Douglass was reunited with Eliza Bailey (1816–c. 1876), who had been sold to her future husband, Peter Mitchell, a free Black man.
5 Douglass was the presiding officer of the National Convention of Colored Men held at Syracuse, New York, on 4–7 October 1864; he addressed the delegates and gave a lukewarm endorsement of Lincoln's re-election.

in England as the black man's view of the state of affairs here. At any rate you can pass this copy around among your friends: it will show that some of us take an intelligent interest in the question of our future in this country. I was never heard, here or elsewhere in this country, more willingly than now. But I will not glory in this, but rather rejoice that through the all-wise and inscrutable workings of Providence, the chains of my long enslaved race are soon to be broken."

FREDERICK DOUGLASS ON THE AMERICAN CRISIS

Manchester, England, *Manchester Times*, 20 May 1865, p. 5

The *Inquirer* publishes the following extracts from a letter of Mr. F. Douglass, to an English friend,[1] dated Rochester, April 18th: –

After expressing the horror and sadness with which the first news of the assassination of the President had filled his mind, Mr. Douglass says: "While I mourn the death of Mr. Lincoln as of a personal friend – for he was to me a personal friend – while I remember the good acts of his life towards my enslaved people, I still think that the man who succeeds him will answer better the stern requirements of the hour than even Mr. Lincoln. He was too much under the dominion of his amiable qualities. He thought the rebels should not be punished, but petted, not conquered but conciliated. The recent victories of the Union armies relaxed all his sterner qualities, and he thought to win back his enemies by his kindness, rather than compel their respect and obedience by his power. He forgave without repentance, and, while murder and assassination were darkly sheltered in rebel hearts and homes, he took the sullen submission of treason as evidence of loyalty, and was willing to concede them everything but their slavery, and allow them still to be the dominant and ruling class at the South. Owning the land as they do, and organized as they are, with their negroes disfranchised, and the poor whites ignorant, the government of the South in their hands, they could easily find a substitute for slavery, and lord it over both white and black as they pleased. Andrew Johnson,[2] the man now at the head of the government, understands this better than Mr. Lincoln, and I hope

---

1 Once again, this is likely to be Julia Griffiths Crofts, or Russell L. Carpenter (who frequently wrote for *The Inquirer*).
2 Andrew Johnson (1808–1875), a Democrat who served as vice president to Abraham Lincoln, becoming president when Lincoln was assassinated.

more of him than I dared to hope from Mr. Lincoln. As a man he is not equal to Mr. Lincoln; but as a ruler I think he will prove superior. Perhaps in Mr. Lincoln's place, during the past four years, he would have done no better; he might have done worse; but that first work is done, and we need men of a different mould for what remains. Nothing short of equality before the laws can give the black man any security in this country; and for nothing less than that do I ask the American people and government. If I had a thousand constitutional guarantees of freedom, they would be a mockery without the ability of the black man to sue and testify in the courts, and vote for the men who are to make the laws. In a country where the great mass of people are disfranchised, it is comparatively easy to be one of that mass. Masses of men can take care of themselves anywhere, but to be deprived of a privilege enjoyed by everybody is a hardship and blight upon the proscribed race. I think Mr. Johnson is in favour of enfranchising the negro. Give the negro this one right, and I ask nothing more for him. Whatever else he may lack after that will come finally, without special effort.

"My greatest fear of Mr. Johnson is that he may be less discreet in his bearing towards European powers than the peace of the world and the conditions of the country requires. Once through with this dreadful rebellion, and the South reorganized, my soul longs for unbroken peace; not the old peace of slavery, for that is but another name for war, but for peace based upon justice, liberty, and human brotherhood. When we shall have any such peace no man can tell . . . Since discontinuing my paper, I have spent most of my time in lecturing, devoting myself to the education of public opinion, and endeavouring to bring it not merely to the point of emancipation, but to the enfranchisement of the coloured people, South and North. By this labour, which is by the way quite laborious, requiring me to be ever on the wing, and leaving me very little time to myself, outside of railway carriages, I not only do something for the cause of my people, but am able to support myself and family. I still have the ear of the American people, and never attracted larger crowds. I am very glad to be able to send you so satisfactory an account of myself, and I am sure you will be glad also.

"I think you have done well, and will do well, to send to Philadelphia what you may obtain in aid of freedmen. My mission for the present is to get the American people to substitute justice for sympathy. The coloured people must always remain a helpless and spiritless people while they are deprived of any rights belonging to manhood. In your country a man is protected whether he has a vote or not; because, though not now a voter, he may be one to-morrow, – and there is nothing in his race or past position to mark him out for abuse or insult. This is not so here. The best work I can do, therefore, for the freed-people, is to promote the passing of just and equal laws towards them. They must have the cartridge box, the jury box, and the ballot box, to protect them . . . The thought of some day visiting England again flies across my mind like a sunbeam into the darkness of the hour, but I dare not allow it a long stay. Time flies: it will be twenty years next August since I first set sail for England. England has entered deeply into my life ever since, and happily so. My friends there have been more thoughtful for me, in my works, than anywhere else."

THE POSITION OF THE BRITISH GOVERNMENT TOWARD LIBERTY

Washington, DC, *New National Era,*
17 August 1871, p. 2

We learn that some members of the English royal family have met with any-thing but a cordial reception in Ireland. No cheering could be drawn from the people, and the visitors were even greeted with hisses. Though this may not have been exactly pleasant for them, it was certainly a very natural and genuine exhibition of the feelings of the Irish people, and it required indeed all the besotted self-infatuation peculiar to royalty, to expect any demonstration of joy and affec-tion from the people toward a family that has never done the least thing to deserve their sympathies – nor, in fact, those of the world generally – a family, which, to support in luxury and idleness, they are heavily taxed, and that is identified with a Government under which almost their very life-blood is extorted, and thousands are every year compelled to leave their homes and cross the ocean, to escape from hopeless poverty and starvation. In our own country the Irish form a troublesome element of the population; but their worst features have their source in the degrada-tion and demoralization consequent upon the oppression and despotism exercised over them by the English Government. It is strange how long fame and reputa-tion may sometimes outlive the real merits on which they were founded. From old times it has been the boast of England to be the most liberal Government, to have the best laws and institutions, and to be unsurpassed in the protection afforded to the rights and liberty of the people. There was some foundation to those claims in former days, when our own republic was one of the faithful colonies of his Majesty; when, on the European continent, the rights of the people were hardly anywhere understood, much less admitted; when absolute, arbitrary, monarchical government had full sway; when law was powerless under the hands of the rulers, and even the life and freedom of citizens were subject to their caprices. Then the English con-stitution was indeed something for the English to be proud of, and to be envied by other nations; but since those times the condition of Europe has greatly changed.

Especially since the latter part of the eighteenth century the march of progress has been more rapid than in any previous one. The French revolution[1] and the establishment of our own republic, the reflex of whose light has spread far over Europe, have exercised a powerful influence; and far behind as the masses yet are in respect to political institutions, great things have been achieved already, and more will be achieved in spite of all reactionary elements. Constitutional government has become the rule in all Europe, with the sole exception of Russia, which, however, is counted only among the half-civilized countries; and especially the elective franchise has been recognized everywhere as one of the principal rights of the people. Nevertheless, the old tradition of the supreme excellence of English institutions and English rule is still upheld and believed in, even among other nations. A close observer, however, cannot fail to see a mere illusion in this belief, and to come to the conclusion that on the contrary, just in this respect England has not kept pace with the rest of Europe, and nowadays, of all countries, has the most illiberal, selfish, and treacherous government, the most unjust and superannuated institutions and laws, enforced with merciless rigor. In saying this, however, we strictly separate the nation, the real people from the Government, as we have to do so in order to render them justice, since the majority of them being disfranchised until quite recently, have never had a share in the making of their laws, or the management of their home and domestic policy, consequently are by no means represented and embodied by the Government. This feature, alone, goes far to demonstrate the groundlessness of the assumption that there is anything like sovereignty of the people. The people, on the contrary, as we know them from personal contact, as well as from their whole social and political record, their literature and science, are as progressive, generous, warm-hearted, and liberal as any other nation. Indeed, all the progress made in this century, all the conquests made on the side of liberty are due to the people, wrung from the government as concessions to dire necessity – safety valves against revolution. In fact the wisdom of government – not a very high one – during more than a century, has consisted chiefly in yielding in the last hour to the most imperious demands of the times, in order to avert the storms and civil strifes of which other countries have been the scene. Thus the new suffrage law – imperfect as it is – was granted, and thus the most odious abuse, the purchase of army commissions has been only abolished after it had become manifest that the British army was utterly incapable to cross arms with any of the European nations, who, thanks to an efficient military system, have astonished the world by their brilliant achievements on the battle-field. In one word: England is following, but no longer leading in the way of improvement and progress.

---

1   The French Revolution was a period of political turmoil that began with the overthrow of King Louis XVI in 1789 and ended a decade later when Napoleon Bonaparte crowned himself French emperor.

Much has been said in praise and admiration of the hospitality of the British Government for affording protection and shelter to the political fugitives of all nations. We are far from depreciating the value of this hospitality, which has been a great benefit to many hunted-down martyrs of liberty; yet we should ascribe it less to any truly liberal tendency than to the proud indifference of a powerful State – that, in the consciousness of its independence and security, can disdain to meddle with the affairs of its weaker neighbors as long as its own interests and sensibilities are not touched. In the darkest days of slavery it was a safe and harmless pleasure to denounce royalty in Charleston; and in Austria, under METTERNICH's rule,[2] every one who chose might have spoken against American slavery to his heart's content. Certain it is that that independent, proud British Government deviated most cowardly from its own self-established rule, when, out of fear of NAPOLEON,[3] at his bidding, it expelled GARIBALDI[4] from England without the slightest pretext for such an unheard-of outrage. The proof, however, that real liberality and generosity do not enter into the policy of Government, is furnished by the treatment which it metes out to its own rebellious subjects in Ireland as well as in the colonies. It is no exaggeration to say that the British rule, wherever established, is about the most tyrannical and oppressive of all – the most cruel and relentless in suppressing and avenging any attempt to throw off its yoke. It is hardly necessary to refer to Ireland and the patriotic advocates of the claims of her people – O'DONOVAN ROSSA,[5] and his associates – the most favored of whom, after long imprisonment, during which the most revolting tortures were inflicted upon them, have been sent into exile, while one was massacred in the name of law and justice, and some others, according to MR. GLADSTONE's own admission, have become insane in jail. Further proof is furnished by the Sepoy insurrection in India, which, provoked by the tyranny and rapacity of the government and its officers, was suppressed with an atrocity not exceeded by the horrors of warfare in the most barbarous ages. The wholesale executions by fastening the victims to the mouths of cannon and blowing them to atoms, will forever remain a dark blot in the name of the British government. The execution of GORDON and his alleged, fellow-conspirators in Jamaica, under GOVERNOR EYRE, forms another dark chapter in the long and bloody record of that most liberal government in Europe.[6]

---

2   Klemens von Metternich (1773–1859), Austrian politician and statesman.

3   Napoleon Bonaparte (1769–1821) was a brilliant army commander in the French Revolution who made himself French emperor and ruled over much of continental Europe until his final overthrow in 1815.

4   Giuseppe Garibaldi (1807–1882), Italian statesman, military general, and supporter of Italian unification.

5   Jeremiah O'Donovan Rossa (1831–1915) was an Irish Fenian and prominent figure in the Irish Republican Brotherhood.

6   In 1865, Governor Edward Eyre (1815–1901) arrested and executed George William Gordon (1820–1865) for his alleged role in the Morant Bay Rebellion in Jamaica.

The religious liberty enjoyed by the people of Great Britain is another of those old traditions, and to be sure, one which never was founded on anything but sham and mockery. The horrid laws, dictated by the very spirit of cruelty, bigotry, and religious persecutions, by which the Irish Catholics were made the Pariahs of society, worthy of the darkest days of fanaticism, disgraced the very name of England as late as about a half century ago, and nearly another half century was allowed to elapse before they were relieved from the intolerable burden of supporting a State Church, which to them is an abomination. The violent opposition of the conservative and Church party to the abolition of the State Church in Ireland is of too recent date to be dwelt upon.

The great remedy for all those evils is certain and not far off. Everywhere in Europe the influence and power of the people are in the ascendency, in spite of all exertions of those who still imagine themselves able to shut out the light [of] progress by artificial means. The English people of late have gloriously asserted their power, and it may safely be predicted that they will not stop where so much is left to be done. The old government is tottering to its fall, but the people are full of vitality and youthful vigor, and will in the course of time work out a new government, a new State, really the representative and embodiment of its sovereignty.

THOUGHTS AND RECOLLECTIONS OF A TOUR IN IRELAND (1886)

A.M.E. *Church Review*, 3 (October 1886),
pp. 136–45. Speech, Article, and Book File,
reel 16, frames 113–20, 189–95, reel 19,
frames 408–14, Frederick Douglass Papers,
Library of Congress

Though a man so wise as the late Ralph Waldo Emerson[1] has told us that they who made Rome worth going to see stayed there, and though a distinguished senator has asked somewhat derisively and petulantly, "What have Americans to do with abroad," as though Americans had reached the utmost limit of possible knowledge attainable by travel among, and contact with, other nations, yet we Americans are found in all lands and languages and do more travelling than any other people of modern times. It is possible that this migratory habit is much in excess of a wise moderation, but that benefits arise from it, cannot be utterly denied. The tendency of mankind is ever towards a higher civilization. To this end there are many agents employed: Art, Science, Commerce, Literature, and even War, are such helps; but there is perhaps, no agency more potent and effective in that direction than the knowledge attained and attainable by travelers who make themselves acquainted with the peoples and institutions other than their own. Imitation, though not the highest of human talents, is, nevertheless, one which plays an important part in the matter of human progress. Men learn what is wisest and best by comparison of one thing with another, and travel affords the best means of such comparison. Besides, men are made broad or narrow by their environments.

---

1   Ralph Waldo Emerson (1803–1882), US lecturer and author.

It is not, however, of the philosophy of travel or of civilization that I propose to write; but of the Emerald Isle – the land of Burke and Sheridan, of Gratton and Curran, of O'Connell and Father Matthew;[2] a land renowned in song and story for its statesmen, orators, patriots, and heroes, but alas! a land which has been for ages the scene of misrule and social misery, and which today is, as it has been in the past, the standing and stubborn puzzle of its own reformers and of British statesmanship. With better intentions, with loftier aspirations, with larger experience or with a more masterly intellect, no British statesman has ever attempted to grapple with what is called the Irish problem, than William E. Gladstone; yet, if that only is a solution which *solves*, his effort has, for the present at least, signally failed. England to-day seems further from accepting his Irish policy than when it was first proposed. The age does not favor the creation of small nationalities. In Great Britain, as in this country, liberty and civilization are thought to be safer in the Union than out of it – safer with the whole than with a part – with the mass of the people acting together under one common government than with the few acting in a separate government. The example of the United States in refusing to be dismembered, and the example of the unification of Italy and of Germany, have exerted a silent, but large influence in this direction.

Naturally enough, however, there is a strong feeling in this country favorable to what is called "Home Rule" for Ireland. The relation we sustain to that country both by geography and population, makes her condition and destiny a matter of deep interest to us. Millions of her sons are our countrymen. They are the ruling element in many of our large towns and cities. In fact, Irishmen are said to rule everywhere except in Ireland. They are powerful in Boston, they control in New York, and they dictate the policy of the Pacific States in relation to Chinamen and other competing laborers. That their rule is just and benignant in all respects cannot be successfully maintained – but the Irish are linked and interlinked with the whole American people in the bonds of common country, patriotism, and liberty. It is, therefore, not strange that the American people, in their all-abounding sympathy for Ireland, should share the resentment of her sons in this country to what they consider the wrongs inflicted upon her by British rule, nor is it strange that this feeling should, in some measure, blind us to the insufficiency of the means proposed as a remedy for her misfortunes. I have often said that of all things in this

---

2 Edmund Burke (1729–1797) was an Irish politician and philosopher; Richard Brinsley Sheridan (1751–1816) was an Irish playwright and poet; Henry Grattan (1746–1820) was an Irish politician, orator, and lawyer; John Philpot Curran (1750–1817) was an Irish politician and orator. Roman Catholic monk Theobald Mathew (1790–1856) was Ireland's leading advocate of total abstinence from alcohol.

world the hardest to obtain, is even and exact justice whether to individuals or nations. It is hard for a Turk to be just to a Christian, hard for a Christian to be just to a Jew, hard for a Californian to be just to a Chinaman, hard for an American to be just to a negro, hard for an Englishman, having dominated Ireland for ages, to be just to an Irishman, and, on the other hand, it is hard for an Irishman, under the influence of a sense of ancient wrongs, to be entirely just in his judgment of measures proposed to remedy the wrongs of his country. As time and events have educated the American people on the negro question, so time and events will have to educate both the English and the Irish people as to what is the wisest and best for both.

Interesting to us by reason of kinship and population, Ireland is, and must always be, interesting to us by reason of our proximity, and our increasing facilities for intercourse with her. Once her shores were separated from us by months, now the separation is measured only by days. Distance may lend enchantment to the view, but it is the land that lies nearest us that has the deepest and strongest hold upon our affections. Ireland is now our next door neighbor. Hers is the first land to greet and gladden the eyes of the American voyager as he nears the shores of Europe. I shall never forget the thrill of pleasure and excitement, the eager rush of passengers from cabin to deck, when on my first voyage abroad, forty-one years ago, it was announced by some keen-eyed mariner that the shores of Ireland were in sight. Our voyage had been a pleasant one and the ocean had been more than kind and gentle to us; but whatever may be the character of the voyage, rough or smooth, long or short, the sight of land, after three thousand miles of sea, ship and sky, is unspeakably grateful to the eye and heart of the voyager. The charms of the ocean easily give place to those of the land. The swiftest steamer is too slow, and the shortest voyage too long for most of us. The roll of the ocean is exhilarating for a time, but the steadiness and stability of the firm old earth, especially if one does not happen to be a good sailor, are far more desirable. The feeling of a transatlantic voyager – upon first landing upon a foreign shore – is that nothing short of the attraction of home could tempt him to recross the sea. We may sing as we please of "the sea, the sea, the deep blue sea," and long for a voyage over its "merry waters," but we shall find in it something wild, desolate and appalling. When we think of its unfeeling way of swallowing up great ships, with cargoes, gallant sailors, helpless passengers, regardless of prayers and tears for mercy, your "deep, blue sea" is not the fairest among ten thousand and altogether lovely.

As the distance decreased between our ship and the shore, and the bold, rugged, ragged outline of the Irish Coast disclosed its character, it was impossible to drive from my mind the gloomy thought now expressed. Here was land, it is true, but it was worn and rent with uncounted ages of conflict with the gigantic billows of the broad Atlantic, and its menacing rocks, aided by darkness and storm, may well be contemplated with a shudder. Many a craft has here gone down to rise no more, and many a gallant sailor has here fought his last battle with the elements. Those who have sailed along the rugged and mountainous coast of the State of Maine from Portland to Bar Harbor may easily form some just idea of the Irish coast and its perils.

As Ireland is the first land to greet and gladden the eye of the transatlantic voy-ager, so it is the last to disappear from the view of the cisatlantic voyager. There is always something sad in seeing the dark blue sea rise between us and the land we are leaving, perhaps for the last time. This is so even with a foreign land. It was certainly so with me. There are few who go abroad who do not make friends and acquaintances from whom it is hard to part forever, and land and people become so associated that in parting we do not separate the one from the other. The separation from the people is not complete till we leave the country, and the land disappears from view forever. I was strongly impressed with this feeling when I looked, for what seemed the last time, on the shores of Ireland. If this is true of one leaving a foreign land, a thousand fold more true is it for one leaving his native land, where the ties are a thousand times stronger. Not even the comforting thought of going to a better and happier country can dispel the bitter anguish of an Irish emigrant, when he sees one after another of the familiar hills and mountains of his beloved native land sink below the distant horizon. It is a moment when strong hearts fail and nature speaks in tears.

If I am asked by your respected readers, as I probably shall be, for most of them are, I doubt not, under forty years old, why I made the voyage to the United Kingdom of Great Britain and Ireland, I suppose I should muster courage to tell them, how-ever humiliating it might seem. It would rather be a proud thing to be able to say, I went abroad as a gentleman and a scholar, to seek pleasure or to enlarge my stock of knowledge by observation and study of the peoples, countries and civilizations older than our own; but truth does not allow me any such high-sounding purposes. The fact is, I went to England and Ireland for the purpose of finding liberty and shelter denied me at home. I was a slave – a fugitive slave, and neither the American flag nor the American eagle could protect me. The going away of a man from a republic in search of liberty in a monarchy was a striking commentary upon the institutions of both countries and the inappropriateness of names signifying things. At that time the republic meant slavery and the monarchy freedom, at least so it was in my case. While, however, abroad for freedom, I will not deny that I gained some knowledge as well. I saw many great and wise people and made many friends.

I have a good word to say for the Irish people just here. However harsh and oppressive the sons of Erin may feel and act towards the oppressed classes when they take up their abode in this country, I am bound to say that I found among them in their own country a warm welcome and safe asylum. Those who go to the

Emerald Isle expecting to find a country given up to lawless violence, from which neither persons nor property are safe, and where only misery and utter destitution prevail, will find how mistaken have been their impressions when they walk the orderly streets of the beautiful city of Dublin, the seat of Ireland's ancient greatness and now the centre of the Irish law, learning, refinement and civilization. To be sure, like other great transatlantic cities, it has a new and an old part, with the characteristics peculiar of each. The old is dark, dilapidated and sinister, abounding in painful evidences of misery and destitution; the other light, clean and elegant, abounding in evidences of wealth, comfort and refinement. Nowhere in the world can extremes more opposite in human conditions be seen than in this fine city of Dublin. Attraction and repulsion, virtue and vice, elevation and depression, do not, like wheat and tares, grow together here, but in their respective localities. In one you see only the mansions of the rich, where all is elegant, refined and beautiful; in the other the wretched hovels of the poor, where all is miserable and repulsive. The contrast between the one section and the other is painful to contemplate, and a sigh comes up from the depths of the soul asking why should these things be and where is the remedy? To this no answer has yet been given. Of course the same extremes of wealth and poverty, of refinement and brutality, may be seen in all large cities, though not so glaringly as I saw it in Dublin, where misery seemed so out of proportion with comfort, the one so much the rule and the other so much the exception. Many of the business streets of Dublin will bear favorable comparison with those of New York and Philadelphia, notably that known as Sackville Street.[3] It is broad, straight, far-reaching and grand. It is, in fact, the pride of Dublin. It is lined on either side with fine stores, laden with the riches of all lands and languages. Dublin can boast of many noble and commanding public buildings. The Custom House, the Parliament House and the Bank of Ireland are buildings that would attract attention and admiration anywhere.

Strolling about in the new and aristocratic part of Dublin, observing its well-clothed men and its elegantly dressed women, the latter models of beauty and refinement; observing its splendid equipages, with servants in livery, you would not expect the appalling extent of wretchedness and misery to be found within its borders, or of the country of which it is the ancient capital. But leave the city, roam among the beautiful Wicklow hills, within one hour's ride of the beautiful city, and you will meet with the most distressing examples of ignorance, pauperism and suffering. Persistent beggars, who can neither be persuaded nor compelled to let you

---

3 Today renamed for Daniel O'Connell, Sackville Street was Dublin's main thoroughfare and commercial hub since the late 18th century.

alone, will dog your every step and assail your ears with tales of deepest woe, against which it is impossible to steel your heart, and equally impossible for you to administer relief. I was told by a friend who was with me on one of these strolls, and who saw me dealing out my pennies to the beggars, that I must stop, that I might empty my pockets every day to the beggars and myself become a beggar like the rest, without at all diminishing the number or the wants of the beggars, – many of whom were, he said, professional. Professional or not I thought, here is no counterfeited misery. There are some things in the world that will tell the truth. Words may lie, but the human voice will tell the truth. Through it the deepest feelings will reach the ear and heart. You will hear in the voices of the poor people here tones that you never heard before, and such as I hope you will not often hear elsewhere. They tell of centuries of oppression and sorrow far more impressively than speech. I was often called upon while in Ireland to speak upon slavery, but I found so much misery in that country that I could not well talk of American slavery. How can I ask these people, who have so many wrongs to redress and so much suffering to relieve at home, to look after wrongs and oppressions abroad, was a question that constantly forced itself upon me at every turn.

I visited many towns and cities in Ireland, both in the north and south of the country. Cork in the south and Belfast in the north are the two cities which may be well enough taken as typical of the civilization of each section. The difference between these is about as distinctly marked as is the difference between the northern and southern sections of our own country, and they show the same superior progress of the one over the other. The cause of the difference between the North and the South in the United States is explained by one word – Slavery. I can only hint at the cause of the difference between the North and South of Ireland. I think that both religion and blood have much to do with the disparity between the two. The south of Ireland is overwhelmingly Catholic and withal distinctly Irish in blood. The quickening influence of foreign admixture had been little felt here. Not only the Irish brogue is heard here, but often the Irish language. Though English is generally spoken, the Irish tongue has not yet been quite forgotten or supplanted.

An amusing story was told me in this connection of Daniel O'Connell. He had been announced to make a great political speech in the south of Ireland, at a time of much political excitement about the repeal of the union between England and Ireland, and in England it seemed very important to hear just what the great Irish agitator was saying to the easily inflammable Irish people. The London "Times," surnamed the "Thunderer," always alert and determined to be equal to this as well as to every other occasion, was at the pains and expense of sending over the Channel an expert verbatim reporter to report the speech. When O'Connell was made aware of the sinister presence he determined to thwart and confound his old adversary. He ordered that a table and a chair should be courteously furnished to the highly-accomplished reporter, and when he was seated, had sharpened his pencils, smoothed down his papers and prepared to catch every word, the wily O'Connell advanced to the front of the platform with a mirthful twinkle in his eye, and, to the amazement and utter confusion of the would-be reporter, harangued his audience and worked them up to the highest pitch of excitement in his own native, unreportable tongue of which the reporter could not understand a single word. The poor fellow was compelled to sit there utterly confounded, and serve as an object of amusement both to the speaker and to the crowd.

No public man was perhaps more beloved by any people than Daniel O'Connell was by the people of his country. The first sight I caught of him, after landing in Ireland, was near Sackville Street Bridge. He was then on his way to Conciliation Hall, where he was to make a speech on essentially the same question which today so deeply agitates the United Kingdom. It was then called Repeal, but meant Home Rule all the same. He was just from Derrynane, his country-seat, where he had been spending several months resting from his arduous labors in the cause of Irish liberty. It was a cool October day, and he was, as usual, wrapped in his cloak, walking at a rapid rate towards the great hall, followed by a squad of ragged little boys shouting in tones of loving admiration, "There goes Dan! There goes Dan!" And the great man beamed upon the ragged urchins with a look of overflowing affection and delight, as though they were his own children greeting his coming to his home after a long absence. A more beautiful and touching picture it has seldom been my good fortune to witness. With all the rest of the world I had heard much of Daniel O'Connell as an orator and as the greatest man of his country, and this day it was my privilege to see the man and to stand upon the platform of Conciliation Hall with him, and to hear him address an expectant crowd of his countrymen. I, with the rest, expected much, and though, in such cases, expectations are seldom realized, the present instance was an exception. I was not only not disappointed in my expectations; but I found them exceeded. I had heard and read much of the great orator and liberator; how he could sway and control the feelings of his people; how he could move them to mirth or tears; how he could rouse to fiercest indignation and wrath; how he could in the open air hold the attention of twenty and even thirty thousand people; still I made allowance for enthusiasm and exaggeration, and tempered my thought accordingly; but a few sentences of this man's deep, rich, musical and almost miraculous voice, as it swept over the vast multitude, uttered without effort, without gestures, with arms folded upon his deep broad chest, dispelled all doubt of the vastness and grandeur of his power with his people, and, indeed, with any people who might come under the spell of his eloquence. In the address delivered on this occasion he showed himself a broad-hearted philanthropist as well as a patriot. I shall never forget his eloquent reference to American slavery, when, drawing himself up to his full height and holding in his hand a copy of O. A. Brownson's Review,[4] he said: "I am here charged with attacking the American Institution, as slavery is called. I am not ashamed of that attack. My sympathy is not confined to the narrow limits of my own Green Island. My spirit walks abroad upon the clement waters. Wherever there is oppression, I hate the oppressor; wherever the tyrant rears his head, I will deal my bolts upon it; and wherever there is sorrow and suffering, there is my spirit to succor and relieve." The worst enemy of Mr. O'Connell could not accuse him of insincerity in his anti-slavery professions. He saw a man in the negro, in spite of his color. In introducing me to this great Repeal meeting, he playfully called me the black O'Connell of America. He was not only a man of words and wisdom, but, like most of the great orators of his country, he was a man of wonderfully ready wit, and had the faculty of giving a man a nick-name that would stick to him through life. Replying to one of the fierce invectives of the great Disraeli, he stigmatized him as the lineal descendant of the impenitent thief upon the cross, and, powerful as Disraeli became afterwards, these terrible words stuck to him through all his future career. The London "Times," desiring to turn the tables upon Mr. O'Connell, and to prove that his denunciation of Irish land-lords should be directed against himself, sent a commissioner to Ireland to spy out and report to the "Times" the condition of tenants holding under Mr. O'Connell, and the report was certainly a most damaging arraignment. It described Mr. O'Connell's tenants as among the most miserable of all the most miserable class in Ireland. In Kircheveen, a village owned by O'Connell, of nine hundred inhabitants, the commissioner stated there was not a single pane of glass to be seen. It was an assemblage of wretched huts, without the least approach to comfort or health. In replying, Mr. O'Connell did not, as I hoped, show that the condition of his tenantry was misrepresented, but simply denounced the commissioner as the "Gutter Commissioner," – and to his statement that there was not a single pane of glass to be seen in his village, he simply said: "I wish he had as many *pains* in his body;" and this mode of dealing with the public accusation seemed altogether satisfactory to his audience. Such a mode of disposing of unpleasant allegations would hardly be deemed convincing in America, though it must be said that this mode is not confined to Ireland.

Mr. O'Connell's method of receiving Americans visiting his country was rough on slaveholders. A gentleman from this country being introduced to the Liberator, and about to extend his hand, was suddenly stopped, as O'Connell withdrew his hand, saying: "Pardon me, sir; but I make it a rule never to give my hand to an American

---

4 Orestes Augustus Brownson (1803–1876), US activist, preacher, writer, and editor of *Brownson's Quarterly Review*.

without asking if he is a slaveholder." The gentleman answered good-naturedly: "No, Mr. O'Connell, I am not a slaveholder, but I am willing to discuss the question of slavery with you." "Pardon me again," said O'Connell; "discuss it with me! Without meaning you the least harm in the world, – should a gentleman come into my study and propose to discuss with me the rightfulness of picking pockets, I would show him the door, lest he should be tempted to put his theory into practice." His quickness to see and turn a point to advantage was as remarkable as the depth and power of his pathos. He could amuse as well as make men feel and think. A sea-captain, who had taken a cargo of iron to the coast of Africa, on his return was invited to dine with O'Connell; while dining, and speaking of his voyage, Mr. O'Connell asked him how he made out with his cargo of iron. "Oh, pretty well," said the captain, "but on land-ing we found the iron terribly worm-eaten." "Indeed," said O'Connell, "but may I inquire what kind of a worm you found on board your ship that could eat iron?" "O," said the captain, "it was very like a bug." "Ah!" said O'Connell, "I understand, we have a bug in Ireland which eats iron, but we call it a humbug!"

One act of this great Irishman deserves to be held in everlasting memory by everybody, and especially by the colored people of the United States. It is this: Certain slaveholders of this country had sent him money to aid him in his agitation of repeal, but with their contributions coupled a protest against his denunciations of American slavery. He sent back the money! He denounced it as stained with inno-cent blood, and said he would not purchase the freedom of Ireland with the price of the negro's blood in America. It was a stinging rebuke. His conduct in this respect was in striking and creditable contrast with that of Mr. John Mitchell,[5] another distinguished Irish Liberator, who had hardly reached the shores of America from banishment and penal servitude before he wished himself the owner of a plantation in Alabama well stocked with negro slaves.

I have spoken of the marked difference of civilization in the North and South of Ireland. This difference will strike the mind of any one travelling through these two sections of that country. The North seemed to me far in advance of the South in all the elements of progress. This is neither due to the differences of climate nor the superior fertility of the soil. In these respects the South would seem to have a decided advantage over the North. All the natural conditions there seem favorable to the development of wealth and prosperity. It is never too hot nor too cold to labor; the country is well supplied with warmth and moisture, – the two great sources of life and well-being. The lack of prosperity in the South is due, I think, to three causes: Religion; want of diversified food; and freedom from foreign

---

5 John Mitchel (1815–1875), an Irish nationalist, journalist, and writer who supported the Confed-eracy during the American Civil War.

ad-mixture. The South is Roman Catholic; its people live mainly on potatoes, and the population is purely Irish. They are agricultural, strangers alike to manufactures and commerce. They attract to themselves neither a mixed diet, nor a mixed population. The great Humboldt[6] has said, that while one acre of wheat will only sustain life in two persons during one year, an acre of potatoes will sustain life in eight persons during the same period, while one acre of bananas will support forty persons during a year. Now, the people in the South of Ireland, owing to the absence of other means of livelihood are compelled by high rents and enforced poverty, to live on small farms, and, as they generally have large families, they are obliged to raise and live on potatoes. Now, I believe it is demonstrated and admitted, that not only from this structure of the human body, but also from the teachings of experience, it is manifest that no people can be strong and flourish, either mentally or physically, upon a single article of diet. Equally does it appear that any race or variety of people will deteriorate which shall remain entirely apart from other races and varieties of men. In fact, it does not appear that oneness, in population, oneness in the matter of religious belief, or oneness in diet, is favorable to progress. Contact, variety, competition, are essential to the life, both of individuals and nations. Uniform religious opinion brings mental quiet, and mental quiet brings mental stagnation, and mental stagnation brings death to human progress. Latin civilization under the influence of one church, one faith, one baptism, was dying, until the Latin races began to invite freedom of thought and opinion – till philosophy began to claim a place beside theology. But, aside from these and other causes, the South of Ireland and the whole of Ireland, are suffering to-day from wrongs inflicted centuries ago, and though many of these wrongs have been long since legally redressed, ages will be required to free that country from their baneful effects. The strong statement of Daniel O'Connell, that the history of Ireland may be traced like a wounded man through a crowd by the blood, will not be disputed by any man who has read any impartial history of that country.

I am not of those who blame England for all the misfortunes of Ireland, but the Catholic population have a terrible indictment to bring against England. The following summary of hardships imposed upon Irish Catholics, is from the pen of Sydney Smith,[7] himself an English clergyman, and one not likely to be too severe upon the behaviour of his country.

"If the child of a Catholic turned Protestant, he was taken away from his father and put into the hands of a Protestant relation. No Papist could purchase a freehold or release for more than thirty years, or inherit it from an intestate Protestant – or

---

6   Alexander Von Humboldt (1769–1859) was a pioneer of modern geographical studies.

7   Sydney Smith (1771–1845), English Anglican minister and writer.

from an intestate Catholic – or dwell in Limerick or Galway – or hold an advowson, or buy an annuity for life.

"Fifty pounds was given for discovering a Popish archbishop, thirty pounds for a Popish clergyman – and ten shillings for a schoolmaster. No one was allowed to be trustee for Catholics; no Catholic was allowed to take more than two apprentices, no Papist to be solicitor, sheriff, or to serve on grand juries. Horses for Papists might be seized for the militia, for which militia Papists were to pay double and to find Protestant substitutes. Papists were prohibited from being present at vestries, or from being high or petty constables; and when residents of town, they were compelled to find Protestant watchmen. Barristers and solicitors marrying Catholics were exposed to the penalties of Catholics. Persons plundered by privateers during a war with any Papish prince were reimbursed by a levy on the Catholic inhabitants where they lived. All Popish priests celebrating marriage contrary to George I, Cap. 3, were to be hanged."

When we remember that a sense of injustice and wrong may be handed down from generation to generation, that it may be increased rather than diminished by admissions and concessions on the part of the oppressor, it does not appear strange that the Catholic part of the population of Ireland, should still look back to the days of their proscription, and nurse their resentment towards England, the power by which they were inflicted. I have favored "Home Rule" for Ireland for two reasons: – First, because Ireland wants "Home Rule," and Secondly, because it will free England from the charge of continued oppression of Ireland. Whether the condition of the Irish people would be improved by the change, is another question; – but whether they are improved or not, the proper judges, and the responsibility should be laid upon them. I am for fair play for the Irishman, the negro, the Chinaman, and for all men of whatever country or clime, and for allowing them to work out their own destiny without outside interference.

A SENTIMENTAL VISIT TO ENGLAND

Baltimore, MD, *Commonwealth*, 1 October 1887, p. 1
Other texts in Speech File, reel 16, frames 223–27,
Frederick Douglass Papers, Library of Congress;
New York *Freeman*, 1 October 1887, p. 1

When Mr. Douglass began, he said friends this is indeed an honor which I had not expected. I am certainly a very proud man to-night, who would not be proud at such a grand ovation as this? I thank you with all my heart; you want to hear something about my trip to Europe and to Egypt, etc., well I will commence at the starting point. The passage from New York to Liverpool on the splendid steamer, *City of Rome*,[1] the largest ship afloat except the *Great Eastern*,[2] was exceedingly pleasant. The winds and waves were in their most amiable mood, and we made the voyage from land to land in seven days. In nothing has there been more progress and improvement than in naval architecture and in navigation. Five and 40 years ago 14 days was a short trip from New York to Liverpool – now it can be made in 6 days. Fifty years ago the great scientist, Dyonisius Lardner,[3] proved by facts and figures to his own satisfaction, that no vessel could carry enough coal to propel her across the Atlantic, but theories amount to nothing against facts accomplished. The *City of Rome* consumes a ton of coal every five minutes during her voyages. She has 60 furnaces and a crew, including all hands, of 250 persons. To walk her decks is like walking a populous street: she is a small town, not on wheels, but on the waves.

---

1   The *City of Rome* steamship traveled across the Atlantic and carried Frederick Douglass and Helen Pitts Douglass to Britain in September 1887.
2   The world's largest ship at the time of its construction in 1858, the London-built *Great Eastern* actually held many records for size into the early twentieth century.
3   Dionysius Lardner (1793–1859), Irish scientist, mathematician, and writer.

Our voyage to Liverpool was marked by two incidents in which you will be interested, since they illustrate the gradual wearing away of race prejudice. There was on board the Rev. Henry Wayland, son of the great Dr. Wayland[4] late president of Brown's University. Mr. Wayland had known me years ago and had been my friend in Rochester. He is one of God's freemen. Through him I was made known to many of the passengers, and this resulted in a strong invitation to address the passengers in the saloon[,] with which I complied. After this I was called upon by Capt. Monroe to move a vote of thanks in a brief speech to Lord Rochester,[5] who had presided at a concert given in the grand saloon by some talented musicians, thus my privacy was at an end, and I had much talking to do which I could not avoid.

A striking contrast between the treatment I received during this voyage and that of 40 years ago, was as striking as it was gratifying. Then I could not obtain a first class passage – even on a British steamship and was compelled to go in the forward cabin. Now I found myself not only welcome in the first cabin, but treated by every body with special marks of interest and esteem. It is true, that although I belonged to the forward cabin 40 years ago I made many friends during that voyage and was then, as on the late voyage, invited to deliver an address on the saloon deck of the *Cambria*, but I did not comply till invited to do so by the captain. There were several slave holders on board and a number of dough-faces from the North. I had hardly been speaking 10 minutes when one of the wildest, bitterest and most devilish rows occurred that I ever saw. It was only put down by the captain calling upon the boatswain to bring up the irons and threatening to put any one in irons who dared to disturb me. A most unfair account of this outbreak of proslavery violence has gone into the history of the Cunard line, denouncing me as the cause of the disturbance on the same principle that the slaves used to be denounced as the cause of the war. The fact is, slave holders at that time were dictators on sea and land, and the Cunard line, although flying the British flag, found it for their interest to yield to slave holding dictation, but I believe I am the last man of color proscribed on even the Cunard line. I made such a noise in England about it at the time that Samuel Cunard himself publicly declared that there should be no more proscription on his ships on account of race and color.

Contemplation of the forces of nature is enlarging. Standing on the deck of the *City of Rome* and moving among its company of passengers so unlike in appearance and character, and then looking out upon the broad, dashing billows of the Atlantic

---

4 Francis Wayland (1796–1865), US minister and president of Brown University. His son Herman Lincoln Wayland (1830–1898) was a Baptist minister, served as a chaplain in the Civil War, and became president of Franklin College in Indiana.

5 Actually Lord Portchester, George Edward Stanhope Molyneux Porchester (1866–1923), who later succeeded his father as Lord Carnarvon and gained celebrity for his support of the archaeological excavation of Egyptian pharaoh Tutankhamun in the 1920s.

suggested to my mind the formula that the types of mankind are various. They differ like the waves, but are one like the sea.

THE HOME RULE QUESTION.

The features of England are too well known to justify me in saying much about my sojourn in that country. It is common now-a-days to speak of England as a declining power in comparison with the rest of the world, and there may be truth in that representation, but the American who travels there will see nothing on the surface to justify that conclusion. Great Britain, though small in territory and limited in population, as compared with our Republic, is still Great Britain – great in her civilization, great in physical and mental vigor, great in her statesmanship, and great in her elements of power and stability. The question uppermost when we landed there, as when we left there, was Home Rule, or coercion for Ireland. No question of modern times has stirred England as deeply as this. It has rent asunder parties, cast down leaders, broken up friendships, and divided families; men who have acted together in politics during nearly half a century have all at once found themselves widely separated on this vast and vital question. There is much strength in [the] positions of each party. As in the case of our maintenance of our union, I believe that good order, liberty and civilization will be better served and better received in the union of Great Britain and Ireland than outside of it. The spirit of the age does not favor small nationalities; extension, organization, unification are more in harmony with the wisdom of the times.

The trouble in Ireland, however, is not its limited population, its destitution of statesmen, or its ability to maintain an independent government, but that there is in reality two Irelands; one loyal to the union, and the other anxious for complete separation. The loyal part of the people of Ireland as a class, are Protestant, and the Home Rule men are largely Catholic; so just here is the bitterest element in the British political cauldron. The Tory party profess to see in the Home Rule the entering wedge to the entire separation of Ireland from England, and handing over the whole loyal Protestant Population into the power of the hostile Catholic – a result they look upon with unaffected horror. It is this which has caused even the generous and noble-minded John Bright to array his powerful influence against Home Rule. A Republican in his sympathies, and in convictions he yet shrinks back in horror from applying the Republican majority rule to Ireland. His great friend, Mr. Gladstone, hitherto far more conservative than Mr. Bright, has no such scruples. He seems quite willing to trust the fairness and justice of the majority. He is bitterly reproached for his change of front. It is said he did not always hold his present liberal views towards Ireland, and that his conversion is far too sudden to be genuine. His answer to this, however, seems to be honest, statesmanlike and conclusive. He tried coercion for Ireland so long as he thought coercion the only remedy for the ills of that country. He treated Ireland as a wise physician would treat his patient; having his health steadily in view, when [he] found that one course of treatment failed to restore health, he tried another. His method was changed, but his object never.

I hardly need say, that I am in sympathy with Home Rule for Ireland, as held by Mr. Gladstone, I am so, both for the sake of England and for the sake of Ireland. The former will throw off a tremendous load both in money and in reputation by granting it. The glory of England will cease to be soiled with shame for the grievances of Ireland, and Ireland will be put upon her good behavior before the world, and made responsible for her own good or ill condition. Though often charged with seeking the dismemberment of the British Empire, I believe Mr. Gladstone is as firm a friend to the Union between England and Ireland as any man in the United Kingdom, but he is for the rule of justice instead of the rule of the bayonet, the rule of love instead of the rule of hate, the rule of trust and confidence instead of the rule of doubt and suspicion.

I wanted to see this famous statesman and orator while in London. It has been my good fortune to hear many of the best speakers in this country and in England. I have heard Webster,[6] Everett,[7] Sumner,[8] Phillips,[9] and other great American Orators, living and dead. I have also heard Sir Robert Peel,[10] Richard Cobden, George Thompson, John Bright, Lord Brougham, O'Connell, and other great speakers in England, and I felt it would be something to hear the peer of any of the greatest of them. Well, the opportunity was afforded me. I heard Mr. Gladstone, under the most favorable conditions. It was on an occasion of his motion in Parliament to reject the infamous Coercion Bill. For weeks the bill had been debated and Mr. Gladstone had borne his full share in that debate and I was anxious to know what he would say further, the tide of public opinion set strongly against him, and the passage of the bill was already assured. The press of the country, for the most part, had kept up a steady fire upon him [and] loaded him with reproaches of the bitterest kind. The House was crowded, and all eyes were turned upon him when he rose to make his last great effort to defeat this force bill for Ireland, which he knew could not be defeated, but Mr. Gladstone had a duty to perform and he performed it admirably.

---

6   Daniel Webster (1782–1852) was a leading Whig senator from Massachusetts and secretary of state for three presidents.

7   Edward Everett (1794–1865) held numerous positions in the Massachusetts and federal governments and was regarded as one of the great orators of his generation.

8   Charles Sumner (1811–1874), US lawyer, politician, and senator based in Massachusetts.

9   Wendell Phillips (1811–1884), US lawyer and abolitionist based in Massachusetts.

10 Twice Conservative prime minister Sir Robert Peel (1788–1850) is best remembered for championing the repeal of the Corn Law.

The first glance at his face impressed me. There was a singular blending of qualities in it, the lamb and the lion, were there: dauntless as a veteran soldier and, yet, meek as a saint. His speech was one of the grandest I ever heard, and was listened to with profoundest silence by the whole House, my expectations were high, very high, but in some respects they were far exceeded. For one hour and a half, without pause, and without once hesitating for a word, he poured out one stream of eloquence, learning and argument which seemed to be irresistible. When he sat down the government benches, as well as the opposite benches[,] were immediately emptied, and poor Mr. Balfour, the secretary for Ireland, was left almost without an audience.

My visit to England was in some respects sentimental, I wanted to see the faces and press the hands of some of the dear friends and acquaintances I met there over 40 years ago. In our meeting there was something pathetic. Neither they nor I were as young and strong as when we met so long ago. I saw the two ladies who [engaged?] Walter Forward of Pittsburgh, and Mr. Merideth, of Philadelphia,[11] and through them bought me out of slavery, secured a bill of sale of my body, made a present of myself to myself and thus enabled me to return to the United States, and resume my work for the emancipation of the slaves. It was a great privilege to see these two good women, and to see others who assisted them in raising the money to ransom me. If I had no other compensation for my voyage across the sea, this would have been ample payment. Of course many of the precious friends who met me in England, Ireland and Scotland 40 years ago have passed away, but I saw some of them through their children and in them recognized their noble qualities.

One of the most interesting places for American tourists is the City of Edinburgh, and it was especially so to me, not only on account of the historical associations that cluster about it, and its many beautiful features, but for the memorable controversy I took part in with the Free Church during my second visit to Scotland – the facts are these: That church had sent a deputation to the United States immediately after separating itself from the established Church of Scotland, to collect money to build churches and support its ministry. That deputation went South and collected several thousand pounds for this purpose in the slave states and presumably from slaveholders. George Thompson, Henry C. Wright and James N. Buffum, lately deceased, made an issue with the church. We felt that it would be good testimony against slavery if we could induce the Free Church to follow the example of Daniel O'Connell in a like case to send back the money. The debate was sharp and long – the excitement was great. Nearly everybody in Scotland, outside the Free Church,

---

11   American Whig Walter Forward (1786–1852) served as secretary of the treasury for President John Tyler and later as US chargé d'affaires to Denmark. Jonathan Meredith (1784–1872) was the Baltimore lawyer who acted as a go-between in the negotiations for Douglass's legal purchase from the Auld family in 1846.

were on the side of freedom, and were sending back the money. This sentiment was written on the pavements and walls and sung in the streets by minstrels. The very air was full of send back the money. Forgetting that I was in a monarchy and not in this Republic I got myself into trouble by cutting, send back the money in the back of a seat. I was soon thereafter arrested for trespassing on the Queen's forests, and only got off by a written apology.

I visited the same spot when over there a few weeks ago, but the friendly grass of 40 years ago had obliterated all trace of the famous formula and my humiliation, as it has also happily blotted out all further need of sentiment itself. The money, however, was never sent back, for Scotchmen do not part with money knowing wherefor – a lesson which colored people will do well to learn, if they ever favorably change their relations to the people and civilization of our age.

I have travelled since I left, not only in England, Ireland and Scotland, but in France, Switzerland, Italy, Athens and Egypt. The most civilized, the best culti-vated, and apparently the most prosperous of these countries is England. Nothing here goes to waste, every inch of fertile soil is cultivated and made to yield abundant harvests. The average crop of wheat is 46 bushels to the acre, exceeding that of our best Western lands. Its fields are pictures in frames of rich hedges adorned with leaves and flowers, its people are well behaved, orderly and strong, its cattle, large, smooth and round, its public buildings, substantial and imposing, its houses, neat, ample and comfortable: everything here exhibits the mark of thoughtful care. The management of its railroads for the comfort of travelers is somewhat clumsy; they lack over there our excellent system of checks, but the protection of life is more complete, and a higher rate, of speed is attained, the railroad crossing[s] for teams are spanned by bridges – no teams cross on the rails, and hence nobody is run over as in free America.

I stopped but a little while in London, the greatest city, with the greatest popula-tion in the world, a population which is just double what it was 42 years ago. It was two and a half hundreds of thousands that flock day after day to see this wonder of the Wild West.

If any American wants to have a vivid impression of human progress, and to shudder at the cruelty and barbarism of England a few centuries ago he has only to go to the Tower of London, and look upon the terrible things he will see there – torture and death are written all over that ancient prison. But I must not stop here with England, otherwise I shall hardly reach in my narrative any one of the other great countries it was my good fortune to visit during my stay abroad even as the matter now stands, I must postpone to another occasion remarks upon other features of my tour.

I AM HERE ADVOCATING THE RIGHTS OF IRELAND

Grand Reception to Arthur O'Connor, Esq.,
M.P. and Sir. Thomas H. Grattan Esmonde,
Bart., M.P., at Masonic Temple, Washington, DC
(Washington, DC: William H. Moore, 1887),
pp. 21–23 Another text in Washington, DC
National Republican, 15 December 1887, p. 1

This is not my hour. England does not want to know what FREDERICK DOUG-
LASS has to say on the subject of Home Rule for Ireland.

Mr. MURPHY:[1] We do.

Mr. DOUGLASS: England did want to know, and does want to know, what such
eminent gentlemen as have addressed you this evening have to say on that subject.
I am only a stripling. I was only emancipated a few years ago myself. (Applause.)

When I received the invitation to come here I thought it a good thing – a good
thing for me and a good thing for that people that I in some measure represent, for I
hold it an honor to sit on this platform. I came not to present myself as a speaker, but
to hear speakers, and I have heard them. I was glad of the opportunity of coming, if
merely to give *color* to the occasion. (Laughter and applause.)

Now, the lateness of the hour calls only for a very short speech, and I never made
a short speech in my life that I was satisfied with, nor a long speech with which
anybody else was satisfied. (Laughter.)

More than forty years ago I had the pleasure and the privilege of standing on the
banks of the Liffey, side by side with the great Daniel O'Connell, (great applause,)

---

1 Washington, DC contractor Maurice Murphy presided over this reception for two visiting Irish
members of parliament.

and at that time I declared, before a vast audience in Conciliation Hall, my conviction of the justice, the wisdom, the necessity, and the final triumph of the repeal of the Union, (applause,) and I had the honor there to receive a word of commendation, a word of eulogy from the lips of that most eloquent man, Daniel O'Connell. (Applause.) He called me then the Black O'Connell of America. (Applause.) He is not the only Irishman from whom I received a compliment.

Speaking in Ohio, some time ago, a good Irishman, after I had got through, walking behind me, said to another Irishman:

"Jimmie, what do you think of that?"

"Faith," said he, "he is only a half nagur." (Laughter.)

"Ah, but," said he, "if a half nagur could make a speech like that, what could a whole one do?" (Great laughter.)

I am not here this evening to fan the flames of Irish animosity, if there be any such animosity, toward England. I am not long from that country. I am not long from Old Ireland – only a few months. I once traveled through it from the Hill of Howth to the Giant's Causeway, and from the Giant's Causeway to Cape Clear. I know something of the Irish heart. I went there forty years ago as an exile. I left my country because there was no valley so deep, no mountain so high, no glen so secluded, no spot so sacred to liberty under the Star-Spangled Banner and in all this broad land where I could set my foot and say, now, by the blessing of God and the humanity of the American people, I am free. (Great applause.)

When I went to Ireland I head a voice in Conciliation Hall which spoke the mind and heart of Ireland, saying: "My sympathies are not confined to the narrow limits of my own green Ireland. My spirit walks abroad upon the clement waters. Wherever there is oppression I hate the oppressor. Wherever the tyrant rears his head I will launch my bolts upon it." These were the words of Daniel O'Connell. (Applause.)

I heard something of the breadth and comprehensiveness of the Irish heart from the lips of that great and good man, and I am, therefore, with every other American, of whatever color or class, an out-and-out Home Ruler for Ireland and an out-and-out Home Ruler for every man in this Republic. The right that I am claiming for Ireland I claim for every man here – North and South. (Applause.)

Now, no political allusions, but this is a night of liberty, (applause,) broad and glorious. I am letting myself loose; beginning to feel at home in the interest of Home Rule. (Applause.) Oh, I know England is listening to-night for some indiscreet or revolutionary sentiment. I don't mean all England, for there are two Englands, distinct and separate, on this question. The line is drawn between them. There is the Liberal England, made up of the bone and sinew of old England, the working classes, the laboring men – the men of Newcastle, the men of Manchester, the men of Birmingham, and the men of Glasgow and Edinburgh. There is one England, one Great

Britain. Then there is the Great Britain of William H. Smith and of Mr. Balfour, (hisses,) and some one said Chamberlain.[2] (Hisses.) No, don't mention him; he is on a beneficent mission here, and I wish him success. (Laughter.) That England is for Home Rule, growing and increasing. Indeed, I have not heard any extravagant speeches here to-night, no word that England could take any very great offence at, except, perhaps, by the Americans – by these cool-headed and clear-headed and eloquent Senators. They have suggested, they have hinted, they have squinted at a warning, if not a threat; but the gentlemen who have come to us from abroad have said not one word that Mr. Balfour, or anybody else over there, will gain the slightest advantage from. (Applause.) It is constitutional agitation. What right has England to complain of these gentlemen for coming over here? When we had the great battle with slavery, why, they welcomed FREDERICK DOUGLASS, and they welcomed any and every other man who came there to ask their sympathy in behalf of the cause of liberty, and you only do that same here. There is no such thing as limiting the spirit of liberty. Liberty! why it is like the sun in the heavens – it shines for all. National lines, geographical boundaries, do not and cannot confine it. It belongs to the whole world, and the whole world has a right to stand up in its behalf, (applause,) for when it is struck down in one direction it is struck down in another and in all directions. (Applause.)

Now, I am not going to speak any longer. I thank you for letting me sit on the platform with these white people. You know it is not the usual thing in America. (Laughter.) I am very glad to be here and to let you look me in the face, and to see that you don't get angry with my wooly head, my high cheek bones and distended nostrils or any of my features, and that you have really discovered that FRED. DOUGLASS is a man. (Applause.)

I am here advocating my rights as well as the rights of Ireland, for I have sometimes found it necessary to do so here and elsewhere.

Mr. Chairman, I thank you. I thank Senator SHERMAN and I thank Mr. SPRINGER for the earnest words they have spoken to-night.[3] My friends over the way know where I stand on this question of Home Rule. I told some of my English

---

2   Conservative politician William Henry Smith (1825–1891) held numerous government offices culminating in First Lord of the Treasury and leader of the House of Commons at the time of his death. Arthur James Balfour (1848–1930), nephew of Lord Salisbury, rose steadily through Conservative Party leadership until achieving the prime ministership (1902–05). Joseph Chamberlain (1836–1914) led the 1886 Liberal Unionist bolt from Gladstone's government over Home Rule. In alliance with later Conservative governments, he advocated for British imperial expansion.

3   The younger brother of famed Civil War general William T. Sherman, Ohio Republican John Sherman (1823–1900) served in the House and Senate before becoming William McKinley's secretary of state. William McKendree Springer (1836–1903) was a Democratic Party congressman who represented Illinois from 1875 until 1895.

friends they were on the wrong side of this question. My old friend, John Bright, was on the wrong side, strangely enough, for he is a great and good man. But I will tell you, also, his sister is on the right side. Two or three of his sisters and his brother are on the right side, (applause,) and his son and his daughter, Mrs. Clark[4] – beg pardon for mentioning the name – is on the right side. The fact is, we are all on the right side, and mean to be until the battle is fought and won. (Applause.)

---

4 Helen Bright Clark (1840–1927), English activist and suffragist, daughter of M.P. John Bright. Douglass gave a lecture at Clark's house in 1887.

EUROPEAN TOUR

Frederick Douglass, *Life and Times of Frederick Douglass, Written by Himself, His Early Life as a Slave, His Escape from Bondage, and His Complete History to the Present Time* (Boston: De Wolfe & Fiske Co., 1892), pp. 674–80

SEPTEMBER, 1886, was quite a milestone in my experience and journey of life. I had long desired to make a brief tour through several countries in Europe and especially to revisit England, Ireland and Scotland, and to meet once more the friends I met with in those countries more than forty years before. I had twice visited England, but I had never been on the continent of Europe, and this time I was accompanied by my wife.

I shall attempt here no ample description of our travels abroad. For this more space would be required than the limits of this volume will permit. Besides, with such details the book-shelves are already crowded. To revisit places, scenes, and friends after forty years is not a very common occurrence in the lives of men; and while the desire to do so may be intense, the realization has to it a sad side as well as a cheerful one. The old people first met there have passed away, the middle-aged have grown old, and the young have only heard their fathers and mothers speak of you. The places are there, but the people are gone. I felt this when looking upon the members of the House of Commons. When I was there forty-five years before, I saw many of England's great men; men whom I had much desired to see and hear and was much gratified by being able to see and hear. There were Sir Robert Peel, Daniel O'Connell, Richard Cobden, John Bright, Lord John Russell,[1] Sir James Graham,[2]

---

1 Lord John Russell (1792–1878) was a Whig Liberal statesman and two-time prime minister (1846–52 and 1865–66).
2 Whig M.P. James Graham (1792–1861) held cabinet posts under Peel's and Aberdeen's governments.

Benjamin Disraeli,[3] Lord Morpeth,[4] and others, but except Mr. Gladstone, not one who was there then is there now. Mr. Bright was alive, but ill health kept him out of Parliament. Five and forty years before, I saw him there, young, robust and strong; a rising British statesman representing a new element of power in his country, and battling as the co-worker of Richard Cobden, against the corn-laws which kept bread from the mouths of the hungry. His voice and eloquence were then a power in Parliament.

At that time the question which most deeply interested and agitated England was the repeal of the corn-laws. Of this agitation Mr. Richard Cobden and Mr. Bright, backed by the anti-corn-law league, were the leaders. The landed aristocracy of England, represented by the Tory party, opposed the repeal with intense zeal and bitterness. But the circumstances were against that interest and against that party. The famine of 1845 was doing its ghastly work, and the people not only of Ireland, but of England and Scotland, were asking for bread, more bread, and cheaper bread; and this was a petition to which resistance was vain. The facts and figures of Cobden and the eloquence of Mr. Bright supported by the needs of the people, bore down the powerful opposition of the aristocracy, and finally won over to repeal the great Tory leader in the person of Sir Robert Peel, one of the most graceful debaters and ablest parliamentarians that England ever had. A more fascinating man than he I never saw or heard in any legislative body. But able and skillful leader as he was, he could not carry his party with him. The landed proprietors opposed him to the last. Their cause was espoused by Lord George Bentinck[5] and Mr. Benjamin Disraeli. The philippics of the latter against Sir Robert were among the most scathing and torturing of anything in their line to which I ever listened. His invectives were all the more burning and blistering because delivered with the utmost coolness and studied deliberation. But he too was gone when I looked into the House of Commons this time. The grand form and powerful presence of Daniel O'Connell was no longer there. The diminutive but dignified figure of Lord John Russell, that great Whig leader, was absent. In the House of Lords, where, five and forty years before, I saw and heard Lord Brougham, all were gone, and he with the rest. He was the most remarkable speaker I ever heard. Such a flow of language; such a wealth of knowledge; such an aptitude of repartee; such quickness in reply to difficult questions suddenly sprung upon him, I think I never saw equaled in any other speaker.

---

3 Benjamin Disraeli (1804–1881) rose through Conservative Party ranks as a moderate reformer who served twice as prime minister (1868, 1874–80).
4 George William Frederick Howard, seventh earl of Carlisle or Lord Morpeth (1802–1864), supported abolition.
5 Lord George Frederick Cavendish-Scott-Bentinck (1802–1848) shifted political alliances frequently but was an outspoken opponent of the repeal of the Corn Law.

In his attitudes and gestures he was in all respects original, and just the opposite of Daniel Webster. As he spoke, his tall frame reeled to and fro like a reed in a gale, and his arms were everywhere, down by his sides, extended in front and over his head; always in action and never at rest. He was discussing when I heard him the postal relations of England, and he seemed to know the postal arrangements of every civilized people in the world. He was often interrupted by "the noble Lords," but he very simply disposed of them with a word or two that made them objects of pity and sometimes of ridicule. I wondered how they dared to expose their lordly heads to the heels of such a perfect race-horse in debate as he seemed to be. He simply played with them. When they came too near he gave them a kick and scampered away over the field of his subject without looking back to see if his victims were living, wounded, or dead. But this marvelous man, though he lived long, was now gone, and I saw in England no man like him filling his place or likely to fill his place.

While in England during this last visit I had the good fortune to see and hear Mr. William E. Gladstone, the great Liberal leader, and, since Sir Robert Peel, the acknowledged prince of parliamentary debaters. He was said by those who had often heard him to be on this occasion in one of his happiest speaking moods, and he made one of his best speeches. I went early. The House was already crowded with members and spectators when Mr. Gladstone came in and took his seat opposite Mr. Balfour, the Tory leader. Though seventy-seven years had passed over him his step was firm and his bearing confident and vigorous. Expectation had been raised by the announcement in advance that Mr. Gladstone would that day move for the indefinite postponement of the Irish Force Bill, the measure of all others to which the Government was committed as a remedy for the ills of Ireland. As he sat in front of the Government leader, an able debater awaiting the moment to begin his speech, I saw in the face of Mr. Gladstone a blending of opposite qualities. There were the peace and gentleness of the lamb, with the strength and determination of the lion. Deep earnestness was expressed in all his features. He began his speech in a tone conciliatory and persuasive. His argument against the bill was based upon statistics which he handled with marvelous facility. He showed that the amount of crimes in Ireland for which the Force Bill was claimed as a remedy by the Government was not greater than the great class of crimes in England; and that therefore there was no reason for a Force Bill in one country more than in the other. After marshaling his facts and figures to this point, in a masterly and convincing manner, raising his voice and pointing his finger directly at Mr. Balfour, he exclaimed, in a tone almost menacing and tragic, "What are you fighting for?" The effect was thrilling. His peroration was a splendid appeal to English love of liberty. When he sat down the House was instantly thinned out. There seemed neither in members nor spectators any desire to hear another voice after hearing Mr. Gladstone's, and I shared this feeling with the rest. A few words were said in reply by Mr. Balfour, who, though an able debater, was no match for the aged Liberal leader.

Leaving public persons, of whom many more could be mentioned, I turned to the precious friends from whom I parted at the end of my first visit to Great Britain and Ireland. In Dublin, the first city I then visited, I was kindly received by Mr. Richard Webb,[6] Richard Allen,[7] James Haughton,[8] and others. They were now all gone, and except some of their children, I was among strangers. These received me in the same cordial spirit that distinguished their fathers and mothers. I did not visit dear old Cork, where in 1845 I was made welcome by the Jennings, the Warings, the Wrights, and their circle of friends, most of whom I learned had passed away.[9] The same was true of the Neals, the Workmans, the McIntyres, and the Nelsons at Belfast.[10] I had friends in Limerick, in Waterford, in Eniscorthy, and other towns of Ireland, but I saw none of them during this visit. What was true of the mortality of my friends in Ireland, was equally true of those in England. Few who first received me in that country are now among the living. It was, however, my good fortune to meet once more Mrs. Anna Richardson and Miss Ellen Richardson, the two members of the Society of Friends, both beyond three-score and ten, who, forty-five years before, opened a correspondence with my old master and raised seven hundred and fifty dollars with which to purchase my freedom.[11] Mrs. Anna Richardson, having reached the good old age of eighty-six years, her life marvelously filled up with good works, for her hand was never idle and her heart and brain were always active in the cause of peace and benevolence, a few days before this writing passed away. Miss Ellen Richardson, now over eighty, still lives and continues to take a lively interest in the career of the man whose freedom she was instrumental in procuring. It was a great privilege once more to look into the faces and hear the voices of these noble and benevolent women. I saw in England, too, Mr. and Mrs. Russell Lant Carpenter, two friends who were helpful to me when in England, and, until within a few days, helpful to me still. During all the time that I edited and published my paper in Rochester, New York, I had the material and moral support of Rev. Russell Lant Carpenter and that of his excellent wife. But now he too has passed away covered with honors. He was one

---

6   A Quaker turned Unitarian, Richard Davis Webb (1805–1872) was a Dublin printer and active
    Garrisonian abolitionist.

7   Brother-in-law of Richard Webb, Richard Allen (1803–1886) was an active member of the Hibernian Anti-Slavery Society.

8   James Haughton (1785–1873) was a leading Irish reformer on behalf of antislavery, temperance
    and other causes.

9   These Irish abolitionists include the sisters Charlotte, Helen, Isabel, and Jane Jennings, all active
    in the Cork Ladies' Anti-Slavery Society; Richard Webb's sister-in-law Maria Waring; and William
    and Jane Wright of Kilworth.

10 Among the Belfast abolitionists alluded to were John R. Neill, Eliza McIntyre (?–1851), and Isaac
    Nelson (1812–1888).

11 Ellen Richardson (1808–1896), a Newcastle-upon-Tyne teacher, joined her sister-in-law Anna in
    purchasing Douglass's 1846 manumission.

of the purest spirits and most impartial minds I ever met. Though a man of slender frame, his life was one of earnest work, and he reached the age of seventy-five. He was the son of Rev. Lant Carpenter, who for a long time was an honored pastor in Bristol. He was also the brother of Philip and Mary Carpenter, and one of a family distinguished for every moral and intellectual excellence.[12]

I missed the presence of George Thompson, one of the most eloquent men who ever advocated the cause of the colored man, either in England or America. Joseph Sturge and most of his family had also passed away. But I will pursue this melancholy enumeration no further, except to say that, in meeting with the descendants of anti-slavery friends in England, Ireland and Scotland, it was good to have confirmed the scriptural saying, "Train up a child in the way he should go and when he is old he will not depart from it."

---

12   The extended Carpenter family were among Douglass's longest and most dedicated British allies. They included Unitarian minister Russell Lant Carpenter (1816–1892), his wife Mary Browne Carpenter (1824–1898), his brother and noted naturalist Phillip Carpenter (1819–1877), and sister and educator Mary Carpenter (1807–1877).

Part IV

"A Comrade in the Fight": British Responses to Frederick Douglass

Douglass's three visits to the British Isles sparked a flurry of artistic and creative activity. Newspaper correspondents reported on the blistering content of his speeches as well as the performer himself. Described as an eloquent orator, Douglass was a "Negro Hercules" whose electric presence on stage and "sonorous" voice never failed to make an impression on his audiences. Most of the language used to define Douglass was unsurprisingly racialised, with several correspondents expressing astonishment that a Black man could speak, act, or write as well as he could. Part of the fascination and popularity surrounding Douglass in Britain, then, cannot be separated from Victorian racial dynamics and how such debates about antislavery, race, and Blackness rested on a white racist schema.

We have reproduced here five newspaper articles, two advertisements, five images, and two obituaries, representing a small fraction of the correspondents who waxed lyrical about Douglass's performances or indeed those who bristled at the controversial debates in which he became involved. While the majority of newspaper coverage was favorable to Douglass and to the antislavery cause, there were other correspondents (from the *Belfast Newsletter*, for example) who were deeply unimpressed with Douglass's rhetoric against the church.

Poetry, sonnets, and songs were constantly published in the transatlantic press, too, and we have published eighteen here. Antislavery activists including William Wells Brown reprinted poems in edited volumes, tracts, and pamphlets; some were inspired by events such as the Fugitive Slave Act of 1850, or the courageousness of fugitive slaves who escaped to the northern states and Canada. Abolitionist books and volumes were littered with poetry, focusing on themes such as slavery's cruelty, the auction block, the mother who mourned her suffering children, the separation of families, and the instruments of torture such as whips and chains. Poems were also published at the close of slave narratives. In the 1848 edition of Moses Roper's narrative, for example, there were several poems written by abolitionists and members of the public who were inspired to write after hearing Roper speak. Significantly, Roper included a poem written by a Black Scotsman in 1838.[1] Douglass's slave narrative

---

1 William Wells Brown, *The Anti-Slavery Harp: A Collection of Songs for Anti-Slavery Meetings* (Boston: Bela Marsh, 1848); Moses Roper, *Narrative of the Adventures and Escape of Moses Roper, From American Slavery* (Berwick-upon-Tweed: Warder Office, 1848). See also Henry "Box" Brown, *Narrative of the Life of Henry Box Brown* (Manchester: n.p., 1851) and James Watkins, *Struggles for Freedom; Or the Life of James Watkins* (Manchester: n.p., 1860); and John Anderson, *The Story of the Life of John Anderson, The Fugitive Slave* (London: n.p., 1863).

and subsequent speaking tour of the British Isles also inspired the British and Irish public to compose songs and poetry. Frances Brown and an anonymous "friend of the Anti-Slavery movement" both wrote poems after reading certain passages from his narrative, in particular focusing on the motifs of freedom and slavery as social death.[2] Douglass's role in the controversy surrounding the Free Church of Scotland in 1846 also led to numerous poems published in the Scottish press. Cries of "Send Back the Money!" and songs in regional dialects were popular amongst the working classes in particular (see "The Boy Tammy's Meditations," republished here).[3]

While the composition of poetry and songs were common and popular within the antislavery movement (and the Victorian period at large), obituaries or memoirs to Black American men were not. Douglass's position as the "leader" of the African American race and one of the most famous men in the world led to numerous obituaries in the British press in the wake of his death in 1895. The radical Quaker journalist Catherine Impey wrote an extensive memoir of Douglass in her newspaper, *Anti-Caste*, and praised his lifelong and unrelenting activism. She described the impact of their meeting in 1887, and how activists on both sides of the Atlantic would forever be inspired by Douglass's life and work. Although other newspaper correspondents were not as fortunate as Impey in knowing Douglass, few were unaware of his significance to transatlantic history. He was remembered as a famous orator, a successful writer, and, most of all, a champion of racial equality. The *London Daily News* eloquently summarized that "his own people have lost a father and a friend, and all good men a comrade in the fight, not only for the legal emancipation of one race, but for the spiritual emancipation of all."[4]

---

2   *Belfast Commercial Chronicle*, 10 January 1846, p. 2; *The Western Times*, 12 September 1846, p. 8.

3   *Elgin Courant and Morayshire Advertiser*, 22 May 1846, p. 4; *The Northern Star*, 24 October 1846, p. 3. *Antislavery Songs* (Edinburgh: J. Fairgrieve & Co., 1846).

4   *The London Daily News*, 22 February 1895, p. 4.

TO THE PEOPLE OF WATERFORD

Waterford Mail, 9 October 1845

To the People of Waterford
On Their Chilling Reception of Frederick Douglass[1]

Shame on ye, heartless of Waterford!
Who, when the slave come to your hearth and home
To thrill your bosoms with his lightning word
Doubtfully question, "Wherefore does he come?"

What unto us the woes of cat and cord?
Of life extinguished, or of soul held dumb?
To, give us rest and peace, our gentle ears
Soothe with bland murmurs, if you speak of wrong.

We're delicate. Mayhap our exquisite tears
Should start if troubled by your "language strong"!
Must Douglass shrink from truth to still your fears?
Deny the cruel torture felt so long?

Blind, craven men! Slaves, slaves in heart and brain!
Your <u>souls</u> are dark – your minds confess the chain.

---

1   See Fenton (2014) and Coughlan, "Frederick Douglass and Ireland," for a brilliant discussion on this poem.

[FOR THE BELFAST CHRONICLE]
LINES, BY FRANCES BROWN

Suggested by a passage in the Life of Frederick Douglass.
Belfast, Ireland, *Commercial Chronicle,*
10 January 1846, p. 2

Mr. Douglass relates, that his first longings for freedom were awakened in his childhood, when, lying under a tree, he watched the birds at play among its branches.

> The boy made his rest where for ages waved on
> One tree, of a forest whose thousands were gone;
> But the soft summer airs through its foliage still played,
> And the wild birds rejoiced in the depth of its shade.
> Oh, broad was the river, and lovely the scene
> That spread where the wilds of that forest had been:
> The noon lay in splendour on field and on wave,
> But the boy knew it shone on the Land of the Slave.
>
> And well might be cast his young limbs on the soil –
> Their grace was for fetters, their strength was for toil, –
> For the current that blent with his life, stream was one
> That burst in far time by the fount of the sun.
> Oh, dark was the midnight that shadowed its course,
> But his eye was still lit by the fire of that source;
> For the changeless old charter that Liberty gave,
> Hath a record still left in the Land of the Slave.
>
> But where might that weary eye rest, when it sought
> Some spot where the brand of his memory was not?

He turned from the fields, with their summer wealth filled,
For he knew in what terror their furrows were tilled.
He looked on the river, and thought of the day
Its waters had wafted his kindred away,
And the tears of the young that had blent in its wave –
But, alas! for bright youth in the Land of the Slave.

He saw the far sky, like an ocean of blue,
And thought of the mother his infancy knew –
Of the love that, through toil and through bondage, she bore,
And the night-coming step that might seek him no more.
Oh, faint was the faith of his future, and dim
The hope that soul-masters had granted to him;
But they said that the grass had grown green on her grave,
And he wished her not back to the Land of the Slave.

Yet ever the birds in the branches above
Sang on, in the joy of their freedom and love –
Their freedom, that sceptre or sword never cleft –
Their love, on which tyrants no foot-print had left.
And oh, for their lot, where a shadow ne'er crossed
The light of the summers his childhood had lost –
For their song, that burst forth like a stream from its cave, –
And their wings, that could waft from the Land of the Slave!

Young lover of freedom, that prayer was not vain,
Though far was the moment that shivered thy chain;
But woe for the heart that can find, in the clime
Of its early remembrance, but deserts of time!
Our isle hath her sorrows – the page of her years
Is dark with the memory of discord and tears –
But she still owns the heart and the hand that would save,
And we welcome thy steps from the Land of the Slave.
Stranoriar, Jan. 1846.

FREDERICK DOUGLASS

Boston, MA, *The Liberator*, 27 March 1846, p. 4

FOR THE LIBERATOR
FREDERICK DOUGLASS

> A God-sent star! Shot out from Southern night,
> Thou seem'st, O Douglass! Freed from bondage dire,
> To stream through Northern heav'ns a startling light,
> And wake the nations with thy tongue of fire.
>
> Thy voice, now pealing truth o'er ocean's main,
> Borne by the waves that heard its silver tones,
> Is echoing back the thrilling sounds again,
> And shaking tyrants on their trembling thrones.
>
> Speak boldly, then, for all the trodden down,
> The word that god may give thee to proclaim,
> And quail not, shrink not, at oppression's frown,
> Till all the foes of man be put to shame.

"SEND BACK THE MONEY, SEND BACK THE MONEY"

Boston Public Library [1846?]

Part IV, no 1 "Send Back the Money, Send Back the Money" (Boston Public Library).

THE BOY TAMMY'S MEDITATIONS

Anti-Slavery Songs (Edinburgh: J. Fairgrieve & Co., 1846)[1]

The following SONG, with the INTRODUCTORY LETTER to the EDITOR, appeared first in the MONTROSE STANDARD:

MR YEDITUR, – on Munonday nicht our Jock gat me enteeced to gang doon on' hear that chiel Douglass. I had cam awa' wantin' ma specks; but frae the luik I gat o' him, he seem't a buirdly fallow, and ane I shouldna like to hae a tussle wi' aither fessecally or intellektually. But to the pint on han'. I cam' hame an' gaed aff to ma bed, leavin' Jock sittin' gey an' dowf-like at the ingle cheek. "Jock," quo' I, "gang your wa's to your bed, an' dinna sit there burnin' coal an'caunie for nae an': ye ken that wab maun be feenesh't the morn." "Oh aye," quo' he, "nae fear o' the wab." Weel, sir, thro' the nicht I'm waukent wi'sumbody roarin' an' singin'. I luiks atower – an' wad ye believ't? – it was Jock, an' it near twa i' the morning'. I was in a pashin – nae wunner – a hale penny caunle brunt! "Ye ne'er-do-weel loon," quo' I, raxin' ower the bed for ane o' ma shoon, "sittin' squeachin there at this time o' the mornin', disturbin' the hale kintra side – this'll no be the gate o't i' the mornin' – there'll be nae harlin ye oot o' yer bed than." Wi' that, Mr Yeditur, I gars the shae play breenge at his head – it skifft his lug – coupit the caunlestick – bruke twa plates – an' foosh doon the tea-tray wi' a reeshle like thunner. Jock was ben the house like winkin', an' the door bar't. I [went?] to see th'extent o' the dawmage, an' fell in wi' [page torn], whilk Jock had drappit in his flicht. Wad ye juist stap it oot o' the gate sume way, Mr Yeditur, for I canna luk at it without thinkin' o' the plates. And oblige,

---

1   See Rice, "Transatlantic Portrayals."

SAUNDERS KENEYQUHAR
Links, March 1846

THE BOY TAMMY'S MEDITATIONS

ONY TUNE YE LIKE

(The Poet indulgeth in the descriptive.)

Oh, Tammy sat lane by his ain fireside,
He luikit dum foundert – he graned and he sighed
As he shuke his long pow – the tears pappin' down came
"There'll never be peace till that siller's sent hame."

(Moral reflections about scourin' bluidy bawbees.)

"I ha'e scoor'd thae bawbees till blabs stan' on my broo –
I may scorr a' may days, but the bluid aye keeks thro';
I maun e'en sen' them back, just to please oor auld dame,
For she'll no be at peace till that siller's sent hame."

(A case o'conscience.)

"Send it hame: lat me see – it gans sair 'gainst my heart;
But it's better wi' siller than conscience to pairt;
Can we haud be't? Na! Douglass has blawn sic a flame,
That we winna hae peace till that siller's sent hame."

(A predic'.)

"It's hard, unco' hard, to confess we've dune wrang;
Ane micht do't – but, oh, an Assembly! – ma sang!
But oor folk are uproarious, and cry 'What a shame,'
And they'll no gi'e us peace till that siller's sent hame."

(A dreary prospect.)

"I ken I've dune wrang – the warl' maks sic a din;
Nae smile frae withoot, and nae comfort within;
The deed stamps eternal disgrace on my name,
And I winna hae peace till that siller's sent hame."

(No go.)

"Thae chiels in Dundee, tho' weel gifted wi' gab,
May talk of the slave-holding patriarch Job;
They kay [page torn] Bible – it comes a' to the same –
[page torn] the sillar's sent hame."

("Random Recollections.")

"Ive play'd mony a queer pliskie, I trow, in my day;
I've belauber't Dissenters – weel, weel, let that gae;
I've run aff frae my Granny, but I've stain'd my fair fame,
And I'll never ha'e peace till the siller's sent hame."

(Real reminiscences.)

"I've danc'd mony a queer reel – aye, and danc'd them wi' pride,
But this is the daftest like e'er I he'e tried;
For The Slavery Strathspey – a back step – (sic a name!) –
Maun be danc'd to the tune o' 'Send that siller hame.'"

(A melancholy state of affairs.)

"My mither cries, 'Tammy, correct the mistak' –
As usual, there's 'Patteraw John' at my back;
While 'The Slave' redds my hair wi' his murderous kaim,
And I'll no be at peace till the siller's sent hame."

("Ah, Tam! ah, Tam!")

"My mither! – puir body! – shares a' my disgrace:
Wi' a tear in her ee, she aye glow'rs in my face;
She gangs aboot dowie, and greetin' for shame,
And she'll no gi'e me peace till the siller's sent hame."

(Tammy jocosely addresseth himself.)

"Aye, Tammy, ma man, ye've a will o' your ain;
To 'Retract e'en a hairbreadth, I ken gi'es ye pain;
But, I doot, ye maun do't, tho' twad coup ilka 'scheme,'
For there'll never be peace till the siller's sent hame."

(Visions.)

Wi' a heartrendin' sigh, and a shot o' his head,
Tammy, sairly perplex't, slippit aff till his bed;
But he raved in his sleep, and cried oot in his drame,
"THERE'LL NEVER BE PEACE TILL THE SILLER'S SENT HAME."

[UNTITLED]

Exeter, England, *Western Times,*
12 September 1846, p. 8

M r. Editor – A friend to the Anti-Slavery movement would strongly recommend the readers of the *Western Times* to procure the shilling narrative of Fred. Douglass.

The facts in the following lines, which are at your service, have been taken from the first chapter of the work by

ALIQUIS.

My name *was* Bailey, born in Tuck-a-hoe,
An heir by birth, of misery and woe,
I would, but am not able, on this page
To leave a record of my birth and age.
Of horses, you may just as well enquire
Their pedigree, as trace a "nigger's" sire.
One cannot learn the birth-day of a slave;
It goes, with most, a secret to the grave.
The *white man's* child could tell his age and name,
So could not I – it fill'd my soul with shame.
To now my age I ventured to enquire,
But only rous'd my master's dreadful ire,
My master was my father – so 'twas thought;
I cannot say, it might be so or not.
A few short months alas! had I been born,
Before my mother from her child was torn,
From nature's yearnings, infant slaves to wean;
The master early snaps the bond in twain;
It would not do to let the children prove
The sweet experience of a mother's love.

Alas! *my mother*, now and then, 'tis true,
Unable, nature's feelings to subdue –
A lengthen'd journey through the night would take,
And brave *all dangers* for her infant's sake.
I never saw her by the light of day;
She came by night – by night she went away.
In sweet repose I lay upon her breast,
But found her gone on waking up from rest.
Thus circumstanc'd I was but little taught –
No friend was there to guide an infant's thought.
Death soon depriv'd me of my transient bliss
I felt in childhood from a mother's kiss.
May I not *hope my* loss to her was gain –
The end of all her hardships, grief, and pain?
Awhile, not e'en a whisper or a breath
Made me acquainted with my mother's death.
Thus suddenly and early call'd away,
Who was my sire I never heard her say,
The odious law of slavery ordains –
The infant of a slave a slave remains,
The *father* may be honor'd, rich, and free,
But slaves the mother and the child shall be.
To gratify their lusts such laws they make,
And immolate the *race* for *mammon's* sake!
Such are the most unfortunate of slaves,
Exposed to greater hardships from the knaves,
Whose anger kindles to a lurid flame,
Attempting to conceal their guilt and shame.
The mistress of the family complains,
And soon the lash with blood the victim stains,
Her husband or her son she'll thus employ,
And see him flog the tortured slave with joy,
Their presence pains her – pride and passion swell,
Till *he* consent, the *hated ones* to sell.
From year to year extends *this mingled race*,
With danger and dismay in every place!
Will not the children *soon unite and claim*
Their right to *freedom* and their *father's name*?
The *mother*, as the father soon shall be,
Tho' *black* the one and *white* the other – *free*!
The laws of population shall compel

The base injustice to return to hell,
I suffer'd from a cruel overseer –
A savage monster, who would curse and swear.
With heavy cudgel and a cowskin – he
Would "slash the womens' heads" most "horribly,"
With unrelenting heart the master too
This cruel work would diligently pursue.
From sleep I've oft been rous'd at dawn of day,
By fearful shrieks which fill'd me with dismay.
From my own aunt heart-rending cries arose
As she receiv'd the lash with heavy blows;
Her naked back, with gashes cover'd o'er,
Until she writhed in agony and gore.
No words nor tears could move his iron heart,
Or cause him from his purpose to depart.
In vain his victim's agonies and prayers
Might plead for pity, with her burning tears,
He whipp'd the harder as *she* louder cried,
And mercy's plea his cruel soul denied.
He whipped the *longest* where the gushing blood
Ran *fastest* to the spot on which he stood.
Whene'er he thought her obstinate or proud
He whipped his victim till she scream'd aloud;
He whipped her *then* to make her hush the noise
That fill'd the monster's breast with fiendish joys.
Till by *fatigue* he was compelled to yield,
His hand the cowskin did not cease to wield.
I witness'd when a child this horrid deed,
And long'd for my poor bleeding aunt to plead.
With awful force it struck my rising soul,
Scarce able *then* its anger to control.
It seemed to *me* the blood-stain'd gate to hell,
When I was doom'd a helpless slave to dwell.

THE AMERICAN "APOSTLES" – THE EVANGELICAL ALLIANCE – AND THE PRESS

Belfast, Ireland, *Belfast Newsletter*, 9 October 1846, p. 2

It has not much surprised us to observe that W. L. Garrison has obtained the support of the *Northern Whig*. "The great American anti-slavery apostle," as, with alliterative elegance and propriety, W. L. Garrison is called by our contemporary, is the whiteheaded boy of the *Whig*, as his friend, F. Douglass, is the "curled darling" of the ladies. They are, in truth, a *par nobile fratrum* – Messers. Garrison and Douglass – *arcades ambo*, and their protector in the press is well fitted to be their panegyrist. The public is told by this journalist that "a considerable portion of Mr. Garrison's speech was taken up with comments upon an *ungenerous* and *unfair* attack made upon him by a Belfast contemporary." "That gentleman, however," adds the writer, "is what may be called 'an ugly customer,' and, as our report shows, he retorted upon his assailant very vigorously." We have already shown that we made no attack upon W. L. Garrison, but if it be "ungenerous" and "unfair" to quote a man's own words, and refer to his own avowed acts, in order to instruct the public as to the kind of "customer" who was coming among them, we plead guilty to the charge. W. L. Garrison called the members of the evangelical churches "mockers," "blasphemers," and "man-stealers." We told the Belfast public so much, and for this we are accused of endeavouring to hunt down a worthy man, and blacken his character! Somehow, these American "apostles" – poor fellows! – have always been dreadfully "hunted." They have ever the same story in their mouth – the same argument, *ad mise ricordiam*. Let the public see, from this instance, how slow it should be in putting much faith in the stories of persecution which are current. The *truth* is, those men have evidently come over in order to *hunt down* the Evangelical Alliance, and to sow the seeds of a fatal scepticism in the field of labour that they have thus hoped to clear for themselves.

The *Whig* defends Mr. Garrison's use of the Infidel Hall in Boston.[1] Mr. Garrison himself, however, seemed to think the step needed an apology, for he tells us he could get no other place to lecture in. He was, he says, accompanied to the infidel platform by a number of the Christian ministers of Boston. How did it happen, then, that these ministers refused him their meeting-houses? We are afraid that, in the words of the celebrated showman of the menagerie, "there must be some mistake here."

We are told that we should have exhibited more forbearance to Mr. Garrison than we did, because that person himself is an editor, and actually "works at case" two days in the week. We can hardly suppose our contemporary to be serious in advancing such a plea. Mr. Garrison may be a very good hand at the case for aught we know; but we know that he uses both his pen and his tongue very badly. He has been a shoemaker and a cabinet maker in his time; and, in short, a jack-of-all trades. We regret, for the sake of the editorial profession, that he did not stick to his last, or keep to his cabinet making. That is all the sympathy we are disposed to afford him.

It will be seen that, on Tuesday evening, there was a second mournful exhibition of bad taste and worse feeling, on the part of the abolition agitators, in which the chief actor was Mr F. Douglass. We shall not characterize the language made use of on this occasion as it deserves. It is sufficient to record that it has totally defeated its real or pretended object – if that object be the strengthening of the cause of Anti-Slavery.

There is only one passage in the letter of the Rev. Mr Nelson, which the reader will find elsewhere, which we wish to notice Mr Nelson's remark, that we were "satisfied at the time" with his interference, is particularly odd, after what we have spoken and written on the subject. We can assure him we were anything but satisfied with the part he acted in the matter. We said we were sure Mr Nelson did not intend to give us offense, but that is very different from an expression of satisfaction.

---

1   William L. Garrison used Julian Hall occasionally for antislavery meetings. It was owned by the Boston Infidel Society.

NEWSPAPER ADVERTISEMENT

Manchester, 1846
University of Manchester

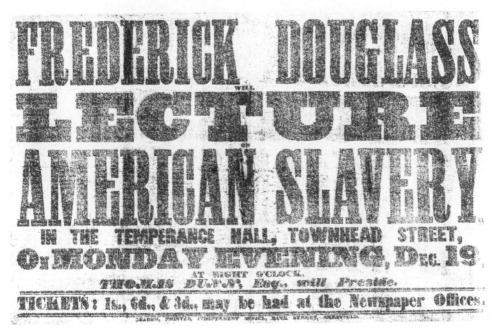

Part IV, no 2 Advert for Frederick Douglass's speech, Manchester, 1846
(University of Manchester).

'GIVE BACK THE MONEY'

A FAMILIAR HOWL IN THE NORTH.
Leeds, England, *Northern Star*, 24 October 1846, p. 3

Another gust – another jet
  Spurts from the yellow tide;
Dividing yet – devising yet
  How yet they may divide.
"Give back the money!" well, give it back,
  The last blood mingled mite;
Or be it scourged from a slaving black, –
  Or wrung of a starving white.
Heaven wills it not, His altar stained
  By the wretch's narrowed share;
What, from hungering heart all strained,
  Had never welcome there.
O, we have seen of labour wan,
  Yon solemn croucher seek
The lonely dole of a withering man,
  Nor care for his sunken cheek.
We've marked the wake of a whining few, –
  Their prim and pious look,
Stride off with a *very farthing* too
  From pauper in his nook.
Ah! then – all this, yea more and more, –
  The groan-earned sin give back;
'Tis murder's wages, O! restore
  To the white slave as to the black.
But who have sundered the sister's heart, –
  Bade parent fondness cease, –

And all life's loveliness depart
   Our lowly homes of peace!
Did Bethlehem's star bode strife below,
   Yon night the seraph sung? –
Or spake its ray of want and woe,
   In Mammon's poisoned tongue?
Give back you may – or you may keep, –
   Tis mockery evermore;
The jewels 'reaved from hearts that weep,
   Ye never may restore.
Divide, and haste ye, – broken Ice
   Melts faster being small,
'Till waxing "beautifully less"
   We find no ice at all.
Then, be the altar, House or Hill,
   The only priests shall be –
Truth, Light, Reason, and Good-will,
   The one Church and the free.
WM. THOM.[1]

---

1 Sottish weaver and poet William Thom (1788–1848).

TO FREDERICK DOUGLASS

Boston, MA, *The Liberator*, 27 November 1846, p. 4

TO FREDERICK DOUGLASS.

Amerigo Vespucci![1] Well was given
Thy name to you, vast continent of lies:
The new-found world, whence sacred truth is driven,
Where men religion love and God despise.

Vain, boastful Florentine! What though thy name
Is stamped upon the world Columbus found?
Thine is the falsehood, his the rightful fame,
If fame may spring from such accursed ground.

Dark was the day on which the vessel sailed,
Which bore thy name, chaste mother of our lord!
Oh, how have lust and cruelty prevailed!
What hecatombs have fleshed the tyrant's swords,

Since holy Mary's barque first touched the shore,
Till then unknown to these, our Eastern climes!
America, go write thy name in gore,
No other ink will suit thy demon crimes.

Land of the bended knee, the vengeful arm!
Land of the crosier and the knotted thong!
Where bondsmen till the low-born freeman's farm;
Where men the weak oppress, and help the strong.

---

1   Amerigo Vespucci (1454–1512), Italian merchant and explorer after whom the Americas are supposedly named.

What though thy name is new in history's page?
A fungus nation, offspring of a night!
Thy deeds are worthy of a bygone age,
When crimes of shame were rife, which shunned the light.

Pizarro! Cortez![2] Ye whose names supply
A byword to the world that loathes your deeds,
Hide your mean heads, to those whom you outvie
In acts at which the stoutest nature bleeds.

Thrice happy those, whom Spain's remorseless hand
Consigned to death, to cold oblivion's power!
Oh blest, thrice blest, that slain, that countless band,
Who rest forgotten, like yon withering flower.

Another race is heir to all your woes,
A race transported from their native soil,
To one through which no stream of kindness flows,
To cheer the pathway of unceasing toil.

Oh what a day was that for Afric's race,
When Spain sent out the restless Genoese,
Commissioned to proclaim redeeming grace
To lands encircled by the Western seas!

Redeeming grace! Oh, mockery profane!
Spain plants the crop, but plants it deep in blood;
Nought fills her bosom but the love of gain –
'tis sordid gold she seeks, not India's good.

Baptized and ground to death, the Indian lies,
His name forgotten and his race destroyed
His people gone, another race supplies
The broken ranks, fills up the deadly void.

Age after age has slowly rolled away,
O'ercharged with Afric's groans and bitter tears;
Her sons the constant, unprotected prey
Of one whose galling yoke in woe she bears.

---

2 Francisco Pizarro (c. 1470s–c.1541) and Hernán Cortés (1485–1547) were Spanish conquistadors.

Rise, Afric, rise! Oh, break the tyrant's band!
Each generous voice will cheer thee to thy right;
Stand up erect – the craven ne'er will stand
Before thine arm in Nature's rightful fight.

DOUGLASS, we welcome thee to England's shore,
A brother-freeman, once a tyrant's thrall,
The planter's chain shall shackle thee no more,
Thy frame ne'er tremble at the driver's call.

Thy tongue, thine arm, thy foot, thy voice, is free –
Free as the air, the light, the mountain stream;
Thrice welcome to this land of liberty –
Look back on bondage as a bygone dream!

Thy tongue is loosened – loosened be the ties
Which held thy brethren in the western shores;
Proclaim their wrongs, denounce the nation's lies,
Where man his brother hates, his God adores!
July 1 1846. L. SABINE.

FREDERICK DOUGLASS

Boston, MA, *The Liberator*, 4 December 1846, p. 4

FOR THE LIBERATOR.
FREDERICK DOUGLASS.

MR. EDITOR:

The following lines, which I transcribe from the Ipswich "Phono Press," a Phonographic Journal, and written by an English lady for FREDERICK DOUGLASS, if you see fit to republish. I would commend to the particular attention of John H. Pearson, the New-England kidnapper.[1] Probably this lady was not aware that New England contained such a 'thing' when she penned these beautiful lines.

J.H.

I'll be free! I'll be free! and none shall confine,
With fetters and chains, this free heart of mine;
From my youth I have learned on my God to rely,
And, despite my oppressor, gain freedom or die.

Though my back is all torn by the merciless rod,
Yet firm is my trust in the right arm of God;
In his strength I'll go forth, and forever will be
'Mong the hills of the North, where the bondman is free.

Let me go, let me go, to the land of the brave,
Where the shackles must fall from the limbs of the slave;
Where Freedom's proud eagle screams wild through the sky,
And the sweet mountain birds in glad notes reply.

---

1 Bostonian John H. Pearson had a reputation for aiding southern slavecatchers, and in 1851 he participated in the rendition of fugitive Thomas Sims.

I'll fly to New-England, where the fugitive finds
A home mid her mountains and deep forest winds;
And her hill-tops shall ring with the wrongs done to me,
Till responsive they sing, "Let the bondman go free!"

New-England! New-England! thrice blessed and free,
The poor hunted slave finds a shelter in thee;
Where should blood-thirsty hounds ever dare on his track,
At thy strong voice, New-England, the monsters fall back.

Go back, then, ye blood-hounds, that howl on my path!
In the land of New-England, I'm free from your wrath;
And the sons of the Pilgrims my deep scars shall see,
Till they cry with one voice, 'Let the bondman go free!'

Great God! hasten on the glad jubilee,
When our brethren in bonds shall arise and be free,
And our blotted escutcheon be washed from its stains,
Now the scorn of the world, with three millions in chains.

O, then shall Columbia's bright flag be unfurled,
The glory of freemen, the pride of the world;
While earth's struggling millions point hither in glee,
To the land of New England, the home of the free.

TO FREDERICK DOUGLASS

Boston, MA, *The Liberator*, 15 January 1847, p. 4

Hail, DOUGLASS, hail! With open hearts and true,
We welcome thee to England's honoured shore,
And in thy path the flowers of Friendship strew,
With Sympathy's sweet dew-drops spangled o'er;
Oh, twine a simple garland from that store!
Bind it around thy brows, and speed thy way;
Tell all the West that here thy name is dear –
That England cherishes *their* cast-away;
And ere that wreath of flowers is dead and sere,
Slavery shall pine and fade in all that hemisphere.

Across the wide Atlantic has thou come,
Bearing the broken chains of slavery,
Flying thy native, though unworthy home,
To greet a land where even *slaves* are free:
Oh! e'en for *Freedom's* sake, we welcome thee!
It was herself who loosed thy iron bands,
Her guardian angel bore thee o'er the sea –
She gently nursed thee in her fostering hands,
And now her sheltering wing broad over thee expands!

Beloved by Freedom, and by knowledge blest,
Thine is a mind which feels for others' woes;
Thou wilt not tamely in the silken nest
Of luxury take up thy soft repose;
Ah no! thy mind with nobler feelings glows;
Thou never, never wilt accept of rest,
Till the whole world, in every region, knows,
No stern oppressor, and no sad oppressed, –
No tyrant's hardened heart, – no Bondman's bleeding breast.

There is a mystery to me, I own –
It is the mystery of iniquity, –
The being who can hear the deep-moan
Escape the lips of wronged humanity
That wrong inflicted by his own decree;
It is a mystery I would not know;
I still will claim the right of sympathy
With every varied form of human woe;
In every land and clime, the heaven's blue vault below.

Oh, thou who, by experience, hast known
The fullness of that cup of bitterness!
Thou, who canst understand the stifled groan,
And read the glance of deep and dark distress, –
The spirit mourning in its dreariness, –
The heart unstrung to every joyful song, –
The soul disconsolate and comfortless, –
Gifted by heaven to lead the heart along,
Teach us to feel aright for Afric's peerless wrong.

Oh for a soul like His, who fondly wept
O'er all the ills of sad Jerusalem,
That whilst thy hand the harp of sorrow swept,
Our hearts might mourn responsive to thy theme;
Nor yet too long indulge an idle dream,
But grasping firmly Truth's unconquered brand,
Let us in spirit cross the Atlantic stream,
And join in fight against Oppression's band,
The noble, faithful few, who love their Fatherland!
Bristol, England, 1846.

WE'LL FREE THE SLAVE

Boston, MA, *The Liberator*, 5 February 1847, p. 4

WE'LL FREE THE SLAVE. AIR: *'Ye banks and braes of bonny Doon.'*

How bright the sun of freedom burns,
From mount to mount, from shore to shore!
"the slave departs, the man returns,"
The reign of force and fraud is o'er:
'Tis Truth's own beam, from sea to sea,
From vale to vale, from wave to wave;
Her ministers this night are we,
To free, to free, to free the slave!

We'll free the slave of every clime,
Whate'er the chain that binds his soul;
And publish forth this truth sublime,
From farthest Indus to the Pole,
That man, how proud soo'er he be,
Is but a poor and paltry knave,
Who joins not now with you and me,
To free, to free, to free the slave!

We'll free the slave, the poisoned bowl
Has fettered to low crime and care;
We'll bid him burst its harsh control,
And break its fetters of despair.
We'll free the slave of Mammon's power;
And War's poor darling, called the brave;
And Tyrants! Yes, form this blest hour,
We'll free, we'll free, we'll free the slave!

Poor Afric's sons, though slaves they be,
Shall spring to freedom and to light;
And what they shall be, you may see, –
*One of those sons is here to-night!**
And ASIA from her sleep supine,
And EUROPE from her feudal grave,
Yes, e'en America shall join,
To free, to free, to free the slave!

You laugh! But, ah! you do not know
How great a power this truth can wield;
Thought always aims the surest blow,
And wisdom is the safest shield.
The spirits of six thousand years
Are round us, and they make us brave;
Come, brother, quell ignoble fears,
And free, and free, and free the slave!
*Frederick Douglass

NEWSPAPER ADVERTISEMENT

Leamington Spa Courier, 20 February 1847
British Library

AMERICAN SLAVERY.

On Tuesday next, February 23rd,
TWO PUBLIC MEETINGS

Will be held, when Addresses will be delivered by

MR. FREDERICK DOUGLASS,

(A FUGITIVE SLAVE,)

AND

GEORGE THOMPSON, Esq., of London.

The MORNING MEETING at the MUSIC HALL, BATH STREET, at 2 o'Clock, when the Rev. DR. MARSH is expected to preside.

The EVENING MEETING at SPENCER-ST. CHAPEL, at 7 o'Clock ; T. H. THORNE, Esq., in the Chair.

Part IV, no 3 Advert for Frederick Douglass's speech, *Leamington Spa Courier*, 20 February 1847, p. 2 (British Library).

ON HEARING FREDERICK DOUGLASS

Northampton Mercury, 3 April 1847, p. 2

On Hearing Frederick Douglass, "*The Run-away Slave*," at Northampton, March 29th, 1847.

I.
It was a glorious spectacle, that crowd
Of minds, in all things various, save one,
And this, Humanity's fine unison. –
By the same feeling of compassion won,
By the same sense of foul dishonour bowed,
To the same deep resolve sacredly vowed,
Those diverse hearts as one were lifted loud
In stern denouncement of the damning crime,
The murder-stain, the plague-spot of our time,
That wraps man's spirit in corruption's shroud,
Turning to bitter all Heav'n meant for sweet,
Making Religion's self a vile deceit,
And Freedom's holy name – no more sublime –
A mockery, a snare, a loathed cheat.
II.
Back to thy brethren, thou, their CHAMPION, go!
And with the fervid eloquence of truth
Move even OPPRESSION'S iron heart to ruth,
And cause its eyes, like ours, to overflow.
Be those eyes thus unsealed, and, happy, so,
Know themselves human; then the spotted SOUTH,
Unleprosied, shall feel her primal youth,
Nor blush when God's free airs around her blow.

The TYRANTS are themselves but erring brothers,
And to expose a wrong is to remove;
No fair aim now its aspirations smothers, –
TRUE effort here wrests blessing from above.
UNCHAINED THYSELF, go, break the bonds of others,
Melting their fetters in the SUN OF LOVE.
Duston.   J. W. DALBY.[1]

---

1   John Watson Dalby (1799–1880), English editor and poet.

FAREWELL TO FREDERICK DOUGLASS

Boston, MA, *The Liberator*, 14 May 1847, p. 4

From Howitt's Journal for April.
   FAREWELL TO FREDERICK DOUGLASS, WHO SAILED FROM ENGLAND FOR AMERICA APRIL 4TH 1847, EASTER SUNDAY.

BLESSINGS be with thee, Freedom's noble son!
Thou leav'st thy Fatherland of Liberty,
Where thou hast dwelt as man should dwell with man,
To seek the cruel Stepdame's blood-stained soil,
Who gave thee for thy birthright stripes and chains,
Nor granted thee, secure, to tread her shores,
Until was paid a paltry sum of gold,
To stamp the patent of nobility
Which god's own hand had set upon thy brow! –
– Farewell! Thou'rt armed with a rich panoply
of sympathy and love from English hearts,
and prayers that rise to heaven in thy behalf.
With this thou wilt not feel the darts of scorn,
Arrows from lying lips, weapons of rage,
That will assail thee. Nobly thou wilt stand
To fight the battle of thy injured race,
Armed with the christian's weapons, faith and hope.
Go forth, our Friend and Brother! Cry aloud,
And with a voice America must hear,
Tell her of all her huge iniquity,
And bid her loose the bands of wickedness,
Set her oppress'd ones free, break every yoke, –
Ere, without mockery, she can keep her fasts,

Or raise to heaven a pure and holy prayer.
And comfort thou thy people, for the lord
Will, in His own good time, be glorified; –
They that delighted in their evil ways,
That cast you out from men, that set their feet
Upon your neck, and e'en blasphemed the name
Of the Most High, to cover o'er their sin,
Their fears shall come upon them, and their shame
Shall sink them in the dust, beneath the glance
Of the offended nations. Still hope on,
For Christ must yet subdue his enemies.
This day the churches ring the gladsome sound,
'the lord of life is risen!' he died to save
the world from its iniquity; – he rose,
that in sure prospect of immortal life,
we might be new in spirit. Come the day,
when a pure light shall beam upon thy race,
e'en from the rising Saviour; when the Sun
of Righteousness shall melt their heavy chains, when with hearts full of joy and
thankfulness,
forgiving their oppressors, they shall join
the severed links of Nature's holy ties,
and taste the bliss of heaven, while yet on earth!
Oh, may'st thou see that day; and may the gifts
In mercy sent thee, of rich eloquence,
A fervent, thankful heart, warm, earnest zeal
That no repulse can cool, And patient trust
In the subduing power of truth and love,
Hasten its glorious coming! – thus, farewell!
Bristol. M.C.[1]

---

1   Possibly Mary Carpenter (1807–1877), social reformer and abolitionist based in Bristol.

THE ADIEU

From the *London Inquirer*.
Boston, MA, *The Liberator*, 14 May 1847, p. 4.

THE ADIEU.

Thou bright star of Liberty, Douglass! Farewell!
Yet how fleeting the glimpse of tiny ray!
Complain not, my soul! – it were folly to dwell
In regions all blazing with day.

Then adieu, noble Douglass! To dark realms benighted
In tyranny, haste thee away:
I would not detain thee, though e'er so delighted –
Yet 'tis bitter to lose thy sweet ray.

Still, Douglass, good-bye! For, hark! Liberty calls,
In slavery's chains, sadly groaning;
Then forth o'er the wave, where the dread tempest howls!
Yes, away to the fettered – the moaning!
April 5, 1847. JAMES.

AMERICA. – BATTLE OF BLACKS AND WHITES

Bristol, England, *Bristol Mercury and Western Counties Advertiser*, 15 May 1847, p. 2
Originally from *Jerrold's Weekly Newspaper*

Often, has it been predicted that America nursed within herself the certainty of a terrible social revolution – a revolution of colour – a contest of black and white. A very brief time, and the battle will begin – Frederick Douglass, Field marshal of all the American negro forces. By this time Mr. Douglass has landed in America, and is on his way to take up his position at Lynn, Massachusetts. There he proposes to open the campaign against the anti-abolitionists; and, with the ammunition of good argument, and the sword of intellect (of late so prettily prattled about by the King of Prussia), to force his way through the treble lines of blasphemy, ignorance, and injustice, in which the enemy lies entrenched. The battle will be fought with all the might of men, but – there will be no bloodshed. It will be a battle of the press; and in such a battle who, in the end, may doubt the result? We are happy to state that contributions will be sent out from this country, that a magnificent piece of artillery – an iron press – may be immediately placed at the general's disposal. Shot – type of all newspaper variety – will be cast, and served out to his troops; all of them black soldiers, enlisted in the cause of emancipation. A broadside (in the shape of a newspaper) will be fired upon the enemy at stated intervals; and rockets and shells, carrying most destructive syllables, will from time to time be scattered among the foe. General Douglass will have at his disposal a far more potent combustible than the celebrated Greek fire – namely, printers' ink. A combustible that makes its way into all places – that burns everywhere – against which nothing can make defence or safeguard:

> "Nor Alps nor Pyrreneaus keep it out,
> Nor fortified redoubt!"

It is not for us to prophecy the duration of the contest: we can only express our hopeful assurance that, with such weapons, General Douglass must ultimately be victorious. From his demeanour in this country we are sure that he will carry on the Printers' War (the only war in which the Devil does good service) with as much forbearance as skill. At his hands we look for the most humane treatment of the disabled; and then, there is this balsamic virtue about printers' ink – it heals even where it has wounded. And then the general does not propose to put anybody to the sword – only to the paragraph. – *Jerrold's Weekly Newspaper.*

LINES ADDRESSED TO FREDERICK DOUGLASS ON HIS RETURN TO AMERICA

Boston, MA, *The Liberator*, 9 July 1847, p. 4
Originally from the Newcastle *Peace Advocate*

LINES ADDRESSED TO FREDERICK DOUGLASS ON HIS RETURN TO AMERICA.

And thou, indeed, art free!
Thy noble spirit never more shall pine
With the dark thought that aught of slavery
Henceforth can e'er be thine!

Homeward thy footsteps turning,
The blue waves waft thee to the land that gave
To thy the young heart, for freedom deeply burning,
The brand that marks the slave!

Yet it is home to thee,
And there thy loved ones gather round the hearth;
Those whom thy spirit long has yearned to see
Smiling around thy path!

Sweet may that meeting be!
And kind friends greet thee, even greet there;
With heart like thine, so warm, and pure, and free, –
Friendship is every where!

Yet, should thy pathway lie
'Mid cruel prejudice, unfeeling, scorning,
oh! lift to heaven a calm and trusting eye,
and hail a brighter morning.

Yes, for that hour must come
When Freedom's land will to herself be true;
A brighter star shall rise, o'er Slavery's tomb,
And kindle hope anew!

And truth's pure light be spread
To injured Afric's sable sons and daughters;
Then shall Columbia find again the bread
She casteth on the waters.

Then shall her sons go forth,
Preaching glad tidings to the world around;
Scattering good seed upon the fruitful earth,
That else were barren found.

But never can she know
The full deep tide of promised blessings given
Unto the merciful, till she shall show
Mercy like that of heaven.

Farewell, a kind farewell;
Heaven shield and succor thee in trial's hour,
And nerve thy *free* heart, boldly still to tell
Of slavery's cruel power.
L.S.[1]

---

1 Possibly another poem from "L. Sabine."

POETRY. FAREWELL SONG of FREDERICK DOUGLASS ON LEAVING ENGLAND. BY T. POWIS GRIFFITHS

Leicester, England, *Leicestershire Mercury*, 17 July 1847, p. 4

Farewell to the land of the free![1]
Farewell to the land of the brave!
Alas! that my country should be
America, land of the Slave!

What if the Negro's despised and degraded,
And scorn and reproach are heap'd on his head?
Perish the thought that would leave him unaided!
American soil shall be that which I tread.
   Farewell to the land, &c.

What if I've drunk of the cup that awaits me
One bitter foretaste already;* shall I
Glean from the prospect no thought that elates me,
If in freedom's great cause counted worthy to die?
   Farewell to the land, &c.

Am I not wanted where warfare is waging?
Shall I, like a coward, not join in the flight?
[S]hrink from the onslaught when battle is raging,
Scared by the enemy's tyrannous might?
   Farewell to the land, &c.

---

1 Julia Griffiths wrote the music for this song and Thomas Powis Griffiths, her brother, wrote the lyrics. Fought, *Women in the World of Frederick Douglass*, p. 340. The song was performed by Jonathan Rhodes and Lee Wright in 2018 at the University of Rochester. See https://www.youtube.com/watch?v=I53djcD77iA. Thanks to Janet Douglas for sending this.

Give me, then, Friends! the weapon that's wielded
Best in the cause I have sworn to uphold,
And I will fight on till the foe shall have yielded,
Or the years of my sojourn on earth have been told.
  Farewell to the land, &c.

*Alluding to the disgraceful reception of Douglass on board the *Cambria*.

FAREWELL TO FREDERICK DOUGLASS

From *Howitt's Journal*
Rochester, NY, *The North Star*, 14 April 1848, p. 4

FAREWELL TO FREDERICK DOUGLASS,
Who sailed from England for America April 4, 1847

Blessings be with thee, Freedom's noble son!
Thou leav'st thy fatherland of liberty.
Where thou hast dwelt as man should dwell with man,
To seek the cruel Stepdame's blood-stained soil,
Who gave thee for thy birthright stripes and chains,
Nor granted thee, secure, to tread her shores,
Until was paid a paltry sum of gold,
To stamp the patent of nobility
Which God's own hand had set upon thy brow! –
Farewell! Thou'rt armed with a rich panoply
Of sympathy and love from English hearts,
And prayers that rise to heaven in thy behalf.
With this thou wilt not feel the darts of scorn,
Arrows from lying lips, weapons of rage,
That will assail thee. Nobly thou wilt stand
To fight the battle of thy injured race,
Arms! with the Christian's weapons, faith and hope,
Go forth, our Friend and Brother! Cry aloud,
And with a voice America must hear,
Tell her of all her huge iniquity,
And bid her loose the bands of wickedness,
Set her oppressed ones free, break every yoke,
Ere, without mockery, she can keep her fasts,

Or raise to heaven a pure and holy prayer.
And comfort thou thy people, for the Lord
Will, in His own good time, be glorified;
They that delighted in their evil ways,
That cast you out from men that set their feet
Upon your necks, and e'en blasphemed the name
Of the Most High, to cover o'er their sin;
Their fears shall come upon them, and their shame
Shall sink them in the dust, beneath the glance
Of the offended nations. – Still hope on,
For Christ must yet subdue his enemies.
This day the churches ring the gladsome sound,
"The Lord of Life is risen!" He died to save
The world from its iniquity; he rose,
That, in sure prospect of immortal life,
We might be new in spirit. Come the day,
When a pure light shall beam upon they race,
E'en from the rising Saviour; when the Sun
Of Righteousness shall melt their heavy chain,
When, with hearts full of joy and thankfulness,
Forgiving their oppressors, they shall join
The severed links of Nature's holy ties,
And taste the bliss of heaven, while yet on earth!
Oh, may'st thou see that day; and may the gifts,
In mercy seat thee, of rich eloquence,
A fervent, truthful heart, warm, earnest zeal
That no repulse can cool, and patient trust
In the subduing power of truth and love,
Hasten its glorious coming! – Thus, farewell!
Bristol, 1847. M.C.[1]

---

1   Possibly Mary Carpenter.

FREDERICK DOUGLASS

Rochester, NY, *The North Star*, 12 May 1848, p. 4

FREDERICK DOUGLASS
On board the Cambria Steamship, April 1847

Blow cheerily, ye eastern gales,
To waft us from the shore, –
The steam is up, and bent the sails,
And leaning on the larboard rails,
Faintly the parting traveller hails
His fading land once more.
But forward flies the dashing keel,
The level sun may scarce reveal,
Upon the far horizon's rim
The cloudy top of mountain dim:
'Tis gone – 'tis lost – the waning light
Is curtained in the robe of night!

Yet, gallantly and fearlessly
The good ship holds her way;
Now bounding on the billows high,
Or deep engulfed the paddles ply,
Whirring, roaring, ceaselessly,
Like demon-sprites at play.
And still along the lonely deep,
That guarded ship her course shall keep,
And vainly shall the midnight storm
Pour down upon her quivering form;
There is a mighty arm upraised,
To shield her from the blast:
A watchful eye that sleepeth not,

A hand unseen, that faileth not,
Shall guide her home at last.

Oh, if in the great world there be,
A place where *must* feel
The presence of the Deity,
'Tis out upon the trackless sea,
Boun! to his fragile keel.
But there are hearts upon that deck –
Cold, selfish hearts, that little reck
Of mercies which the common day
Showers thick around their heedless way
Yet proud in their vain littleness,
Deem Heaven's sore care themselves to bless;
Nor cast on others' weal a thought,
So they may reach the destined port.

The sabbath sun is shining
On the wild Atlantic waves,
With golden net-work lining
The hollow ocean-caves:
It is the solemn hour,
When the voice of prayer should rise,
From the lonely ship upon the waste
Up to the vaulted skies.

The swinging bell tolls heavily, and soon
The gathering crowd shall throng the gay saloon:
One, 'mid the rest, of bold and manly brow,
Barred from those ranks, would fain approach them now,
To mingle, with the hymns that heavenward roll,
The grateful homage of a rescued soul;
But hark! loud murmurs rise – "Go back! go back"
"Can white men worship with a slave – a black?"
Yes, he will go; but from his scornful eye
The kindling fire-glance bears his proud reply:
"Vain hypocrites! That bow the bended knee
In mockery to the God of Liberty!
Think ye the passport of your boasted skin
The scats of heaven for you alone shall win?
Oh, contemptible! and will ye dare
To call upon 'Our Father's' name in prayer,

And know that ye have spurned a brother man,
Like some foul scum of earth? Why, if ye can,
Unwarned of conscience, kneel before His throne,
To whom the secrets of all hearts are known,
May his stern justice – nay, I will not call
For vengeance – rather let forgiveness fall
Upon your impious hearts!"
He turns away,
And in his lonely cabin kneels to pray:
"O God of mercy! let thine eye
Behold with pitying sympathy,
The outcasts of the world, who lie
In hopeless, helpless misery!
Teach this unlettered tongue to tell
The story of their wrongs so well,
That slumbering justice shall awake,
And thunder till the mountains shake,
And coward tyranny be hurled
For ever from a righted world!"

Ay, and the prayer of that once slave,
Ascending from the desert wave,
Shall yet be heard! To misery's cry
Unnumbered hearts shall yet reply,
And brand America's proud name
With deep imperishable shame,
So long as Freedom's banner holds
A lie upon its crimson folds.
F. T. Mott[1]
LEICESTER (Eng.)

---

[1] Possibly an early work by Frederick Thompson Mott (1825–1908), a Leicester merchant, botanist, and poet.

"THE GREAT PLEA FOR FREEDOM"

My Bondage and My Freedom (Edinburgh, 1855), National Library of Scotland

Part IV, no 4 "The Great Plea for Freedom," *My Bondage and My Freedom* (Edinburgh, 1855). National Library of Scotland.

LITERATURE: MY BONDAGE AND MY FREEDOM

Edinburgh, Scotland, *The Scotsman*,
13 February 1856, p. 3

This is a book of deep interest and of great ability. It is also, in many respects, a precious literary curiosity. Considering what Frederick Douglass is, under what circumstances he was educated, this book is perhaps one of the most remarkable that has ever been given to the world. It is not simply its great excellence that renders it so very remarkable as its kind of excellence – its whole character. The publication of Frederick Douglass's book will mark a step in advance to the destruction of American slavery. By exchanging the platform for the press, the author has extended the influence which his talents are sure to command wherever he is listened to. There are many persons who will read a book regardless of the colour of the hand that penned it, who would never think of going to a public meeting to hear a black man speaking. There are many persons, even in this free country, who would hold their principles as compromised if they were to be seen in a meeting of the friends of Frederick Douglass, who yet, it may be hoped, will, in the privacy of their closets, be induced to take a glance at the pages of a volume which, if they once commence reading, they will if they are readers at all, feel compelled to read to the end. Amidst the feelings with which the book will be read, one of the strongest will be the feeling of surprise. To those who have had the pleasure of hearing Frederick Douglass's speeches, the surprise felt at reading his book will not be so unbounded as that of those who have now the mind of the author for the first time laid before them. When we are told that a man of black colour, of African race, of great genius and great eloquence, but born and brought up in slavery, is delivering lectures against slavery, what is it, with all our faith in the report of his genius and eloquence, that we expect to listen to? Great genius and great eloquence certainly, but mingled with what, under the circumstances, would be so excusable and so natural, great faults, tawdry ornament, inflated declamation, unsound reasoning, an Asiatic exuberance of words, an African viciousness of taste, or something of that Hibernian style of oratory which, with its faults as well as its beauties, is most natural to minds more fervid than well balanced – more inflamed by excitement than disciplined by the contemplation of chaste and symmetrical models. Instead of all this, or any part of this, those who listened to Frederick Douglass heard an orator who, from the first moment that he opened his lips, appeared to look stead-fastly to the attainment of the one great object of all true eloquence – the conviction of his hearers; placing no value on their mere admiration. His audience listened to an address singularly devoid of figures of rhetoric or flowers of oratory, without a para-graph or sentence of mere useless adornment – an address distinguished by a severe simplicity of language, which went direct towards the object aimed at – the convinc-ing of the understanding and winning the hearts of his hearers to the great purpose which lay nearest to the orator's own heart. Those who listened felt themselves in the condition of the hearers of the great orator of Athens, and the criticism made on his eloquence might in spirit be passed on that of Frederick Douglass. When other orators concluded their addresses, the people said "How beautifully he has spoken!" When Frederick Douglass made his appeal to humanity in the cause of humanity, the people said, "Arise, let us march to the overthrow of slavery!" People felt that against the bare stern eloquence of the man whose body had been lacerated by slavery, the contention of the heartless and wordy sophistry which was arrayed in defence of the trade in the flesh and blood of men was the contention of the chaff with the consuming flames.

A foretaste of the character and spirit of the book now before us was given in the author's speeches. The style of a writer is always the picture of his mind. The great char-acteristics of Frederick Douglass's mind are those which do not often mark out a man as a public orator. His strong points are soundness of judgment, closeness of reasoning, and, above all, a decided and refreshing manliness. To these faculties his other gifts are all wisely subordinated. He has pathos, wit, and sarcasm, but he never unnecessar-ily uses them, or overlabours them. His satire is generally insinuated in a single quiet phrase, which no doubt often escapes the notice of readers of less acute sensibility than his own. But, above all, manliness, masculine strength, is the characteristic of his mind.

An ancient poet, speaking of a slavery which was freedom itself when compared to American slavery, tells us with melancholy truth that "man loses half his virtues that day he becomes a slave." And amongst the few virtues which we could con-ceive still retaining a place in the heart of a slave, would it not look something like madness and mockery to look for manliness? How, then, are we to account for this miracle, that from the age of six years, from the very day that Frederick Douglass discovered that he was a slave, manliness was the guiding and all-elevating feature in his character? From that moment, though violently subjected to slavery, he never consented not even in thought, to his subjection. From that moment his clear rea-son saw at once that the relation between him and his master was a criminal rela-tion, which it was his duty to break as soon as he was able. The sophistries which bewildered the feeble judgments of other slaves, and which were daily preached to them by divines of the most flaming reputation for piety, and by ladies and gentlemen who constantly held the hymn-book in one hand and the scourge in the other, never imposed on the sound understanding of Frederick Douglass, or made him doubt for a moment that it was his duty to plot and conspire, and use every necessary means to break his fetters and the fetters of his fellow-slaves.

Frederick Douglass never knew who was his father, and scarcely did more than just see his mother to his knowledge, and never ascertained the year of his birth. With a white father and a black mother, prejudice will be inclined to trace the intellect to the paternal side. Against this conclusion, the opinion of Frederick Douglass himself is arrayed. His regret at his separation from his mother is expressed in simple language, which some will not call eloquent, but most people will feel to be so.

The detail of the means by which at length Frederick Douglass made his escape, he buries in silence, regretting the evil consequences that have arisen from the publicity given to the accounts of the escapes of other slaves. The opening of the second part of his work finds him a free man in New York. In the summer of 1841, he made his first public speech at Nantucket. A humorous divine and ardent Abolitionist present introduced him to the audience as "a graduate from the Peculiar Institution, with his diploma written on his back." In 1845, Douglass came to England. On his passage, and during his residence in Britain, considerable opposition to his cause was manifested even by parties of high religious professions; but Douglass shows that the hostility of the friends of slavery, not less than the support of the friends of liberty, tended to increase his influence, and to surround him with public favour . . .

There is one strange and painful feeling which will not fail to arise in all thinking minds on the perusal of these deeply-interesting pages. This perusal of these increase the public conviction of the horrible nature of American slavery – above all slavery that ever existed. In any other country, ancient or modern, in the world, where slavery exists, a slave of the intellect of Frederick Douglass would have risen to honour, wealth, or power, or all combined. In the heathen world, the slave Phaedrus became the freedmen and the friend of Augustus; the slave, the African slave, Terence, was the companion of Scipio and Lelius, of all that was noble in rank and refined in character in Rome; the slave Epictetus became the counsellor of Hadrian and the teacher of Arrian.[1] In Christian America, the body of Frederick Douglass has been tortured by slaveholders of the lowest intellect and the most brutalised

---

1   The correspondent mentions specific enslaved people who reached eminent positions of power in Ancient Rome. Phaedrus was born enslaved *c*. 15 BCE and was freed by Augustus, Emperor of Rome. Terence, an African playwright, was born enslaved *c*. 195/185 BCE and freed by Terentius Lucanus, a Roman senator. Epictetus was born enslaved *c*. AD 50 and became a teacher and friend to Emperor Hadrian.

character. His pre-eminence in mental endowments, over the ablest of those writ-ers who have prostituted and degraded their pens to the perpetration of the most hideous system of cruelty and obscenity that ever existed in any part of the world, will not bear questioning. If it were the case that superiority of intellect gave one human being a right to treat another as a brute, which of the defenders of slavery in America or in Britain, male or female, would be entitled to hold Frederick Douglass in bondage? Would it be any of those "converted men" who, according to a slavery-defending divine of our city, are more common amongst the American slaveholders than such men are in Scotland, and whose names have been consigned by Frederick Douglass to an immortality of infamy?

TO FREDERICK DOUGLASS

Edinburgh, Scotland, *Caledonian Mercury*, 19 August 1865, p. 2

William Meillar, the Dalkeith Poet.[1]

We append one of his sonnets, most appropriate to the times – that to Frederick Douglass: –

> Once tortured, alighted, and insulted slave,
> Soul-scorned, thought-fettered, and like felon chained,
> We bid thee Welcome o'er the Atlantic wave,
> Where freeborn man can wander unrestrained,
> Where mental worth is honoured, not disdained.
> Now, happily, thou bear'st a freeman's name,
> The rights of freedom gloriously can claim.
> No longer by the scourge of slavery pained,
> Thy genius, like a lark new fledged and free,
> Cans't mount at will the sky of liberty!
> Self-taught, self-cultured, and by self refined,
> Thy mental powers display a polished mind!
> Thou to the world giv'st proof what slave may be
> If brother man would set his brother free.

---

1 Scottish cabinetmaker William Miller (1819–1872) gained renown for his poetry, often directed toward juvenile readers.

FREDERICK DOUGLASS

London, England, *Daily News*, 21 October 1886, p. 3

Somewhat unceremoniously I was yesterday morning ushered into the reading room of the Cannon-street Hotel.[1] I had inquired for Mr Frederick Douglass, and the waiter merely pulled open the door of the room and said, "There he is." The gentleman I had come to see was engaged with two ladies, and apologising as well as I could for my abrupt intrusion, I backed out from the presence of a man whose name all England is familiar with as the name of a runaway slave, but whose venerable appearances, courtly dignity of demeanour, and powerful but beneficent face had instantly impressed me with the conviction that I had stepped into the presence of a man who was both great and good. The world moves very fast in these days. Event succeeds event with bewildering rapidity. Already the reverberations of the tremendous crash down of American slavery have died away in the far distance, and the chief actors in the terrible drama have become dim and distant figures in history. Comparatively few persons in England can now very clearly recall the events which led up to the great American civil war and there may be some who do not very distinctly recollect the part taken in that great movement by this remarkable man.

To-day Frederick Douglass stands by universal consent the head and representative of his race in America. With a splendid physique, tall and powerfully built, the swarthy complexion of the mulatto, an abundant crop of negro hair white as snow, and features which, of the negro type, are nevertheless full of emotional fire and intellectual force, he looks every inch a man born for distinction. His father he never knew. His mother was a black slave, and he was born on a remote plantation lying on the banks of the Choptauk River, "amid the laziest and muddiest of streams, surrounded by a white population of the lowest order and among slaves who, in point of ignorance and indolence, were fully in accord with their surroundings." It

---

1 Originally the City Terminus Hotel designed by Edward M. Barry, the Cannon Street Hotel fronted a terminal for both the London Underground and the South Eastern Railway.

is a remarkable fact that there was one, and apparently only one, exception to the general laziness and ignorance of the black population in the midst of which he was born, and that one exception was his mother. She could read; though how she could have learned has ever been a mystery to her son. Infinitely pathetic is his story of his love for his cabin home, of his being carried off to a distance when quite a child, of being brutally beaten and starved, of the last visit from his mother, who, after her day's work, walked twelve miles to see him, and then hurried back to be in time for the overseer's horn at sunrise next morning, never to be seen by him again. All the world is more or less familiar with the slave life of America, and the only exceptional feature of Frederick Douglass's career was the fact of his being a high spirited, bright, and intelligent mulatto, with a consuming desire for knowledge and freedom. A lady incautiously taught him his alphabet, and although the peril of it was speedily discovered, and every effort made to extinguish the light thus kindled, the efforts were in vain. Douglass learned to read and write, and by-and-bye he resolved to be free. It is difficult to realize the desperate character of such a resolution. He knew something of theology but nothing of geography, and did not know whether there was a spot on that side the Atlantic where he could be safe. However, he and four or five others made their plans, were betrayed, and were plunged into more hopeless depths of slavery. At 23 years of age he succeeded in escaping, and 41 years ago he came to this country a fugitive slave. Two Quaker ladies of Newcastle raised 150 l. for the purchase of his freedom, and as he himself pithily puts it, provided with this title to his own body he went back to fight the battle of his race. How he fought and how the battle was won, how he became, under the impulse of his all-devouring theme, one of the finest orators of America, and rose to high official rank, everybody knows on the other side the Atlantic, and thousands know here.

It need hardly be said that a man who has been Marshal of the United States has nothing of the typical negro about him. In appearance, in voice, accent, language, and conversation Frederick Douglass is the highly-cultured gentleman, and it is strange indeed to English ears to sit and listen to the stories he has to tell of the varied and distinct lives he has led. Especially interesting is his account of his return, after he had attained to high official life, to the scenes of his slave life and to the bedside of his old master.

"He had struck down my personality, had subjected me to his will, made property of my body and soul, reduced me to a chattel, hired me out to a noted slave-breaker to be worked like a beast and flogged into submission. He had taken my hard earnings, sent me to prison, offered me for sale, broken up my Sunday school, forbidden me to teach my fellow slaves to read on pain of nine and thirty lashes on my bare back; he had sold my body to his brother and had pocketed the price of my flesh and blood without apparent disturbance of conscience." To the bedside of this man he was summoned, and he asked the dying ex-slaveowner what he thought of this running away. "Frederick," said the dying man, "I always knew you were too smart to be a slave, and had I been in your place I should have done as you did."

Douglass went over the old plantation on which he had been one of a thousand slaves. He stood in the kitchen where he had last seen his mother; went to the window where he used to sing, when hungry, in hopes that a little bread would be given him, and to the closet where as a child he remembered that he had slept in a bag. As the venerable negro chief sits and talks of this, and of the baronial splendour of the great slaveowner's establishment, one may almost fancy that even now his voice is tremulous, and that he is again imagining himself back in that Maryland plantation. It is strange, indeed to listen to such a voice, such words; to observe the gentle, dignified demeanour of the man, and to think of him as the slave who was beaten and starved, hired out like a horse and sold as chattel.

"But it is all a thing of the past."

Mr. Douglass sadly shakes his head. He has no desire to be hard in his criticisms of his country, but on the other hand, he cannot pretend to be satisfied. How can he be? Slavery has been abolished in name and in theory all over the Union; but the prejudice against his colour is still at times very painfully manifest. His whole life is a battle with it, and he is now here in England for rest, and in order for a time to escape from the stream which he is always conscious of struggling against in his own country.

At this point, Mrs. Douglas, who is an American lady, young and fair, puts in her word for the honour of her country. She gently reminds her husband that not long ago they travelled together 2,600 miles through the States, and everywhere Mr. Douglas had met with kindness and courtesy. Very cordially he admits it. Even on the Hudson steamboats, where thirty years ago another lady[2] who is present testifies to his having been forcibly ejected from the saloon in which he had presumed to sit down to dinner with his friends from England, though they sat at a table by themselves, he was permitted in the course of this journey to pass without any interference on account of his colour. Indeed he had a very agreeable distinction. The coloured waiters on board the vessel refused to take his money. He had done so much for them, they said, that his money would not pass them. Yes; he fully recognised the change that time had brought, but nevertheless it was true that within the past two years the mere rumour that he had taken a sitting in a Presbyterian church of Washington raised a ferment throughout the city, and filled the newspapers with angry and excited letters.[3] This highly gifted and heroic man, whom Abraham Lincoln distinguished with his

2   Julia Griffiths Crofts.
3   Douglass often attended the Fifteenth Street Presbyterian Church in the District of Columbia and delivered many lectures there.

friendship, who has been Marshal of the United States, and has just retired from the position of Registrar of Deeds for the district of Columbia, who has edited and owned influential newspapers, and in whom a whole continent recognises a man of consummate ability and stainless integrity, has nevertheless a swarthy skin, and he must not take a sitting with other Christians.

"And are you really conscious of a different social atmosphere here in England?"

"Oh, dear, yes!" is the ready response, "entirely different. I have in America my own wide circle of friends, and my official position had reduced friction and unpleasantness to a minimum; but here in England there is no friction or unpleasantness. I am free, and I feel myself free to go anywhere, or to mingle in any society."

I gently suggest that even here in England prejudices are not wholly unknown. Even here there are changes going on. There is a greater commingling of classes than there was, and time, it is reasonable to hope, may wear out the unworthy antagonism in America. To this Mr Douglass cordially assents. He sees very clearly himself, he says, that the change I allude to is taking place among ourselves, and time and the uplifting of the negroes may, he agrees, to a greater extent dissipate the prejudices which to a man of his breadth of sympathy and nobility of nature must appear as incomprehensible as it is galling.

"Are the negroes dying out, Mr Douglass?"

"Certainly not. At the time of the abolition there were about four millions of them. Taking the last census as a basis I calculate that there are now seven millions."

"And what progress are they making?"

In reply to this Mr. Douglass dwells a good deal on the circumstances under which they started on their career of freedom. When Russia emancipated her serfs every man had land allotted to him. When the Israelites went out of Egypt they spoiled the Egyptians; but when the slaves of America were freed they were turned out destitute to the open sky, and with their late owners exasperated with them for the part so many had taken in the struggle. The wonder is, not that they have made so little progress, but that they have made so much. The salvation of the negro, however, was his possession of all the muscle of the community. When Mr. Douglass went through the Southern States recently he found that the negroes were still the only men at work. When emancipation was impending there were wild threats of importing Chinamen and Irishmen, and labourers from various odd corners of the earth. The negroes were to be driven out of the community, and in some cases it was actually attempted. The mistake, however, was soon apparent. In getting rid of the negroes they were getting rid of the hands while they kept the mouths. The negroes were really indispensable, and they are making, Mr. Douglass believes, advances in many ways. Nevertheless, there is much sadness in his general review of the condition of the Southern State negroes. They are no longer slaves in name; but, in fact, their slavery is still a terrible reality, and great changes have yet to be made before the great work of emancipation can be considered complete. Here we have banished the "truck system." It is illegal to pay wages in goods. But in the Southern States the system largely prevails. By means of it great numbers of blacks are held in bondage, which virtually ties them down to the soil on which they are oppressed almost as effectually as ownership in them would do. There is another atrocious method of re-establishing slavery that has been extensively resorted to. Negroes convicted of the pettiest offences are hired out as convict labourers, and under the guise of a system of justice slavery is still the lot of many unfortunate negroes. Still, the work of emancipation is slowly progressing, and though to the vehement heart of a man like Frederick Douglass the process must no doubt appear painfully slow, it is, he believes, going on, and his people will yet show that their inferiority is not in their race, but in the embruting and debasing conditions slavery has imposed upon them.

Mr. Douglass has now left for the continent. The winter he purposes spending in France and Italy, and it is his intention to return to London in time for the May meetings, at some of which he will no doubt be present.

FREDERICK DOUGLASS

Image in *The Graphic*, 13 November 1886
British Library

FREDERICK DOUGLASS
The Negro Champion and Orator

Part IV, no 5 Frederick Douglass, *The Graphic*, 13 November 1886 (British Library).

A FUGITIVE SLAVE

Newcastle, England, *The Newcastle Daily Chronicle*, 20 June 1887, p. 4

"A FUGITIVE SLAVE." [BY A CORRESPONDENT.] The laying of the foundation stone of the College of Science will be remembered by many from the fact that there they first saw Frederick Douglass.[1] To a few his presence recalled a far-off time laden with controversies now settled for ever. It is forty-one years since I heard the apostle of emancipation. He had recently come to England with William Lloyd Garrison and Mr. Buffum. Of Garrison, I need not speak – a simpler or more self-forgetful great man I never met. Mr. Buffum was the embodiment of New England's anti-slavery enthusiasm, and in all ways an honour to "the Old Bay State." It was Frederick Douglass, however, to whom I was specially attracted. The fact that he had escaped from slavery and that he possessed the power to make the story of his wrongs familiar to the world, give him an *eclat* with which few public men, whether white or black, had the fortune to be invested. It was in Kilmarnock, in the immediate vicinity of the spot where "A man's a man for a' that" was originally published, that I first heard the great American anti-slavery orator. The church in which Frederick Douglass made his most noteworthy speech in that bright Ayrshire town, has for those familiar with the poetry of Burns a deeply historic interest. There most of the heroes of "The Holy Fair" had successfully preached. The antique building was densely crowded when Douglass spoke, not less than 2,000 people being present on the occasion. The orator was at his best, in the full flush of life, mental and physical. The story he told had intensely stirred the hearts of a people who saw and felt that they had not listened to a merely eloquent speaker, but to a really great man. It fell to Dr. James Morison[2] to say a

---

1 Possibly Newcastle University.
2 The Reverend James Morrison (1816–1893) was a Scottish minister expelled from the United Secession Church for unorthodox theology.

few words by way of thanks to the orator. Douglass had described what he was by American law, and contrasting fact with legal right. Dr. Morison – himself an oratory of the highest powers – indignantly asked: "Is this a chattel, is this a thing to be bought and sold?" The emphatic "No!" with which the vast audience answered the interrogation, seems still to reverberate over the waste of years which separate this day from that memorable night.

THE MISSION OF FREDERICK DOUGLASS.

During the past week Frederick Douglass has been quietly sojourning in Newcastle among friends greatly beloved. The old anti-slavery phalanx is now sadly thinned in Northumbria, but a few of the veterans still survive, and by them Douglass has been visited. Speaking with respect to his special work, it may be said "His warfare is accomplished." The foe he fought is vanquished, and peace now lies like a shaft of light across the sea. But in 1846 it was far otherwise. The struggle with slavery had then risen to fever heat in America. Events were nearing a crisis. Ultimately the Supreme Court of the United States decreed that "a slave had no rights which a white man was bound to respect."[3]

At that time, the Disruption in the Scottish Church was still a recent event. The liberality with which its friends had contributed to render it a success, marks an epoch in the development of willinghood. But in quest alike of sympathy and of supplies, several of its most distinguished ministers crossed the Atlantic and sought assistance from the southern slaveholders. When these men sent their dollars to O'Connell, the Liberator sent back the money. It was thought that what O'Connell had done, the leaders of the Free Church should do. Frederick Douglass made it his mission to enforce this view. In a short while, the cry "Send back the money" re-echoed over Scotland. The leaders of the Free Church were men of power, of culture, and of character. But they had made a false step, and in most of the towns and cities of Scotland Frederick Douglass denounced the policy to which they had committed themselves. He quite understood the difficulties of his task, and did not make the mistake of underrating his antagonists. Dr. Chalmers was then in feeble health. His potent eloquence was therefore no longer at command of his friends. The whole weight of the defence fell on Cunningham and Candlish, and it is thus that Douglass speaks of these intellectual gladiators. "No shoulders in the Church were broader than theirs; and I must say, badly as I detested the principles laid down and defended by them, I was compelled to acknowledge the vast mental endowments of the men." Hitherto no one had ventured to confront those who at the call of duty had abandoned the State Church. "The Claim of Right" had remained

---

3   A quote from the Dred Scott decision.

unanswered, and in intellectual force and moral earnestness the Disruption leaders occupied a unique position. But the fugitive slave had touched a weak joint in their armour, and for once their popularity was overshadowed. "'Send back the money,' in huge capitals, stared from every street corner. 'Send back the money' adorned the broad flags of the pavements. 'Send back the money' was the chorus of the popular street song." It was felt that this was virtually a continuation of the old anti-slavery struggle, the slaveholders being no longer Englishmen but Americans. How well Frederick Douglass understood the situation is indicated by a reminiscence of his which vividly recalls the great debates in Tanfield Hall. "Dr. Cunningham rose, and his rising was the signal for tumultuous applause. It may be said that this was scarcely in keeping with the solemnity of the occasion. But, to me, it increased its grandeur and gravity. It seemed thundered up from the vast audience like the fall of an immense shaft flung from shoulders already galled by its weight. The Doctor proceeded with his speech – abounding in logic, learning, and eloquence, and apparently bearing down all opposition; but at the moment – the fatal moment – when he was bringing all his arguments to a point, and that point being that neither Jesus Christ nor his holy apostles regarded slave holding as a sin, George Thompson in a clear, sonorous, but rebuking voice, broke the stillness of the audience, exclaiming, 'Hear! Hear! Hear!' The effect of this simple exclamation was as if a granite wall had been suddenly flung up against the advancing current of a mighty river. For a moment speaker and audience were brought to a dead silence. Both the Doctor and audience seemed appalled by the audacity and the fitness of the rebuke." A few years later Dr. Candlish was thoroughly in sympathy with the struggle of the North.

MANUMISSION.

The fugitive slave had lectured in all the large cities and towns of the United Kingdom, and, in fact, had become a power in England. But though free to go anywhere in the Queen's dominions, he was liable to capture the moment he set his foot on the soil of the Republic. It had not occurred to any one of his numerous friends that it might be well legally to secure the freedom which Frederick Douglass enjoyed. But there were two ladies in Newcastle with practical genius to whom the thought suggested itself, and this is his account of the transaction: – "Miss Ellen Richardson, an excellent member of the Society of Friends, assisted by her sister-in-law, Mrs. Henry Richardson – a lady devoted to every good word and work – the friend of the Indian and the African, conceived the plan of raising a fund to effect my ransom. They corresponded with the Hon. Walter Forward, of Pennsylvania, and through him ascertained that Captain Auld would take £150 sterling for me; and this sum they promptly raised and paid for my liberation, placing the papers of my manumission into my hands before they would tolerate the idea of my return to my native land."

Some people thought this arrangement a violation of anti-slavery principles, and, in fact, a concession of the right to hold property in man. With just as much reason might it be contended that to give a brigand the ransom which he claims for the liberty of his captive is a recognition of brigandage. By this common-sense policy Frederick Douglass was empowered to do in America what he had done in England. By tongue and pen he proved himself an eloquent apostle of emancipation, while as a journalist he was distinguished by equal ability and earnestness. Before the war, he had lectured in every northern town of the Union. He was the confidant of John Brown, and but for a timely retreat to England would have shared the fate of that hero. The story of his bondage was told in a little book published many years ago, and in a volume given to the world in 1881 this story is supplemented by details of his after life.[4]

SUCCESS OF DOUGLASS.

That one born a slave should have become a Marshal of the United States, and held important official appointments under three Presidents, illustrates the marvellous transformation that has taken place in the social and political life of America. Frederick Douglass is now about seventy years of age, and few have known so well the vicissitudes of life. There is a graphic humour in this description of the place of his birth: "In Talbot County, Eastern Shore, State of Maryland, near Easton, the county town, there is a small district of country, thinly populated and remarkable for nothing that I know of more than for the worn-out sandy desert-like appearance of its soil, the general dilapidation of its farms and fences, the indigent and spiritless character of its inhabitants, and the prevalence of ague and fever. It was in this dull, flat, and un-thrifty district or neighbourhood, bordered by the Choptank river, among the laziest and muddiest of streams, surrounded by a white population of the lowest order, indolent and drunken to a proverb, and among slaves who, in point of ignorance and indolence, were fully in accord with their surroundings, that I, without any fault of my own, was born, and spent the first years of my childhood." The mother of Frederick Douglass was a woman of remarkable character, and the only slave in the region where she dwelt who could read. How she acquired that accomplishment her son never knew. But he prefers to trace his love of letters to the African rather than the Anglo-Saxon elements in his nature. His mother was tall and finely proportioned, of dark glossy complexion, and amongst the slaves was remarkably sedate and dignified. These characteristics of the parent have been reproduced in the son. Like many others, ultimately distinguished as orators, Frederick Douglass

---

4 Douglass, *Life and Times of Frederick Douglass* (1881).

was first known as a Methodist local preacher. John Wesley pronounced "slavery the sum of all villainy," and had his followers faithfully upheld that creed Frederick might have been with them to this day.

HIS OLD MASTER.

In the picture of slavery which he gave to the world shortly after his escape, things were said which could not have been very agreeable to his former master. But, though nothing extenuating, neither was there aught set down in malice. It chanced that in revisiting the district where he had been held as a slave, Captain Auld, hearing of the fact, expressed to a friend a desire to see him. Frederick had made the Captain's name and deeds familiar to the world in four languages, yet after four decades had passed, master and slave met again.[5] The fugitive was now United States Marshal of the District of Columbia. "Captain Auld was on his bed, aged and tremulous, drawing near the sunset of life. But, though broken by age and palsy, his mind was clear and strong." The old man, addressing Frederick as Marshal Douglass, had the formal nature of their meeting broken up by this prompt reply, "Not Marshal, but Frederick to you as formerly." The good taste of this greeting was eminently characteristic. Captain Auld, when asked his opinion as to Frederick's escape, said, "I always knew you were too smart to be a slave, and had I been in your place I should have done as you did."

BRITISH ORATORY

When Frederick Douglass was about to visit England for the first time, Wendell Phillips, knowing something of his appreciation of orators and oratory, said to him, "Although Americans are generally better speakers than Englishmen, you will find in England individual orators superior to the best of ours." In his "St. Stephen's," the late Lord Bulwer has a remarkable passage descriptive of the witchery of the Liberator's oratorical powers.[6] But here is an estimate of them by Douglass: "Daniel O'Connell welcomed me to Ireland and to Conciliation Hall, and there I first had a specimen of his truly wonderous eloquence. Until I heard this man, I had thought that the story of his oratory and power were greatly exaggerated. I did not see how anyone could speak to twenty or thirty thousand people and be heard by any consid-

---

5 This brief reunion with former enslaver Thomas Auld occurred at St. Michael's, Maryland, on 17 June 1877.

6 Edward George Earle Lytton Bulwer (1803–1873) published the poem "St. Stephen's" in 1860. It contained praise of Daniel O'Connell's oratory.

erable number of them; but the mystery was solved when I saw his person and heard his musical voice. His eloquence came down upon the vast assembly like a summer thunder shower upon a dusty road. He could stir the multitude at will to a tempest of wrath, or reduce it to the silence with which a mother leaves the cradle side of her sleeping babe."

It is nine months since Frederick Douglass came to Europe. But during the greater portion of that time he has been on the Continent. He has not spoken in England, but in Naples they had a taste of his quality as an orator. To those who heard him while yet the dew of youth was still fresh upon him it would be a surpassing pleasure to hear him anew. Though well stricken in years, Frederick Douglass seems to have lost little of his physical power. It would be almost as hazardous an enterprise now as it proved forty years ago, for the gallant little captain who then proposed to be *one of a number, one of an indefinite number,* to throw Douglass out of the Cambria. Could not some arrangement be made by which in the city where dwell those who secured the manumission of this great man, Newcastle might have an opportunity of listening to his superb eloquence. I understand that the quondam United States Marshal leaves the city to-day for Scotland, but he might perchance be persuaded to return. He has much to tell of all the great movements that have recently taken place in the great Republic. On educational and social problems he has thought long and deeply, while his knowledge of the condition of the coloured population is of the most comprehensive and far-reaching character.

FREDERICK DOUGLAS

Dundee, Scotland, *Dundee Courier*,
22 February 1895, p. 2

By the death of Frederick Douglas, the dark races have lost a warm and enthusiastic friend. It would be difficult to over-estimate the service which Douglas accomplished in the anti-slavery crusade. As an orator he produced a deep effect in this country, and many who before they heard him had but a dim impression of the horrors and shamefulness of slavery, were touched to the quick by his appeals, and became the friends of the slaves, and used their influence to bring about their freedom. It was after one of his visits to Great Britain that his admirers here purchased his liberty for him. He lived long enough to see the gladsome fruits of the Civil War in America, and to congratulate the African race on their emancipation. His life work was a great work well and nobly performed.

OBITUARY

London, England, *Daily News*, 22 February 1895, p. 4

Frederick Douglass – WE publish to-day a telegram announcing the sudden death, in America, of the venerable Frederick Douglass, the famous coloured champion of the freedom of the slave. His history belongs to the great day of Wendell Phillips and Lloyd Garrison, of John Brown, and of Harriet Beecher Stowe.[1] He was born a slave, he died as full of honours as of years. He was an ex-Minister of the United States, and he had held other offices of only inferior dignity. At one time he was a familiar figure on English platforms, and he was regarded on both sides of the Atlantic as the representative of all that was best in his race. The purity of his life and the brilliancy of his talents as an orator and a man of letters, were in themselves, and without regard to the noble ends to which he made them subservient, among his highest services to the negro cause. They showed of what the negro was capable under freedom, fair advantages, and generous treatment. In his early experience he stood for everything that was most tragic in the fate of the slave; in his later career of public honour and of public consideration he showed to what eminence of every kind the despised race wanted only the opportunity to attain. He was born in Maryland, and, as he conjectured in 1817. But he never knew the exact date of his birth, as he never knew so much as the name of his father. His mother was a slave, and that determined his own condition of servitude. He was separated from her when he was still an infant, as though he had been destined from the outset to exhibit in his circumstances all the typical sorrows and miseries of the bondsman's life. Mother and child were on neighbouring plantations, and she died soon after walking twelve miles out and twelve miles home to have a glimpse of her boy.

His earliest recollections were of brutal butcheries of negro men and women, in fits of anger or in mere gusts of temper, which, in other communities, would hardly have justified the killing of a dog. He was taught to read, by the kindness of a lady,

---

1 Harriet Beecher Stowe (1811–1896), US activist and author of *Uncle Tom's Cabin* (1852).

and this part of his education had gone too far to prevent him from doing the rest for himself when his teacher had been warned not to give such dangerous accomplishments to a slave. He was but a lad when he was hired out by his owner for a term of service to a notorious "negro breaker," who undertook to enslave the mind as well as the body by his merciless brutalities. This man tried his hand on his new charge, and at first had matters all his own way. But one day the victim turned, in his desperation of suffering and of shame, and returned the thrashing with so much interest that the cowardly tyrant was glad to escape with his life. The ruffian might easily have called in the aid of the law, but he was unwilling to make public confession of his discomfiture by a boy of sixteen. Douglass soon found a better master, but this did not prevent him from forming plans of escape. He has told us, in his autobiography of his councils with his fellow slaves, and of the system of secret correspondence by which they made seemingly harmless phrases from their hymn books serve as the passwords of their conspiracies for freedom. At length, after one disastrous failure, which nearly cost him his life, he found his opportunity, and, after enduring all sorts of hardships, contrived to plant his feet in the free soil of the North. He married; and he changed the name which had been given to him by his mother to the one by which he was ever afterwards known. He was befriended by Garrison, and by other notable persons, then in the very thick of that dire struggle for emancipation, which was ultimately to find its end in the Civil War. But his friends were hard-pressed, and they were not sufficiently sure of their ground to feel that any part of the United States was a safe harbourage for the runaway. He came to this country, then convulsed by the twin agitations for the Repeal of the Corn Laws and the Repeal of the Union. The leader of the Irish people introduced him to a meeting as "the black "O'Connell," and he became conspicuous among the platform orators of that stirring time. But he soon resolved to return to America to work in the cause of emancipation; and, to give him greater confidence in the venture, his freedom was purchased of his last American owner, by a subscription raised by an English quakeress. It was a rather cumbrous procedure. He was transferred by due form of law from one owner to another, and from the second to himself.

He went back to add Mrs. Stowe, and that sublime fanatic of freedom, John Brown, to the list of his helpers and friends. Brown was soon ready for his desperate and glorious raid of emancipation at Harper's Ferry. He failed, and his reward was the martyr's death. His martyr's blood became the seed of Freedom, and his martyr's name the refrain of the marching song of the conquering North. Douglass was deep in his confidence, and, when he heard of his discomfiture, he fled precipitately across the Canadian border, and finally to England, to escape the vengeance of the slaveowners. The war at length brought him to his final and conclusive reckoning with the enemies of human liberty, and its triumphant termination gave him the full freedom of the soil in the land of his birth. His place in public life was waiting for him. He rose rapidly in honours and in dignities. He was sent on a mission to San Domingo, appointed a Member of Council, and subsequently Marshal, of the District of Columbia, and a representative elector for the State of New York. In later years he was appointed United States Minister to Hayti. No great public celebration of national importance was considered complete without him. As an orator, or as a writer for the Press, his utterances reached to the farthest extremities not only of his own country, but of ours. He had but one great theme – the amelioration of the lot of his race. He pleaded with them as well as for them, and he never ceased to teach them the precious lesson of self-help. "I have aimed," he said, "to assure them that knowledge can be obtained under difficulties; that poverty may give place to competency; that obscurity is not an absolute bar to distinction, and that a way is open to welfare and happiness for all who will resolutely and wisely pursue it; that neither slavery, stripes, imprisonment, nor proscription need extinguish self-respect, crush manly ambition, nor paralyse effort; that races, like individuals, must stand or fall by their own merits; that the fault is not in our stars, but in ourselves, that we are 'underlings,' and that 'who would be free, themselves must strike the blow.'" His final efforts on behalf of his race brethren devoted to that anti-lynching crusade of which Miss Ida Wells[2] in America, and Miss Florence Balgarnie and other ladies of position in this country, are the generous champions.[3] One of his latest literary labours was an article on that cause in the American Church Review, which was justly described as a splendid specimen of impassioned eloquence. From first to last it was a noble life. His own people have lost a father and a friend, and all good men a comrade in the fight, not only for the legal emancipation of one race, but for the spiritual emancipation of all.

---

2   Ida B. Wells-Barnett (1862–1931), US journalist, editor, activist, and anti-lynching campaigner.
3   Florence Balgarnie (1856–1928), English reformer, feminist, and suffragist.

FREDERICK DOUGLASS

Anti-Caste, February 1895
British Library

SPECIAL MEMORIAL NUMBER.

Anti=Caste.

Assumes the Brotherhood of the entire Human Family, and claims for the Dark Races of Mankind
their equal right to PROTECTION, PERSONAL LIBERTY, EQUALITY OF OPPORTUNITY,
AND HUMAN FELLOWSHIP.

| VOL. VII. | APRIL—MAY, 1895. | For Free Distribution. |

FREDERICK DOUGLASS.

SKETCH OF THE LIFE OF FREDERICK DOUGLASS.

CHIEFLY COMPILED FROM HIS AUTOBIOGRAPHY AND A FEW OF HIS LETTERS AND SPEECHES.

CHILDHOOD.

It was probably in the month of February, 1817, that Frederick Douglass, as he afterwards called himself, was born at Tuckahoe, a slave plantation lying on the banks of the Choptank river in Maryland. The farm belonged to Capt. Anthony, who lived twelve miles away, occupying the "Home plantation," and being chief agent for Colonel Edward Lloyd, the owner of a vast estate and a thousand slaves.

Frederick Douglass was the child of a white father, whom he never knew, and a slave mother—a cruelly overworked field hand, tall, dignified, intelligent, even able to read, though how she learned was ever a mystery to her son. Accounted the property of "old master," as much at his disposal as cow and calf, her baby was early taken from her to be brought up with a number of others in charge of its grandmother, who, being a skilful nurse, was allowed the privilege of living in a log cabin apart from the slave "quarters," and supporting herself by fishing, growing vegetables, and making fishing-nets. Those childish days with his kind and clever old grandmother were among the happiest of his life. He remembered that sometimes his tired mother stole in after her long day's work in the fields to see him.

Part IV, no 6 Frederick Douglass, *Anti-Caste*, February 1895 (British Library).

SKETCH OF THE LIFE OF FREDERICK DOUGLASS.
CHIEFLY COMPILED FROM HIS AUTOBIOGRAPHY AND A FEW OF HIS LETTERS AND SPEECHES

Street, England, *Anti-Caste*, 7
(April–May 1895), pp. 1–16[1]

CHILDHOOD.

It was probably in the month of February, 1817, that Frederick Douglass, as he afterwards called himself, was born at Tuckahoe, a slave plantation lying on the banks of the Choptank river in Maryland.[2] The farm belonged to Capt. Anthony, who lived twelve miles away, occupying the "Home plantation," and being chief agent for Colonel Edward Lloyd,[3] the owner of a vast estate and a thousand slaves.

Frederick Douglass was the child of a white father, whom he never knew, and a slave mother – a cruelly overworked field hand, tall, dignified, intelligent, even able to read, though how she learned was ever a mystery to her son. Accounted the property of "old master," as much at his disposal as cow and calf, her baby was early taken from her to be brought up with a number of others in charge of its

---

1   *Anti-Caste* was created and edited by Catherine Impey (1847–1923), an English Quaker and activist who invited Ida B. Wells to Britain in 1893.

2   Throughout his life, Douglass tried in vain to find an accurate record of his birth; he chose Valentine's Day and estimated the year to be 1817, but in reality, his birth year was 1818.

3   Edward Lloyd V (1779–1834) was one of Maryland's largest owners of both plantation land and enslaved people.

grandmother, who, being a skilful nurse, was allowed the privilege of living in a log cabin apart from the slave "quarters," and supporting herself by fishing, growing vegetables, and making fishing-nets. Those childish days with his kind and clever old grandmother were among the happiest of his life. He remembered that sometimes his tired mother stole in after her long day's work in the fields to see him.

When he was seven years old, the poor grandmother, according to orders, took him up to the master's house, a long and tiring walk, during which she gave him many bits of kindly admonition. Playing about the rough kitchen of the house were a number of bigger children, among them an unknown brother and sister of his own, and while he was timidly watching them at play, the poor grandmother slipped away without venturing a goodbye. When the sensitive child discovered that he was left behind, a prolonged passion of grief and despair swept over him, which lasted til, exhausted with sorrow, he at length fell asleep.

IN SLAVERY ON THE HOME PLANTATION.

His experiences of slave life had begun in earnest. The favourite cook of the establishment, a fierce virago, had charge of all the children. Frederick, ill clad, half-starved, cuffed and beaten, used to crawl into an old meal bag for warmth at night, or lie with his feet in the ashes of the kitchen fire. Once in a while the master's daughter, Miss Lucretia,[4] took pity, and gave him a crust of bread and butter, or Col. Lloyd's little son[5] would share a bun with him. Infinitely pathetic is the story he told of the last visit ever paid him by his mother. The woman in charge had refused him food during a whole day in punishment for some childish offence, and at night he was crying with hunger when his mother came in. She had walked the twelve miles after her hard day's work in the fields, and had to hurry back to be in her place when work began at sunrise next morning. He never forgot "the look of deep tender pity in her glance" as she folded him in her arms, nor "her fiery indignation" with the cruel woman. Happily the lecture she read her was never forgotten.

Not far from their master's house stood Col. Lloyd's slave quarters, where, without regard to decency, men and women, young and old, married and single, and swarms of children slept on the common mud floor, – a miscellaneous herd of weary and wretched human beings. In sharp contrast with their embruted condition, Col. Lloyd's family lived at the "Great House" in almost princely magnificence. The stately portico with its rows of pillars, the well-kept lawns, the splendid sweep of the carriage drive, with the beautifully timbered deer park beyond, all greatly impressed

---

4 Lucretia Planner Anthony Auld (1807–1827).
5 Daniel Lloyd (1811–?) was the youngest son of Edward Lloyd V.

the child Frederick. Within the house was a continual scene of feasting. Behind the tall-backed, carved chairs stood fifteen servants – men and maidens – chosen for their grace and agility and captivating address. Some fanned the ladies, others, with their fawn-like steps, anticipated every want on the part of the numberless guests. These servants "constituted a sort of black aristocracy among the slaves,["] in dress as well as in form and feature, in manners and speech, in taste and habits, the distance between these favoured few and the sorry and hunger smitten multitude of the quarters was immense.

The thirty beautiful horses for riding and driving were in charge of two valuable slaves – father and son – who were not ostlers merely, but also veterinaries and farriers. Col. Lloyd, like most slave-owners, was a captious and irritable master, caring far more for the well-being of horses and hounds than for that of his slaves. To the ceaseless fault-finding no explanations were allowed; escape from unmerited humiliation was impossible. One day Frederick was greatly shocked to see the faithful elder foreman made to kneel bare-headed and bare-backed before his angry master while he cruelly lashed him with his riding whip for some trivial offence.

The Colonel once meeting on the high road one of his young slaves who did not recognise him, asked him, "Well, boy, who do you belong to?" "To Col. Lloyd, sir." "Well, does the Colonel treat you well?" "No, sir," was the reply. "What, does he work you hard?" "Yes, sir." "Well, don't he give you enough to eat?" "Yes, sir, he gives me enough to eat, such as it is." The Colonel rode on. For this innocent exposure of his discontent, the poor young fellow, without warning, was torn from his home and friends, and sold to the Georgia traders, whence no slave had ever been known to return, consequently a terrible and dreaded fate to their ignorant minds.

But the worst sufferings came from the vile product of slavery, the overseers, or drivers, of whom there were some thirty employed on this estate – men who, while the slaves toiled wearily on the land, "rode or strutted about, whip in hand, dealing heavy blows that left gashes on the flesh of men and women." Against these brutal and profligate men, appeals to the master were vain. Frederick saw Capt. Anthony roughly dismiss a poor outraged woman who had fled to him covered with blood and bruises from Tuckahoe for protection. The Captain himself, too, committed outrages deep, dark, and nameless. Frederick, from his sleeping place in a cupboard, was once awakened by the piercing cries of a beautiful slave girl, Esther (his own young aunt) whom he could see tied to a beam while his master laid blow on blow of the lash on her soft and tender shoulders as she writhed and shrieked in her agony – the cause of her offence being her faithful attachment to a forbidden negro lover, and her abhorrence of the base overtures of the master.

Such scenes, and others equally terrible, filled the young child's soul with horror and indignation, and deeply impressed him with the brutalizing influences of slavery upon the master class. His Aunty Jenny succeeded in running away. From that day forward Frederick, too, in spirit "ran away." Life seemed unbearable, and, child though he was, he longed to die.

It was thought by many that the slaves were happy when they sang, but the songs sung by the slaves were not songs of joy, he says; – rather, like tears, they gave relief to their aching hearts, and breathed the prayer and complaint of souls overflowing with bitterest anguish.

IN BALTIMORE.

At nine years old a fortunate change took place in the boy's career. He was hired out to a connexion of the family, Mr. Hugh Auld, a ship builder in Baltimore, where he was to be the companion and caretaker of his little boy. Mrs. Auld[6] had never been connected with slavery, and shewed the little stranger great kindness. She was a truly religious woman – very unlike her husband – and once, when reading the Bible to the children, Frederick asked her to teach him to read it. "Without hesitation," he says, "the dear woman began her task." He was quick to learn, and soon mastered his letters and the shorter words, and Mrs. Auld was recounting to her husband her success in making a Bible reader of Frederick, when she was struck dumb by his stern rebuke. It was not only unlawful, but dangerous to teach a slave to read, he said; it made them discontented and likely to run away. Frederick heard all this, and treasured in his heart the idea that education was the key to freedom; although every hindrance was henceforth put in his way, the step could not be recalled, and he soon taught himself not only to read but to write also. At thirteen he bought for himself (with pennies earned by shoe-blacking) a book of speeches of great Englishmen, with a dialogue between a master and his slave, the reading of which still further strengthened his longing for freedom.[7]

During the seven years that he lived in Baltimore, the religious side of his nature became deeply awakened. "I felt a love for all mankind," he says, "slaveholders not excepted, though I abhorred slavery more than ever." He formed a loving attachment to a pious old coloured man named Lawson, "the very counterpart of Uncle Tom," who was a great stay and comfort to him in his young religious life. He also attended a Sunday School for free coloured children; and at night, when others slept, he wrote and studied in his little attic room. By day he now worked in the shipyard.

When he was about sixteen, his owner, Capt. Anthony, died, and the property, including thirty slaves, was called together, valued and apportioned between the son

---

6   Sophia Keithley Auld (1797–1880), wife of Hugh Auld.
7   *The Columbia Orator* (1797), a primer edited by Caleb Bingham.

and daughter (Miss Lucretia, now Mrs. Thomas Auld). Frederick fell to the lot of the daughter; the poor grandmother, now very aged, to the son – a drunken, brutal young man, who built for her a miserable little hut with mud chimney in the woods, and there left her to live or die.

PLANTATION LIFE.

Miss Lucretia had allowed Frederick to go back to Baltimore, but it was not for long, for she died soon after, and a difference having arisen between her husband and his brother, the Mr. Auld, with whom Frederick lived, he was once more torn from friends and home, and put to plantation life near a low, drunken, little fishing village called St. Michaels. Here his life was extremely miserable. The treatment was harsh and exasperating, and his new mistress – for Mr. Auld had already married again – provided such scanty fare for her slaves that they were miserably pinched with hunger, and were almost obliged to steal (or help themselves), from dire necessity. They were allowed to attend the Methodist Church to which the family belonged, but in spite of the high religious professions of their master, the slaves were often shamefully ill-used. The Bible-class which Frederick had started in the village – his one consolation – was broken up by a mob with sticks and staves, led by two Methodist class-leaders and his "Christian" master. A cripple girl, a cousin of Frederick's, was sometimes hung up by her wrists for hours together, and cruelly lashed on the bare back, as if in hope that she might die and be off their hands. Being useless and a burden she was at last given her freedom (to save the cost of her keep).

Burning with indignation, the boy Frederick often *looked* the things he dared not speak, and, at last, his master having become exasperated at his frequent visits to a neighbouring plantation, where he went for bits of food which a kind woman sometimes gave him, and finding that repeated whippings made little impression on the hungry youth, hired him out for a year to one Covey,[8] a notorious "Negro-breaker," a hard and crafty man, who made him drink the cup of slavery to the very dregs. By unspeakable brutality, which kept him stiff and aching in every limb, and by rigorous and ceaseless labour, Frederick was reduced to a state of utter wretchedness, both physical and mental. One terrible day, covered with wounds and drenched in blood, he fled to his owner for protection, only to be sternly ordered back, but when the brutal coward would have tied him down to flog him, the lad in desperation seized his tormentor by the throat and, after a desperate struggle, threw him upon his back in the cow yard. Covey never attempted to beat him again, though he had six months yet to serve.

---

8 Maryland yeoman farmer Edward Covey (1806–1875).

For the following year he was hired to a kinder master – a gentleman – where he revived in spirit, and resumed his Sunday Bible teaching. He and his companions became lovingly attached, but the longing to escape from slavery led five of them, including himself, to make an unsuccessful attempt. On the very morning they had planned to start, they were betrayed and dragged off to jail amid the jeers and shouts of the onlookers. Here, racked with fears as to their future, the victims of insult and indignities from a swarm of loathsome traders who came to inspect them with a view to purchase, they were, after a week of misery, unexpectedly liberated, Mr. Auld sending Frederick back to Baltimore, as the slaveholders of the neighbourhood had threatened to shoot him, unless removed, considering him a dangerous example.

On his return to the city, Frederick was placed in the ship-yards to learn calking, and was soon earning from six to eight dollars a week (24/- to 32/-), all of which he had of course to carry to his master, an injustice to which he was keenly alive. Moreover he soon became an object of fierce and bitter persecution in the ship-yards from the white mechanics, who, in their jealousy of slave labour, made, more than once, a murderous assault upon their unfortunate coloured comrades, in which Frederick barely escaped with his life. He endured these wrongs, though more or less restive under them, for about three years, but in the year 1838, when he was just twenty-one years old, he managed, unobserved, to leave Baltimore behind him, and escape to the city of New York.[9]

COMPARATIVE FREEDOM.

A fugitive, fearful of betrayal, hiding among the barrels on the wharves at night, he was at last taken by a kind sailor to the secretary of the Anti-Slavery Committee, Mr. D. Ruggles,[10] who kindly sheltered him and sent him on to New Bedford, in Massachusetts. But before leaving New York he had sent to the free coloured girl in Baltimore, to whom he had become attached, to meet him, and they were married.

At New Bedford it was somewhat of a shock to him to find that, though they met with many kind friends, he would be unable to work at his trade, owing to the refusal of white artisans to work with him, but must content himself with the earnings of a day labourer. He joined the Methodist Church, but not being allowed to sit with the white members either at the ordinary services or the Lord's Supper, he withdrew, and joined a small body of Coloured Methodists, amongst whom he became a local preacher.

---

9   Douglass could not have escaped slavery without the integral help of his wife Anna Murray. See Douglass (ed. Bernier), *Narrative*, and Fought, *Women in the World of Frederick Douglass*.

10 David Ruggles (1810–1849) was an African American writer, activist, and conductor on the Underground Railroad.

His first introduction to the Anti-Slavery cause was at a Convention held at Nantucket in 1841, under the auspices of the leading Abolitionists, to whom he was as yet unknown. On being called on for a few words he rose, trembling in every limb. W. L. Garrison writing of this first speech says: "I shall never forget the extraordinary emotion it excited in my own mind, the powerful impression it made upon a crowded auditory completely taken by surprise. There stood one in physical proportions and stature commanding respect, in intellect richly endowed."

At the close of the Convention the Committee of the Massachusetts Anti-Slavery Society engaged this surprising young orator as one of their agents, and forthwith he entered upon his public life. Their cause was terribly unpopular, but in spite of this and the ceaseless persecution to which he was subjected on account of his colour – again and again being dragged from the cars, refused accommodation at hotels and lodging-houses, or berth on the steamboats, forcibly removed from public dining tables, chased, threatened by mobs, even in one instance (and this was worse than all) left without food or shelter in an unfriendly city by the very Anti-Slavery friends under whose auspices his speeches were delivered – still he continued everywhere to plead the cause of those whom he had left behind in slavery.

His power was promptly felt in the United States, and "under the influence of his devouring theme he became one of the finest orators of America."

IN ENGLAND.

In 1845, leaving wife and children in America, he came to England with the object of concentrating against American slavery the moral and religious sentiment of its people, then eminently clear and strong on the subject, in consequence of having but recently passed through our own long Anti-Slavery struggle. Thousands flocked to hear him, and the counsel and sympathy of the veterans of their great victory in the West Indies cheered and strengthened his course.

This enthusiasm in the cause of liberty, and the respect with which he was welcomed in England, contrasted so strongly with his "long and bitter experience in the United States," that he looked with amazement on the transition. "I live a new life," he wrote in a letter to W. L. Garrison; "No longer a fugitive slave, liable to be hunted any moment like a felon, no longer doomed by inveterate prejudice to insult and outrage . . . I am seated beside white people, I am shown into the same parlours, I eat at the same tables and no one is offended, and when I go to church I am met by no scornful lip to tell me 'We don't allow niggers in here.'"

Resolutions were passed at his great English meetings urging the religious bodies of Great Britain to refrain from all fellowship with slave-holding Churches in America. The great Free Church of Scotland – then but just freeing itself from State control, and heroically forfeiting support from State funds – had just accepted a rich contribution from these slave-holding American Churches. When Douglass came to their assembly with his vivid picture of slavery a cry arose to send back the blood-stained offering from the Southern States. "Send back the money!" became the watchword for a great and brave effort at non-complicity on the part of a large minority, but alas, the need of money was pressing, policy prevailed, and the money was kept.

In the State of Indiana a large section of the Society of Friends had repudiated the action of their Yearly Meeting (Annual Assembly), on account of its action in proscribing the whole of its members engaged in the Abolition movement, and prohibiting the use of meeting-houses for Abolition meetings; England's "Yearly Meeting" – being but incompletely informed, and owing to distance but partially alive to the vital issues involved – had sent a deputation to make peace. Great indignation was felt by Garrison, Douglass and other leaders of the Anti-Slavery cause, when this deputation, instead of reproving the lamentable action of the majority, treated that of the brave party of protest as an unjustifiable schism, urging their return to (unconditional) allegiance!

In Bristol a special meeting, attended by thousands of people, was held to hear F. Douglass speak on the attitude of the Churches to the Anti-Slavery cause – so we see from an old Bristol newspaper of the day (1845).[11] George Thomas presided, and Elihu Burritt was among the speakers. The policy of total non-complicity on the part of England for which Douglass pleaded was applauded to the echo; those who were put forward as apologists were few, and seemed ashamed of their cause.

Before his return to the United States, where he was liable, if recognised, at any moment to re-capture, two Quaker ladies at Newcastle, Ellen and Anna Richardson, raised the £150 purchase money needed to release him from the claims of his so-called owner, Mr. Thos. Auld, and set him free.

This visit of Douglass to England was pronounced by the Anti-Slavery leaders in America to have "rendered most valuable services to the cause of his oppressed countrymen."

RETURN TO AMERICA.

It was extremely painful to Frederick Douglass even on board the vessel by which he returned to America to be met with rude exhibitions of prejudice from fellow passengers. He was, however, too great a man, too full of inspiring purpose, to be turned aside by the smallness of others. The more his way was hedged in by unjust restrictions, the more stoutly did he strive to cut a way through – not for himself alone,

---

11   This address occurred at the Broadmead Public Rooms in Bristol on 2 September 1846.

but that he might clear the path for others of his colour. He lived for his people and humanity. "I never rise before an American audience," he said, "without something of a feeling that my failure or success will bring blame or benefit to my whole race."

Besides making him a free man his friends in England had given him a printing press, believing with him, that a good newspaper edited and managed by a Negro, would go far to refute the charge of the intellectual inferiority of the race. It was painful that his New England friends, incredulous of his success, entirely disapproved the scheme. Still he persevered, and settling at Rochester, near Lake Ontario, he began to publish his *North Star*, afterwards called *Frederick Douglass' Paper*, and resolutely continued his struggle for human rights.

"As the Anti-Slavery cause gained in strength, the opposition to it became more powerful . . . Prominent men opposed it, and this gave encouragement to the lower classes who possessed the mob spirit. When Frederick Douglass made his first lecturing tour through the West he had to contend with prejudice expressed in the most insulting manner." (See *Reminiscences of an Abolitionist* by Levi Coffin.[12]) The whole party was subject to violent attack, their meetings were dispersed, their lives endangered, but their courage rose proportionately.

While in the Northern States the human rights of the Negroes were being thus nobly advocated, Southern politicians fiercely and furiously maintained that the slave-holders' property in human flesh was part of the "property" to which "protection" was guaranteed by the Constitution, and could not be interfered with without violation of national pledges and national honour, forgetting that underneath the Constitution lay the noble Declaration of Independence, in which it was declared that *all men* were born free and equal, and had an equal right to life, liberty, and the pursuit of happiness. As slavery had existed prior to the Union, and the adoption of the Constitution, there were many even in the North who held that there was some ground for Southern contention, and in the year 1850 the nation, instead of repairing its past neglect of the Negro's rights, determined to conciliate the angered Slave Power by adopting the "Fugitive Slave Law," whereby the nation, pledged itself to return to slavery those free coloured people who had escaped in past years from their oppressors and had made themselves houses in the Northern States.

One of the darkest chapters of American history is that in which these trusting people were allowed to be hunted down by officers of the law, or by kidnappers under cover of law, and resold into captivity, even the Northern pulpit endorsing this policy. Thousands of fugitives fled into Canada, while at risk of their lives and liberty Douglass and old Levi Coffin, and a number of sturdy Quakers and other

---

12   Levi Coffin (1798–1877) was a US Quaker, author, abolitionist, and conductor on the Underground Railroad.

Abolitionists scattered through the country, sheltered and secretly helped these parties of fugitives on their way, many humane persons contributing in money or in kind towards the cost entailed.

These were anxious times, and led to the formation among the Abolitionists of what became known as "the Underground Railroad," a system of secretly transferring the fugitives from shelter to shelter, Douglass's home at Rochester being *one* of their regular stations or depôts.

Writing, lecturing, travelling hither and thither, persecuted, mobbed, Douglass's life was one ceaseless battle against slavery and proscription. It was said by coloured travelers that they could feel the influences of his humanizing work for fifty miles round Rochester.

"In the midst of these fugitive slave troubles came Mrs. Stowe's *Uncle Tom's Cabin*, with its marvelous depth and power, to touch the American heart." It seemed to the Abolitionists "an inspired production . . . Its effect was instantaneous and universal."

Mrs. Stowe, who had become an object of interest and admiration, was soon afterwards invited to England. But before leaving home she sent for F. Douglass to confer with him as to how she might best contribute part of the money she expected to receive for the permanent good of the coloured race.

A School and workshops for teaching handicrafts to the "free" coloured people of the North was what he earnestly advised. These people, he urged (and alas! this is still largely their condition in Northern States), were "shut out from all lucrative employments, and compelled to work at wages so low that they could lay up little or nothing. Their poverty kept them ignorant, and their ignorance kept them degraded." . . . "Colleges have been opened to coloured youths in this country during the last dozen years, he adds, yet the few comparatively who have acquired a classical education . . . have found themselves educated far above a living condition, there being no methods by which they could turn their learning to account . . . White people will not employ them to the obvious embarrassment of their cause . . . Hence educated coloured men . . . are at a very great discount."

"There is little reason to hope that any considerable number of free coloured people will ever be induced to leave this country, he adds, even if such a thing were desirable. The black man (*unlike* the Indian) loves civilization. He likes to be in the midst of it, and prefers to share its most galling evils to encountering barbarism. Dear Madam, we are *here*, and here we are likely to remain. Individuals emigrate – nations never."

"Prejudice against the free coloured people in the United States has shown itself nowhere so invincible as among mechanics. The farmer and the professional man cherish no feeling so bitter as that cherished by these. The latter would starve us out of the country entirely. At this moment I can more easily get my son into a lawyer's office to study law, than I can do into a blacksmith's shop to blow the bellows and wield the sledge hammer. Denied these means of learning useful trades, we are pressed into the narrowest limits to obtain a livelihood.

We once enjoyed a monopoly in menial employments, but even these are rapidly passing out of our hands. "The fact is that coloured men must learn trades; must find new employments, new modes of usefulness to society, or they must decay under the pressing wants to which their condition is rapidly bringing them." . . .

"We have our orators, authors, and other professional men, but these reach only a certain class, and get respect for our race only in certain select circles. To live here as we ought, we must fasten ourselves to our fellow-countrymen through their everyday cardinal wants. We must not only be able to *black* boots, but to *make* them. At present we are unknown in the Northern States, as mechanics, and the fact that we make no show of our ability is held conclusive of our inability to make any; hence all the indifference and contempt with which incapacity is regarded fall upon us, and that too when we have had no means of disproving the infamous opinion of our natural inferiority."

"Now, firmly believing as I do that there are skill, invention, power, industry and real mechanical genius among coloured people, which only need the means to develop them, I am decidedly in favour of the establishment of such a college or institution as I have named."

We regret to say that Mrs. Stowe, although warmly approving the proposal at the time, on her return to America appears to have entirely abandoned this excellent and practically beneficent scheme.

Douglass was constantly accused by the South of fomenting insurrection among the slaves. He was well known to be in frequent intercourse with John Brown, and after the defeat of "that noble-hearted fanatic," Governor Wise, of Virginia, on behalf of the enraged slaveholders, sent a requisition to the Governor of Michigan, demanding the person of Frederick Douglass. Although he had always dissuaded John Brown from his raid on Harper's Ferry, so great was the excitement and so little was justice to be expected from a court of slave-holders should he be captured by them, that he left the country and again spent a time in England.

The death of his beloved daughter Annie,[13] "the light and life" of his house, caused him to return home about six months later, though this was not generally known at the time. He found the country much quieter. John Brown had behaved so nobly in the face of death – when confession had been looked for, uttering grand words of rebuke and warning to the nation, that already he was looked upon as a

---

13 Annie Douglass (1849–1860), fifth child of Frederick and Anna Murray Douglass, who tragically died after John Brown's rebellion and during her father's tour of Britain 1859–60.

martyr in the North, and the John Brown song – saying that though his body was mouldering, his soul was marching on, was being sung all over the land. "What the South slew last December (wrote Victor Hugo) was not John Brown, but slavery. Between the North and South stands the gallows of Brown – Union is no longer possible, such a crime cannot be shared."[14]

THE WAR.

F. Douglass had never fully embraced the Peace principles of his early friends, Whittier[15] and Garrison, and when, in the spring following his return, the war between North and South broke out, believing that the triumph of the North would involve the destruction of Slavery, he flung himself into the struggle. It was largely through his efforts that free coloured men were at length *allowed* to enlist on equal terms (though in separate regiments) – to wear the same uniform, share the same dangers and responsibilities, and ultimately receive the same pay, as their white comrades.

When thus given equal opportunity, their conduct and courage were so marked that a distinct step towards their recognition as men among men, was felt to have been gained. Hitherto they had merely been thought of as cheap material for economizing the lives of white soldiers in fever districts, perilous positions, &c., and had been paid at half the regular rate.

During this war time, Douglass, by his manly and unselfish care for the rights of others, won the friendship and high regard of Abraham Lincoln, who found in him a wise and helpful counsellor in all that concerned the race. President Lincoln, Douglass tells us, was "pre-eminently the white man's President." Though he hated slavery, yet he thought it was "in the bond" and was "ready and willing at any time during the first years of his administration to deny, postpone, sacrifice the rights of humanity in the coloured people, to promote the welfare of the white people of the country." "The race to which we belong was not his special object," he says again "he shared the prejudices common to his countrymen towards the coloured race."[16]

The notion "that they were fighting an abolition war" was at first scornfully denied by the North, and for three years, had the South accepted the terms of peace that were offered, the North would have conceded the right of the Slaveholder to hold property in his fellow men. Lincoln's Proclamation emancipated only the

---

14   French novelist Victor Hugo (1802–1885) wrote this description about John Brown in a 2 December 1859 letter to *The Times* of London.

15   John Greenleaf Whittier (1807–1892), journalist, abolitionist, and poet.

16   Douglass originally made these remarks in a speech at the dedication of the Freedmen's Memorial to Lincoln in Washington, DC, in 1877.

slaves of those in rebellion against the National Government, yet "There's a divinity that shapes our ends, rough hew them how we will"; and at the close of this terrible and bloody civil war, Slavery, in so far as it existed by *law*, had been abolished.

"Can any coloured man ever forget," said Douglass, "the night which followed the first day of January, 1863, when the world was to see if Abraham Lincoln was as good as his word? I shall never forget that memorable night, when in a distant city (Boston), I waited and watched at a public meeting with three thousand others not less anxious than myself for the word of deliverance. Nor shall I ever forget the outburst of joy that rent the air when the lighting brought to us the emancipation proclamation." We were too thankful to criticise.

AN OLD LETTER.

A discoloured letter lies before me, written by F. Douglass to a friend in England, from Rochester, April 20, 1865, the time of Lincoln's Assassination.

Its tone reflects the gloom into which the nation was plunged by this terrible and cowardly act, and the writer's sorrow at the death of so kind and amiable a friend.

Amid the general gloom, however, there came to Douglass and his race a sense also of an averted danger, and apprehension lest "Lincoln in his extreme amiability towards his white opponents, might, if confronted with apparent repentance on their part endorse a re-union on terms that '*boded no good to the coloured race.*' Once let the South ask for terms as a condition of return to the Union, then will be the real trial of Northern virtue," says the letter, "I believe," it adds, "that Mr. Johnson (the suddenly promoted Vice-President), understands better than Lincoln did the necessity of putting down not only slavery, but the slave power, which owning the land of the South, possessing the influence which education gives, and which it has so long wielded, as an aristocracy in favour of slavery, would be dangerous to liberty even after the fall of slavery. This, Mr. Johnson (himself a Southerner), will understand. *I hope much of him.* I hope he will see to it that the negro is made everyway equal before the laws of the South; without the ballot freedom for the negro in the Slave States will be but little better than a name.". . .

"You speak of the efforts in behalf of freed men. My opinion is that all such efforts would be rendered unnecessary in two years after the war, if the American people will give the negro the elective franchise. The great evil is that the American people desire to make their pity a substitute for justice. I want you and other good friends of my race in England, to be on the look out for those [presumably white men. Ed. *Anti-Caste*] who come to ask alms of you in the name of my race, to tell them *from me* that they would do far better to work for the negro by staying at home, and exerting their influence in favour of giving the negro the means of protecting himself by giving him the ballot box. We have been greatly wronged as slaves. We are not likely to be equally wronged by persons in the garb of friendship, representing us as a helpless race. Truly, yours always,

FREDERICK DOUGLASS."

In a postscript he adds . . . "I have lived this winter (1864–5), almost constantly on railroads and platforms. Never was more sought for, and listened to with more interest . . . ."

THE FREEDMEN.

It was not long after the above letter was written that the war was brought to an end, and slavery finally prohibited by the organic law of the land.

For a short time Douglass felt a strain of sadness mingling with his exceeding joy. His occupation seemed gone, his voice no longer wanted, the great happiness he had enjoyed of meeting with kindred spirits in the great work was to be a memory only. He thought of buying a little farm and tilling it. But at this juncture unexpected invitations began to pour in from colleges, literary societies, etc., some offering him a hundred and even two hundred dollars (£40), for a single lecture on social and historical topics. He gladly entered upon this new field of labour, finding in it a double satisfaction "for that in this too I was in some measure helping to lift my race into consideration" he says.

I soon found that "the negro had still a cause," he adds, "and that he needed my voice and pen with others to plead for it. The American Anti-Slavery Society, under the lead of Mr. Garrison, had disbanded, its newspapers were discontinued, and all systemic effort by abolitionists abandoned. Many of the Society, Mr. Wendell Phillips and myself amongst the number, differed from Mr. Garrison as to the wisdom of this course. I felt that the work of the Society was not done, that it had not fulfilled its mission, which was not merely to emancipate, but to elevate the enslaved class; but against Mr. Garrison's leadership, and the surprise and joy occasioned by the emancipation, it was impossible to keep the association alive, and the cause of freedom was left mainly to individual effort and to hastily extemporized societies of an ephemeral character brought together under benevolent impulse but having no history behind them . . ."

Though legalized slavery was abolished, the wrongs of his people were not ended. Their condition was in fact most pitiable. It is true they were freed from bondage to any one master, (such is the freedom of a dog without an owner), and their children were their own, and could not be sold from them. But how did their liberty fare, and how did they live? The land all belonged to their masters. In Russia when the serfs were freed, each was granted three acres of ground. Here three millions of people of all ages, men, women, children, aged persons, young infants, had found themselves turned loose, naked, homeless, penniless, hungry, under the bare sky, "free" to starve or return to their wrathful masters, – who had resented their emancipation as an act of hostility to themselves and were still more embittered by the fact of some of their class having borne arms against them, – and beg them such insufficiency of food and covering as they might deign to offer. The thought of paying cash for labour that hitherto they could extort by the lash was foreign to the men of whom they had to seek employment, and "freed men" though they were, they were powerless to negotiate fair terms.

Seeing their opportunity, the owners of the soil offered them land on shares, the tenants to do the work, the landowner to lend tools, and advance necessary food, etc., till the crop ripened, then to have a settlement. The crop is sold, the master pockets the whole money, and is careful moreover to show a balance in his own favour in the account. He has "charged for rent a sum that would have bought the land, has charged four times its price for each pound of bacon" and so forth; and now if the tenant attempts to quit, he finds he is in a net. He can be arrested for leaving in debt, or perhaps if troublesome will be shot, for the negro was always in the eyes of his soul-degraded masters, a sort of cattle with "no rights that the white man is bound to respect."

Under this terrible system (which largely prevails to-day in the rural districts of the South, although here and there, especially in districts where it has been possible to purchase land, somewhat better conditions prevail), the ardent hopefulness inspired of freedom drooped; it was all hopeless poverty, hopeless debt, where was the use of hard work?[17]

THE STRUGGLE FOR NEFRO SUFFRAGE.

Douglass foresaw all this and more, he knew that "no class of men, however humane, can be safely trusted with absolute power over the liberties of any other class." He saw that he to whom it can be said "you shall work for me or starve," is in bitter truth a slave, and the man who can say it his master. From the first he saw "no chance of bettering the condition of the freedman except he should cease to be a freedman, and should become a citizen, possessed of civil powers wherewith to protect and maintain [h]is new-born freedom." Douglass was a staunch believer in the Republican form of government, and he recognized, as many do not, that not in any race or sex, nor in any physical qualifications lie the basis of true Government, but in moral intelligence, and the ability to discern good from evil, right from wrong, and the power to choose between them. When their ignorance was urged "I used to answer, if the negro knows the way to pay taxes, he knows enough to vote, and if he knows

---

17 "It is important to note, however, that while vast masses are still helplessly in the grip of the landowner, education goes on apace. From 185 colleges, 75,000 teachers and graduates have gone forth throughout the towns and cities of the South as teachers, preachers, doctors, lawyers, and the like."

as much when sober as an Irishman knows when drunk, he knows enough to vote," moreover "the ballot in his hands is necessary to open the doors of the school."

With the whole force and energy of his nature he gave himself to the advocacy of the new demand – suffrage for the negro – a demand so vastly in advance of those hitherto made for the negro, at first struck men as preposterous. Even W. L. Garrison was not quite ready for it, though Wendell Phillips not only saw the justice, but the necessity of the measure, and gave it his full support. The agitation grew with surprising rapidity.

Unintentionally President Johnson brought the question fully before the nation by the repellent attitude he assumed towards a deputation of prominent coloured men, of whom Douglass was chief spokesman. After hearing the purport of their visit he had made them a long hostile speech and then abruptly dismissed them without permitting a reply. They at once, on retiring, issued their reply through the press, reminding him and the nation that "peace between races is not secured by giving power to one race and withholding it from another, but by maintaining a state of equal justice between all classes."

The question now took its place among the practical politics of the day. Ere long a committee of the Senate was reporting upon it and recommending that it be dealt with according to the option of the several States, a measure stoutly opposed by Douglass and others, who presented to the Senate in person, a great memorial against it, and by the efforts of Senator Sumner, and other friends of the race, it was defeated. Sumner – of whom Douglass speaks as "the most clear-sighted, brave, and uncompromising friend of my race who had ever stood upon the floor of the Senate, and was to me a loved, honoured, and precious personal friend, a man possessing the exalting and matured intellect of a statesman, with the pure and artless heart of a child."

Another great incident of the struggle for the suffrage was when in 1866, F. Douglass was elected by the city of Rochester, as its representative to the National Loyalist Convention at Philadelphia, "a city remarkable for the depth and bitterness of its hatred of the abolition movement, where Anti-Slavery meetings were mobbed, and Pennsylvania Hall burned down for opening its doors to people of different colour on terms of equality!"[18] Douglass's election was clamourously opposed by the Republicans, who feared it would bring on their party the charge of favouring amalgamation and social equality. Influential deputations waited on him on his way to the Convention, to urge him to retire, knowing "as he must do, that there was a

---

18　An anti-Andrew Johnson political meeting held on 4–7 September 1866. An anti-abolitionist mob burned down this building on 17 May 1838 to prevent it from hosting a female antislavery convention.

strong and bitter prejudice against his race in the North, as well as the South." He firmly declined to withdraw, however, and proceeded to Philadelphia, where a new difficulty awaited him, a monster procession of the delegates was to walk two and two through the city. Douglass stood among the gathering assemblage alone and shunned by all, till at last, a young man named Theodore Tilton,[19] poet, scholar, and editor of the weekly journal with the largest circulation of any in New York, came to him in his isolation, and seizing him by the hand in a most brotherly way, proposed to walk with him in the procession. "I have been in many awkward and disagreeable positions in my life," Mr. Douglass wrote years afterwards, "but I think I never appreciated an act of courage and generous sentiment more highly that I did that of this brave young man. How was my presence regarded by the populace? I will tell you, the people had made more progress than their leaders. An act for which those leaders expected to be pelted with stones only brought them unmeasured applause. Along the whole line of march my presence was cheered repeatedly and enthusiastically. I was myself utterly surprised." Negro franchise became the burning question of the occasion; on it the Convention split.

Called on by the Pro-suffrage party to speak, Douglass responded with all the energy of his soul. He says, "For I looked upon the suffrage to the negro as the only means which could prevent him from being thrust back into slavery."

It was reserved for "President Grant,[20] with his characteristic nerve and clear perceptions of justice," to finally recommend to the Senate the 14th and 15th amendments to the Constitution, by which coloured men are to-day invested with the right to vote and be voted for in the American Republic.

SOUTHERN ATROCITIES.

On the South there fell a sullen silence – the masters holding fiercely aloof from the public office, and compelling the freedmen all unaided to legislate for both. (Be it remembered to the honour of these that amidst all the blunders and shortcomings of their short reign it was they who gave to the South her public school system, for hitherto she had none.) All too quickly the storm burst, a wild tornado of persecution and slaughter. White men held no trick too mean, no deed too atrocious that might once more secure to them their solid supremacy, and many hundreds of the brightest and bravest of the coloured race were horribly murdered.

---

19 Theodore Tilton (1835–1907), US poet, journalist, and abolitionist.
20 Ulysses S. Grant (1822–1885), general in the Union Army during the American Civil War and
    18th president of the United States (1869–77).

With horror and indignation at his heart over the outrages attendant on their enfranchisement, Douglass still held that unutterably worse would it have been for them had the nation withheld "the means of self-protection granted to others, making the rich strong and the poor weak." The evils he believed would be temporary, the good attained permanent. The fact that the old master-class felt that their interests were opposed, was to his clear mind a powerful reason for their enfranchisement. "Until it shall be safe," he said, "to leave the lamb in the den of the lion . . . it will not be safe to leave a newly-emancipated people completely in the power of their former masters, especially when such masters have not ceased to be such from enlightened moral convictions, but by irresistible force."

DOUGLASS REMOVES TO WASHINGTON.

During that spell of "Negro supremacy," as it was called, Douglass was earnestly urged to remove to some Southern district and stand for Congress, but his increasing years, and his repugnance to "living among people in order to gain their votes" induced him not to yield to the temptation. He believed that the Southern freedman needed his voice more in the Northern States, where, as he said, he had an audience ready made, than in the halls of Congress.

When, however, some time later, a weekly paper in the interest of their cause was needed at the National Capital he consented to become its editor, and to take up his abode at Washington, where he lived for the remainder of his life.

On his departure from Rochester a loving tribute was paid to him by his friends, his marble bust being placed in the hall of the University. They wrote of him that "great in his gifts, he was greater in utilising them; great in his inspirations he was greater in his efforts for humanity; great in the persuasion of his speech, yet greater in the purpose that informed it."

Appointed to various posts of honour by succeeding Presidents, his pen and voice were still ceaselessly exerted in behalf of human rights.

SPEECH AT WASHINGTON.

Speaking of the then condition of his people at a great public meeting held at Washington in April, 1886, F. Douglass indignantly refers to the disregard of their rights by the nation. The following are a few brief extracts from this memorable address, taken from a local paper of the day: –

(In the South) "Lynch law, violence and murder [are as frequent as before] and without the least show of federal interference or popular rebuke. The Constitution has been openly violated with the usual impunity, and the coloured vote has been as completely nullified (suppressed) as if the fifteenth amendment [conferring the franchise] formed no part of the Constitution, and as if every coloured citizen of the South had been struck dead by lighting."

"The number of outrages committed against the civil rights of coloured citizens [travelling] by land and water, and by the courts of the country, under the decision of the Supreme Court of the United States, have shown the same disposition to punish the innocent and shield the guilty as during the (former) Presidency. While I gratefully remember the important services of the Republican party in emancipating and enfranchising the coloured people of the United States I do not forget that the work of that party is most sadly incomplete . . . We are yet as a people only half free. The promise of liberty remains unfulfilled. We stand to-day only in the twilight of American liberty. *The mission of the Republican party will not be ended until the persons, the property and the ballot of the coloured man shall be as well protected in every State of the American Union as are such rights in the case of white men.*"

. . . "The Preamble to the Constitution of the United States, as adopted by the founders of the Republic in 1789, sets forth the cardinal objects to be attained as follows: –

First. – To form a more perfect Union.
Second. – To establish justice.
Third. – To provide for the common defense.
Fourth. – To ensure domestic tranquility.
Fifth. – To promote the general welfare.
Sixth. – To secure the blessings of liberty to ourselves and our posterity.

Perhaps there never was an instrument framed by men at the beginning of any national career designed to accomplish nobler objects than these. They are objects worthy of those who gave to the world the immortal "Declaration of Independence," in which they asserted the equal rights of man, and boldly declared in face of all the divine-right Governments of Europe, the doctrine that Governments derive their right to govern from the consent of the governed." . . . I now undertake to say that neither the Constitution of 1789, nor the Constitution as amended since the war is the law of the land. *So far as the coloured people of the country are concerned the Constitution is but a stupendous sham.*"

[Both political parties] "have promised us law and abandoned us to anarchy, and the Federal Government so far as we are concerned has abdicated its functions. When, where and how has any attempt been made to enforce or establish justice in any one of the late Slave-holding States?

. . . "According to the highest legal authorities justice is the perpetual disposition to secure to every man by due process of law, protection to his person, his property and his political rights[.] Due process of law has a definite and legal meaning. It means the right to be tried in open court by a jury of one's peers and before an impartial judge. It means that the accused shall be brought face to face with his accusers; that he shall be allowed to call witnesses as in his defence, and that he shall have the assistance of counsel. It means that preceding his trial he shall be safe in the custody of the Government, and that no harm shall come to him for any alleged offence till he is fairly tried, convicted and sentenced by the Court. This protection is given to the vilest white criminal in the land. He cannot be convicted while there is even a reasonable doubt in the minds of the jury as to his guilt. But to the coloured man accused of crime in the Southern States a different rule is almost everywhere applied. With him to be accused is to be convicted. The Court in which he is tried is a lynching mob. This mob takes the place of "due process of law," of judge, jury, witness and counsel. It does not come to ascertain the guilt or innocence of the accused, but to hang, shoot, stab, burn or whip him to death. Neither courts, jails nor marshals are allowed to protect him. Every day brings us tidings of these outrages. Their name is legion.[21] Everybody knows that what I say is true, and that no power is employed by the Government to prevent this lawless violence.

. . . "I appeal to our white fellow-country-men. The power to protect is in their hands. If they can protect the rights of white men they can protect the rights of black men. If they can defend the rights of American citizens abroad they can defend them at home . . . The only trouble is the will! the will! the will! Here as elsewhere, 'Where there's a will there's a way.'

"As to removing the people *en masse* from the South, I for one say 'Away with such impotent substitutes for the justice and protection due to us.' The first duty that the National Government owes to its citizens is protection.

. . . "We are used to the shedding of innocent blood, and the heart of this nation is torpid, if not dead, to the natural claims of justice and humanity, where the victims are of the coloured race . . . Where are the defenders of the Constitution? What hand in the House or Senate, what voice in all our Court or Cabinet is uplifted to stay this tide of violence, blood, and barbarism? It is the old story verified;

> 'Vice is a monster of such frightful mien;
> That to be hated, needs but to be seen;
> But seen too oft, familiar with its face,
> We first endure, then pity, then embrace.'[22]

Our chief magistrates and other officers continue to go through the solemn mockery of swearing by the name of Almighty God, that they will execute the laws and the

---

21   Douglass quotes Mark 5:9.
22   Douglass quotes from "An Essay on Man" by Alexander Pope (1688–1744).

Constitution, (but) neither Governors, Presidents, nor Statesmen have yet declared that these barbarities shall be stopped. On the contrary, they all confess themselves powerless to protect our class."

"In view of this confessed impotency of the Government, and this apparent insensibility of the nation to claims of humanity, do you ask me why I expend time and breath in denouncing these wholesale murders? I answer, 'How can any man with a heart in his breast do otherwise, when louder than the blood of Abel the blood of his fellow-men cries from the ground?'

"In other days we had a potent voice in the South – Sumner, Wilson, Conkling and others.[23] These did not exhaust the justice and humanity of American States-manship. There is heart and eloquence still left in the councils of the nation, and these will, I trust, yet make themselves potent in having both the Constitution of 1789 and the Constitution with the fourteenth and fifteenth amendments made practically the law of the land for all the people thereof."

LAST VISIT TO EUROPE.
INTERVIEWED BY "DAILY NEWS."

In the year 1884, Mr. Douglass being then a widower, had married miss Helen Pitts,[24] one of those brave Northern women, who, after the war, had gone into the South as teachers among the Freedmen.

Two years later, in 1886–7, he brought his wife with him, on his third visit to Europe – this time to rest[25] . . .

VISITS STREET.

My own first call on Mr. Douglass was during this same visit of his to England. He was then in London. Our conversation was largely on the colour question, and Mr. Douglass seemed surprised to find English people so deeply concerning them-selves with the question of the negroes' rights, and said in his fatherly fashion, "My child, I am very much interested, I want to see you again." To my great plea-sure I found that he was about to visit Mrs. Helen Bright Clark, at Street, and a few weeks later Mrs. Clark kindly invited her friends and neighbours to meet and spend the evening with Frederick Douglass. During the evening Mr. Douglass

---

23 Massachusetts politician Henry Wilson (1812–1875) represented that state in the US Senate from 1855 until his election as Grant's second vice president. Roscoe Conkling (1829–1888) repre-sented New York in the House and Senate and was one of Douglass's allies in the Republican Party.

24 Helen Pitts Douglass (1838–1903) became Douglass's second wife in 1884, after the death of Anna Murray in 1882.

25 Impey quotes from the London Daily News article, published earlier in the volume.

gave us a luminous half-hour's address on the present condition of the coloured population in America, speaking of the caste barriers that everywhere blocked their way, of the iniquitous truck system, their oppression and their total inability to protect themselves without the ballot, of which they had been deprived by cruel persecution, and the fraudulent manipulation of the ballot boxes.

The gloom of this picture was only relieved by his trust in God, who had brought his people so far out of their bondage in the past, and surely would not desert them till their emancipation was complete. Looking upon the waters of the Atlantic he had thought, he said, how Humanity was "One, like the ocean, though many and varied as its heaving waves."

Before we separated he asked me never again to visit America without paying him and his wife a visit at their home on Anacostia Heights (near Washington),[26] an invitation which it was my privilege to accept in the autumn of 1892. I venture on another page to append a few leaves from my journal at the time. In a letter home I wrote, "We have been a large party of coloured and white (most valuable experience[)] . . . F. Douglass says I *must* come again next summer for us to hold a convention on the new movement!" [Referring to the National Citizens' Rights movement, inaugurated by Judge Tourgée,[27] of which we had been talking hopefully during the latter days of my stay.][28]

LAST WORDS ON POLITICS. HIS DEATH.

Mr. Douglass was profoundly moved by the report brought to him by Miss Ida B. Wells of the growth of lynching outrages in the South, from whence she came bearing her living and lurid testimony of what she had seen and searched into.

"Brave Woman!" he wrote of her, "you have done your people and mine a service which can be neither weighed nor measured. There has been no word equal to yours in convincing power. I have spoken, but my word is feeble in comparison.

"If the American conscience were only half alive; if the American Church and Clergy were only half christianized; if American moral sensibility were not hardened by persistent infliction of outrages and crime against coloured people, a scream of horror, shame and indignation would rise to heaven whenever your pamphlet shall be read!"[29]

---

26 In 1878 Douglass purchased a 15-acre estate, which he and Anna named Cedar Hill, in the Anacostia neighborhood of the District of Columbia.

27 Albion W. Tourgée (1838–1905), US lawyer, civil rights activist, and writer.

28 *Anti-Caste* met with Douglass's warm approval from the beginning, and he contributed liberally to its support.

29 "His own last powerful utterance on this question, issued but a few months before his death, we are republishing in pamphlet form for free distribution."

His death was a heavy blow to the brave young champion of her persecuted race. "I have no words at command to express my sense of personal loss," she wrote, "the blinding tears will not let me attempt at this time to narrate a tenth part of his personal goodness to me and his help to the cause. My heart is desolate over the realization that for the first time since the burden of race defence was laid upon me I cannot have the help and support of Frederick Douglass."

Mr. Douglass retained to the last a vivid interest in current events, and in spite of its lamentable shortcomings he still belonged to what is still fondly called by many the "Party of Freedom." Only the day before his death he wrote sadly to a Northern friend – "Though I am glad that the Democratic party has met with defeat, I have my fears that the victory of the Republicans may make them ever a little more indifferent about protecting human rights under the constitution than when they were in power before. It is to the shame of the Republican party that it could protect the rights of American citizens everywhere but at home. It made no earnest effort to see that the Constitution was obeyed in the Southern States and the ballot box protected. The fourteenth amendment declares that when any State shall deprive any of its citizens of the Elective Franchise, representation shall be reduced, &c. No attempt has been made to enforce this provision by the Republican party or any other, yet all swore to support the Constitution."

A writer in the London *Friend* thus describes his last hours: –

"Frederick Douglass had been in attendance at the Women's National Council, in session at Washington.[30] He sat as a specially welcomed guest through the business session of its Executive Committee on Wednesday, the 20th February last, full of interest and sympathy and (seemingly) in the best health. At the conclusion of the meeting he rode out to his home. He had an engagement to lecture at a neighbouring church in the evening, and while waiting for the carriage to take him thither he was giving his wife an animated account of the day's proceedings, when in the midst of the description he fell forward. She soon perceived that he was dying, and summoned assistance, but he did not rally, and in a short time breathed his last. A sudden attack of the heart disease was the verdict of the physicians. Thus ended a useful, noble life."

The funeral service was held at the Metropolitan African Methodist Church at Washington, at which he was a regular attender. The burial took place at his old home, Rochester (N.Y.). As the above writer says, "his best and most lasting memorial will be found in the improved condition of the people in whose enfranchisement (in so far as it is yet accomplished) he was, under the blessings of God, so mighty a factor."

---

30 The National Council of Women of the United States had been founded in 1888 by Frances Willard, Susan B. Anthony, and other suffragists.

"Born a slave," writes Professor Crogman,[31] of Atlanta, "subjected in his early youth and manhood to the degrading, stultifying, demoralizing influences of slavery, he has left behind him after a public life, long, varied, and stormy, a name as clean and spotless as driven snow."

We cut from a Southern Negro Journal, *The Planet*, the following appropriate remarks quoted from the *Philadelphia Press*: –

"The death of Frederick Douglass has been followed by wide public notice of the honours he had received, the consideration with which he has been treated, and the position he has filled.

"But it is worth while remembering, in the interest of justice and equality, twin duties of the Republic, that these honours and this consideration were both infinitely less than he would have received in any other civilized country in the world.

"In France he would have found Dumas,[32] a man darker than himself, honoured through life in every social circle, and after death one of the few whose statue stands in the Theatre Français. If, as might easily have been the case, Douglass had been elected to the French Academy, he would have found there, now and in the past, men of his race. In no corner of France and in no part of Europe would have found the hotel, the theatre, the railroad car, the school, or the home, in which he would not have been accepted on his merits as a man and his manners as a gentleman.

"This simple equality and justice exists in all other civilized nations. When like even-handed justice is dealt here, the Negro question will be solved, and no other solution can give peace, because none other is just."

"ANTI-CASTE."

Published for Free Distribution, by Voluntary Subscriptions.
Free by post to all subscribers of 1s. (25 cents) and upwards to the funds of the movement.
[Contributions may be sent by Stamps, Greenbacks, or Money Orders.]
All communications to be addressed to
CATHERINE IMPEY,
Street, Somersetshire, (England).
Subscriptions in aid of this growing work are earnestly invited.

Extracts
FROM THE
Editor's Diary of a Visit to
"Cedar Hill."

---

31   William H. Crogman (1841–1931) was a professor at Clark University in Atlanta.
32   Alexandre Dumas (1802–1870), famed French novelist, had an enslaved grandmother.

Sept. 14, 1892. – After a tiring night journey [from Mayville, near Lake Erie, the home of Judge Albion W. Tourgée and his wife, where I had been delightfully spending the last few days,] I arrived at Washington, and with the aid and counsel of a kind negro porter, mounted a street car that took me out to Anacostia, a suburban village lying across the broad Potomac river, a few miles to the south-west of the city. There leaving the cars, I walked up, tired and sleepy, to F. Douglass's beautifully-situated home on its wooded knoll ("Cedar Hill"), to find him away till night, and my telegram of early the day before, announcing the time of my arrival, never having come. I was met at the door by Miss Pitts, Mrs. Douglass's sister,[33] who showed me into the reception-room on the left of the entrance, a pleasant room with two deep bay windows to the south, shaded by great magnolia and other trees, and two long windows opening on to the verandah. The study opened from it to the back. Mrs. Douglass soon came and kindly welcomed me, and as I was very hungry she soon had a little meal served for me in the dining-room (which opens back from the right-hand parlour) by a quaint, little, old and very black negress, who smiled lovingly into my face and called me kindly names. She wore very short skirts and a turban, and looked a most quaint and picturesque figure to my English eyes.

Mrs. Douglass (who it will be remembered is a Northern white lady) had two lady guests already visiting her (two Mrs. Ws.); Miss Pitts and a young friend (Miss Foy)[34] live with the family; also two granddaughters of Mr. Douglass's, so that I soon found we were to be an interesting mixed family, as to colour.

During the afternoon, while Mrs. Douglass and her guests went for their afternoon drive, they kindly allowed me to sleep. The granddaughters (Annie and Estelle Sprague) joined us at the early supper. After a little music and conversation we retired about 9.30.[35]

Thursday, 15 Sept. – Woke early. I feel it very warm again, alas! We breakfast at 7 o'clock – seemingly a usual hour in this country. Miss Sprague goes to her office work in the Treasury department. F. Douglass had come home in the night. What a grand majestic figure it is. Fine features, with a crown of white hair like the Egyptian monarchs of old. He was strolling in the garden under the shade of the trees before we came down. At table he led the talk in a quiet repressed voice. Finding how shy we all were, and conversation often flagging, he said quietly, "We shall become better acquainted before long."

---

33 Eva M. Pitts (1849–1901), sister of Helen Pitts Douglass.
34 Possibly Amelia Foy.
35 Rosine Sprague Morris (1864–1893) was the oldest child of Nathan and Rosetta Douglass Sprague. She married Douglass's secretary Charles Morris. Estella "Stella" Irene Sprague Weaver (1870–1927) became a teacher.

After breakfast I took my note book out on to the lawn in front, seated myself under a cedar, and began my sketch of the house. Trees grow all around – a fir grove, with a few oaks and chestnuts, and grass under foot. You approach the house when walking, by two steep flights of steps with a light handrail, under the shade of tall tulip trees. The scene from the veranda, where hammocks and rockers and garden seats tempt one to rest, is magnificent, away over the city with its dazzling white dome and obelisk, and its masses of red-brick and other buildings, the broad, sluggish Potomac, spanned by bridges, spreading on its lazy way between us and it, and woods and rolling land everywhere as far as the eye can reach, into Maryland.

The drive has been cut in spiral fashion round the knoll. There is a glen or valley on each side [of] the house, down the sides of which slope the vegetable gardens, where later on F. Douglass took me to see the sweet potato plants, growing like cucumber vines in a tangle over the ground, among an orchard of young pear trees, &c.

Rising behind the garden to the west is a cornfield – "Indian corn" as we call it in England – where the huge sheaves stand 8 feet high baking in the sun. Near it are carriage-house, stables, and a small barn.

I had not been long sketching before F. Douglass came and asked me to stroll round with him, and then we rested in this barn – he in an old chair and I on a truss of hay – and we talked, while the pleasant negro woman passed about doing some repairs, &c. F. Douglass was very weary from the exertion of making a long speech to a monster open-air gathering the day before at the Coloured People's State Fair (or agricultural show) at Richmond, Virginia, so we just idled and talked quietly. He showed me his odd little den, too, a small brick room out in the hot sunshine, where he sometimes hides to be quiet and write. He told me a good deal about his family, of those who had died, especially a beloved daughter, and of his one daughter still living (Mrs. Sprague), whom he evidently holds very dear.[36]

In the afternoon we visited the Art gallery near the White House (F. Douglass and party of six ladies). We were just starting, when two more guests arrived – a Mrs. Lee and her daughter, from Chicago (coloured), Miss Lee proving a skilled musician and singer. In the gallery I went the round with Mr. and Mrs. Douglass, and he pointed out to me his favourite pictures. Two he especially called my attention to were "The helping hand" – a merry, happy little child helping an old sailor grandfather to row the boat. The other, a sympathetically-drawn household scene in a negro cabin, in which there is an entire absence of the element of ridicule or caricature, so usual in American pictures of negro life.[37]

---

36 Rosetta (1839–1906), the first child of Anna and Frederick Douglass, worked as a teacher before marrying Nathan Sprague in 1863 and having six children.

37 Probably works held in the Corcoran Gallery of Art, located until 1897 at the corner of 17th Street and Pennsylvania Avenue.

The gallery closed at 4 o'clock. Some went home, Mrs. W., Miss Pitts, Miss Foy and I went through the White House gardens, enjoying the beautiful water lilies and foliage plants and the shade; and then out on to the "White Lot" – white now with army tents, for the great living remnant of the Northern Army was gathering here for a grand parade and reunion the coming week, and all was excitement.[38] Every place was decorated, and grand stands and seats being put up everywhere. The whole city and neighbourhood was swarming with sightseers.

In the evening F. Douglass had out his beloved violin and played, while his grand-daughter (Annie) accompanied on the piano, two of his very favourite hymns. One was from an old Methodist hymn book with music, which he afterwards brought across to me that I might handle it. It was the one book he had brought away with him in his escape from slavery, so greatly did he prize it. It was a picture to remember, his tall majestic old figure bending over his beloved violin, swaying to the music. Then we all sang together "Nearer my God to Thee."

Friday, Sept. 16. – I stayed near home all day expecting Mr. Mitchell (editor of the Richmond *Planet*).[39] The other ladies went off on a long day's excursion with the carriage and its two black horses. I finished my sketch, and then F. Douglass came and told me to stroll with him and talk. I fetched his stick for him (he is old enough to like being waited on) and we strolled away back through a neighbour's garden (the convenience of having no fences) and up through the beautiful woods and sweet odorous places to a disused fortress, where a little calf was tethered, and two little girls played together. There with a grand panorama around us we sat down under a little tree, and after talking of the scene before us he pointed out to me the valley below us to the west, which Gen. Howard purchased (it being waste land then) and gave to the contraband negroes who had followed the army from the South and were starving.[40] They have settled down and worked and paid off what was advanced to them for building their little houses, and some raise vegetables and a little fruit for the city market, and others go into the city to work by day, and come back to their picturesque valley, and the houses strewn among the coppice wood. Some thrifty ones have good houses now. There are two large schools and some chapels, stores, &c., and so the little community of outcasts is "coming up," as they say here.

When we were tired of talking, I read aloud to Mr. Douglass a pamphlet he had brought with him on the culture and civilization of ancient Ethiopia, showing how

---

38 Over seventy thousand Union Army veterans encamped on the "White Lot," now known as the Ellipse, in Washington, DC, for a Grand Army of the Republic celebration.

39 John Mitchell, Jr. (1863–1929) edited the African American weekly *Richmond Planet* from 1884 until his death.

40 Probably the former "contraband" camp located in southern Anacostia near Battery Carroll and Fort Greble, named for Union General O. O. Howard, head of the Freedmen's Bureau.

it preceded and gave birth to Egyptian civilization and architecture, and extended through India in a pre-Aryan era. We stopped to discuss and comment as we read. He was grateful to be read to – gets so tired with reading letters, &c. At last it was time to return to lunch, and we wandered down by a fresh path through the woods, resting awhile on a fallen tree. "Let us be silent awhile and listen to nature," he said, and I heard the gentle falling of dried leaves, the small chirp of distant grasshoppers, and it felt like a prayer, and I longed that this might be a blessed and useful preparation for the future conflict.

Before tea Stella Sprague kindly took me down to call on Miss S., a friendly correspondent of mine in Anacostia, whom I had never met. I found she was a thoughtful young teacher at the large village schools (at the General Howard Place), her parents having been some of those very "contrabands" coming up out of slavery. It was down on the sandy levels, not in the wild old valley, that they had built however, and Oh the heat! The sun does so scald and melt one through! Miss S. walked back to Cedar Hill with us, and as we walked the two girls told me sadly of several cases of injustice and proscription from which they and their companions had suffered in Washington, on account of their colour, exclusion from technical and other classes in which they had hoped or even begun to study and learn to earn their living, and of the separate school system, etc. We talked about Judge Tourgée and the National Citizen's Rights Association.[41] Their enthusiasm is quite fired about it as well as my own.

Saturday, Sept. 17. – That morning, a lovely bouquet of garden flowers was sent me by my teacher friend. In the morning, as Mrs. Douglass was going in the buggy to do some errands, I drove about with and held the "lines" for her. We went up that negro settlement, and oh, the pitiful little dwellings some were, and so ruinous, and showing signs of such hopeless struggling poverty. A poor woman Mrs. Douglass called on to try to get her to help in the kitchen, and who couldn't well manage it, having a little shop whose custom was destroyed if she shut her door for a few days, stood and talked to me as I sat waiting for Mrs. D.

In the afternoon, Miss Lee and some of the young folk went to a concert, in the city, escorted by Joseph Douglass, a music-loving grandson of F. Douglass. In the evening, Estelle ("Stella") sang to Mr. Douglass some of his favourite hymns, which seemed restful to him.[42]

Sunday, Sept. 18. – Mr. Douglass announced at breakfast, that he should go to the Presbyterian Church.[43] I asked if he meant a "coloured one!" He parried my

---

41 Founded by Albion Tourgeé in 1891, the National Citizens' Rights Association was a precursor to the NAACP.

42 A classically trained violist, Joseph Henry Douglass (1871–1935), son of Charles R. and Libbie Douglass, was perhaps Douglass's favorite grandchild.

43 Probably the Fifteenth Street Presbyterian Church.

question, but wanted to know who wished to go. I believed he wished to take us there for some wise purpose and at once said I would like to. Both the Mrs. W's said ditto, and Mrs. Lee, and Mrs. Douglass, so in due time we were driven down by "York," their very black negro driver, by whom it was my portion to sit and from whom I learned a little about the poorer negro community, their rate of wages, etc.

At the church, carriages with their negro drivers were thronged about the street under the shade trees; this is a fashionable coloured church. F. Douglass said "Ladies, I will lead the way, if you please," and his splendid presence preceded us up the aisle, where the ushers took him and his wife and train of friends to a very front seat. Behind the preacher's platform and raised a step, was the seat for the choir (of five trained and select voices), who sometimes sang to the congregation and sometimes led in a hymn. To my English Quaker eyes the place was luxuriously upholstered. It had long coloured lancet windows, crimson Brussels carpet and cushioned seats throughout; an amphitheatre in form and arrangement. The audience of about 700 persons were apparently all "coloured" except four of our party; some fair complex-ioned, some plain, and a few even, to our eyes ugly, but many magnificently hand-some, with their wondrous soft black eyes.

The preacher, refined and sensitive looking, a man of perhaps 35 to 40, light in colour, and altogether very English in appearance[.] His manner was quiet and dignified, his sermon a written discourse on Whittier. Whittier, the poet reformer, the champion of their liberties, who has just passed to his rest, so that the preacher felt he could not but take this opportunity to review his life-work, before a rising generation to whom slavery in its grosser forms is already tradition of the past. Some of the poems quoted were the very finest. I find Whittier loved here much more than Lowell.[44]

After the regular service closed, some little children were brought forward by their parents to be baptized. A simple brief ceremony of dedication on the part of the parents and of exhortation from the minister. We stood near the front, I watch-ing the greetings etc., as the people dispersed. I was then introduced to the preacher (Dr. Grimke[45]) and his wife, a very, very gentle attractive looking lady. That I might enjoy more of their company, Mr. Douglass kindly invited them both to dine with us, and on the way home on the street cars Mr. D., Mr. G. and I had a deeply inter-esting discussion upon points of the caste question.

From this conversation it was evident that the distinct opinion existed, among leading members of the coloured race, that *caste* is *tightening its grasp*, that pro-fessedly Christian society in America is deliberately accepting it as the only and

---

44 James Russell Lowell (1819–1891), US poet and editor.
45 Francis James Grimké (1850–1937), a South Carolina-born enslaved relative of the abolitionist Grimké sisters, became a prominent Presbyterian clergyman and early civil rights leader.

"necessary" means of preventing honourable intermarriage – "intermarriage" not amalgamation – that goes on almost without rebuke, as a matter of course. The higher the coloured generations advance in civilization, the more stringent is the repression. Later in the day I had some very interesting talk with Mrs. Grimke about National Citizens' Rights Association (Judge Tourgée's plan of enrolment for a new Anti-Slavery Crusade, adapted to present conditions), of which she earnestly approves, and had been in correspondence with Judge Tourgée respecting it. In the afternoon we were sitting round the parlour and Mr. Douglass was telling us incidents of the old Anti-Slavery struggle, and said some strong things too, against Caste. Mr. Douglass's daughter, Mrs. Sprague, had joined our party since the morning, and all day callers, driving or on foot, kept coming and going, so many being in the city to see the "Grand Army Review." We counted afterwards 45 visitors, all "coloured!" Among them were three old people of the regular country farmer class, from Maryland, one being a cousin of F. Douglass, and the other fellow slaves from his own old master's estate, from which he had escaped to freedom so remarkably.

The Grimkes left about four o'clock, and another visitor came to stay over the festivities, from New York. In the dark of the warm evening, when most were gone, the Mrs. Ws. and Miss Foy and I sat on the verandah alone, and quiet, Mrs. W. telling us thrilling stories of her teacher life in Virginia during and after the war time. Before the war she had been governess in a slaveholder's family in the South.

One day talking quietly, Mr. Douglass was recalling how before speaking to the audiences who gathered at their Anti-Slavery meetings he used to ask to be alone, and his preparation was to recall the horrors and cruelties suffered by those he had left in slavery. It would all rise up before him like an actual presence, and he would go before the audience quivering with the sympathy it stirred in him. The effect on his hearers was as if they too saw what he saw inwardly. It wrought a marvelous effect on them. He could feel every being before him swayed with his emotion, and multitudes would be weeping. Sometimes he felt unable so to speak, and often feared his quieter efforts were failures. At such a moment Wendell Phillips would be so kind, so encouraging and say "Frederick, so-and-so was well said." . . . Once he and W. L. Garrison and Wendell Phillips had to make a night journey on some steamboat, and he was refused a berth, and had to walk the deck all night. He had not been long thus left alone, when Wendell Phillips came from his room, and taking his arm, walked with him. "I could not sleep and leave you to walk alone," he said.

Sept. 19. – I was quite busy saying my goodbyes from the kitchen upward, and the whole family were on the verandah to see me off, and were all so kind and affectionate I felt quite overwhelmed. Mrs. Douglass said I must make theirs my home for a good long time when I came next, and I felt, what I was assured, that I was leaving friends.

Mr. Douglass and his daughter went with me to the city to see me off, and at the crowded Railway Station we parted.

FREDERICK DOUGLASS MURAL

Belfast, Ireland

Part IV, no 7 Frederick Douglass Mural, Belfast, Ireland, Flickr, Laurence's Travels.

Select Bibliography

Primary Sources

American Slavery: Report of a Public Meeting Held at Finsbury Chapel, Moorfields, to Receive Frederick Douglass, the American Slave, on Friday, May 22, 1846 (London: Christopher B. Christian & Co., 1846).

Correspondence Between The Rev. Samuel H. Cox and Frederick Douglass, A Fugitive Slave (New York: Office of the American Anti-Slavery Society, 1846).

Farewell Speech of Mr. Frederick Douglass Previously to Embarking on Board the Cambria (London: Ward and Co., Paternoster-Row, 1847).

Free Church Alliance with Manstealers: Send Back the Money, Great Anti-Slavery Meeting in the City Hall (Glasgow: George Gallie, Buchanan Street, 1846).

The Proceedings of the World's Temperance Convention (London: Charles Gilpin, 1846).

Report of Proceedings at the Soiree given to Frederick Douglass, Delivered in London (London: R. Yorke Clarke and Co., 1847).

Report on the Proceedings of the Evangelical Alliance, held at Freemason's Hall, London, 19 August to 2 September, 1846 (London: n.p., 1847).

Carlyle, Thomas, "Occasional Discourse on the Negro Question," *Fraser's Magazine for Town and Country*, XL (February 1849), pp. 527–38.

Douglass, Frederick, *Narrative of the Life of Frederick Douglass, an American Slave* (Dublin: Webb and Chapman, 1845).

Douglass, Frederick, "What to the Slave is the 4th of July?" (5 July 1852), available via the University of Rochester Frederick Douglass Project, <http://rbscp.lib.rochester.edu/2945> (last accessed 11 October 2020).

Douglass, Frederick, *My Bondage and My Freedom* (New York: Miller, Orton & Mulligan, 1855).

Douglass, Frederick, *Life and Times of Frederick Douglass: His Early Life as a Slave, His Escape from Bondage, and His Complete History to the Present Time* (Hartford: Park Publishing Co., 1881).

Douglass, Frederick, *Diary of Europe and Africa 1886–1887*, Frederick Douglass Papers, Library of Congress.

Douglass, Frederick, *Life and Times of Frederick Douglass, Written By Himself* (Boston: De Wolfe & Fiske Co., 1892).

Douglass, Helen Pitts, *Diary of Europe in 1886*, Frederick Douglass Papers, Library of Congress.

Douglass, Helen Pitts, *In Memoriam: Frederick Douglass* (Philadelphia: John C. Yorston & Co., 1897).

Lobb, John, *Talks with the Dead: Luminous Rays from the Unseen World, Illustrated with Spirit Photographs* (John Lobb: London, 1907).

MacNaughtan, John, *The Free Church and American Slavery: Slanders Against the Free Church Met and Answered, in a Speech* (Paisley: Alex. Gardner, 1846).

Warburton, James, *Hochelega, or England in the New World* (London: Henry Colburn, 1847).

Wright, Henry Clarke and Frederick Douglass, *Letter to Frederick Douglass with His Reply* (London: n.p., 1846).

Frederick Douglass's papers

Boston Public Library Anti-slavery Collection, <https://www.bpl.org/archival_subject/anti-slavery-movement/>

Frederick Douglass Papers, Library of Congress, <www.loc.gov/collections/frederick-douglass-papers/>

Frederick Douglass Project, University of Rochester, <https://rbscp.lib.rochester.edu/2496>

Blassingame, John (ed.), *The Frederick Douglass Papers – Series One: Speeches, Debates and Interviews, Vol. 1, 1841–1846* (New Haven: Yale University Press, 1979).

Blassingame, John (ed.), *The Frederick Douglass Papers – Series One: Speeches, Debates and Interviews, Vol. 2, 1847–1854* (New Haven: Yale University Press, 1982).

Blassingame, John (ed.), *The Frederick Douglass Papers – Series One: Speeches, Debates and Interviews, Vol. 3, 1855–1863* (New Haven: Yale University Press, 1985).

Blassingame, John, and John McKivigan (eds.), *The Frederick Douglass Papers – Series Two Autobiographical Writings, Vol. 2: My Bondage and My Freedom* (New Haven: Yale University Press, 1999).

Foner, Philip (ed.), *Life and Writings of Frederick Douglass, Vol. 1* (New York: International Publishers, 1950).

McKivigan, John R. (ed.), *The Frederick Douglass Papers – Series One: Speeches, Debates and Interviews, Vol. 5, 1881–1895* (New Haven: Yale University Press, 1992).

McKivigan, John R. (ed.), *The Frederick Douglass Papers – Series Three: Correspondence, Vol. 1, 1842–1852* (New Haven: Yale University Press, 2009).

McKivigan, John R. (ed.), *The Frederick Douglass Papers – Series Two: Autobiographical Writings, Vol. 3, Life and Times of Frederick Douglass* (New Haven: Yale University Press, 2012).

McKivigan, John R. (ed.), *The Frederick Douglass Papers – Series Three: Correspondence, Vol. 2, 1853–1865* (New Haven: Yale University Press, 2018).

Frederick Douglass's newspapers

The North Star
Frederick Douglass' Paper
Douglass' Monthly
New National Era

British newspapers

Aberdeen Journal
Anti-Caste
The Barnsley Chronicle
Belfast Commercial Chronicle
Belfast Newsletter
The Birmingham Daily Post
Bradford and Wakefield Observer, and Halifax, Huddersfield, and Keighley Reporter
The Bristol Mercury, and Western Counties Advertiser
Bristol Times and Mirror
The Bury Times
Caledonian Mercury
Cambridge Independent Press
Carlisle Journal
Carlisle Patriot
Coleraine Chronicle
The Cork Examiner
Cornwall Royal Gazette
Coventry Herald
The Derby Mercury
The Devizes and Wiltshire Gazette
Dumfries and Galloway Standard
Dundee Courier
Dundee, Perth and Cupar Advertiser
Elgin Courier
The Evening Packet
Exeter and Plymouth Gazette
Falkirk Herald
Fife Herald and Kinross, Strathearn and Clackmannan Advertiser
The Freeman's Journal
The Glasgow Herald
The Graphic
The Hampshire Advertiser
Hampshire Telegraph and Sussex Chronicle
Hertford Mercury
The Huddersfield Chronicle
The Hull Packet and East Riding Times
The Inquirer
Kendal Mercury
Leamington Spa Courier
The Leeds Times
Leicester Chronicle
Leicestershire Mercury

The Liberator
The Limerick Reporter
Lincoln, Rutland and Stamford Mercury
Liverpool Mercury
Lloyds Weekly London Newspaper
London Daily News
London Standard
Manchester Courier and Lancashire General Advertiser
The Manchester Examiner
The Manchester Times
Montrose, Arbroath, and Brechin Review
The Morning Post
New National Era
Newcastle Daily Chronicle
The Newcastle Guardian
Norfolk News
North-Eastern Daily Gazette
Northampton Mercury
Northern Star
The Northern Warder
Northern Whig
Nottingham Review
The Nottinghamshire Guardian
The Paisley Herald and Renfrewshire Advertiser
The Perthshire Advertiser
Preston Chronicle and Lancashire Advertiser
The Rochdale Observer
The Saturday Press
The Scotsman
Sheffield and Rotherham Independent
The Southern Reporter
The Spectator
Stirling Observer
Sunderland Daily Echo
The Vindicator
The Washington Post
Waterford Mail
The Western Daily Press
The Western Times
Worcestershire Chronicle and Provincial Railway Gazette
The York Herald
Yorkshire Evening Post

Secondary Sources

Books and articles

Adams, Amanda, *Performing Authorship in the Nineteenth-Century Transatlantic Lecture Tour* (Farnham: Ashgate, 2014).

Andrews, William L., *To Tell a Free Story: The First Century of Afro-American Autobiography, 1760–1865* (Chicago: University of Illinois Press, 1986).

Andrews, William L., *Frederick Douglass: The Oxford Reader* (Oxford: Oxford University Press, 1996).

Augst, Thomas, "Frederick Douglass: Between Speech and Print," in Frederick J. Antczak, Cinda Coggins, and Geoffrey D. Klinger (eds.), *Professing Rhetoric: Selected Papers From the 2000 Rhetoric Society of America Conference* (Mahwah, NJ: Lawrence Erlbaum Associates, 2002), pp. 53–61.

Barker, Hannah, *Newspapers and English Society 1695–1855* (London: Routledge, 2000).

Barnes, L. Diane (ed.), *Frederick Douglass: A Life in Documents* (Charlottesville: University of Virginia Press, 2003).

Baxter, Terry, *Frederick Douglass's Curious Audiences: Ethos in the Age of The Consumable Subject* (London: Routledge, 2004).

Beasley, Edward, *The Victorian Reinvention of Race: New Racisms and the Problem of Grouping in the Human Sciences* (New York: Routledge, 2010).

Bennett, Bridget, "Frederick Douglass and Transatlantic Echoes of 'The Color Line,'" in Kevin Hutchings and Julia M. Wright (eds.), *Transatlantic Literary Exchanges 1790–1870* (Surrey: Ashgate Publishing Limited, 2011), pp. 101–15.

Bernier, Celeste-Marie, "From Fugitive Slave to Fugitive Abolitionist: The Oratory of Frederick Douglass and the Emerging Heroic Slave Tradition," *Atlantic Studies*, 3:2 (2006), pp. 201–24.

Bernier, Celeste-Marie, "A 'Typical Negro' or a 'Work of Art'? The 'Inner' via the 'Outer Man' in Frederick Douglass's Manuscripts and Daguerreotypes," *Slavery & Abolition*, 33:2 (2012), pp. 287–303.

Bernier, Celeste-Marie, *Characters of Blood: Black Heroism in the Transatlantic Imagination* (Charlottesville: University Press of Virginia, 2012).

Bernier, Celeste-Marie, "'His Complete History'? Revisioning, Recreating and Reimagining Multiple Lives in Frederick Douglass's *Life and Times* (1881, 1892)," *Slavery & Abolition*, 33:4 (2012), pp. 595–610.

Bernier, Celeste-Marie, "'Iron Arguments': Spectacle, Rhetoric and the Slave Body in New England and British Antislavery Oratory," *European Journal of American Culture*, 26:1 (2007), pp. 57–78.

Bernier, Celeste-Marie, "A Visual Call to Arms against the 'Caracature [sic] of My Own Face': From Fugitive Slave to Fugitive Image in Frederick Douglass's Theory of Portraiture," *Journal of American Studies*, 49:2 (2015), pp. 323–57.

Bernier, Celeste-Marie, John Stauffer, and Zoe Trodd, *Picturing Frederick Douglass: An Illustrated Biography of the Nineteenth Century's Most Photographed American* (New York: W. W. Norton & Co., 2015).

Bernier, Celeste-Marie, "To Preserve My Features in Marble: Post-Civil War Paintings, Drawings, Sculpture, and Sketches of Frederick Douglass – An Illustrated Essay," *Callaloo*, 39:2 (2016), pp. 372–99.

Bernier, Celeste-Marie and Bill Lawson (eds.), *Pictures and Power: Imaging and Imagining Frederick Douglass, 1818–2018* (Liverpool: Liverpool University Press, 2017).

Bernier, Celeste-Marie and Andrew Taylor, *If I Survive: Frederick Douglass and Family in the Walter O. Evans Collection* (Edinburgh: Edinburgh University Press, 2018).

Black, Christopher Allan, "Frederick Douglass, Daniel O'Connell, and the Transatlantic Failure of Irish American Abolitionism," *Making Connections: Interdisciplinary Approaches to Cultural Diversity*, 12:1 (September 2010), pp. 17–25.

Blackett, R. J. M., *Building an Antislavery Wall* (Baton Rouge: Louisiana State University Press, 1983).

Blackett, Richard, *Beating Against the Barriers: The Lives of Six Nineteenth-Century Afro-Americans* (New York: Cornell University Press, 1986).

Blackett, Richard, "African Americans, the British Working Class and the American Civil War," *Slavery & Abolition*, 17:2 (1996), pp. 51–67.

Blackett, R. J. M., "Cracks in the Antislavery Wall: Frederick Douglass's Second Visit to England (1859–1869) and the Coming of the Civil War," in Alan J. Rice and Martin Crawford (eds.), *Liberating Sojourn: Frederick Douglass and Transatlantic Reform* (Athens: University of Georgia Press, 1999), pp. 187–207.

Blackett, R. J. M., *Divided Hearts: Britain and the American Civil War* (Baton Rouge: Louisiana State University Press, 2001).

Blackett, R. J. M., "'And There Shall Be No More Sea': William Lloyd Garrison and the Transatlantic Abolitionist Movement," in James Brewer Stewart (ed.), *William Lloyd Garrison at Two Hundred: History, Legacy, and Memory* (New Haven: Yale University Press, 2008), pp. 13–40.

Blight, David W., "For Something Beyond the Battlefield': Frederick Douglass and the Struggle for the Memory of the Civil War," *The Journal of American History*, 75:4 (1989), pp. 1156–78.

Blight, David W., *Frederick Douglass's Civil War: Keeping Faith in Jubilee* (Baton Rouge: Louisiana State University Press, 1989).

Blight, David W., *Race and Reunion: The Civil War in American Memory* (Cambridge, MA: Harvard University Press, 2002).

Blight, David W., *Frederick Douglass: Prophet of Freedom* (New York: Simon & Schuster, 2018).

Bowler, Peter J., *Evolution: The History of an Idea*, revised edn. (Berkeley: University of California Press, [1983] 1989).

Bradbury, Richard, "Frederick Douglass and the Chartists," in Alan J. Rice and Martin Crawford (eds.), *Liberating Sojourn: Frederick Douglass and Transatlantic Reform* (Athens: University of Georgia Press, 1999), pp. 169–89.

Bric, Maurice, "Debating Slavery and Empire: The United States, Britain and the World's Anti-Slavery Convention of 1840," in William Mulligan and Maurice Bric (eds.), *A Global History of Anti-Slavery Politics in the Nineteenth Century* (Basingstoke: Palgrave Macmillan, 2013), pp. 59–77.

Buccola, Nicholas, *The Political Thought of Frederick Douglass: In Pursuit of American Liberty* (New York: New York University Press, 2012).

Burke, Ronald K., *Frederick Douglass: Crusading Orator for Human Rights* (New York: Garland Publishing, Inc., 1996).

Carpio, Glenda, *Laughing Fit to Kill: Black Humor in the Fictions of Slavery* (Oxford: Oxford University Press, 2008).

Chaffin, Tom, *Giant's Causeway: Frederick Douglass's Irish Odyssey and the Making of an American Visionary* (Charlottesville: University of Virginia Press, 2014).

Chesebrough, David B., *Frederick Douglass: Oratory from Slavery* (Westport: Greenwood Press, 1998).

Deacon, Andrea, "Navigating 'The Storm, The Whirlwind, and The Earthquake': Re-assessing Frederick Douglass, the Orator," *Rocky Mountain Review of Language and Literature*, 57:1 (2003), pp. 65–81.

DeLombard, Jeanne, "'Eye-witness to the Cruelty': Southern Violence and Northern Testimony in Frederick Douglass's 1845 Narrative," *American Literature*, 73:2 (2001), pp. 245–75.

Dickerson, Vanessa, *Dark Victorians* (Chicago: Chicago University Press, 2008).

Diffley, Kathleen, "Splendid Patriotism: How the *Illustrated London News* Pictured the Confederacy," *Comparative American Studies: An International Journal*, 5:4 (2007), pp. 385–93.

Dilbeck, D. H., *Frederick Douglass: America's Prophet* (Durham: University of North Carolina Press, 2018).

Douglas, Janet, "A Cherished Friendship: Julia Griffiths Crofts and Frederick Douglass," *Slavery & Abolition*, 33:2 (2012), pp. 265–74.

Douglass, Frederick, *Narrative of the Life of Frederick Douglass, an American Slave*, ed. Celeste-Marie Bernier (New York: Broadview Editions, 2018).

Douglass, Frederick, *My Bondage and My Freedom*, ed. Celeste-Marie Bernier (Oxford: Oxford University Press, 2019).

Doyle, Don, "Slavery or Independence: The Confederate Dilemma in Europe," in Cornelis A. van Minnen and Manfred Berg (eds.), *The US South and Europe: Transatlantic Relations in the Nineteenth and Twentieth Centuries* (Lexington: University Press of Kentucky, 2013), pp. 105–24.

Eckel, Leslie Elizabeth, "'A Type of his Countrymen': Douglass and Transatlantic Print Culture," in Leslie Elizabeth Eckel (ed.), *Atlantic Citizens: Nineteenth-Century American Writers At Work in the World* (Edinburgh: Edinburgh University Press, 2013), pp. 71–98.

Ernest, John (ed.), *Douglass In His Own Time* (Iowa City: Iowa University Press, 2014).

Ernest, John (ed.), *The Oxford Handbook of the African American Slave Narrative* (Oxford: Oxford University Press, 2017).

Fagan, Benjamin, "The North Star and the Atlantic 1848," *African American Review*, 47:1 (Spring 2014), pp. 51–67.

Fanuzzi, Robert, "The Trouble with Douglass's Body," in Audrey Fisch (ed.), *The Cambridge Companion to the African American Slave Narrative* (Cambridge: Cambridge University Press, 2007), pp. 27–49.

Fenton, Laurence, *Frederick Douglass In Ireland: The Black O'Connell* (Cork: The Collins Press, 2014).

Fenton, Laurence, *"I was Transformed": Frederick Douglass – An American Slave in Victorian Britain* (Amberley: Stroud, 2018).

Ferreira, Patricia J., "All But 'A Black Skin and Wooly Hair': Frederick Douglass's Witness of the Irish Famine," *American Studies International*, 37:2 (June 1999), pp. 69–83.

Ferreira, Patricia J., "Frederick Douglass and the 1846 Dublin Edition of His Narrative," *New Hibernia Review*, 5:1 (2001), pp. 53–67.

Fisch, Audrey, *American Slaves in Victorian England: Abolitionist Politics in Popular Literature and Culture* (Cambridge: Cambridge University Press, 2000).

Fisch, Audrey (ed.), *The Cambridge Companion to the African American Slave Narrative* (Cambridge: Cambridge University Press, 2007).

Foner, Philip S., *Frederick Douglass* (New York: Citadel Press, 1964).

Foner, Philip S. and Robert James Branham (eds.), *Lift Every Voice: African American Oratory 1787–1900* (Tuscaloosa: University of Alabama Press, 1998).

Foster, Frances Smith, *Witnessing Slavery: The Development of Ante-Bellum Slave Narratives* (Madison: University of Wisconsin Press, 1979).

Fought, Leigh, *Women in the World of Frederick Douglass* (New York: Oxford University Press, 2017).

Fox-Amato, Matthew, *Exposing Slavery: Photography, Human Bondage and the Birth of Modern Visual Politics in America* (London: Oxford University Press, 2017).

Franchot, Jenny, "The Punishment of Esther: Frederick Douglass and the Construction of the Feminine," in Eric J. Sundquist (ed.), *Frederick Douglass: New Literary and Historical Essays* (Cambridge: Cambridge University Press, 1990), pp. 141–65.

Fulkerson, Gerald, "Exile as Emergence: Frederick Douglass in Great Britain, 1845–7," *The Quarterly Journal of Speech*, 60:1 (1974), pp. 69–82.

Gamber, Francesca, "The Public Sphere and the End of American Abolitionism, 1833–1870," *Slavery & Abolition*, 28:3 (2007), pp. 351–68.

Ganter, Granville, "He Made Us Laugh Some': Frederick Douglass's Humor," *African American Review*, 37:4 (2003), pp. 535–52.

Gibbs, Jenna, *Performing the Temple of Liberty: Slavery, Theater, and Popular Culture* (Baltimore: Johns Hopkins University Press, 2014).

Giles, Paul, "Narrative Reversals and Power Exchanges: Frederick Douglass and British Culture," *American Literature*, 73:4 (December 2001), pp. 779–810.

Giles, Paul, "Douglass's Black Atlantic: Britain, Europe, Egypt," in Maurice S. Lee (ed.), *The Cambridge Companion to Frederick Douglass* (Cambridge: Cambridge University Press, 2009), 779–810.

Goldner, Ellen, "Allegories of Exposure: The Heroic Slave and the Heroic Agonistics of Frederick Douglass," in Ellen J. Goldner and Safiya Henderson-Holmes (eds.), *Racing & (E)Racing Language: Living with the Color of Our Words* (New York: Syracuse University Press, 2001), pp. 31–55.

Gough, Kathleen M., *Kinship and Performance in the Black and Green Atlantic: Haptic Allegories* (London: Routledge, 2014).

Grace, Daniel, "Infidel America: Puritan Legacy and Antebellum Religious Persecution in Frederick Douglass's Transatlantic Speeches 1841–1849," *American Literature*, 90:4 (2018), pp. 723–52.

Gray, Elizabeth Kelly, "'Whisper to Him the Word 'India': Trans-Atlantic Critics and American Slavery, 1830–1860," *Journal of the Early Republic*, 28:3 (Fall 2008), pp. 379–406.

Griffin, Matthew, "George Thompson, Transatlantic Abolitionism and Britain in the American Civil War," 40:3 (2019), pp. 564–74.

Hamilton, Cynthia S., "Frederick Douglass and the Gender Politics of Reform," in Alan J. Rice and Martin Crawford (eds.), *Liberating Sojourn: Frederick Douglass and Transatlantic Reform* (Athens: University of Georgia Press, 1999), pp. 73–93.

Harrell, Willie J., Jr., *Origins of the African American Jeremiad: The Rhetorical Strategies of Social Protest and Activism 1760–1861* (Jefferson: McFarland & Company, Inc, 2011).

Harwood, Thomas F., "British Evangelical Abolitionism and American Churches in the 1830s," *The Journal of Southern History*, 28:3 (1962), pp. 287–306.

Heartfield, James, *The British and Foreign Anti-Slavery Society 1838–1956: A History* (New York: Oxford University Press, 2016).

Hobbs, Andrew and Claire Januszewski, "How Local Newspapers Came to Dominate Victorian Poetry Publishing," *Victorian Poetry*, 52:1 (2014), pp. 65–87.

Howard-Pitney, David, *The African American Jeremiad: Appeals for Justice in America* (Philadelphia: Temple University Press, 2005).

Husband, Julie, *Antislavery Discourse and Nineteenth-Century American Literature* (New York: Palgrave, 2010).

Huzzey, Richard, "Free Trade, Free Labour, and Slave Sugar in Victorian Britain," *The Historical Journal*, 53:2 (June 2010), pp. 359–79.

Huzzey, Richard, *Freedom Burning: Anti-Slavery and Empire in Victorian Britain* (Ithaca: Cornell University Press, 2012).

Jackson, Cassandra, *Violence, Visual Culture, and the Black Male Body* (New York: Routledge, 2011).

Jasinski, James, "Constituting Antebellum African American Identity: Resistance, Violence, and Masculinity in Henry Highland Garnet's (1843) 'Address to the Slaves,'" *Quarterly Journal of Speech*, 93:1 (2007), pp. 27–57.

Jeffrey, Julie Roy, *Abolitionists Remember: Antislavery Autobiographies and the Unfinished Work of Emancipation* (Chapel Hill: University of North Carolina Press, 2008).

Jenkins, Lee, "Beyond the Pale: Frederick Douglass in Cork," *The Irish Review*, 24 (Autumn 1999), pp. 80–95.

Jones, Douglas A., Jr., *The Captive Stage: Performance and the Proslavery Imagination of the Antebellum North* (Ann Arbor: University of Michigan Press, 2014).

Kachun, Mitch, "Our Platform Is As Broad As Humanity': Transatlantic Freedom Movements and the Idea of Progress in Nineteenth-Century African American Thought and Activism," *Slavery & Abolition*, 24:3 (2003), pp. 1–23.

Kerr-Ritchie, Jeffrey R., "Black Abolitionists, Irish Supporters, and the Brotherhood of Man," *Slavery & Abolition*, 37:3 (2016), pp. 599–621.

Kinealy, Christine, *Daniel O'Connell and the Anti-Slavery Movement* (London: Routledge, 2011).

Kinealy, Christine (ed.), *Frederick Douglass and Ireland: In His Own Words*, 2 vols. (Abingdon: Routledge, 2018).

Koditschek, Theodore, *Liberalism, Imperialism and the Historical Imagination: Nineteenth-Century Visions of a Greater Britain* (Cambridge: University of Cambridge Press, 2011).

Lampe, Gregory P., *Frederick Douglass: Freedom's Voice 1818–1845* (East Lansing: Michigan State University Press, 1998).

Lawson, Bill E. and Frank M. Kirkland (eds.), *Frederick Douglass: A Critical Reader* (Oxford: Blackwell Publishers Ltd, 1999).

Lee, Maurice (ed.), *The Cambridge Companion to Frederick Douglass: A Critical Reader* (Malden, MA: Blackwell Publishers, 1999).

Leeman, Richard W., "Frederick Douglass and the Eloquence of Double-Consciousness," *Howard Journal of Communications*, 29:3 (2018), pp. 282–98.

Leone, Mark P. and Lee Jenkins, *Atlantic Crossings in the Wake of Frederick Douglass*, (Leiden: Brill Rodopi, 2017).

"Letters to Antislavery Workers and Agencies: 2," *The Journal of Negro History*, 10:3 (1925), pp. 367–93.

"Letters to Antislavery Workers and Agencies: 4," *The Journal of Negro History*, 10:3 (1925), pp. 419–44.

Levecq, Christine, *Slavery and Sentiment: The Politics of Feeling in Black Atlantic Antislavery Writing, 1770–1850* (Lebanon: University of New Hampshire Press, 2008).

Levine, Robert S., "Identity in the Autobiographies," in Maurice S. Lee (ed.), *The Cambridge Companion to Frederick Douglass* (Cambridge: Cambridge University Press, 2009), pp. 31–45.

Levine, Robert S., *The Lives of Frederick Douglass* (Cambridge, MA: Harvard University Press, 2016).

Lockard, Joe, *Watching Slavery: Witness Texts and Travel Reports* (New York: Peter Lang Publishing Inc., 2008).

Lorimer, Douglas A., *Colour, Class and the Victorians: English Attitudes to the Negro in the Mid-Nineteenth Century* (Leicester: Leicester University Press, 1978).

Maclear, J. F., "Thomas Smyth, Frederick Douglass, and the Belfast Antislavery Campaign," *The South Carolina Historical Magazine*, 80:4 (October 1979), pp. 286–97.

Mailloux, Steven, "Re-Marking Slave Bodies: Rhetoric as Production and Reception," *Philosophy & Rhetoric*, 35: 2 (2002), pp. 96–119.

Martin, Waldo E., Jr., *The Mind of Frederick Douglass* (Chapel Hill: University of North Carolina Press, 1984).

Mason, Matthew, "The Battle of the Slaveholding Liberators: Great Britain, the United States, and Slavery in the Early Nineteenth Century," *The William and Mary Quarterly*, 59:3 (2002), pp. 665–71.

McBride, Dwight A., *Impossible Witnesses: Truth, Abolitionism, and Slave Testimony* (New York: New York University Press, 2001).

McDaniel, W. Caleb., "Saltwater Anti-Slavery: American Abolitionists on the Atlantic Ocean in the Age of Steam," *Atlantic Studies: Global Currents*, 8:2 (2011), pp. 141–63.

McDaniel, W. Caleb, *The Problem of Democracy in the Age of Slavery: Garrisonian Abolitionists and Transatlantic Reform* (Baton Rouge: Louisiana State University Press, 2013).

McFeely, William S., *Frederick Douglass* (New York: W. W. Norton & Co., 1991).

McKivigan, John R., "Capturing the Oral Event: Editing the Speeches of Frederick Douglass," *Documentary Editing*, 10:1 (1988), pp. 1–5.

McKivigan, John R., *The War against Proslavery Religion: Abolitionism and the Northern Churches, 1830–1865* (Ithaca: Cornell University Press, 1984).

McKivigan, John R. and Jason Silverman, "Monarchical Liberty and Republican Slavery: West Indies Emancipation Celebrations in Upstate New York and Canada West," *Afro-Americans in New York Life and History*, 10:1 (1986), pp. 7–19.

Meer, Sarah, "Competing Representations: Douglass, the Ethiopian Serenaders, and Ethnic Exhibition in London," in Alan J. Rice and Martin Crawford (eds.), *Liberating Sojourn: Frederick Douglass and Transatlantic Reform* (Athens: University of Georgia Press, 1999), pp. 141–65.

Meer, Sarah, "Douglass as Orator and Editor," in Maurice S. Lee (ed.), *The Cambridge Companion to Frederick Douglass* (Cambridge: Cambridge University Press, 2009), pp. 46–59.

Meer, Sarah, "Public and Personal Letters: Julia Griffiths and *Frederick Douglass' Paper*," *Slavery & Abolition*, 33:2 (2012), pp. 251–64.

Merrill, Walter M. (ed.), *The Letters of William Lloyd Garrison, Vol. 3: No Union with Slaveholders 1841–1849* (Cambridge, MA: Harvard University Press, 1973).

Morgan, Simon, "The Political as Personal: Transatlantic Abolitionism *c.* 1833–67," in William Mulligan and Maurice Bric (eds.), *A Global History of Anti-Slavery Politics in the Nineteenth Century* (Basingstoke: Palgrave Macmillan, 2013), pp. 78–97.

Mulligan, Adrian N., "'As a Lever Gains Power by its Distance from the Fulcrum': Tracing Frederick Douglass in the Irish Atlantic World," *Social & Cultural Geography* 18:3 (2017), pp. 395–414.

Murray, Hannah-Rose, *Advocates of Freedom: African American Transatlantic Abolitionism* (Cambridge: Cambridge University Press, 2020).

Murray, Hannah-Rose, "'The Birth Place of Your Liberty': Purchasing Frederick Douglass's Freedom in 1846," *New North Star*, 2 (2020), pp. 63–65.

Neary, Janet, *Fugitive Testimony: On the Visual Logic of Slave Narratives* (New York: Fordham University Press, 2017).

Newbury, Michael, "Eaten Alive: Slavery and Celebrity in Antebellum America," *ELH*, 61:1 (Spring 1994), pp. 159–87.

Nowatzki, Robert, *Representing African Americans in Transatlantic Abolitionism and Blackface Minstrelsy* (Baton Rouge: Louisiana State University Press, 2010).

O'Neill, Peter, "Black and Green Atlantic Crossings in the Famine Era," *Journal of Transnational American Studies*, 8:1 (2017), pp. 32–54.

Pettinger, Alasdair (ed.), *Always Elsewhere: Travels of the Black Atlantic* (London: Cassell, 1998).

Pettinger, Alasdair, "Send Back the Money: Douglass and the Free Church of Scotland," in Alan J. Rice and Martin Crawford (eds.), *Liberating Sojourn: Frederick Douglass and Transatlantic Reform* (Athens: University of Georgia Press, 1999), pp. 31–56.

Pettinger, Alasdair, *Frederick Douglass and Scotland, 1846: Living an Antislavery Life* (Edinburgh: Edinburgh University Press, 2018).

Pryor, Elizabeth S., *Colored Travelers: Mobility and the Fight for Citizenship Before the Civil War* (Chapel Hill: University of North Carolina Press, 2016).

Putzi, Jennifer, "'The Skin of an American Slave': African American Manhood and the Marked Body in Nineteenth-Century Abolitionist Literature," *Studies in American Fiction*, 30:2 (2002), pp. 182–206.

Quarles, Benjamin, *Frederick Douglass* (New York: Da Capo Press [1948], 1997).

Quinn, John F., "'Safe in Old Ireland': Frederick Douglass's Tour, 1845–1846," *Historian*, 64:3–4 (2002), pp. 535–50.

Quinn, John F., "Expecting the Impossible? Abolitionist Appeals to the Irish in Antebellum America," *The New England Quarterly*, 82:4 (December 2009), pp. 667–710.

Qureshi, Sadiah, *Peoples on Parade: Exhibitions, Empire, and Anthropology in Nineteenth-Century Britain* (Chicago: University of Chicago Press, 2011).

Ray, Angela G., "Frederick Douglass on the Lyceum Circuit: Social Assimilation, Social Transformation?" *Rhetoric and Public Affairs*, 5:4 (2002), pp. 625–47.

Riach, Douglas C., "Daniel O'Connell and American Anti-Slavery," *Irish Historical Studies*, 20:77 (1976), pp. 3–25.

Rice, Alan, *Radical Narratives of the Black Atlantic* (London: Continuum, 2003).

Rice, Alan, "The Cotton That Connects, The Cloth That Binds," *Atlantic Studies*, 4:2 (2007), pp. 285–303.

Rice, Alan J., "Transatlantic Portrayals of Frederick Douglass and his Liberating Sojourn in Music and Visual Arts 1845–2015," in Celeste-Marie Bernier and Bill E. Lawson (eds.), *Pictures and Power: Imaging and Imagining Fredrick Douglass 1818–2018* (Liverpool: Liverpool University Press, 2017), pp. 167–88.

Rice, Alan J. and Martin Crawford (eds.), *Liberating Sojourn: Frederick Douglass and Transatlantic Reform* (Athens: University of Georgia Press, 1999).

Rice, Alan J. and Martin Crawford, "Triumphant Exile: Frederick Douglass in Britain 1845–1847," in Rice and Crawford (eds), *Liberating Sojourn: Frederick Douglass and Transatlantic Reform* (Athens: University of Georgia Press, 1999), pp. 1–15.

Rice, C. Duncan, *The Scots Abolitionists 1833–1861* (Baton Rouge: Louisiana State University Press, 1981).

Ripley, Peter (ed.), *The Black Abolitionist Papers, Vol. I: The British Isles, 1830–1865* (Chapel Hill: University of North Carolina Press, 1985).

Ritchie, Daniel, "Abolitionism and Evangelicalism: Isaac Nelson, the Evangelical Alliance, and the Transatlantic Debate over Christian Fellowship with Slaveholders," *The Historical Journal*, 57:2 (2014), pp. 421–66.

Ritchie, Daniel, "Transatlantic Delusions and Pro-Slavery Religion: Isaac Nelson's Evangelical Abolitionist Critique of Revivalism in America and Ulster," *Journal of American Studies*, 48:3 (August 2014), pp. 757–76.

Ritchie, Daniel, "'The Stone in the Sling': Frederick Douglass and Belfast Abolitionism," *American Nineteenth Century History*, 18:3 (2017), pp. 245–72.

Rodgers, N., *Ireland, Slavery and Anti-Slavery: 1612–1865* (Basingstoke: Palgrave, 2007).

Rohrbach, Augusta, "Making it Real: The Impact of Slave Narratives on the Literary Marketplace," *Prospects*, 26 (2001), pp. 137–62.

Roth, Sarah N., "'How a Slave was Made a Man': Negotiating Black Violence and Masculinity in Antebellum Slave Narratives," *Slavery & Abolition*, 28:2 (2007), pp. 255–75.

Rusert, Britt, "The Science of Freedom: Counterarchives of Racial Science on the Antebellum Stage," *African American Review*, 45:3 (2012), pp. 291–308.

Salenius, Sirpa, "Troubling the White Supremacy – Black Inferiority Paradigm: Frederick Douglass and William Wells Brown in Europe," *Journal of Transatlantic Studies*, 14:2 (2016), pp. 152–63.

Sekora, John, "Black Message/White Envelope: Genre, Authenticity, and Authority in the Antebellum Slave Narrative," *Callaloo*, 32 (1987), pp. 482–515.

Sekora, John, "'Mr. Editor, If You Please': Frederick Douglass, My *Bondage and My Freedom*, and the End of the Abolitionist Imprint," *Callaloo*, 17:2 (Spring 1994), pp. 608–26.

Selby, Gary S., "The Limits of Accommodation: Frederick Douglass and the Garrisonian Abolitionists," *Southern Journal of Communication*, 66:1 (2000), pp. 52–66.

Selby, Gary S., "Mocking the Sacred: Frederick Douglass's 'Slaveholder's Sermon' and the Antebellum Debate over Religion and Slavery," *Quarterly Journal of Speech*, 88:3 (2002), pp. 326–41.

Shepperson, George, "The Free Church and American Slavery," *The Scottish Historical Review*, 30:110, Part 2 (October 1951), pp. 126–43.

Shepperson, George, "Thomas Chalmers, The Free Church of Scotland and the South," *The Journal of Southern History*, 17:4 (November 1951), pp. 517–37.

Shortell, Timothy, "The Rhetoric of Black Abolitionism: An Exploratory Analysis of Antislavery Newspapers in New York State," *Social Science History*, 28:1 (2004), pp. 75–109.

Sinha, Manisha, *The Slave's Cause: A History of Abolition* (New Haven: Yale University Press, 2016).

Smith, Stephanie, "Heart Attacks: Frederick Douglass's Strategic Sentimentality," *A Criticism: A Quarterly for Literature and the Arts*, 34:2 (Spring 1992), pp. 193–216.

Smith, Valerie, *Self-Discovery and Authority in Afro-American Narrative* (Cambridge, MA: Harvard University Press, 1991).

Sood, Arun, *Robert Burns and the United States of America: Poetry, Print, and Memory, 1786–1866* (Cham: Palgrave Macmillan, 2018).

Sood, Arun, "The Burnsian Palimpsest: Robert Burns in American Cultural Memory, c. 1840–1866," *Symbiosis: A Journal of Transatlantic Literary and Cultural Relations*, 22:1 (August 2018), pp. 49–73.

Spiers, Fiona, "Black Americans in Britain and the Struggle for Black Freedom in the United States 1820–70," in Jagdish Gundara and Ian Duffield (eds.), *Essays on the History of Blacks in Britain* (Aldershot, 1992), pp. 81–98.

Stauffer, John, "Frederick Douglass's Self-Fashioning and the Making of a Representative American Man," in Audrey Fisch (ed.), *The Cambridge Companion to the American Slave Narrative* (Cambridge: Cambridge University Press, 2007), pp. 201–17.

Stauffer, John, "Douglass's Self-Making and the Culture of Abolitionism," in Maurice S. Lee (ed.), *The Cambridge Companion to Frederick Douglass* (Cambridge: Cambridge University Press, 2009), pp. 13–30.

Stepto, Robert, *From Behind the Veil: A Study of Afro-American Narrative* (Chicago: University of Illinois Press, 1979).

Stepto, Robert, "Narration, Authentication and Authorial Control in Frederick Douglass's Narrative of 1845," in Dexter Fisher and Robert B. Stepto (eds.), *Afro-American Literature: The Reconstruction of Instruction* (New York, 1979), pp. 178–92.

Stockton, Carl R., "Conflict among Evangelical Brothers: Anglo-American Churchmen and the Slavery Controversy 1848–1853," *Anglican and Episcopal History*, 62:4 (1993), pp. 499–513.

Sweeney, Fionnghuala, "Mask in Motion: Dialect Spaces and Class Representations in Frederick Douglass's Atlantic Rhetoric," in Joanna M. Braxton and Maria I. Diedrich (eds.), *Monuments of the Black Atlantic Slavery and Memory* (New Brunswick: Transaction Publishers, 2004), pp. 29–43.

Sweeney, Fionnghuala, *Frederick Douglass and the Atlantic World* (Liverpool: Liverpool University Press, 2007).

Sweeney, Fionnghuala, "Other Peoples' History: Slavery, Refuge and Irish Citizenship in Donal O Kelly's *The Cambria*," *Slavery & Abolition*, 29:2 (2008), pp. 279–91.

Sweeney, Fionnghuala, "Common Ground: Positioning Ireland within Studies of Slavery, Anti-Slavery and Empire," *Slavery and Abolition*, 37:3 (2016), pp. 505–20.

Tamarkin, Elisa, "Black Anglophilia; or The Sociability of Antislavery," *American Literary History*, 14:3 (2002), pp. 444–78.

Tamarkin, Elisa, *Anglophilia: Deference, Devotion and Antebellum America* (Chicago: University of Chicago Press, 2008).

Taylor, Clare, *British and American Abolitionists: An Episode in Transatlantic Understanding* (Edinburgh: Edinburgh University Press, 1974).

Taylor, Yuval (ed.), *I Was Born A Slave: An Anthology of Classic Slave Narratives: Vol. 1, 1770–1849* (Edinburgh: Payback Press, 1999).

Temperley, Howard, *British Antislavery 1833–1870* (Longman: London, 1972).

Thomas, Julia, *Pictorial Victorians: The Inscription of Values in Word and Image* (Athens: Ohio University Press, 2004).

Turley, David, *The Culture of English Antislavery* (London: Routledge, 1991).

Turley, David, "British Unitarian Abolitionists, Frederick Douglass, and Racial Equality," in Alan J. Rice and Martin Crawford (eds.), *Liberating Sojourn: Frederick Douglass and Transatlantic Reform* (Athens: University of Georgia Press, 1999), pp. 56–73.

Waters, Hazel, *Racism on the Victorian Stage: Representation of Slavery and the Black Character* (Cambridge: Cambridge University Press 2007).

Whyte, Iain, *Send Back the Money! The Free Church of Scotland and American Slavery* (Cambridge: James Clarke & Co., 2012).

Wiener, Joel H., *The Americanization of the British Press, 1830s–1914* (New York: Palgrave, 2011).

Williams, Daniel G., *Black Skin, Blue Books: African Americans and Wales 1845–1945* (Cardiff: University of Wales Press, 2012).

Wong, Edlie, "Anti-slavery Cosmopolitanism in the Black Atlantic," *Victorian Literature and Culture*, 38 (2010), pp. 451–66.

Wood, Marcus, *Blind Memory: Visual Representations of Slavery in England and America 1780–1865* (Manchester: Manchester University Press, 2000).

Wood, Marcus, *Slavery, Empathy, and Pornography* (Oxford: Oxford University Press, 2002).

Wood, Marcus (ed.), *The Poetry of Slavery: An Anglo-American Anthology 1764–1865* (Oxford: Oxford University Press, 2003).

Wright, Tom F., *Lecturing the Atlantic: Speech, Print, and an Anglo-American Commons 1830–1870* (New York: Oxford University Press, 2017).

Yacovone, Donald, "The Transformation of the Black Temperance Movement, 1827–1854: An Interpretation," *Journal of the Early Republic*, 8:3 (Autumn 1988), pp. 281–97.

PhD theses

Coughlan, Ann, "Frederick Douglass and Ireland, 1845: The 'Vertiginous Twist[s]' of an Irish Encounter," University College Cork (2015).

Fulkerson, Raymond Gerald, "Frederick Douglass and the Anti-Slavery Crusade: His Career and Speeches 1817–1861," University of Illinois (1971).

McDaniel, William Caleb, "Our Country is the World: Radical American Abolitionists Abroad," Johns Hopkins University (2006).

Websites

Black Abolitionist Walking Tours, <www.blackabolitionistwalkingtours.wordpress.com>

Bulldozia: Research Projects in Transatlantic History and Literature, <www.bulldozia.com/projects/index.php?id=260>

Frederick Douglass in Britain and Ireland, <www.frederickdouglassinbritain.com>

Frederick Douglass in Edinburgh, National Library of Scotland, <https://geo.nls.uk/maps/douglass/>

Ordinary Philosophy, <https://ordinaryphilosophy.com>

Strike for Freedom, National Library of Scotland, <https://www.nls.uk/exhibitions/treasures/frederick-douglass>

Index

Note: Page references in *italics* indicate figures; 'n' indicates footnotes; place names refer to places in Britain or Ireland unless otherwise stated; FD = Frederick Douglass.